American Profile

Hometown Cookbook

Edited by
Mary Carter • Susan Fisher • Candace Floyd

Rutledge Hill Press®
Nashville, Tennessee
A Division of Thomas Nelson Publishers
www.ThomasNelson.com

Published by Rutledge Hill Press, a Division of Thomas Nelson, Inc., P.O. Box 141000, Nashville, Tennessee 37214.

Rutledge Hill Press books may be purchased in bulk for educational, business, fundraising, or sales promotional use. For information, please email SpecialMarkets@ThomasNelson.com.

Library of Congress Cataloging-in-Publication Data

American profile hometown cookbook / edited by Mary Carter, Susan Fisher, and Candace Floyd.
    p. cm.
Includes index.
   ISBN 1-4016-0221-5 (trade paper)
   1. Cookery, American. I. Title: American profile home town cookbook. II. Carter, Mary, 1957- III. Fisher, Susan, 1954- IV. Floyd, Candace, 1953-
   TX715.A508165 2006
   641.5973—dc22

2005030695

Printed in the United States of America

06 07 08 09 10—9 8 7 6 5 4 3 2

For the 7 million readers of *American Profile* across the nations—especially the thousands who have shared their cherished recipes with us.

Contents

Acknowledgments

THIS PROJECT—BRINGING MORE THAN 400 RECIPES TO PRINT, many for the first time—required the work of a dedicated group of people.

We would like to thank the staff at Rutledge Hill Press, including publisher Pamela Clements, typesetter Stacy Clark, recipe editor Laurin Stamm, copy editor Jamie Chavez, proofreader Michelle Adkerson, proofreader Norma Bates, and indexer Heidi Blough. Also, our thanks goes to Bruce Gore of Gore Studios for the beautiful cover design.

At Publishing Group of America, our thanks to Stephen Duggan, chief financial officer, Charlie Cox, executive editor, and Steve Minucci, director of business development, all of whom envisioned this project as a great compilation of American cookery and cleared the way for it to be done.

Thanks to Stuart Englert, senior editor, and Richard McVey, editor, who steered many of the recipes republished here into print in the pages of American Profile. Also, thanks to David Mudd, photo editor, who located photographs of festivals, and Jane Srygley, assistant editor, who edited the festival stories.

Our most heartfelt thanks goes to editor Geoff Stone of Rutledge Hill Press. His careful leadership kept this team on track, and his knowledge and skill kept our energies directed toward the goal of producing a cookbook that, we believe, truly represents the American heartland.

Introduction

"I know the look of an apple that is roasting and sizzling on the hearth on a win-
ter's evening, and I know the comfort that comes of eating it hot, along with some
sugar and a drench of cream. . . . I know how the nuts taken in conjunction with
winter apples, cider, and doughnuts, make old people's old tales and old jokes
sound fresh and crisp and enchanting, and juggle an evening away before you
know what went with the time."

Mark Twain (1835–1910)
From the *Autobiography of Mark Twain*

HEARTH AND HOME. FAMILIES AND FRIENDS.

America's love of food stems, in part, from our most basic desires for comfort and
fellowship.

For proof, look no further than the pages of *American Profile* magazine. For the past four
years, we have invited our readers to share their recipes and send us the stories behind them.
Over the years, we've amassed a huge collection, and our column, "Hometown Recipes," continues to be our most popular feature. Now we offer, for the first time, more than four hundred of these recipes in this one volume.

We've learned from our readers how some recipes have been passed down through the
generations, how others were traded between beloved friends, and still others provide an
opportunity to spend time in the kitchen with grandchildren.

Many of the recipes in this book are family favorites—wholesome, inexpensive recipes that
please a family around a dinner table. One reader tells us that as a young bride she learned to
make breaded pork chops from her mother. Another explains that she experimented over the

Introduction

years with various ingredients to prepare a dish that was not only tasty, but also economical. Another shares special memories of her mother-in-law sitting under a shade tree while eating a dish prepared with the potatoes, peppers, and tomatoes she grew in her own garden.

Holidays and special occasions evoke cherished memories from our readers. Anita Doucette shares her recipe for Tourtière, a French pork pie that was served on Christmas Eve throughout her childhood. Leonard Gardner shares his grandmother's recipe for *latkes,* which he prepares for his family every year during Chanukah. Jo Ann Reid tells us that whenever she takes her caramel cream cookies to a party, she comes home with an empty container and many requests for her recipe.

In the pages of this book, American favorites—buttermilk and Charleston coconut pies, hoe cakes, and oven-fried chicken—take their place beside ethnic traditions—enchiladas, Hungarian chicken paprika with spaetzle, and Swedish nut cake. To food lovers everywhere, regional and ethnic foods are opportunities to try new tastes, new ways of preparing familiar ingredients. They also point out similarities among all cultures—the American hamburger, the Polish pierogi, the Chinese egg roll, and the Mexican taco are all variations on the theme of filling served inside bread.

But recipes alone do not paint a complete picture of food in American hometowns. We've also included stories about food festivals across the nation—from a sidewalk egg-frying contest in Oatman, Arizona, to the Lobsterfest and Sea Harvest in Mystic, Connecticut, from a French omelet celebration in Abbeville, Louisiana, to a Pennsylvania Dutch festival in Kutztown, Pennsylvania.

Cultural critics once described American society as a great melting pot where various ethnic groups meet and meld together. No longer in favor, that concept has been replaced with another food metaphor. Now critics talk about the salad bowl—where different cultures come together, each retaining its own taste while adding its unique flavor to the whole.

With this cookbook, *American Profile* celebrates the salad bowl—along with the main dish and dessert—and we honor our treasured readers who have contributed their own prized hometown recipes to the groaning board of American cookery.

Breakfast Pizza

Yield: 3 to 6 servings

"This is an especially great recipe for teenagers. They tend to avoid breakfast, but when breakfast is pizza . . ."

1	(8-ounce) can crescent rolls	1½	cups shredded Cheddar cheese
6	eggs, beaten	1	(4-ounce) can sliced mushrooms,
½	pound bacon, cooked and crumbled		drained

Preheat the oven to 375 degrees. Lightly grease a 12-inch pizza pan. Unroll the crescent roll dough, and press it into an even layer to completely cover the bottom of the prepared pan. Combine the eggs, bacon, cheese, and mushrooms, and pour the mixture evenly over the dough. Bake for 20 minutes, or until the eggs are firm and the crust is golden.

DONNA JO HINSON | KISSIMMEE, FLORIDA

Tips From Our Test Kitchen:

Sliced tomatoes, olives, pepperoni, sliced peppers, and green onions are all great toppings.

Eggs Newport

Yield: 8 to 12 servings

"This recipe came to me more than twenty-five years ago. It's been cooked for Easter brunch and many other breakfast functions where I serve it with baked ham and a fruit compote."

18	hard-cooked eggs	8	ounces sour cream or mayonnaise
3	(10¾-ounce) cans condensed cream	½	teaspoon garlic salt
	of mushroom soup	⅛	teaspoon cayenne pepper (omit if
1½	cups milk		using pepper Jack cheese)
1	cup shredded Monterey Jack cheese	½	teaspoon black pepper
	or pepper Jack cheese	8	English muffins, split

Preheat the oven to 350 degrees. Butter a 13 x 9-inch baking dish. Slice the eggs and layer them in the prepared pan. Combine the soup, milk, cheese, sour cream, garlic salt, cayenne pepper, and black pepper in a large bowl. Mix well and spoon evenly over the sliced eggs. Bake for 45 to 50 minutes, or until bubbly and lightly golden. Serve over hot, toasted and buttered English muffins.

MARNA DUNN | BULLHEAD CITY, ARIZONA

Tips From Our Test Kitchen:

Garnish this dish with chopped green onion, black olives, grated Cheddar cheese, chiles, mushrooms, or crumbled bacon.

Southwest Oven Omelet

Yield: 6 to 8 servings

"I've prepared this tried-and-true recipe for over twenty years. This hearty dish, with its Southwestern flair, is a real crowd-pleaser."

16	ounces grated Monterey Jack cheese	1	(12-ounce) can evaporated milk
2	(41/2-ounce) cans green chiles	2	tablespoons all-purpose flour
2	(4-ounce) jars mushrooms	8	eggs
1	pound diced ham		

Preheat the oven to 300 degrees. Generously butter a 13 x 9-inch baking dish. In a medium bowl, mix together the cheese, chiles, mushrooms, and ham. Spoon the mixture evenly over the bottom of the baking dish. In the same bowl whisk together the evaporated milk, flour, and eggs. Pour over the cheese mixture and bake for 1 hour.

JOANNE SANDLIN | PRESCOTT VALLEY, ARIZ.

Stuffed Eggs with Cheese Sauce

Yield: 2 servings

Tips From Our Test Kitchen:

Season the sauce with 1 teaspoon curry powder, or try a bagel or English muffin instead of the toast.

2	slices bread, toasted and cut in half diagonally	1	tablespoon all-purpose flour
4	stuffed egg halves, any recipe	1/3	cup milk
4	green pepper slices, in rings	1/2	pound sharp Cheddar cheese, shredded
1	tablespoon butter		Salt and pepper
		1	tablespoon chopped fresh parsley

Preheat the oven to 350 degrees. Place the toast points on a baking sheet. Place an egg half and a green pepper ring on each slice of toast. Bake just until warm while making the sauce. Melt the butter in a medium saucepan. Add the flour and stir over medium heat until well mixed. Add the milk and stir until the mixture is thick and free of lumps. Add the cheese and stir over low heat until melted. Season with the salt and pepper to taste. Place the warmed toast points with the egg halves and pepper rings on two plates. Quickly pour one-fourth of the sauce mixture over each egg. Garnish with the chopped parsley.

AUDREY MISNER | PRICE, UTAH

Breakfast Casserole

Yield: 6 servings

6	slices white bread	1	teaspoon Worcestershire sauce
1	pound bulk pork sausage	1/4	teaspoon salt
1	teaspoon dry mustard	1/4	teaspoon pepper
5	eggs	2	cups grated Swiss cheese
2	cups milk		

Grease a lasagna pan large enough to hold the slices of bread laid out flat. Brown the sausage, drain the grease, and stir in the dry mustard. Beat the eggs and milk together with the Worcestershire sauce, salt, and pepper. Place the bread slices in the lasagna pan, spoon the sausage over the bread and then sprinkle the cheese over the sausage. Pour the egg mixture over all. Refrigerate for 6 to 8 hours or overnight. When ready to bake, preheat the oven to 350 degrees and bake for 30 to 45 minutes.

PAMELA MILLER | GOSHEN, VIRGINIA

Breakfast Soufflé

Yield: 12 servings

"This recipe is great to serve weekend guests. It's a very convenient, make-ahead meal. Serve it with toast and juice."

1 1/2	pounds bulk pork sausage	1 1/2	teaspoons dry mustard
9	eggs, beaten	1	teaspoon salt
3	cups milk	1 1/2	cups grated Cheddar cheese
3	slices white bread, quartered		

Preheat the oven to 350 degrees. Butter a 13 x 9-inch baking dish. Brown the sausage. Drain and cool. Stir together the beaten eggs, milk, bread pieces, mustard, salt, cheese, and sausage. Pour into the prepared pan. Bake uncovered for 1 hour.

BETTE K. TUMIATI | TAYLORVILLE, ILLINOIS

Tips From Our Test Kitchen:

Grated Swiss or mozzarella cheese can be substituted for Cheddar. Green onion, sliced olives, and chopped fresh parsley are colorful and flavorful additions to this recipe.

Green Chile Bake

Yield: 8 to 10 servings

"I make this recipe for breakfast or brunch. My sons-in-law like it with hot salsa. Our five granddaughters like it with mild."

10	eggs	1	teaspoon baking powder
4	cups shredded Monterey Jack cheese	1/2	teaspoon salt
2	cups cottage cheese	2	(4-ounce) cans chopped green chiles, drained
1/2	cup butter or margarine, melted		
1/4	cup all-purpose flour		

Preheat the oven to 350 degrees. Lightly oil a 13 x 9-inch baking dish. Beat the eggs in a large mixing bowl. Stir in the Monterey Jack, cottage cheese, butter, flour, baking powder, salt, and green chiles. Pour into the baking dish, and bake for 35 minutes, or until the eggs are set. Cool for 10 minutes. Cut into squares and serve with salsa.

SALLY VANDER LINDEN | PLEASANTVILLE, IOWA

Tips From Our Test Kitchen:

This dish also works well as a hearty dip when served with sturdy corn chips or toasted pita bread triangles. It's good with 1/2 cup chopped olives on top.

My Corny Quiche

Yield: 6 servings

"I'm eighty-two years old and have done a lot of cooking. I like to make this recipe. The corn muffin mix seems to give a really different taste."

1	cup corn muffin mix	1/3	cup vegetable oil
3	cups thinly sliced zucchini	4	eggs, well beaten
1	small onion, chopped	1	cup salad dressing (regular or low-fat)
1/2	cup grated Parmesan cheese		Salt and pepper

Preheat the oven to 350 degrees. Lightly grease a 10-inch pie pan or quiche pan. Mix the muffin mix, zucchini, onion, cheese, oil, eggs, dressing, and salt and pepper to taste together in a large mixing bowl. When well blended, pour the mixture into the prepared pan. Bake for 45 minutes, or until a knife inserted in the center comes out clean.

BONITA GAMBLE | COLUMBIA CITY, INDIANA

Tips From Our Test Kitchen:

Chopped fresh basil, oregano, or chives go well with this dish. Serve with sliced fresh tomatoes and hearty bread.

Oatman's Eggs 'n' Burros 'n' Such

Every Fourth of July, instead of bowing to firecracker hot temperatures that might deter visitors, Oatman, Arizona, embraces the staggering heat. Independence Day heralds the town's annual Sidewalk Egg-Fry competition.

Contestants display ample creativity in their cooking methods. Some preheat their cast-iron skillets in the desert sun or trap hot air radiating from the sidewalk with a box covered with plastic wrap. Challengers from as far away as New York and Canada use magnifying glasses and reflectors with mixed results in the anything-goes contest.

But this unusual contest has an unusual problem: wild burros, descended from those left behind by gold mining prospectors in Mohave County, are welcome guests in Oatman, and they sometimes walk on the sidewalk stove. Jack, Strawberry, Jessie, and a half-dozen other burros move freely along the streets and sidewalks and even take cover in the shade to watch the 1:30 p.m. and 3:00 p.m. gunfight reenactments. Burros have the right-of-way in Oatman, and few motorists seem to mind when traffic backs up because of a stalled donkey. However, a burro on the egg-frying "stove" cannot be tolerated, and organizers encourage the slow-moving creatures to move on.

The town's 150 residents, give or take a few, happily accommodate the burros and tourists but also maintain their close-knit community. Once a bustling town of 3,500, the town has weathered three major fires, mine closings, and the building of Interstate 40, which drew traffic off Route 66 that runs through town.

About a half-million visitors tour the shops and mines of Oatman each year. Some book a room in the 1902 Oatman Hotel, where movie stars Carole Lombard and Clark Gable stayed after they were married in Kingman, about twenty miles northeast, in 1939. Eventually, the tourists drive off on Route 66, now designated both a historic and a scenic route.

The annual egg-fry isn't the only big draw to Oatman—named for Olive Oatman, who, in 1851 at age thirteen, survived after being kidnapped by Yavapai Indians. The town also touts bed races in January and the Christmas Bush Festival in December.

For more information about the egg-fry competition, log on to www.oatmangoldroad.com or call (928) 768-6222.

Terri Likens is a freelance writer from Flagstaff, Arizona.

Crustless Crab Quiche

Yield: 4 to 6 servings

"A friend shared this light and tasty recipe with me when I was searching for a festive brunch dish. We enjoy this quiche with fruit and muffins."

1	cup shredded Cheddar cheese	2	tablespoons all-purpose flour
8	ounces flaked crabmeat (real or imitation)	1/2	teaspoon salt
1	cup milk		Black pepper
4	eggs, beaten	1/4	cup chopped green onions (optional)

Preheat the oven to 350 degrees. Coat a 9-inch pie pan with cooking spray. Arrange the cheese evenly over the bottom of the pie pan. Top with the crabmeat. Mix together the milk, eggs, flour, salt, pepper to taste, and green onions, if desired. Pour this mixture evenly over the cheese and crabmeat. Bake for 35 to 40 minutes, or until a knife inserted in the center comes out clean. Let stand for 10 minutes before serving.

KATHY GRAHAM | STERLING, COLORADO

Tips From Our Test Kitchen:

This quick and tasty dish is also good with a dash of cayenne pepper.

Ham and Cheese Quiche

Yield: 6 servings

"This recipe is so easy and delicious for breakfast, lunch, or dinner. I love it, and so do my guests."

2	cups shredded sharp Cheddar cheese	2	eggs, beaten
1	cup chopped ham	1/2	cup mayonnaise
1/4	cup finely chopped yellow onion	1/2	cup evaporated milk
1	(9-inch) deep-dish piecrust, thawed		

Preheat the oven to 375 degrees. Toss together the cheese, ham, and onion. Spoon the mixture into the piecrust. Whisk together the eggs, mayonnaise, and milk until well blended. Pour this over the ham and cheese mixture. Bake for 45 minutes, or until golden and a knife inserted in the center comes out clean.

DEE DEE CLARK | METTER, GEORGIA

Spinach-Cheese Breakfast Squares

Yield: 8 to 10 servings

"I like to bring these breakfast squares to the school where I work. Everyone loves them. They never last more than ten minutes."

4	tablespoons butter	1	cup milk
3	eggs	16	ounces sharp Cheddar cheese, grated
1	cup all-purpose flour	2	(10-ounce) packages frozen spinach, thawed and well drained
1/2	teaspoon salt		
1	teaspoon baking powder		

Preheat the oven to 350 degrees. Melt the butter in a 13 x 9-inch baking dish in the oven. In a large mixing bowl beat the eggs with the flour, salt, and baking powder. Stir in the milk. Add the cheese and spinach. Spread the mixture evenly into the baking dish. Bake for 25 minutes, or until golden and set in the center. Cool and cut into squares. This dish can be served warm or reheated.

JANE ZADNICK | MANCHESTER, CONNECTICUT

Tips From Our Test Kitchen:

For additional zip, chop and sauté an onion and add it to the spinach mixture.

Sylvester Graham, born in West Suffield, Connecticut (pop. 1,350), invented the graham cracker in 1829. A Presbyterian minister, Graham touted the benefits of unsifted, coarsely ground wheat (graham) flour. He advocated a health regimen of hard mattresses, cold showers, and a diet of homemade bread, rough cereals, fruits, and vegetables.

Cheddar-Apple Breakfast Lasagna

Yield: 6 servings

"Everyone who has tried this recipe really likes it. It is easy to assemble and ready in no time. It's especially quick if the French toast is prepared ahead or if you use the frozen variety."

Topping:

1 cup sour cream
1/2 cup firmly packed brown sugar

Lasagna:

12 slices French toast
1 (8-ounce) package sliced ham
2 cups shredded sharp Cheddar cheese
1 (20-ounce) can apple pie filling
1 cup granola

For the topping, blend the sour cream and brown sugar in a small bowl and place in the refrigerator to chill.

Preheat the oven to 350 degrees. Layer six pieces of the French toast in a buttered, 13 x 9-inch baking dish. Layer the ham and half the cheese over the toast. Place the remaining slices of French toast on top. Spread the apple pie filling over the toast, and sprinkle the remaining cheese and granola on top. Bake for 25 to 35 minutes, or until warm through. Serve with a generous dollop of the sour cream topping.

DEBBIE MULLIS | CONCORD, NORTH CAROLINA

The Big Coffee Pot in a village in Winston-Salem, North Carolina, was built in 1860. The twelve-foot hunk of metal advertised not coffee, but a silversmith.

Baked Cinnamon-Bread Custard

Yield: 8 to 10 servings

"This is a favorite recipe for breakfast or dessert. It's easy to prepare and is delicious with fresh fruit."

14	slices cinnamon bread, 1/2-inch thick	3	cups milk
6	whole eggs	2	cups half-and-half
3	egg yolks	1	teaspoon vanilla extract
1	cup sugar		Confectioners' sugar

Preheat the oven to 375 degrees. Arrange the bread in a double layer in a lightly greased 13 x 9-inch baking pan. (Cut the bread as needed to cover the bottom of the pan.) Whisk together the eggs, egg yolks, and sugar. Gradually add the milk and half-and-half, and stir in the vanilla. Pour the mixture over the bread. Bake for 25 to 30 minutes, or until a knife inserted in the center comes out clean. Dust with confectioners' sugar while still warm.

JOANN PARKER | COZAD, NEBRASKA

Tips From Our Test Kitchen:

For a nice flavor twist, add 1 tablespoon orange zest to the egg mixture.

Baked Custard

Yield: 6 servings

"We serve this custard at our bed and breakfast, Bonnie's Parsonage, in Holland, Michigan. It is delicious with fresh berries on top."

3	eggs, beaten	1/2	cup sugar
3	cups milk	1/2	teaspoon ground nutmeg

Preheat the oven to 300 degrees. Mix the eggs, milk, and sugar until smooth. Pour into six 3-inch ramekins or custard cups. Dust with a pinch of nutmeg. Place the cups in a glass baking dish filled halfway with water. Bake for 1 hour and 15 minutes, or until a knife inserted in the center comes out clean.

BONNIE VERWYS | HOLLAND, MICHIGAN

Tips From Our Test Kitchen:

If you like vanilla, add 1 teaspoon vanilla extract to the uncooked egg mixture. This custard also is good served cold as a light dessert.

Baked Rice

Yield: 6 servings

"This recipe was handed down through four generations of my family. It's good, quick, and easy to make. And it makes the house smell really great."

2	cups uncooked instant rice	1/4	teaspoon salt
3	eggs	1/4	teaspoon vanilla extract
1	cup sugar	2	tablespoons cinnamon sugar
3	cups milk		

Cook the rice until tender, according to the package instructions. Preheat the oven to 350 degrees. In large ovenproof dish, beat the eggs and whisk in the sugar, milk, salt, and vanilla. Add the cooked rice. To prevent the rice from sticking to the sides, place the dish in a larger ovenproof pan filled with 2 inches of water. Bake for 30 minutes. Sprinkle the cinnamon sugar over the rice. Bake an additional 30 minutes, or until a knife inserted in the center comes out clean.

RICHARD ROSSIO | THE VILLAGES, FLORIDA

Caramel Pecan French Toast

Yield: 6 servings

"This simple recipe is easy to assemble the night before and bake in the morning. I was served a similar dish at a bed and breakfast. I've made some changes to suit my family."

1/2	cup butter, melted	3	eggs, beaten
1/2	cup maple syrup	2/3	cup whole milk
1	teaspoon vanilla extract	1/4	teaspoon salt
1	loaf French bread, cut into	1/4	teaspoon black pepper
	1-inch-thick slices	3/4	cup chopped pecans

Combine the butter, syrup, and vanilla in a small bowl. Pour into a 13 x 9-inch baking dish. Place the bread in a single layer over the syrup mixture. Whisk together the eggs, milk, salt, and pepper, and pour the mixture over the bread. Sprinkle the pecans on top. Cover with plastic wrap and refrigerate 6 to 8 hours or overnight.

When ready to bake, preheat the oven to 350 degrees. Uncover the dish and bake for 1 hour.

MARY BISHOP | NORTH PLATTE, NEBRASKA

Spiced Apple Pancakes

Yield: 2 to 4 servings

"I love the taste of gingerbread and anything with apples in it. I decided to combine them for a flavorful and hearty pancake."

1	cup all-purpose flour		1	egg
2	tablespoons sugar		3/4	cup milk
2	teaspoons baking powder		2	tablespoons molasses
1/2	teaspoon cinnamon		1	tablespoon vegetable oil
1/4	teaspoon ground ginger		2	apples, peeled and diced
1/4	teaspoon allspice			

Combine the flour, sugar, baking powder, cinnamon, ginger, and allspice in a large bowl. In another bowl, beat the egg and mix in the milk, molasses, and oil until well blended. Pour the egg mixture into the flour mixture and stir until just evenly blended. Fold in the apples. Lightly grease and heat a griddle. Pour 1/4 cup batter onto the griddle and cook for 2 to 3 minutes on each side, making certain the center is cooked through.

HELEN SAWECKI | LIVONIA, MICHIGAN

Tips From Our Test Kitchen:

Serve with confectioners' sugar, applesauce, or traditional maple syrup.

Granola Wraps

Yield: 1 sandwich

"Wraps are so quick and easy to make. You can put just about anything in them. This is an after-school and lunchbox favorite."

1	(10-inch) flour tortilla	Granola cereal
	Peanut butter	Bananas
	Honey	

On a tortilla spread a thin, even coating of peanut butter and honey, leaving about one-half inch uncovered around the edge. Sprinkle a thin layer of granola over the peanut butter and honey. Slice a banana in half from end to end, and place it in the tortilla's center. Roll up the tortilla and slice into spirals for a snack, or keep it whole to eat as a sandwich.

ERIN JONES | BRENTWOOD, TENNESSEE

Tips From Our Test Kitchen:

The granola can be replaced with raisins, and the honey can be omitted or replaced with a fruit spread. A thin layer of cream cheese sprinkled with cinnamon sugar makes a great wrap. Cut it into spirals, and toast until just warm in a toaster oven.

Abbeville's Omelette Celebration
Is All It's Cracked Up to Be

Making an omelette takes on new proportions at an Abbeville, Louisiana (pop. 11,887), festival. Chefs crack 5,021 eggs for the Giant Omelette Celebration, held on the first weekend in November in Magdalen Square. They also add in 50 pounds of chopped onions, 75 chopped green bell peppers, 52 pounds of butter, more than 6 gallons of milk, 4 gallons of chopped green onions, and 2 gallons of finely chopped fresh parsley.

But the omelette wouldn't be complete in Cajun country without the addition of Louisiana crawfish and Tabasco. It's then cooked over an open wood fire in a twelve-foot-diameter stainless steel skillet. Organizers say the omelette ends up being more like scrambled eggs, but that doesn't stop approximately 5,000 people who line up each year for a taste. Best of all, it's free.

This unique festival also offers a morning walk-a-thon, arts and crafts, Cajun food and music, antique car and farm implement shows, and home tours.

But the omelette and its history remain the centerpiece of this community festival. According to legend, when Napoleon and his army were traveling through the south of France, they decided to rest for the night near the town of Bessières. Napoleon feasted on an omelette prepared by a local innkeeper. The meal was such a culinary delight that he ordered the townspeople to gather all the eggs in the village and to prepare a huge omelette for his army the next day.

From this beginning, the omelette became a traditional dish to feed the poor of the village at Easter. It has also become the symbol of a worldwide fraternity, rich in friendship, tradition, and cultural exchange, known as the Confrerie.

In 1984, three members of the Abbeville Chamber of Commerce (Emery "Bichon" Toups, Tracy Kays, and Sheri Meaux) attended the Easter Omelette Festival in Bessières, France, and were knighted the first of Abbeville's chevaliers. They returned home determined to bring

Photo courtesy of the Abbeville Giant Omelette Festival. Used by permission.

Abbeville closer to its French heritage by hosting an omelette festival, joining the sisterhood of cities who celebrate the omelette—Bessières, and Frejus, France; Dumbea, New Caledonia; and Granby, Quebec, Canada. (Malmedy, Belgium, and PiGue, Argentina, later joined, bringing to seven the number of locations that annually celebrate this festival.)

Abbeville's Giant Omelette Festival is truly an international event. Every year, representatives from each of the seven cities are invited to Abbeville to be knighted as chevaliers into Abbeville's Confrerie. Beneath majestic moss-covered live oak trees in historic Magdalen Square, they help to prepare the giant omelette. They also come to experience the area's *joie de vivre*, to share its rich culture, to meet and mingle with its people, and to make memories and friendships that last a lifetime. In return, members of the Abbeville Confrerie are

Photo courtesy of the Abbeville Giant Omelette Festival. Used by permission.

invited to visit in each of the participating countries.

For more information, log on to www.giantomelette.org or call (337) 893-0013.

Arlene White is president of Utila Tours, Inc., and the Confrerie d'Abbeville in Abbeville, Louisiana.

Apple-Sausage Pancakes with Apple Syrup

Yield: 4 servings

"These pancakes are a real crowd-pleaser at breakfast or at dinner. Initially, this recipe did not appeal to me. But as they say, 'The proof is in the eating.'"

Syrup:

1/2	cup sugar
1	tablespoon cornstarch
1/8	teaspoon pumpkin pie spice
1	cup apple juice or apple cider
1	tablespoon lemon juice
3	tablespoons butter

Pancakes:

1	egg
1	cup complete pancake mix (requires only water to be added)
2/3	cup milk
2	tablespoons vegetable oil
1/2	teaspoon cinnamon
1	cup peeled and shredded apples
1/2	pound bulk pork sausage, browned, drained, and crumbled

For the syrup, mix the sugar, cornstarch, spice, apple and lemon juices, and butter in a saucepan. Bring to a boil and then reduce the heat. Continue simmering while preparing the pancakes.

Preheat a griddle to 350 degrees. For the pancakes, in a large bowl combine the egg, pancake mix, milk, oil, and cinnamon. Fold in the apples and sausage. Fry on the griddle until the first side is brown. Fry the other side until the center is cooked through. Serve with the warm apple syrup.

BETH CONRAD | VALLEY CITY, OHIO

Tips From Our Test Kitchen:

This hearty dish is the ideal "breakfast for dinner" recipe. Be certain to cook this thick batter all the way through before serving.

Sour Cream Coffeecake

Yield: 8 to 10 servings

"I've been baking this coffeecake for over twenty-eight years. It's no-fail, it freezes beautifully, and everyone loves it."

1 1/4	cups plus 2 heaping teaspoons sugar	8	ounces sour cream
1	heaping teaspoon cinnamon	2	cups all-purpose flour
1	cup (2 sticks) butter, softened	1	teaspoon vanilla extract
2	eggs	1	teaspoon baking soda

Tips From Our Test Kitchen:

Spread 1 cup chopped walnuts or pecans along with the cinnamon sugar mixture over the first half of the batter. This coffee cake also is delicious with a confectioners' sugar glaze.

Preheat the oven to 350 degrees. Grease a Bundt pan very well. Mix together 2 heaping teaspoons of the sugar with the cinnamon. Sprinkle half the cinnamon-sugar mixture over the entire Bundt pan until coated.

In a medium mixing bowl, beat together the butter and 11/4 cups of the sugar until smooth. Add the eggs and sour cream. Mix well. Add the flour 1 cup at a time. Stir in the vanilla and baking soda until evenly mixed. Pour half the batter into the coated pan. Sprinkle the remaining cinnamon-sugar mixture over the batter. Spoon the remaining batter on top. Bake for 45 minutes. Turn the cake out of the pan onto a plate immediately.

MARSHA MADERE | WRIGHT CITY, OKLAHOMA

Blueberry Coffeecake

Yield: 8 servings

"Though I stay busy working as a nurse's aide for the elderly, I find time to cook and write down my favorite recipes to share. This coffeecake is easy to make and so good."

Coffeecake:
- 1/2 cup solid vegetable shortening
- 1 cup sugar
- 2 eggs
- 1 teaspoon vanilla extract
- 21/4 cups all-purpose flour
- 1 tablespoon baking powder
- 2/3 cup milk
- 2 cups fresh or frozen blueberries

Topping:
- 2/3 cup sugar
- 2/3 cup flour
- 1/2 cup butter or margarine
- 1/4 teaspoon almond extract

Preheat the oven to 350 degrees. Lightly grease and flour two 9-inch-round baking pans. For the coffeecake, beat the shortening and sugar together until light and fluffy in a large mixing bowl. Add the eggs and vanilla. Beat well. In another bowl stir together the flour and baking powder. Add this alternately with the milk to the egg mixture. When smooth, divide the batter between the two baking pans. Spoon 1 cup blueberries over the batter in each pan.

For the topping, combine the sugar, flour, butter, and almond extract and mix until crumbly. Sprinkle over the blueberries. Bake for about 35 minutes, or until the center is cooked. Cool slightly and cut into wedges.

CEOLA RIVERS | ATMORE, ALABAMA

George Washington Carver helped reinvigorate agriculture in the South by developing hundreds of useful products derived from peanuts, soybeans, sweet potatoes, and more while teaching at Tuskegee Institute, now Tuskegee University, in Alabama from 1896 until his death in 1943.

Cranberry Swirl Coffeecake

Yield: 8 servings

"I have kept this recipe a secret until now. This coffeecake has been enjoyed by friends and family on many occasions. It is absolutely delicious."

Tips From Our Test Kitchen:

Serve this festive cake at brunch or for dessert.

Coffeecake:

1/2	cup (1 stick) margarine, softened
1	cup granulated sugar
2	eggs
2	cups all-purpose flour
1	teaspoon baking powder
1	teaspoon baking soda
1/2	teaspoon salt
1	cup sour cream
1	teaspoon almond extract
1	cup whole cranberry sauce
1/2	cup chopped walnuts

Glaze:

3/4	cup confectioners' sugar
1/2	teaspoon almond extract
1	to 2 tablespoons water or milk

Preheat the oven to 350 degrees. Grease and flour a 9-inch tube pan. For the coffeecake, beat together the margarine and granulated sugar with an electric mixer until smooth. Beat in the eggs one at a time until fluffy. In a separate bowl combine the flour, baking powder, baking soda, and salt. Add the flour mixture alternately with the sour cream to the creamed mixture until blended. Do not overmix. Stir in the almond extract. Spoon half the batter into the prepared pan. Spoon half the cranberry sauce and half the walnuts on top. Repeat with the remaining batter, cranberry sauce, and walnuts. Swirl through the batter just once with a butter knife. Bake for about 55 minutes, or until the center springs back to the touch.

For the glaze, stir together the confectioners' sugar, almond extract, and water until smooth. Ice the coffeecake while still warm.

SHIRLEY DOUCETTE | MILTON, NEW HAMPSHIRE

Overnight Coffeecake

Yield: 8 to 10 servings

"Westphalia, Iowa, is a German colony on the National Register of Historic Places, and many times we serve dinner to tour groups. For dessert, I decided we must have something 'German-ish,' so I used my old never-fail recipe for Apfelkuchen. It is an overnight coffeecake that can be served at breakfast."

2	cups all-purpose flour	1	cup granulated sugar
1	teaspoon baking powder	1/2	plus 1/2 cup firmly packed brown sugar
1	teaspoon baking soda	2	eggs
1/4	teaspoon salt	1	cup buttermilk or sour milk
1	plus 1 teaspoon cinnamon	1	cup peeled, cored, and chopped apples
2/3	cup butter or margarine, softened	1/2	cup chopped black walnuts or pecans

Grease a 13 x 9-inch baking dish. Mix the flour, baking powder, baking soda, salt, and 1 teaspoon of the cinnamon in a bowl. In another bowl beat the butter with the granulated sugar and 1/2 cup of the brown sugar. Mix in the eggs, buttermilk, and flour mixture. Fold in the apples. Pour into the prepared pan.

For the topping, combine the remaining 1/2 cup brown sugar with the walnuts and the remaining 1 teaspoon cinnamon, and sprinkle the mixture over the batter. Cover with foil and put in the refrigerator until the next morning.

Preheat the oven to 350 degrees. Uncover the baking pan, and let the batter stand at room temperature for about 30 minutes. Bake for 45 minutes. This coffeecake is best served warm. Try drizzling it with a thin confectioners' sugar frosting before serving.

SYLVIA GOESER | WESTPHALIA, IOWA

Since the 1920s, Stanton, Iowa (pop. 714), has had a 40,000-gallon water tower, which was later reshaped like a coffeepot. Another water tower completed in June is shaped like a coffee cup and holds 150,000 gallons of water.

Take a Coffee Break in Stoughton

When customers stop into the Koffee Kup diner in Stoughton, Wisconsin (pop. 12,354), for a mid-morning respite or afternoon pick-me-up, they're carrying on a tradition that's more than 130 years old.

Stoughton is the birthplace of the coffee break, and townspeople have known the value of a cup of joe since the town's Norwegian immigrants began roasting their own coffee beans to save money in the mid-1800s.

To honor its coffee-loving heritage, Stoughton celebrates with the Coffee Break Festival at Mandt Park each August. The festival features an art fair, vintage car show, the Java Jog, children's activities, handmade souvenir coffee mugs, and, of course, gallons of free coffee.

Lorraine Hawkinson, a Stoughton native and retired local newspaper columnist for the *Stoughton Courier Hub*, came across a story, written during the 1950s, about the town's coffee break tradition. By the early 1870s, T. G. Mandt's Wagon Works was the town's major industry, attracting Norwegian immigrants to Stoughton to work in the factory. Because Mandt's factory employed all the available men, leaving other manufacturers with a labor shortage, Osmund Gunderson, a local tobacco warehouse owner, found it necessary to recruit the women in the community for seasonal tobacco work during the fall and winter.

According to the story, the women, many of whom lived on Coffee Street, agreed to work in Gunderson's warehouse on one condition: they had to be allowed to take a break every morning and afternoon. On their breaks, the women would run home, check on their children, start a meal, and have a cup of coffee.

Coffee Street, now called Hillside Avenue, earned its name long before Gunderson's acquiescence, however. When doing their shopping, the frugal homemakers would purchase green coffee beans because they were cheaper than roasted ones. The women would roast the beans in large pans in wood-burning stoves, and the resulting aroma gave the street its moniker.

The coffee break isn't the only tradition Norwegian immigrants contributed to Stoughton. The town honors its Norwegian history each spring with a Syttende Mai celebration. *Syttende Mai* means "seventeen May," the date on which the Norwegian Constitution was signed in 1814 and Norway got its independence after 500 years of Danish rule. Naturally, the event showcases everything Norwegian, including exhibits of the traditional folk arts of *hardanger* (needlework) and *rosemaling* (stylistic painting on wood). Festival-goers enjoy parades, folk dancing performances, a Viking encampment, a smorgasbord of Norwegian foods.

For more information, log on to www.stoughtonwi.com or call (608) 873-7912.

Mary Lou Santovec is a freelance writer in Jefferson, Wisconsin.

Texas Blueberry Muffins
Yield: 24 medium or 12 large muffins

"We grow our own blueberries on our farm. I searched for the perfect blueberry muffin recipe and ended up creating this one. It's been a hit for years."

Muffins:

4 cups all-purpose flour

6 teaspoons baking powder

1 cup sugar

1/2 teaspoon salt

1 cup butter or margarine

2 large eggs, slightly beaten

1 cup plus 3 tablespoons milk

1 teaspoon vanilla extract

2 teaspoons almond extract

3 teaspoons grated orange rind (optional)

2 cups blueberries, fresh or frozen

Topping:

1/4 cup sugar

4 tablespoons all-purpose flour

1 teaspoon ground cinnamon

2 tablespoons cold butter

Preheat the oven to 375 degrees. Grease and flour muffin tins—24 cups for medium or 12 cups for large muffins. Combine the flour, baking powder, sugar, and salt in a large bowl. Cut in the butter until the mixture resembles small peas. Make a well in the center, and add the eggs, milk, vanilla and almond extracts, and orange rind if using. Mix gently just until the liquid is absorbed. Gently fold in the berries. Fill the prepared tins.

For the topping, blend the sugar, flour, cinnamon, and butter together, and sprinkle the mixture evenly over the top of each muffin.

Bake the muffins for 23 to 30 minutes, or until the center springs back to the touch. The larger muffins will take a bit longer.

HELEN WORONIK | SALEM, CONNECTICUT

Tips From Our Test Kitchen:

The batter will seem stiff compared to others. These muffins freeze beautifully.

While living in Torrington, Connecticut (pop. 35,202), Gail Borden, founder of the Borden Milk Company, produced the world's first commercially available condensed milk, patented in 1856. Its use spread during the Civil War as the military made it available to civilians.

Bran Muffins

Yield: 48 muffins

"This recipe is more than thirty years old. It was developed by the Kansas State Home Economics Department as a nutritious school-breakfast offering. School children and everyone else I've baked them for just love these wholesome muffins."

2	cups raisins	4	cups (1 quart) buttermilk
2	cups boiling water	5 1/2	cups sifted all-purpose flour
5	teaspoons baking soda	4	cups All-Bran cereal
1	cup (2 sticks) butter or margarine	2	cups Bran Flakes cereal
2	cups sugar	1	teaspoon salt
4	eggs, beaten	1	cup chopped pecans or walnuts

Combine the raisins with the boiling water and baking soda. Grease the cups of tins for 48 muffins. Preheat the oven to 375 degrees. In a large bowl beat the margarine and sugar until smooth. Combine the beaten eggs with the buttermilk in a separate bowl. Mix together the flour, cereals, salt, and nuts in another bowl. Alternately add the dry and wet ingredients to the sugar mixture until just moistened. Stir in the raisin mixture last. When ready to bake, fill the cups of the muffin tins three-quarters full and bake for 20 to 25 minutes.

BETTE MEYER | DELAWARE, OHIO

Enriched Muffins

Yield: 12 muffins

"I add variety to my meals by experimenting. Muffins are a favorite, so I tried some 'different' ingredients. My husband was impressed."

1	egg	1	cup self-rising flour
1/4	cup margarine, softened	1/2	cup bran
1/2	cup sugar	1/4	teaspoon baking soda
1/4	cup grape juice	1/2	cup dried cranberries
1/4	cup half-and-half		

Preheat the oven to 400 degrees. Grease a 12-cup muffin tin. Using an electric mixer, blend the egg, margarine, and sugar in a bowl. Mix in the grape juice and half-and-half. In a separate bowl

Tips From Our Test Kitchen:

White grape juice may be substituted for purple. To cut calories, use skim milk instead of the half-and-half. If desired, sprinkle the muffins with bran cereal before baking.

combine the flour, bran, baking soda, and cranberries. Stir the dry ingredients into the egg mixture. Fill the muffin tins and bake for about 12 minutes.

BRENDA ADAMS, | WEATHERFORD, TEXAS

The reputation of Crystal City, Texas (pop. 7,190), as a major shipping point for fresh vegetables—particularly spinach in the 1920s and 1930s—earned it the nickname "Spinach Capital of the World."

Pumpkin-Applesauce Muffins

Yield: 24 muffins

"These muffins are very moist and delicious. They're good for breakfast with a glass of milk."

2/3	cup solid vegetable shortening	2	teaspoons baking soda
22/3	cups sugar	1/2	teaspoon baking powder
4	eggs	11/2	teaspoons salt
1	cup applesauce, any style	1/2	teaspoon nutmeg
1	cup pumpkin (not pumpkin pie filling)	1	teaspoon cinnamon
2/3	cup apple juice	1/2	teaspoon mace
31/3	cups all-purpose flour	1	cup finely chopped walnuts

Preheat the oven to 350 degrees. Grease 24 cups of muffin tins. Beat together the shortening and sugar until smooth. Add the eggs one at a time. Stir in the applesauce and pumpkin until well mixed. Add the apple juice, flour, baking soda, and baking powder. Don't overmix. When just smooth, add the salt, nutmeg, cinnamon, and mace. Stir in the walnuts. Pour into the prepared muffin tins until two-thirds full. Bake for 20 minutes, or until a toothpick inserted in the center comes out clean.

CHERI MARCOVITCH | SANTA CLARITA, CALIFORNIA

Tips From Our Test Kitchen:

Try these cake-like treats with apple butter. They're also sweet enough to be served as cupcakes with cream cheese frosting.

Television chef Julia Child was born in Pasadena, California, in 1912. Her inaugural show, *The French Chef*, first aired in 1963. Much beloved for her exuberant spirit and passion for cuisine, Child was featured in a PBS television special called *Julia Child's Kitchen Wisdom*, which still is shown in some markets.

Oven-Baked Doughnuts

Yield: 12 doughnuts

"This simple oven-baked doughnut is more healthful than the deep-fried variety."

Doughnuts:
1/2 cup sugar
21/2 tablespoons solid vegetable shortening
2 eggs
2 cups all-purpose flour
2 teaspoons nutmeg
1/2 teaspoon salt

2 teaspoons baking powder
6 tablespoons milk

Coating:
1/2 cup sugar
1 teaspoon cinnamon
1/2 cup (1 stick) butter, melted

Preheat the oven to 400 degrees. Grease 12 cups of muffin tins. For the doughnuts, beat the sugar and shortening until smooth. Add the eggs, flour, nutmeg, salt, baking powder, and milk. Stir well. Using a small ice cream scoop, spoon the dough into the prepared tins until two-thirds full. Bake for 15 to 20 minutes, or until centers are no longer gooey.

For the coating, stir together the sugar and cinnamon. Remove the baked doughnuts from the muffin tins, dip them in the melted butter, and coat them with the sugar mixture. Serve while still warm.

RUTH DREXLER | FAIRBURY, NEBRASKA

Cinnamon Rolls

Yield: about 24 cinnamon rolls

"I came up with this recipe myself. These cinnamon rolls are a big hit for breakfast or anytime."

3/4	cup hot water	1/2	teaspoon salt	
2	(1/4-ounce) packages active dry yeast	1	cup plus 3 tablespoons butter, softened	
1	cup lukewarm milk	41/2	cups all-purpose flour	
1	plus 3/4 cups sugar	2	tablespoons cinnamon	
2	eggs, beaten			

Tips From Our Test Kitchen:

These delicious rolls are also good with a glaze and chopped nuts on top.

Mix the water with the yeast and allow the yeast to dissolve for 5 minutes. Add the milk, 3/4 cup of the sugar, the eggs, salt, and 3 tablespoons of the butter. Mix well. Add the flour a little at a time. Mix again. Knead for 5 to 7 minutes. Place in a lightly greased bowl. Cover with plastic wrap and allow the dough to rise in a warm place until doubled in size.

On a large surface roll out the dough into a large rectangle, using additional flour as needed to keep the dough from sticking to the surface. When the dough is about 1/4 inch thick, spread the remaining 1 cup softened butter evenly over the surface to within about one-half inch of the edges. Sprinkle the buttered surface evenly with the remaining 1 cup sugar and the cinnamon. Roll up jelly-roll style, and slice into 11/2-inch-thick discs. Place in a large baking dish with sides. (Two 13 x 9-inch pans result in a good fit; one larger pan can be used instead.) Place the rolls in a warm place, and allow them to rise until doubled in size again. Preheat the oven to 350 degrees. Bake the rolls for about 25 to 30 minutes, or until light golden with the centers cooked through. Brush the rolls with butter while hot.

LORIE JONES | LEBANON, MISSOURI

Two vendors thought fast during the 1904 St. Louis, Missouri, World's Fair, and the results are iced tea and the waffle cone. Englishman Richard Blechynden's tea concession wasn't doing well, and since it was a sweltering day, he added ice. The waffle ice cream cone was invented when an ice cream vendor ran out of cups and asked a waffle vendor to help by rolling up waffles to hold the ice cream.

Danish Puff

Tips From Our
Test Kitchen:

This pastry is great for breakfast or dessert.

"This winning recipe was given to me by a dear, dear friend, now deceased. She prepared it for our annual church bake sale. It never made it to the table of goodies because there was a standing order to have it saved for the parish priest."

Base:
1   cup all-purpose flour
1/2 cup margarine
2   tablespoons water

Egg layer:
1/2 cup margarine
1   cup water
1   teaspoon almond extract

1   cup all-purpose flour
3   eggs

Icing:
2   cups confectioners' sugar
1   teaspoon almond extract
     Milk
     Slivered almonds
     Maraschino cherries

Combine the flour, margarine, and water for the base, and roll the mixture into a ball. It will be slightly sticky. Use a bit more flour if needed. Divide this dough into two balls. Shape each ball into a 12 x 3-inch strip on a cookie sheet. Preheat the oven to 350 degrees.

For the egg layer, bring the margarine and water to a boil in a saucepan. Remove from the heat and stir in the almond extract. Stir the flour into the hot liquid quickly to prevent lumping. When smooth and thick, add the eggs one at a time, beating after each addition until smooth. Spread this evenly over the two base strips of dough. Bake for 1 hour. Set aside to cool.

For the icing, stir together the sugar, almond extract, and just enough milk to make a thick glaze. Spoon this evenly over the cooled pastries. Sprinkle with the slivered almonds and maraschino cherries.

JULIA BURNS | BATAVIA, NEW YORK

Appetizers & Beverages

Garlic Cheese Roll

Yield: 12 servings

*"This is one of my favorites. I entered it in a cooking contest back in 1958.
Everyone has always liked it."*

1 1/2	pounds sharp Cheddar cheese, grated	1	teaspoon seasoning salt
1/2	pound processed cheese (like Velveeta)		Garlic powder
1	(3-ounce) package cream cheese		Chili powder
1/2	cup finely chopped pecans		

Mix the Cheddar, processed, and cream cheeses into a bowl. When the cheeses are soft enough,
mix them with your hands. Add the pecans, seasoning salt, and garlic powder to taste. When
well blended, divide the cheese into four parts. Roll each part into a cylinder about 2 inches in
diameter and 3 inches long. Roll each cylinder in the chili powder. Refrigerate for several hours
before serving. Slice the rolls into 1/4 to 1/2-inch discs and serve with crackers.

DORIS STURGES | MT. PLEASANT, TEXAS

*Tips From Our
Test Kitchen:*

The cheeses are easier
to work with when they
are not cold. This dish
should be served at
room temperature.

Marinated Cheese

Yield: about 25 servings

*"I've been in a gourmet group for about ten years. We meet once a month and
love to serve new and different recipes. This is one of my favorites."*

1	(3/4-ounce) envelope dry Italian dressing mix	1 1/2	teaspoons sugar
1/2	cup vegetable oil	1	(8-ounce) block Monterey Jack cheese
1/4	cup white vinegar	1	(8-ounce) block sharp Cheddar cheese
2	tablespoons water	1	(8-ounce) block cream cheese
2	tablespoons minced green onions	1	(4-ounce) jar diced pimientos, drained
			Chopped fresh parsley for garnish

Combine the dressing mix, oil, vinegar, water, onions, and sugar in a jar. Cover and shake vig-
orously until well blended. Slice the blocks of cheese into 1/4-inch strips, and halve each strip to
form two cubes. Assemble them side-by-side in a 2-quart glass dish, alternating the Cheddar,
Monterey Jack, and cream cheese, stacked like dominoes on their sides. Make two rows. Pour
the marinade over the top. Cover and refrigerate 6 to 8 hours or overnight. Drain and place on
a platter. Top with the pimientos and parsley. Serve with crackers.

JANEY STUBBS | STARKVILLE, MISSISSIPPI

*Tips From Our
Test Kitchen:*

Remember to bring the
cheese to room temper-
ature before serving to
bring out its full flavor.

Ginger Cheese Ball

Yield: 1 cheese ball

"I received this recipe from a coworker, Frances Rose, back in 1964 when we both worked for an insurance company. I make several of these every Christmas."

2	tablespoons ginger preserves	1	cup chopped pecans
1	(8-ounce) package cream cheese, softened		

Mix the preserves and cream cheese by hand or with a hand mixer until well blended. Form into a ball and roll in the chopped pecans. Chill until time to serve.

LaVonne C. Whitaker | Cleveland, Tennessee

Party Cheese Ball

Yield: 1 cheese ball

"This is a favorite when I make it for church dinners. Everyone goes for it."

1	(8-ounce) package grated Cheddar cheese	2	tablespoons dried chives or 3 tablespoons finely chopped fresh chives
1	(8-ounce) package cream cheese, softened	2	tablespoons mayonnaise
1/2	medium onion, minced	1	cup finely chopped pecans or walnuts

Mix together the Cheddar cheese, cream cheese, onion, chives, and mayonnaise, and form into a ball. Roll the ball in the nuts until evenly coated. Chill until time to serve.

Anna Mae Campbell | Elizabethton, Tennessee

Tips From Our Test Kitchen:

Chopped candied ginger, available at Asian or health food stores, can be substituted if you can't find ginger preserves. Serve this slightly sweet cheese ball with ginger snaps or garlic toast.

Tips From Our Test Kitchen:

Serve with crackers or garlic toast. To enhance the appearance, add 1/2 cup chopped fresh parsley to the nuts.

In Search of Mesick's Famous Fungus

Mesick, Michigan (pop. 447), the self-proclaimed "Mushroom Capital of the World," began celebrating the morel in 1959 when the Mesick Area Chamber of Commerce organized the town's first mushroom festival. In 1998, the Lion's Club began hosting the festival to keep the tradition alive.

Each spring, when flowers begin blooming and songbirds return from their winter migration, mushroom hunters can be found trekking through the woods around Mesick, searching for the wild and delectable morel mushroom. Veterans advise new hunters to look under the brush near ash and apple trees and to keep their eyes fixed on the ground just ahead. The mushrooms resemble small sponges and can be found growing among the new green foliage or hiding behind last fall's leaves.

Mushroom hunting season starts in early April in Illinois, Indiana, Missouri, and Ohio. It creeps northward into Michigan, Minnesota, and Wisconsin as temperatures warm and are accompanied by spring rain or melting snow. Morel season in northern Michigan normally begins in early May and runs through early June, drawing mushroom hunters from across the country in pursuit of the sometimes elusive fungus.

About 5,000 people attend the festival, scheduled on Mother's Day weekend each year. While some people scour nearby woods for mushrooms, others enjoy the parade, flea market, and carnival rides or participate in the softball, volleyball, or card tournaments.

During the event, some people ask for permission to hunt mushrooms on private property, while others venture onto nearby state and federal lands in search of morels. When dried, the mushrooms can sell for as much as $12 an ounce in gourmet stores or on the Internet. Because of their high water content, it can take up to a pound of fresh mushrooms to make an ounce of dried morels.

Successful hunters often stop by Ken's IGA, one of the town's grocery stores, to have their largest specimens measured. The person who finds the biggest morel receives a monetary prize, along with the all-important bragging rights.

It's the hope of finding that perfect specimen that draws visitors to the annual festival—that and the pastie sale, fish fry, softball tournament, horseshoe contest, and grand parade that round out the celebration.

For more information, log on to www.mesick-mushroomfest.org or call (231) 885-3200.

Terri Hughes-Lazzell grew up in Mesick and now lives in Ossian, Indiana.

Fiesta Bean and Beef Dip

Yield: 9 to 12 servings

1   pound ground beef
1   medium onion, chopped
1   package taco seasoning

1   (10-ounce) can tomatoes and
    green chiles (like Ro-Tel)
1   (15-ounce) can pinto beans, mashed
1   pound processed cheese (like Velveeta)

Brown the meat with the onion. Drain the grease. Add the taco seasoning and the amount of water suggested on the packet. Add the tomatoes and green chiles, beans, and cheese. Heat thoroughly. Serve immediately with tortilla chips, or keep warm in a slow cooker.

ZEE ANNE REISHUS | WOOD LAKE, MINNESOTA

Among inventions and products born in Minnesota are the Bundt cake pan, Green Giant vegetables, and Cream of Wheat cereal.

Tips From Our Test Kitchen:

For a vegetarian dip, use two cans of beans and omit the meat. Serve with a swirl of sour cream and fresh cilantro on top.

Cheesy Black Bean and Artichoke Dip

Yield: 6 to 8 servings

"I am always searching for ways to reduce fat and calories. When using low-fat cheese and baked tortilla chips, this appetizer is just right."

2   (15-ounce) cans black beans, drained
1   (10-ounce) package frozen spinach,
     thawed, drained, and chopped
1/2 cup medium-hot salsa
1   (4-ounce) can chopped green chiles,
     undrained

1   teaspoon minced garlic
2   cups shredded low-fat Cheddar cheese
1   (14-ounce) can artichoke hearts,
     chopped
1/2 cup shredded pepper Jack cheese

Preheat the oven to 350 degrees. Combine the beans, spinach, salsa, chiles, garlic, Cheddar cheese, and artichoke hearts in a 1-quart casserole dish. Sprinkle the pepper Jack cheese on top. Bake for 30 minutes, or until the cheese is bubbly and golden.

LARITA LANG | LINCOLN, NEBRASKA

Tips From Our Test Kitchen:

This high-fiber, lower-fat dip can be assembled ahead of time and baked at the last minute. Serve it with your favorite chips or on pita bread.

Creole Corn Salsa

Yield: 4 1/2 cups or 8 to 10 servings

"We love the fresh foods grown in our summer garden. This recipe is made often in the height of tomato season. It's popular with my family as a chilled dip."

1	(15-ounce) can whole kernel corn, drained	1/4	cup chopped green pepper
1	cup drained chopped tomatoes	2	tablespoons olive oil
1/2	cup chopped onions	2	tablespoons lime juice
1/2	teaspoon minced garlic	2	tablespoons cider vinegar
		1	teaspoon Creole seasoning

In a large bowl mix the corn, tomatoes, onions, garlic, and green pepper. In a separate bowl whisk together the olive oil, lime juice, vinegar, and Creole seasoning. Pour the dressing over the vegetables and blend well. Cover and refrigerate for 1 to 2 hours before serving. Serve with tortilla chips.

MARY SHIVERS | ADA, OKLAHOMA

Italian Spinach Dip

Yield: 3 1/2 cups or 6 to 8 servings

"I'm a working mom who loves to cook. This is one of my favorite appetizers. My family just loves this dip with crackers."

1	(3/4-ounce) envelope dry Italian dressing mix	1	cup sour cream
1	(10-ounce) package frozen spinach, thawed, chopped, and well drained	1	cup grated mozzarella cheese
		1/2	cup chopped red bell pepper

Combine the dressing mix, spinach, sour cream, cheese, and pepper. Cover and refrigerate for several hours before serving. Serve with your favorite crackers.

LINDA MCCUISTON | ROCKINGHAM, NORTH CAROLINA

*Tips From Our
Test Kitchen:*

This dip is also great with celery sticks, baby carrots, and other veggies.

33

Tomato Sauce and Garlic Toast Appetizer

Yield: 20 pieces

"Spoon the sauce onto garlic toast, and serve some ripe red Italian olives on the side."

Sauce:

1   (15-ounce) can diced tomatoes, drained well
2   tablespoons chopped onions
1   tablespoon capers
1   tablespoon teriyaki sauce
2   tablespoons olive oil
1   to 2 tablespoons chopped fresh basil or 1/2 teaspoon dried basil
1/4 teaspoon salt
1/4 teaspoon black pepper

Toast:

1   (24-ounce) loaf French or Italian bread
1/4 cup (1/2 stick) butter, melted
1/4 cup olive oil
4   garlic cloves, minced
1   teaspoon dried basil
1   teaspoon dried oregano

For the sauce, in a bowl combine the tomatoes, onions, capers, teriyaki sauce, olive oil, basil, salt, and pepper in the order given. Adjust the seasonings to suit your taste. Allow the mixture to stand overnight in the refrigerator, but serve at room temperature.

For the garlic toast, preheat the oven to 400 degrees. Slice the bread into about 20 pieces. Place the slices on a cookie sheet. Toast for 8 to 10 minutes, or until light golden. Combine the butter, olive oil, garlic, basil, and oregano. Brush a layer of the butter mixture on the top of each toast round. Place the rounds back in the oven, and bake until golden brown, about 10 minutes. Cool before serving.

W.R. VALENTINE | ROGERS CITY, MICHIGAN

Started by Michael Bowerman in 1813, Willow Orchards near Romeo, Michigan (pop. 3,721), is Macomb County's oldest family-owned farm and the third oldest in the state.

Deep-in-the-Woods Beef and Sausage Dip

Yield: 10 cups or 12 hearty servings

"I serve this dip every year at the 'Fantasy Football League' draft party at my house. I have to make several copies of the dip recipe each time to hand out to the guys."

3/4	pound lean ground beef	2	(15-ounce) cans kidney beans, undrained
3/4	pound mild bulk pork sausage		
1/2	large yellow onion, chopped	2	cups grated Cheddar cheese
1	cup ketchup	1	cup sliced black olives
4	teaspoons chili powder	1/2	cup chopped green onion
3	teaspoons sweet paprika		

Preheat the oven to 350 degrees. Brown the beef, sausage, and onion in a medium-sized skillet. Drain the excess fat. Add the ketchup, chili powder, paprika, and beans. Mix well. Place the mixture in a 13 x 9-inch baking dish. Bake for 15 minutes. Sprinkle the cheese, olives, and green onions on top. Bake for an additional 5 to 10 minutes, or until the cheese is melted. Serve with your favorite chips.

PAT NUGENT | EATONTON, GEORGIA

Tips From Our Test Kitchen:

This hearty dip can also be served with small slices of sourdough bread.

Mom's Ham Dip

Yield: about 2 cups or 6 to 8 servings

"My mom has made this dip for over thirty years. I guarantee that your company will want the recipe. Once you dip, you won't quit!"

1/4	cup mayonnaise	1	teaspoon parsley flakes
1	(8-ounce) package cream cheese, softened	1	teaspoon onion flakes
1/2	cup thinly sliced and chopped ham	1/4	teaspoon dry mustard

Combine the mayonnaise, cream cheese, ham, parsley flakes, onion flakes, and dry mustard. Mix until well blended. Chill. Spoon the mixture into a hollowed-out bread "bowl." Serve with your favorite crackers.

BRIDGET DREY | IDA GROVE, IOWA

Tips From Our Test Kitchen:

Adjust the seasonings to suit your taste. A dash of hot sauce or some chopped green onions work well with the flavors in this dip. It's a good dip for raw veggies too.

Pepperoni Pizza Dip

Yield: about 31/2 cups or 6 to 8 servings

"This recipe is from my mother."

8	ounces ricotta cheese	1/4	cup finely chopped pepperoni
1	cup mayonnaise	1	teaspoon garlic powder
1	plus 1/2 cup shredded mozzarella cheese	1	teaspoon Italian seasoning
1/4	cup grated Parmesan cheese	1/8	teaspoon crushed red pepper

Preheat the oven to 350 degrees. Combine the ricotta, mayonnaise, and 1/2 cup of the mozzarella. Stir in the Parmesan, pepperoni, garlic powder, Italian seasoning, and red pepper. Mix well and spoon into an ungreased ovenproof casserole dish. Sprinkle the remaining 1 cup mozzarella on top. Bake for 25 to 30 minutes, or until the cheese is bubbly and golden. Serve the dip hot with wedges of Italian bread.

AMY COLLINS | FORT VALLEY, VIRGINIA

*Tips From Our
Test Kitchen:*

Hard-core pepperoni fans can double the pepperoni. This dip is also great served with sliced vegetables.

Salmon Dip

Yield: about 11/2 cups or 4 to 6 servings

"This recipe came from my mother-in-law. She loved it. I serve it at showers and parties, but I also like to make it and eat it myself on crackers."

1	(15-ounce) can salmon	1	tablespoon lemon juice
1	(8-ounce) package cream cheese, softened	1/2	teaspoon prepared horseradish
1/3	small onion, chopped	1/4	teaspoon liquid smoke
			Salt

Remove the skin and bones from the salmon. Mix the salmon with the cream cheese, onion, lemon juice, horseradish, liquid smoke, and salt to taste. Refrigerate until ready to serve. Serve with crackers.

VIOLA PARKER | RUSSELLVILLE, KENTUCKY

*Tips From Our
Test Kitchen:*

This dish is best if allowed to chill for at least a few hours in the refrigerator to let the flavors blend. A few chives make a complementary garnish.

Shrimp-Crabmeat Spread

Yield: 1 1/2 to 2 cups or 4 servings

"This recipe is good when served with crackers or in small phyllo pastry cups."

1 (6-ounce) can tiny shrimp, drained
1 (6-ounce) can crabmeat, drained
1 small onion, finely chopped
1/4 to 1/3 cup mayonnaise

1 (3-ounce) package cream cheese, softened
3 celery stalks, finely chopped

Stir together the shrimp, crabmeat, onion, mayonnaise, cream cheese, and celery until well blended. Before serving, refrigerate for several hours to allow the flavors to blend.

DONNA BATTEN | ALLIANCE, OHIO

Tips From Our Test Kitchen:

For a creamier dip, double the cream cheese. Add a dash of hot sauce, if desired.

Shrimp Dip

Yield: about 2 cups or 4 to 6 servings

"A simple and delicious dip for when you have friends over."

2 (6-ounce) cans small shrimp, drained
1 (8-ounce) package cream cheese, softened
1/2 small onion, grated

2 tablespoons ketchup
1 tablespoon prepared horseradish
Salt and pepper

Combine the shrimp, cream cheese, onion, ketchup, horseradish, and salt and pepper to taste and stir together. Refrigerate for 4 hours before serving with crackers.

ANNA CHEPLICK | COOLDALE, PENNSYLVANIA

Tips From Our Test Kitchen:

If the dip is too thick, add more ketchup.

The first product bottled by Henry J. Heinz, founder of the Heinz Company, in the basement of his home was horseradish. In 1869, he opened his first factory in Sharpsburg, Pennsylvania (pop. 4,021).

Popping a Tasty Tradition in North Loup

The familiar mouth-watering fragrance of popping corn wafts from the fire hall in North Loup, Nebraska (pop. 339), where volunteers are turning a ton of golden kernels into a fluffy white snack and simultaneously honoring local farmers who have grown the crop for more than a century.

Visitors who arrive for the town's annual Popcorn Days celebration have no need to ask for directions to the 104-year-old event; they just follow their nose to the free bags of freshly popped corn.

Popcorn Days, which was started in 1901 by North Loup businessmen as a way to celebrate the important local crop, is the longest continuously running celebration in Nebraska.

For nearly forty of those years, Chuck Lundstedt, a retired mechanic, has helped run the event's natural-gas-operated popping machine and used scoop shovels to mix giant batches of popcorn, butter, and salt. "I just enjoy popping the corn," Lundstedt says. "Otherwise, I wouldn't have helped out this long."

During the three-day August event, 20,000 to 30,000 bags of free popcorn are handed out to thousands of popcorn lovers, says Terry Christensen, the 2004 Popcorn Days Association chairman. The celebration also features a talent show, music and dancing, a carnival on Main Street, and a huge parade.

Both the celebration and the crop are time-honored traditions in the fertile Loup River Valley, where farmers have grown popcorn since the 1890s. Chuck Zangger's family has grown popcorn since his grandfather planted their first crop in 1924. In those days, North Loup was considered the "Popcorn Center of the World."

"There's still about 1,500 acres of popcorn grown around here," Zangger says of the North Loup area. "There are quite a few farmers who are second- or third-generation popcorn growers." Today, Nebraska is the nation's top popcorn-producing state, with more than 326 million pounds produced in 2003.

The weather and soil in the valley are perfect for growing popcorn, Zangger says. "In August, we have cool nights that allow the plant to convert sugars to starch" making for kernels that pop better. Zangger not only raises popcorn that he sells to processors for food, but he also developed his own hybrid popcorn seed that is planted by farmers around the country.

Having popcorn growers so close to home is good news for Mormac, the town's only popcorn processor. The company, which donates the tasty treat for Popcorn Days, purchases popcorn from growers and distributes it to movie theaters and other food companies, which repackage it as microwave popcorn and products such as caramel corn and cheese corn.

On the first day of the event, it's traditional for residents to vote for a Popcorn Days Queen. When North Loup celebrated its Popcorn Days centennial in 2001, most of the living former queens returned home for special recognition.

The 1966 queen, Susan Hudson Traudt, now lives in nearby Grand Island, Nebraska, but she brings her family back to the celebration every year. For Traudt, it's a family affair because her sister and her aunt also were queens. "It was an honor to be chosen," Traudt says, "being from a small town and picked by the people of North Loup."

Formerly, Popcorn Days was held mid-week. "Classes were called off at school so the kids could help with activities," Christensen says. In recent years, officials have turned the event into a Friday through Sunday festival, although classes are still dismissed on Friday to allow students to participate. "When you live in a small community, everyone pitches in together," Cox says. And no one goes home hungry!

For more information, call (308) 496-4781.

Curt Arens is a farmer and freelance writer in Crofton, Nebraska.

Spinach Balls

Yield: about 60 balls or 20 servings

"This recipe is a favorite because so many friends like these spinach balls, even those who don't care for spinach. After a job-related move, I attended a newcomers' gathering where these were served. I have been making them ever since, and they are always a big hit."

2	(10-ounce) boxes frozen chopped spinach	4	eggs
2	cups herb stuffing	3/4	cup (1 1/2 sticks) margarine, melted
1	small onion, chopped	1/2	teaspoon garlic powder
		1/2	cup grated Parmesan cheese

Cook the spinach as directed on the box and drain well. Combine the herb stuffing, onion, eggs, margarine, garlic powder, and Parmesan cheese. Add the spinach. Chill.

Preheat the oven to 350 degrees. Lightly grease a baking sheet. Shape the mixture into balls, and place them on the baking sheet. Bake for 20 minutes. Serve warm.

LINDA ROBERTS | THE VILLAGES, FLORIDA

Tips From Our Test Kitchen:

Make sure the spinach is drained well by squeezing out as much excess water as possible. Sausage would be a good addition to these bite-size hors d'oeuvre.

Spinach Triangles

Yield: 8 to 10 servings

"When raising my five kids, we enjoyed trips to the Parthenon Greek restaurant in Chicago. I tried to duplicate these favorites at home."

1	(8-ounce) package frozen phyllo dough	1	medium yellow onion, chopped
1/2	cup (1 stick) butter, melted	8	ounces feta cheese, crumbled
1	(10-ounce) package frozen chopped spinach, thawed	1	tablespoon dried oregano
3	tablespoons olive oil		Salt and pepper

Preheat the oven to 350 degrees. Thaw the phyllo dough according to the package instructions. Brush a layer of melted butter in a 13 x 9-inch pan. Layer the pan with the phyllo dough sheet, overlapping to completely cover the bottom of the pan. Alternate layers of the phyllo dough sheets and melted butter until half the dough and butter is used.

Squeeze the excess liquid from the spinach. Heat the olive oil and sauté the onion. Add the spinach to the onion. Combine the feta cheese, oregano, and salt and pepper to taste. Add the feta mixture to the spinach mixture and stir while over the heat to combine and warm. Spread the mixture evenly over the prepared phyllo dough sheets. Layer the remaining dough sheets and butter over the spinach mixture. Bake for 40 minutes, or until golden brown. Cool slightly and cut into triangles.

MARSHA MCCLOSKEY | LONG BEACH, INDIANA

Tomato Cups

Yield: 12 tomato cups or 6 servings

"I won first place in a recipe contest with this dish. That was my third try. My mother always said the third time's the charm. She was right."

1	(16-ounce) can large flaky biscuits (like Grands)	1	(10-ounce) can tomatoes and green chiles (like Ro-Tel), drained
1/2	cup mayonnaise	1	teaspoon dried basil
1	cup shredded cheese (mozzarella and Cheddar blend)	1/2	onion, chopped
		10	slices bacon, cooked and crumbled

Preheat the oven to 350 degrees. Lightly grease the cups of a 12-cup muffin tin. Separate each biscuit into two or three layers. Place and press a biscuit layer evenly into each cup. Combine the mayonnaise, cheese, tomatoes and green chiles, basil, onion, and bacon and mix well. Spoon the filling on top of the biscuit layers. Bake for 20 to 25 minutes, or until golden.

IRENE TUCKER | GRENADA, MISSISSIPPI

Crystal Springs, Mississippi (pop. 5,873), once known as the "Tomatopolis of the World," was a major supplier of produce, particularly tomatoes, during the mid-1800s. Citizens moved the town several miles in 1858 to be closer to the railroad and to enable easier produce shipping.

Barbecue Beef Cups

Yield: 8 servings

"I found this recipe many years ago in the food section of our local newspaper. I have been making these little gems ever since for parties, picnics, or just snacking."

1	egg, beaten	2	(12-ounce) cans refrigerated buttermilk biscuits
1/2	cup barbecue sauce		
1	pound ground beef, browned and drained	1	cup grated Cheddar cheese

Preheat the oven to 350 degrees. Stir together the egg, barbecue sauce, and ground beef. Separate the biscuits to make 16 pieces and press them into the bottom and sides of lightly greased muffin tins. Spoon the beef mixture into each shell. Top with the cheese. Bake for 8 to 12 minutes, or until golden brown.

ANNELIESE DEISING | PLYMOUTH, MICHIGAN

*Tips From Our
Test Kitchen:*

Top with sour cream, chopped tomatoes, green onions, or chopped lettuce.

Fancy Covered Meatballs

Yield: 8 servings

"My sister discovered this recipe in an old recipe book used as a fund-raiser a long time ago. It is an appetizer she uses for special dinner parties, but it can be used anytime. My family enjoys it whenever I make it."

1	pound lean ground beef	1	package refrigerated crescent rolls
1	package dry onion soup mix		

Preheat the oven to 375 degrees. Mix the ground beef with the onion soup mix and form into sixteen 1-inch meatballs. Open the rolls on a cutting board. Cut the rolls down the middle, making 16 pieces. Press each one with the palm of your hand to flatten. Place a meatball on the wide side of each triangle and roll up, bringing the sides together. Place the wrapped meatballs on a cookie sheet and bake for 13 to 15 minutes, or until lightly browned.

ROBERTA BINDMAN | SILVER SPRING, MARYLAND

Tips From Our Test Kitchen:

Spray the covered meatballs with a non-stick spray (to help the toppings adhere better), and sprinkle them with Italian seasoning, poppy seeds, or sesame seeds. Bake as directed. Serve with dipping mustard or other sauces.

Ham Balls with Tangy Mustard Glaze

Yield: about 40 meatballs or 16 to 20 servings

"My mother made this recipe while I was growing up some fifty years ago. My grown children like it especially as part of a brunch menu."

Glaze:

1/2	cup firmly packed brown sugar
1/2	to 1 teaspoon dry mustard
2	tablespoons fruit juice

Ham balls:

1	pound cooked ham, ground
1	pound bulk pork sausage
2/3	cup cracker crumbs
1/4	to 1/2 cup milk
1/4	cup chopped onion
1	egg, beaten
	Black pepper

For the glaze, stir together the brown sugar, mustard, and juice in a small bowl.

For the ham balls, combine the ham, sausage, cracker crumbs, milk, onion, egg, and pepper to taste and mix well. Roll the mixture into golf ball shapes. (Adjust the amount of milk to encourage easy rolling and firmness.) Cook the ham balls in a large skillet over medium-high

Tips From Our Test Kitchen:

Try hot sausage if you desire more spice. Add more mustard and a dash of hot sauce for a tangier glaze.

heat, turning occasionally to brown on all sides. When cooked through, drain the grease and pour the glaze over the ham balls to coat well. Keep the ham balls warm in a slow cooker or chafing dish. Serve with toothpicks.

JAN SUPPLE | CASCADE, IOWA

In 1921, five beekeepers pooled $200 and 3,000 pounds of honey to form the Sioux Honey Association in Sioux City, Iowa. The association now has more than 350 members nationwide who produce 40 million pounds of honey annually.

Sausage-Stuffed Mushrooms

Yield: about 30 mushrooms or 10 servings

"I always make a double batch when I prepare this recipe, and I've never had any left over. My grown sons are especially fond of them."

1½ pounds medium mushrooms (about 30)	1/2 cup shredded mozzarella cheese
1/2 pound bulk pork sausage	1/2 cup shredded pepper Jack cheese
1/4 cup chopped onion	1/4 cup seasoned bread crumbs

Preheat the oven to 450 degrees. Remove the mushroom stems from the mushroom caps, and chop the stems very finely. Place the mushroom caps in a shallow baking dish in a single layer.

In a skillet brown the sausage and drain well on paper towels. Reserve a small amount of sausage grease in the pan. Crumble the sausage. In the reserved grease, lightly brown the onion. Add the chopped mushroom stems and cook until tender. Remove from the heat. Stir in the cheese, bread crumbs, and sausage. Spoon the filling into the mushroom caps. Bake for 15 minutes. Serve hot.

JANICE HEIDEN | MASON, ILLINOIS

Tips From Our Test Kitchen:

Be sure to choose a baking dish in which the mushrooms caps fit snugly. This will keep them upright.

Wonton Sausage Appetizers

Yield: 12 servings

"I'm asked to share this recipe each time I bring it to a church supper or family gathering."

1   (25-count) package wonton wrappers
1   pound bulk sausage, cooked and well drained

1½ cups shredded Cheddar cheese
1   cup shredded pepper Jack cheese
3/4 cup ranch dressing

Preheat the oven to 350 degrees. Press a wonton wrapper into each of 25 muffin-tin cups. Bake for 5 minutes. Remove from the oven and place the wonton cups on a cookie sheet. Mix the sausage, Cheddar cheese, pepper Jack cheese, and dressing until well blended. Spoon the mixture into the cups. Bake for 5 to 10 minutes, or until bubbly.

LOIS DEARWESTER | LOOGOOTEE, INDIANA

*Tips From Our
Test Kitchen:*

For bite-size appetizers, use a package of 50-count wonton wrappers, and bake them in mini-muffin tins. This doubles the yield.

Roll-Ups

Yield: about 36 roll-ups

"My daughter gave me this recipe. It's become a favorite for parties and family get-togethers."

1   (8-ounce) package cream cheese, softened
4   (9-inch) flour tortillas
1   bunch lettuce, any kind
8   ounces mozzarella, thinly sliced

1/2 to 1 pound deli-sliced turkey, beef, or ham
1   red or green bell pepper, finely chopped

Spread 2 ounces of the cream cheese evenly over the entire surface of each tortilla. Layer several leaves of lettuce over the cream cheese. Evenly divide and layer the mozzarella, meat, and pepper over the lettuce. Roll each wrap very tightly into a large cigar shape. Cut the rolls into 1-inch slices and place on a serving platter. Discard the ends.

CAROLYN CHEEK | LONDON, KENTUCKY

*Tips From Our
Test Kitchen:*

This recipe can be tailored to suit your taste by using spinach leaves instead of the lettuce. You might also add pimientos, jalapeños, spices, olives, tomatoes, or blue cheese.

Chicken Fingers

Yield: 6 to 8 servings

"These are great for a main dish, an appetizer, or a snack. Everybody loves them."

21/2	pounds skinless, boneless chicken breasts	1	cup vegetable oil
1	cup milk	1/2	cup (1 stick) butter
1	egg	1/4	cup Louisiana hot sauce (or more
1	cup all-purpose flour		to taste)
	Salt and pepper		

Preheat the oven to 350 degrees. Cut the chicken into 2- to 3-inch slices. Beat together the milk and egg. In a separate bowl mix together the flour, salt, and pepper. Dip the chicken slices into the egg mixture. Then dip them into the seasoned flour. Heat the oil in a large frying pan and brown the chicken in the oil. Melt the butter in a large baking dish and stir in the hot sauce. Place the browned chicken fingers in the dish, cover with aluminum foil, and bake for 30 minutes.

EDWANNA CHENAULT | WINCHESTER, KENTUCKY

*Tips From Our
Test Kitchen:*

If you like it real spicy,
add more hot sauce.

Silver Spoon Wings

Yield: 12 to 18 servings

"We have six children and plenty of grandchildren. They are all crazy about these chicken wings."

1/2	cup sugar	1	teaspoon ginger
1/2	cup water	1/2	teaspoon garlic powder
1/2	cup soy sauce	2	to 3 pounds chicken wings, cut at the
1/4	cup pineapple juice		joints and tips discarded
2	tablespoons vegetable oil		

In a large bowl combine the sugar, water, soy sauce, pineapple juice, vegetable oil, ginger, and garlic powder, and whisk until well blended. Add the chicken wings and coat them well. Cover and refrigerate for at least one day, stirring occasionally.

When ready to bake, preheat the oven to 350 degrees. Place the wings on a baking sheet, and bake for about 40 minutes, or until golden brown. Baste the wings with the marinade several times while baking.

DOROTHY KROUSE | CADOTT, WISCONSIN

Tips From Our
Test Kitchen:

The breading mixture
coats the chicken best
if it is processed to
resemble coarse meal.
Be certain to get the
vegetable oil hot.

Prairie-Fire Chicken Strips

Yield: 20 strips or 10 servings

"I came up with this recipe for a football party at my church several years ago. It's been the hit of every party where it's been served since."

Marinade and chicken:

1	cup sour cream
1	tablespoon lemon juice
1	tablespoon celery seed
1/2	teaspoon seasoned salt
1/4	teaspoon white pepper
2	garlic cloves, minced
10	chicken tenders, halved

Breading:

1	cup uncooked quick or old-fashioned whole oats
1	cup plain granola (without fruit or nuts)
1	cup finely chopped pecans
1/2	cup drained and chopped pickled jalapeño peppers
1/2	cup seasoned salt

Dipping sauce:

1/3	cup Dijon mustard
2	tablespoons mayonnaise
1/2	cup honey
1	garlic clove, minced
1	tablespoon chopped fresh parsley
1	teaspoon cayenne pepper
1/2	teaspoon white pepper
2	tablespoons sour cream
4	to 5 drops hot sauce
3	to 4 cups vegetable oil for frying Black pepper

For the marinade and chicken, combine the sour cream, lemon juice, celery seed, salt, pepper, and garlic in a large bowl and mix well. Add the chicken tenders. Refrigerate for several hours or overnight.

For the breading, combine the oats, granola, pecans, jalapeños, and salt in a shallow dish and mix.

For the dipping sauce, combine the mustard, mayonnaise, honey, garlic, parsley, cayenne pepper, white pepper, sour cream, and hot sauce in a food processor and blend well.

In a heavy, deep skillet or fryer heat the oil to 400 degrees. While it's heating, evenly coat both sides of the marinated chicken in the breading mixture. Fry several pieces of chicken at a time until lightly browned on both sides. Drain on paper towels. Sprinkle lightly with the black pepper to taste. Serve hot with the dipping sauce.

GWEN BEAUCHAMP | LANCASTER, TEXAS

Rick's Chicken

Yield: 8 to 10 servings

"This makes an attractive platter since the cheese and jalapeño in the center grab your attention. This is a mainstay at our parties. Guests love it."

12	to 16 skinless, boneless chicken thighs	1	pound sharp Cheddar cheese
	Cavender's Greek Seasoning	1	pound bacon
12	to 16 small jalapeño peppers		Toothpicks

Prepare the grill for cooking. Rinse the chicken thighs, and coat them lightly with the seasoning.

Wearing gloves to protect your hands, slice the peppers lengthwise and remove the seeds. Slice the cheese into pieces that will fit inside the peppers. Stuff each pepper with a piece of cheese.

Pound the chicken thighs with a meat tenderizer to flatten. Wrap each pepper with a chicken thigh. Then wrap a piece of bacon around each chicken piece. Secure well with toothpicks. Grill over low heat for 40 to 45 minutes, turning as the bacon cooks. The bacon will shrink and hold everything together. Allow the chicken to cool. Remove the toothpicks and slice into 1/2-inch rounds. Arrange on a platter to serve.

RICK DYKES | GRANBURY, TEXAS

Spinach and Chicken Crescents

Yield: 4 servings

"This recipe is quick and delicious."

1	cup well-drained chopped spinach, canned, frozen, or fresh	1	cup chopped cooked chicken
		2	tablespoons minced onion (optional)
1	cup shredded cheese (Cheddar, mozzarella, or pepper Jack)	1/2	cup mayonnaise
		1	(8-ounce) can crescent rolls

Preheat the oven to 350 degrees. Lightly grease a cookie sheet. Mix the spinach, cheese, chicken, onion, and mayonnaise until well blended. Unroll the crescent dough and separate it into triangles. Spoon the spinach mixture onto the triangles and wrap each triangle as securely as possible. Place them on the cookie sheet and bake for 20 minutes.

RENA WORKMAN BURK | JAMESTOWN, TENNESSEE

Maryland Crab Cakes

Yield: 4 servings

"When blue crabs were swimming in the Chesapeake Bay, I would catch them and steam them, setting aside the meat. Then my mother, Tess, would make her special Maryland crab cakes."

1	egg		Pinch of white pepper
1/2	cup mayonnaise	1	slice white bread without crust,
1	tablespoon chopped fresh parsley		crumbled
1	teaspoon dry mustard	1	pound back fin crabmeat
1/2	teaspoon Old Bay Seasoning		Vegetable shortening or butter
1/2	teaspoon baking powder		for sautéing
1	teaspoon Worcestershire sauce		

Combine the egg, mayonnaise, parsley, mustard, Old Bay Seasoning, baking powder, Worcestershire, and pepper in a bowl and mix. Fold in the bread crumbs and crabmeat gingerly. Form the mix into four cakes. Heat the shortening and sauté the crab cakes.

BOB PETERS | NOKOMIS, FLORIDA

Tips From Our Test Kitchen:

To reduce the cost of this dish, substitute canned lump crabmeat. Tabasco is delicious as a condiment, as are tartar sauce and cocktail sauce mixed with mayonnaise.

Seared Scallops

Yield: 5 servings

"This recipe is part of our Christmas Eve appetizer buffet. I developed it from a favorite entrée. It's important to season the scallops lightly. They should be enhanced rather than inundated."

10	large fresh scallops		Steak seasoning
2	tablespoons lime juice	4	tablespoons water
2	tablespoons butter		

Rinse the scallops in cold water and place them in a small bowl with the lime juice. Turn them several times to coat well. Allow the scallops to marinate for 10 minutes. Rinse the scallops in cold water and drain.

Melt the butter in a heavy skillet. When the pan is coated with the butter, add the scallops, and sprinkle them very lightly with the steak seasoning. Sear on medium-high heat until half cooked. The scallops will become slightly cracked on the edges, will be more firm, and will

Tips From Our Test Kitchen:

This delicacy is delicious with sautéed fresh spinach and pasta.

begin to change color. Turn them with tongs and cook until almost done. Add 2 tablespoons of the water and turn the heat up to high. Shake the pan occasionally until the liquid is reduced and the scallops are glazed. Turn again and add the remaining 2 tablespoons of the water. Proceed as before until the scallops are seared and glazed. Serve immediately with cocktail forks or toothpicks.

MOLLY B. HAUCK | EAST AURORA, NEW YORK

It takes about thirty-six apples (New York's state fruit) to create one gallon of apple cider. Standard apple trees bear fruit eight to ten years after being planted, whereas a dwarf tree starts bearing in three to six years.

Salmon Pinwheels

Yield: about 24 servings

"This recipe is very special to me because each time I prepare it for entertaining, I get great compliments on it. And the pinwheels are gone in a flash."

1	(15-ounce) can salmon or 2 cups cooked fresh salmon	1	teaspoon cilantro
1	(8-ounce) package cream cheese, softened	2	tablespoons chopped fresh parsley
		4	tablespoons mild or hot salsa
1/4	teaspoon cumin	8	(8-inch) flour tortillas
			Fresh dill (optional)

Drain the salmon and remove the skin and bones. If using fresh salmon, remove the bones and skin, and flake it.

In a small bowl combine the salmon, cream cheese, cumin, cilantro, parsley, and salsa. Mix well. Spread about 2 tablespoons of the mixture over each tortilla. Roll up each tortilla tightly and wrap individually with clear plastic wrap. Refrigerate for 2 to 3 hours.

Slice each tortilla roll into bite-size pieces. (To prevent the tortilla from flattening, roll it as you slice.) Garnish with the dill, if desired.

MARIANNE SUMMERS HOYT | TELLICO PLAINS, TENNESSEE

Tips From Our Test Kitchen:

Crabmeat can be substituted for the salmon.

West Coast Salmon Cakes with Tangerine-Tarragon Sauce

Yield: 8 servings

"My husband brings home pounds and pounds of salmon from his annual fishing trip in British Columbia. This is one of our favorite original salmon recipes."

Salmon cakes:

1	pound fresh salmon
1	tangerine, juice and zest
1	large egg, beaten
1	tablespoon heavy cream
1	teaspoon Dijon mustard
1/4	teaspoon ground red pepper
1	tablespoon chopped tarragon
1/2	cup crushed buttery crackers (such as Ritz)
1/2	cup plain bread crumbs
	Vegetable oil for frying

Sauce:

1/2	cup fresh tangerine juice
2	tablespoons fruit-flavored vinegar
2	shallots, peeled and minced
1/2	teaspoon sea salt
1/2	teaspoon ground red pepper
3/4	cup (1 1/2 sticks) unsalted butter, cut into cubes
1	tablespoon heavy cream

Preheat the oven to 350 degrees. Place the salmon on a large square of heavy-duty foil. Squeeze the tangerine juice over the salmon and sprinkle it with the zest. Bake for 20 minutes, or until the fish flakes. Remove the skin and bones from the salmon and flake the salmon into a glass bowl. Add the egg, cream, mustard, red pepper, tarragon, and crackers. Mix well. Divide the mixture into eight patties. Coat each side with bread crumbs and refrigerate for 30 minutes.

While the salmon cakes are resting in the refrigerator, prepare the sauce. Boil the tangerine juice, vinegar, and shallots in a small saucepan until the liquid is reduced to about 2 tablespoons. Add the salt and red pepper. Add the butter, several cubes at a time, whisking constantly. Remove from the heat as soon as all the butter is incorporated. Whisk in the cream. Keep the sauce warm (a thermos works great) until the salmon cakes have finished frying.

Fry the salmon cakes in the oil (four at a time) until golden brown, 3 to 4 minutes per side. Garnish with the warm tangerine sauce.

MICHAELA ROSENTHAL | WOODLAND HILLS, CALIFORNIA

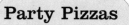

Sugared Pecans

Yield: 3 1/2 cups

"Folks always think I spent the whole day preparing them. Really, they're easy to make."

1	egg white	1	teaspoon salt
1	tablespoon water	1	teaspoon cinnamon
1	cup sugar	1	pound pecan halves

Preheat the oven to 300 degrees. Beat the egg white and water until frothy. In a large zip-lock plastic bag, combine the sugar, salt, and cinnamon. Dip the pecans in the egg white and then drop them into the bag containing the sugar mixture. Shake the bag until the pecans are well coated. Place the pecans on a well-greased, shallow baking sheet. Bake for 40 minutes, or until the egg white is dry. Stir every 10 minutes. Cool on wax paper.

MARY ALLEN | LEBANON, INDIANA

Party Pizzas

Yield: 12 to 16 rounds

"I made this back when my children were small because it fits well in small hands. It caught on with adults and has been popular with family and friends for many years."

1/2	pound sharp Cheddar cheese, grated	1	teaspoon salt
2	hard-cooked eggs, chopped	1/2	cup drained and chopped black olives
3	green onions, chopped	1 1/2	teaspoons sugar
1	large garlic clove, minced	1	(8-ounce) can tomato sauce
1	tablespoon balsamic or red wine vinegar	1	loaf French bread, sliced into 1/2-inch-thick rounds
1/4	cup olive oil		

In a large bowl combine the cheese, eggs, onions, and garlic. Add the vinegar, olive oil, salt, olives, sugar, and tomato sauce and stir until well blended. Chill 6 to 8 hours or overnight.

When ready to bake, preheat the oven to 325 degrees. Place the bread slices on an ungreased baking pan with sides. Spoon the cheese mixture evenly on the top of the bread slices. Bake for about 25 minutes, or until golden and bubbly.

MARY LOUISE GIAMFORTONE | LA MARQUE, TEXAS

Tips From Our Test Kitchen:

Toss a few of these pecans on top of a sundae or a salad. They freeze well.

Tips From Our Test Kitchen:

To freeze, place the unbaked pizza rounds on a cookie sheet and place the cookie sheet in the freezer. When frozen, transfer the pizza rounds into freezer bags until needed. When ready to eat, allow the pizza rounds to thaw for about 5 minutes and then bake as directed. Top with a slice of pepperoni, if desired.

Any Way You Slice It,
Cheese Is Tops in Little Chute

Little Chute, Wisconsin, celebrates the state's dairy industry and area cheese producers in a big way the first weekend in June. In observance of June Dairy Month, the Great Wisconsin Cheese Festival nearly doubles Little Chute's population of 10,476 as 10,000 visitors pour into the village.

Festival-goers are treated to three days of pure entertainment at Doyle Park. In the Celebrity Cheese-Curd-Eating Contest, area notables from government, business, and media compete in consuming a half-pound of cheese curds, while cheesecake lovers flock to the cheesecake contest for a taste of the cake slices sold after the competition. Another big attraction is the cheese-carving demonstration, in which artisans show off their talents by carving creations from forty-pound blocks of cheese.

Also not to be missed are the music, Big Cheese parade, cheese tasting, carnival rides, children's games and entertainment, and the Big Cheese Breakfast.

The festival, which began in 1988, attracted national attention its first year with its contest between Wisconsin and New York cheese makers. In a local newspaper's editorial, objections

Photo courtesy of Doug Alft / travelwisonsin.com. Used by permission.

were raised when Rome, New York, was selected as the site for a national cheese museum. Wisconsin state senator Walter Chilsen penned a poem that promoted the Dairy Capital as the home for such a museum and claimed that the state made the most and the best cheese. New York responded by holding a "cheese off" and declaring its cheese the best. Citizens of Little Chute challenged that decision and offered to hold another "cheese off" at the first Wisconsin Cheese Festival. The Folks of Little Chute invited Rome Mayor Carl Eilenberg to attend and even sent him a plane ticket.

During the contest, Wisconsin cheese won in all categories and was dubbed "Best Cheese in the USA." Mayor Eilenberg filed a protest claiming the tasting was unfair, since the cheeses were easily identifiable as "Wisconsin" and "New York." He requested a blind tasting on live television and proceeded to blindfold a television reporter on the scene. The reporter picked the Wisconsin cheese as the best.

Coordinated by Little Chute employees and community volunteers who make up the Board of Directors, the festival benefits the community. Since its inception, more than $300,000 has been donated to community organizations, projects, and schools.

For more information, log on to www .littlechutewi.org or call (920) 788-7390.

Vicki Karch is deputy clerk of the Village of Little Chute, Wisconsin.

Holiday Spiced Tea

Yield: 1 gallon

"This is one of my favorite recipes. It's good served hot or cold."

5	small tea bags	1	(12-ounce) can frozen orange juice concentrate
1/2	gallon plus 2 cups water		Juice of 3 lemons
3	teaspoons whole cloves		
2	cups sugar		

Brew the tea in 1/2 gallon of water. Brew the cloves separately in the remaining 2 cups water until the water is amber-colored and has a strong clove scent. This brewing process will take longer than the tea. Strain the clove water. Add the sugar to the tea and stir until it dissolves. Add the orange juice, lemon juice, and clove water. Pour all into a gallon jug. Add enough additional water to fill the jug.

ALICE POUNCEY | DECATUR, MISSISSIPPI

Tips From Our Test Kitchen:

Adjust the sugar and lemon juice to your taste. The sweet-tart balance is up to you. This tea is a very popular choice for special luncheons any time of year.

Summertime Fruit Slush

Yield: about 2 quarts

"This fruit slush is an excellent thirst-quencher passed on from my sister-in-law, Catherine. It always hits the spot and is well worth the effort."

3	plus 11/2 cups water	1	(10-ounce) jar maraschino cherries
3	cups sugar	1	(12-ounce) can frozen orange juice
1	(151/2-ounce) can crushed pineapple		concentrate
6	bananas, cubed		

In a large pan boil 3 cups of the water and the sugar for 10 minutes. Add the pineapple, bananas, and cherries. Set aside to cool.

In another bowl mix the orange juice and the remaining 11/2 cups of the water. Place in the freezer to chill, but do not freeze. Remove the orange juice from the freezer, and mix in the fruit. Freeze. When ready to serve, partially thaw the mixture.

MARIE MONFORTE | FONTANA, CALIFORNIA

*Tips From Our
Test Kitchen:*

If you prefer a drink
that is less sweet, use
1 cup sugar and 1 cup
honey instead of 3 cups
sugar. Save a few
maraschino cherries to
use as a garnish.
Skewer fresh pineapple,
bananas, and cherries
for a colorful garnish.

Nanny Punch

Yield: about 11/2 gallons

"This is a summertime favorite at our house."

6	medium-size ripe bananas	3	cups light rum (optional)
2	(6-ounce) cans frozen lemonade concentrate, thawed	1/2	cup honey
63/4	cups water	2	quarts (1.89 liters) ginger ale, chilled
1	(6-ounce) can frozen orange juice concentrate, thawed	4	cups assorted melon balls (optional)
		1	lime, cut into thin slices

Slice the bananas into a blender jar. Add the lemonade concentrate. Cover and blend on high speed until smooth. Pour into a large bowl. Stir in the water, orange juice concentrate, rum (if desired), and honey. Mix well. Pour into shallow pans or freezer containers. Freeze until slushy, about 2 hours. Pour the slush mixture into a large, chilled punch bowl. Just before serving, stir in the ginger ale. Add melon balls if using. Garnish with the lime slices.

J.P. YARBOROUGH | ELON, NORTH CAROLINA

*Tips From Our
Test Kitchen:*

If desired, use limeade
instead of lemonade
and garnish with fresh
berries.

Holiday Mulled Wine

Yield: 2 1/2 quarts

"This is a traditional family favorite during the holiday season."

4	cups water		Rind of 1 orange	
3	cups sugar		Rind of 1 lemon	
12	whole cloves	2	cups orange juice	
1	(4-inch) cinnamon stick	1	cup lemon juice	
6	whole allspice berries	3 1/3	cups Burgundy wine	
1/2	teaspoon ground ginger			

Combine the water, sugar, cloves, cinnamon, allspice, ginger, and orange and lemon rinds in a large pot. Bring to a boil and cook over medium heat until the sugar dissolves. Remove from the heat and strain out the spices and rinds. Set aside for 1 hour. Place the mixture back into the pot and add the orange juice, lemon juice, and wine. Heat gently, but do not boil. Serve warm.

CAROLYN FISHER | COLUMBIA, TENNESSEE

Tips From Our Test Kitchen:

This delicious drink will warm you up and delight your taste buds. If you don't have Burgundy wine, another red wine can be used.

Wassail

Yield: about 20 cups

"This hot fruit drink provides a charming way to greet your guests on a cold day. It's great before, during, and after a celebration feast. Everyone loves it."

1	quart (.95 liters) cranberry juice	1/2	cup sugar
1	(6-ounce) can frozen lemonade concentrate	3	cinnamon sticks
1	(12-ounce) can frozen orange juice concentrate	3	quarts water

In a large pot combine the cranberry juice, lemonade, and orange juice and bring to a boil. Add the sugar and cinnamon sticks and slow boil for 5 minutes. Add the water, bring just to a boil, and then keep warm over low heat.

DIANE HAMPTON | GAYLORD, MICHIGAN

Tips From Our Test Kitchen:

Whole cloves (about 1 tablespoon) and orange and lemon slices can be added to the pot. They look pretty and add a flavor kick.

Whipping Cream Biscuits

Yield: 10 biscuits

"I can't make biscuits the way Mama used to make them, but I have good luck with these melt-in-your-mouth biscuits. They are a breeze to make, and my family really enjoys them."

2	cups plus 1 1/2 teaspoons all-purpose flour	1	tablespoon sugar
1 1/3	tablespoons baking powder	1/4	cup (1/2 stick) unsalted butter
1/4	teaspoon salt	1	cup plus 1 tablespoon whipping cream

Preheat the oven to 425 degrees. Lightly grease a baking sheet. Combine 2 cups of the flour with the baking powder, salt, and sugar in a mixing bowl. Cut in the butter, using a pastry blender, until the texture resembles cornmeal. Add the whipping cream and stir until the dry ingredients are moist. Shape into a ball. Dust a flat surface with 1 1/2 teaspoons of the flour. Knead the dough five or six times. Roll out the dough until it is 1/2-inch thick. Cut with a 2 1/2-inch round biscuit cutter. Place on the prepared baking sheet and bake for 10 to 12 minutes, or until golden.

CHARLOTTE A. BRYANT | GREENSBURG, KENTUCKY

Tips From Our Test Kitchen:

These biscuits are ideal for breakfast, served with stews and soups, and to show off home-made preserves.

Clint's Hobo Hoe Cakes

Yield: 6 large or 8 to 12 small hoe cakes

"Since I came up with this recipe, I haven't had leftovers to bring home. Everybody else's cornbread is still sitting, and my hoe cakes are gone."

8	tablespoons self-rising cornmeal	1	(12-ounce) can whole kernel corn, drained
4	tablespoons self-rising flour	1/2	pound crisply cooked bacon, chopped
1	bunch green onions, chopped	1/2	cup buttermilk
1	egg		Vegetable oil or bacon grease

Combine the cornmeal, flour, green onions, egg, corn, and bacon and mix well. Stir in the buttermilk, 1/4 cup at a time. Use just enough buttermilk to hold the batter together. Heat 2 to 4 tablespoons of oil in a medium-size skillet. Shape the batter into patties. They can be small or large, but be certain that they are not too thick or they will not cook evenly. Turn the hoe cakes when the first side is golden brown. Fry the second side. Add additional oil to the pan if needed for a second or third batch. Serve the hoe cakes while they're still hot.

CLINT RAINES | MIDDLEBORO, KENTUCKY

Tips From Our Test Kitchen:

Test the skillet temperature with one hoe cake to start. Adjust the heat and amount of oil if necessary. Omit the bacon for a hearty vegetarian side dish.

No-Knead Refrigerator Rolls

Yield: about 30 rolls

"This is my mother's recipe. I've used it for many years. It's very easy and very good."

2/3	cup canola oil	1/4	cup sugar
1	tablespoon salt	1/2	cup wheat germ
2	cups warm water	2	eggs (optional)
2	packages active dry yeast (dissolved in an extra 1/4 cup warm water)	6	cups all-purpose flour or 5 cups if you omit the eggs

In a large bowl combine the oil, salt, water, dissolved yeast, sugar, wheat germ, and eggs, if desired. Mix well. Add the flour 1 cup at a time, stirring after each addition. Cover with plastic wrap, and place in the refrigerator for at least 2 hours before using. This dough lasts up to five days in the refrigerator.

When ready to bake, make 2-inch balls from the dough. Place them on a greased baking sheet and cover with a damp cloth. Let the rolls rise until doubled in size. Preheat the oven to 375 degrees. Bake for about 20 minutes, or until golden. Invert on a rack to cool slightly and serve warm.

LULA PETERSEN | NIWOT, COLORADO

Oatmeal Rolls

Yield: 24 rolls

"As a pastor's wife and school music teacher, I have made these rolls for many potlucks. People always ask for the recipe. I hope you enjoy it."

1/2	cup quick oats	1	tablespoon plus 1 teaspoon granulated sugar
1/2	cup old-fashioned oats		
3	tablespoons margarine, softened	2/3	cup firmly packed brown sugar
2	cups boiling water	1 1/2	teaspoons salt
2	packages active dry yeast	5	cups all-purpose flour
1/3	cup warm water		

In a large bowl combine both the oats and margarine. Pour the boiling water over the oat mixture. Stir and cool to lukewarm. In a small bowl dissolve the yeast in the warm water and 1 teaspoon granulated sugar. Add the yeast mixture along with the remaining 1 tablespoon of the granulated sugar, the brown sugar, and salt to the oat mixture. Knead in the flour, 1 cup at a time. Allow the dough to rise in a warm place for 1 hour. Punch down.

Preheat the oven to 350 degrees. Grease a 13 x 9-inch baking pan. Divide the dough into 24 balls and place in the prepared baking pan. Allow to rise again for 20 to 30 minutes. Bake for 20 to 25 minutes, or until golden brown.

CAROL A. MEYER | LINCOLN, NEBRASKA

Superb Squash Bread

Yield: 2 loaves

"I came up with this recipe when my children were toddlers, and they refused to have anything to do with the yellow squash from our garden. I've always called it 'cinnamon bread.' They didn't know that they were happily eating their least favorite vegetable."

3	eggs	3	cups self-rising flour
2	cups sugar	1	tablespoon cinnamon
1	cup vegetable oil	2	cups finely grated squash
2	teaspoons vanilla extract		

Preheat the oven to 325 degrees. Grease two 8 1/2 x 4 1/2-inch loaf pans. Beat the eggs in a large bowl on medium speed until fluffy. Mix in the sugar, oil, and vanilla. Slowly stir in the flour and cinnamon until just mixed. Stir in the squash until evenly mixed. Pour into the prepared loaf pans. Bake for 45 minutes, or until the bread is firm and light brown. If you use loaf pans, add about 10 minutes to the baking time.

SANDY DRIVER | ALBERTVILLE, ALABAMA

Tips From Our Test Kitchen:

This recipe works great with either zucchini or yellow squash. One cup of chopped walnuts or pecans makes a nice addition.

Gardendale, Alabama (pop. 9,251), founded in the 1830s, originally was called Jugtown because of a crockery jug factory there. The name was changed in 1906 to better reflect the area.

Kutztown Celebrates Pennsylvania Dutch Food and Folklore

The Pennsylvania Germans (also called "Pennsylvania Dutch") are famous for their food, and there probably is no other place in the nation where visitors can find more original Pennsylvania Dutch delicacies than at the Kutztown Pennsylvania German Festival.

The nine-day folklife festival in Kutztown, Pennsylvania (pop. 5,067), is always scheduled around the Fourth of July and draws more than 100,000 attendees.

Believed to be the oldest continuing folklife festival in the nation, the festival traces its roots to 1950 when a group of local farmers and educators banded together to introduce the area's Pennsylvania Dutch customs to a wider public. Today the festival continues to have a strong community presence, with the participation of numerous local clubs and organizations and utilizing more than 200 volunteers from the local area.

Food has always been an important part of the festival, and surveys show that it is one of the major reasons people attend. The recipes for some of the scrumptious Pennsylvania Dutch food enjoyed here are many generations old, some dating to the eighteenth and early nineteenth centuries when Germans first settled in southeastern Pennsylvania.

But there is much more to the festival than its delicious food offerings. The festival emphasizes traditions in America that date back at least two hundred years, and at the same time it provides a full day of fun and entertainment for visitors of all ages. Folklife presentations on Pennsylvania Dutch history, religion, music, meal preparation, clothing, folk medicine, and family life, as well as living history programs, immerse festival-goers in the region's history. More than two hundred nationally recognized folk artists and traditional American craftspeople demonstrate their skills and invite questions from visitors during the juried arts and crafts show. The crafts include pottery, metalwork, wood carvings, clothing, weavings, brooms, *scherenschnitte* (cut paper art), *fraktur* (ink and watercolor folk art drawings), folk instruments, hex signs, sundials, beeswax candles, and much more.

Nearly 2,000 locally handmade Pennsylvania German quilts are on display and for sale, and the quilt auction held on the second Saturday of the festival draws bidders from hundreds of miles around Kutztown. In addition, continuous music and dancing are provided on six stages, and festivalgoers can enjoy shopping for antiques and collectibles. A wide range of children's activities, including a barnyard theater, mule-drawn carousel, and a petting zoo, round out the offerings.

Traditional old-fashioned cooking takes place at the Summer Kitchen. Here visitors learn how to make meals from recipes that have been handed down through generations of a Pennsylvania German family. Cooking is done on authentic, century-old cooking appliances.

And visitors who are at the Summer Kitchen at the right time get to sample some of these tasty offerings.

Following a long-held tradition, bread is baked daily in a nineteenth-century outdoor oven, one of the oldest in Pennsylvania, and the wonderful aroma draws visitors to the bake oven.

Perhaps the most celebrated of all traditions may be the ox roast, familiar to generations of people who have attended the festival. The ox roast has its origin in the traditional Pennsylvania Dutch harvest celebrations. Everyone loves a good picnic, and the Pennsylvania Germans always looked forward to a wonderful feast following the harvest of their summer crops but before the fall planting.

Homemade Pennsylvania Dutch apple butter doesn't go unnoticed either. Fresh batches of this delicacy are available daily, made from newly picked apples, cinnamon, and other seasonings.

Food-to-go at the festival runs the gamut from the finest beef and pork to be found anywhere to liver pudding, Braunschweiger, tripe, and an assortment of unpronounceable Pennsylvania Dutch treats.

It's a Pennsylvania Dutch tradition that meals should be tasty and plentiful, and this fact is fully understood at the festival. Delicious selections abound, with items ranging from snacks to lunches and dinners. There are full-course, all-you-can-eat Pennsylvania Dutch family-style ham and chicken dinners, as well as a variety of homemade soups, sandwiches, and favorites such as sausage, chicken pot pie, corn fritters, funnel cakes, shoo-fly pie, and apple dumplings.

For more information, log on to www .kutztownfestival.com or call (888) 674-6136 or (610) 683-1597.

Dave Fooks is director of the Kutztown German Festival.

Photo courtesy of Kutztown German Festival. Used by permission.

Friendship Bread

Yield: 2 loaves

"Some years ago, a neighbor presented me with a loaf of Amish Friendship Bread, the recipe, and 'starter' dough with which I could subsequently bake my own. When I ran out of the starter, I concocted this recipe and have baked dozens of loaves for delighted friends and neighbors."

	Cinnamon sugar		
1	cup vegetable oil	2 1/2	cups all-purpose flour
1 1/2	cups sugar	1 1/4	cups milk
1	teaspoon vanilla extract	1/2	teaspoon baking soda
3	large eggs	1	(3 1/2-ounce) box instant vanilla pudding
1/2	teaspoon salt	1 1/2	teaspoons baking powder
2	teaspoons cinnamon	1/3	cup chopped black walnuts (optional)

Preheat the oven to 325 degrees. Grease two 9 x 5-inch loaf pans and sprinkle the cinnamon sugar over them. Combine the oil, sugar, vanilla, eggs, salt, and cinnamon in a large bowl. Add the flour, milk, baking soda, pudding mix, baking powder, and walnuts, if desired. Mix well. Pour the batter into the prepared loaf pans and sprinkle any leftover cinnamon sugar on top. Bake for 1 hour.

JIM EVANS | KENSINGTON, MARYLAND

Fresh Apple Bread

Yield: 2 loaves

"I'm a housewife and proud mom, and I won second place at our county fair with this delicious recipe."

2	cups sugar	1/4	teaspoon baking powder
3/4	cup vegetable oil	1	teaspoon baking soda
2	eggs	2	cups all-purpose flour
1 1/2	teaspoons cinnamon	4	cups peeled and diced apples
2	teaspoons vanilla extract	1 1/2	cups chopped walnuts
1	teaspoon salt		

Preheat the oven to 350 degrees. Grease and flour two 8 1/2 x 4 1/2-inch loaf pans. Whisk together the sugar, oil, eggs, cinnamon, vanilla, salt, baking powder, and baking soda in a large mixing bowl. Stir in the flour just until it is evenly mixed. Add the apples and walnuts. Stir together until well blended. Pour into the prepared loaf pans and bake for 55 minutes to 1 hour and 5 minutes, or until the center is set.

KELLY INGRAM | PLACERVILLE, CALIFORNIA

Applesauce Nut Bread

Yield: 2 loaves

"I received this recipe twenty-eight years ago from a coworker. Since then I've made it every Christmas to give to my family and friends."

1	cup plus 1 tablespoon granulated sugar	1	teaspoon baking soda
1	cup applesauce	1/4	teaspoon salt
2	eggs	1/2	teaspoon baking powder
1/2	cup canola oil	1/2	teaspoon cinnamon
3	tablespoons milk	11/2	cups walnut halves
2	cups all-purpose flour	1/4	cup brown sugar

Preheat the oven to 350 degrees. In a large bowl mix 1 cup of the granulated sugar with the applesauce, eggs, oil, and milk. Combine the flour, baking soda, salt, baking powder, and cinnamon in a separate bowl. Mix the contents of both bowls together and stir in the nuts. Pour the batter into two 81/2 x 41/2-inch loaf pans. Mix the brown sugar with the remaining 1 tablespoon granulated sugar and sprinkle evenly over the top of each loaf. Bake for about 1 hour, or until a toothpick inserted in the center comes out clean. Cover the tops of the loaves with foil for the final 30 minutes if they begin to get too brown.

JEANETTE HOAGLAND | McHENRY, ILLINOIS

Tips From Our Test Kitchen:

This perfect companion for a cup of coffee or tea is also good with 1 teaspoon grated lemon zest added to the batter.

Lender's Bagel Bakery made the world's largest bagel on July 23, 1998, when it created a 718-pound blueberry bagel during Bagelfest, an annual celebration in Mattoon, Illinois (pop. 18,214).

Bettye's Best Banana Bread

Yield: 2 loaves

"After years of tasting dry and flavorless banana breads, I worked out my own recipe. The secret is in using the ripest of bananas . . . almost too ripe to handle."

Bread:

13/4	cups all-purpose flour
1/4	teaspoon salt
1	teaspoon baking soda
3/4	cup (11/2 sticks) butter or margarine, softened
11/2	cups granulated sugar
2	eggs
1/4	cup buttermilk
1	teaspoon vanilla extract
1/2	to 1 cup chopped walnuts
1	cup well-mashed overripe bananas

Glaze:

1	cup confectioners' sugar
2	to 3 tablespoons lemon juice

Preheat the oven to 350 degrees. For the bread, grease and flour two 81/2 x 41/2-inch loaf pans. Combine the flour, salt, and baking soda. Beat together the margarine and granulated sugar until light and fluffy. Add the eggs one at a time, beating well after each addition. Stir in the flour mixture and buttermilk alternately. Beat the batter for 2 to 3 minutes. Stir in the vanilla, nuts, and bananas. Spoon into the prepared loaf pans. Bake for about 50 minutes, or until the center is done. Cool before adding the glaze.

For the glaze, stir the sugar and lemon juice together until there aren't any lumps. Pour it over the cooled loaves.

BETTYE BRUNER | MOUNTAIN VIEW, ARKANSAS

Mom's Cranberry Bread

Yield: 1 loaf

"My mom made this every year for the holidays. Mom passed it on to me. I passed it on to my daughter. It's the best."

1	orange (juice and rind)
2	cups all-purpose flour
1	cup sugar
1/2	teaspoon salt
11/2	teaspoon baking powder
1/2	teaspoon baking soda
2	tablespoons shortening, melted
1	egg, beaten
1	cup fresh cranberry halves
1	cup chopped walnuts

Preheat the oven to 325 degrees. Grease and flour one 9 x 5-inch loaf pan or two smaller loaf pans. Using a grater with small holes, grate the rind off the orange. Squeeze the juice into a measuring cup. Add the rind and enough hot water to equal 3/4 cup. Sift the flour, sugar, salt, baking powder, and baking soda in a medium mixing bowl. Add the orange juice, with water and rind, the shortening, and the egg to the dry ingredients. Mix well. Stir in the berries and nuts. Pour into the prepared loaf pan. Bake for 45 to 60 minutes, or until a toothpick inserted in the center comes out clean.

KATHY ANTUS | VIOLA, ARKANSAS

Strawberry Bread

Yield: 2 loaves

"This recipe is easy to make, and I have made it with leftover strawberries in the fridge. It's very tasty."

3	cups all-purpose flour	4	beaten eggs
2	cups sugar	11/4	cups vegetable oil
1	teaspoon baking soda	2	(10-ounce) packages frozen
1	teaspoon salt		strawberries, thawed and chopped
1	teaspoon cinnamon		

Preheat the oven to 350 degrees. Grease and flour two 81/2 x 41/2-inch loaf pans. Combine the flour, sugar, baking soda, salt, and cinnamon in a large bowl. Form a shallow well in the center of the mixture. Combine the eggs, oil, and strawberries and pour into the well. Stir well. Spoon the batter into the prepared loaf pans. Bake for 1 hour. Cool for 10 minutes before removing from the pans.

GERALDINE LATHAM | ELIZABETHTON, TENNESSEE

Tips From Our Test Kitchen:

This bread is also good with 1 cup chopped pecans or walnuts.

Established in 1902, Dutch Maid Bakery in Tracy City, Tennessee (pop. 1,679), is considered Tennessee's oldest family bakery. Founder John Baggenstoss, a Switzerland native, spoke Deutsch, or German, so the name became Dutch Maid.

A Heavenly Slice of Americana in South Pittsburg

The National Cornbread Festival (NCF), held the last full weekend of April in South Pittsburg, Tennessee (pop. 3,295), casts lasting impressions on organizers, volunteers, and visitors.

The reason behind the NCF's decade of success is as simple as pinto beans, onions, and cornbread.

"There's such a sense of community everywhere you go," says Louis Mahoney, food writer for the *Richmond Times-Dispatch*, who served as a judge of the 2005 National Cornbread Cook-off. "The people are proud of what they have, they know the worth of what they have, and they value it. It's a heavenly slice of Americana that has been lost."

Like many small towns in the country, in the early 1990s South Pittsburg was struggling to recapture its financial and cultural heritage. Half a century earlier, the city was the home of U.S. Stove Company, which employed more than 700 local residents. Lodge Manufacturing was another major employer, making cast iron cookware that was and remains the pride of the nation. A cotton gin, lumber mill, woolen mill, concrete company, and other companies made the city the economic heartbeat of southeastern Tennessee and northeastern Alabama.

But by the late 1980s, U.S. Stove and other companies had either shut down or relocated. Only Lodge, Sequatchie Concrete, and two textile plants remained. Community leaders became even more frustrated when a by-pass removed traffic from the central shopping district. Fortunately, links to the past jump-started South Pittsburg into the future.

"We had been toying with the idea of a festival," says Ed Fuller, president of the NCF. "But we couldn't think of anything that said 'South Pittsburg.' And then we thought of a cornbread festival. What's more Southern than cornbread and Lodge Manufacturing?"

Teaming with Lodge, Martha White, Brown Stove, and several other Tennessee companies, the NCF has become a favorite destination for locals and tourists from throughout the nation. Arts and crafts, music, the National Cornbread Cook-Off, the Celebrity Cook-Off, Cornbread Alley (tasting area), and other food vendors meld along Cedar Avenue to create a two-and-a-half-day extravaganza.

Pivotal to the success of the NCF has been the National Cornbread Cook-Off, with Martha White and Lodge annually hosting ten finalists out of approximately 1,000 entrants. Participants prepare main dish cornbread recipes, using Martha White cornmeal, Lodge cast iron cookware, and a Brown Five Star range.

The setting is as much the catalyst for success as the format, says Linda Carman, Southern baking expert for Martha White. "You have a great location in a small town that is accessible to much of the South. The town is charming and vibrant, with the volunteers pitching in and making it all happen."

From one judge's perspective, the frenzy of the competition on the cook-off stage is more heated than the Five Star ranges preparing the recipes. "At most cook-offs the whole process is sequestered. The participants don't interact with the folks in the bleachers," says *Southern Living* food editor Scott Jones, a judge for the 2005 event. "That's what's so cool about the Cornbread Festival: they're up on the stage, and the judges and audience can see the whole process. It doesn't have an influence with the final choice, but it sure puts a lot of pressure on the competitors."

"The connection with the cook-off is fascinating," says Carman of audiences watching the competition. "Not only do audiences learn how to cook cornbread, they celebrate cast iron cooking and maintain the Southern tradition of trading recipes with friends. It's exactly what we were hoping for when we started the festival."

Festival organizers developed a game plan to reinvest NCF proceeds into the community. Grants have been designated for the restoration of an old theater, the redevelopment of a community park, and projects of many other local organizations. In 2003, the City of South Pittsburg received an award from the Tennessee Municipal League in recognition of the spirit of volunteerism exemplified by the NCF.

"We've always had a generous spirit," says Bob Sherrill, mayor of South Pittsburg during the festival's first eight years. "Volunteers pick up trash, prepare food, host tours, play music, and host raffles for their organizations. The volunteers have made this the biggest thing that has ever happened to South Pittsburg."

As the popularity of the NCF has grown, so have the crowds, with an estimated 50,000 attending the eighth annual event in 2004. Food, crafts, and music may dominate the itinerary of folks, but other factors have come into play as well.

"We've become an annual destination," NCF Vice President Teena Hewgley said after the 2005 event. "This year a family from north Georgia returned for their third Cornbread Festival, and they brought friends. It's an annual event for them. Several of my friends who grew up locally return to volunteer; there's such a sense of pride in everything related to the festival."

Lodge chairman and CEO Bob Kellermann views the blend of community attributes and festival planning as the recipe for the NCF's success. "Small towns built America," says Kellermann, who along with his second cousin, Henry Lodge, is the fourth generation to follow in the management footsteps of founder Joseph Lodge. "On any given day we live and work as a community we cherish. Come cornbread time, we welcome the world, and they've all joined our love affair with cornbread."

For more information, log on to www.nationalcornbread.com or call (423) 837-0022.

Mark H. Kelly is the marketing communications manager of Lodge Manufacturing in South Pittsburg, Tennessee.

Pear Bread

Yield: 2 loaves

"We have three pear trees that really bear fruit! I've never done much canning, so I created this recipe to use our fresh pears. My family loves this simple and delicious bread."

3	cups all-purpose flour	3/4	cup vegetable oil
1	teaspoon baking soda	2	cups sugar
1/4	teaspoon baking powder	2	cups peeled and chopped pears
1	teaspoon salt	2	teaspoons vanilla extract
11/2	teaspoons cinnamon	1	cup chopped pecans (optional)
3	eggs, slightly beaten		

Preheat the oven to 325 degrees. Grease and flour two 81/2 x 41/2-inch loaf pans. Combine the flour, baking soda, baking powder, salt, and cinnamon in a medium bowl. In a separate bowl, mix the eggs, oil, sugar, pears, and vanilla. Add this mixture to the dry ingredients, stirring until just moistened. Stir in the pecans, if desired. Spoon into the prepared loaf pans. Bake for about 1 hour, or until a toothpick inserted in the center comes out clean. Cool for 10 minutes before removing from the pans. Slice when cool.

JAN WILES | HOLLY HILL, SOUTH CAROLINA

Tips From Our Test Kitchen:

Be certain that this ultramoist bread is cooked through before removing it from the oven. Serve it as a tea bread or as an elegant dessert with ice cream on top.

Tropical Bread

Yield: 2 loaves

"My family loves this sweet quick bread. It is easy to make. We eat it for breakfast, an afternoon snack, or dessert. It is a great hit at potluck dinners."

Bread:

1/2	cup granulated sugar	13/4	cups self-rising flour
2	eggs	1/4	teaspoon baking soda
1/2	cup vegetable oil		
1	cup mashed bananas (about 2 medium bananas)	**Frosting:**	
1/2	cup flaked coconut	1	cup confectioners' sugar
		1	tablespoon milk
			Coconut

Tips From Our Test Kitchen:

This bread is also good with 1 cup chopped pecans or walnuts.

70

Preheat the oven to 350 degrees. For the bread, grease two 8½ x 4½-inch loaf pans. Beat together the granulated sugar, eggs, and oil in a large bowl. Stir in the bananas and coconut. Combine the flour and baking soda in a separate bowl. Add to the banana mixture. Pour into the prepared pans and bake for 35 to 40 minutes, or until a toothpick inserted in the center of the loaf comes out clean. Cool slightly and frost with the confectioners' sugar frosting. Store the bread covered to keep it from drying.

For the frosting, sift the confectioners' sugar and mix with the milk in a small bowl until smooth. Spread over each cooled loaf and sprinkle the coconut on top.

FLO BURTNETT | GAGE, OKLAHOMA

Pork and Bean Bread

Yield: 3 loaves

"Ten years ago a friend gave me a loaf of this bread with the recipe. She told me not to tell anyone that the main ingredient is canned pork and beans. No one has yet guessed the secret ingredient, but many have enjoyed this bread."

1	cup raisins	1	teaspoon vanilla extract
1	cup boiling water	3	cups all-purpose flour
1	(15-ounce) can pork and beans	1	teaspoon cinnamon
2	cups sugar	1/2	teaspoon baking powder
3	eggs, beaten	1	teaspoon baking soda
1	cup vegetable oil	1	cup chopped pecans

Preheat the oven to 325 degrees. Grease and flour three 9 x 5-inch loaf pans. Soak the raisins in the boiling water for about 10 minutes. Mash the beans with a fork until very smooth. Add the sugar, eggs, oil, and vanilla. Mix well. Sift together the flour, cinnamon, baking powder, and baking soda and fold into the egg mixture. Drain the raisins. Fold the raisins and nuts into the batter. Spoon the batter into the prepared loaf pans. Bake for 50 to 60 minutes, or until a knife inserted in the center comes out clean.

ROSE BLANCO | ESCALON, CALIFORNIA

Tips From Our Test Kitchen:

A slice of this bread is delicious spread with cream cheese, butter, or honey.

Aunt Lillian's Pumpkin Bread

Yield: 2 loaves

"My aunt wrote this recipe on a card for me forty-six years ago. I still have her original handwritten card. We honor her every Christmas Eve when we include this bread on our menu. Three cheers for Aunt Lillian!"

2 eggs	1/2 cup vegetable oil
13/4 cup sugar	1/3 cup water
1 cup canned pumpkin	1 teaspoon baking soda
1/2 teaspoon salt	13/4 cups all-purpose flour
1 teaspoon cinnamon	1 tablespoon vanilla extract
1 teaspoon freshly grated nutmeg	1 cup chopped black walnuts

Preheat the oven to 350 degrees. Grease and flour two 9 x 5-inch loaf pans. In a large mixing bowl, combine the eggs, sugar, pumpkin, salt, cinnamon, and nutmeg. Stir in the oil, water, baking soda, flour, vanilla, and walnuts until well blended. Divide the batter equally in the pans. Bake for 45 minutes. Reduce the oven temperature to 250 degrees, and continue baking the loaves for an additional 15 minutes, or until a toothpick inserted in the center comes out clean. Serve with real whipped cream and a dash of freshly ground nutmeg.

SHAY SOUTHWICK THUROW | NORTH PORT, FLORIDA

Tips From Our Test Kitchen:

If you are unable to find black walnuts, regular walnuts or pecans can be substituted.

Pecan Pie Muffins

Yield: 30 to 36 muffins

"A friend gave me this recipe when she was visiting us. I tried it and have been making it ever since. Everyone who eats it wants the recipe, so I will just share it with everyone at American Profile. The secret, of course, is in using real butter."

1 cup firmly packed light brown sugar	2/3 cup butter, melted (I use salted butter)
1/2 cup all-purpose flour	1 cup chopped pecans
2 eggs	

Preheat the oven to 350 degrees. Grease the cups of mini-muffin tins. Mix the sugar, flour, eggs, butter, and pecans in a bowl with a wooden spoon. Pour into the muffin tins, filling each cup two-thirds full. Bake for 12 to 15 minutes.

Tips From Our Test Kitchen:

Garnish each muffin with a pecan half.

CAROLYN HAYS | ATHENS, ALABAMA

Nutty Rhubarb Muffins

Yield: 12 muffins

"I make these at least twice a week during rhubarb season. My family loves them."

Muffins:

3/4	cup firmly packed brown sugar
1	egg, beaten
1	teaspoon vanilla extract
1/3	cup vegetable oil
1/2	cup buttermilk
2	cups all-purpose flour
1/2	teaspoon baking soda

1/2	teaspoon salt
1	cup diced rhubarb
1/2	cup chopped nuts

Topping:

1/4	cup firmly packed brown sugar
1/4	cup chopped pecans or walnuts
1/2	teaspoon ground cinnamon

Preheat the oven to 375 degrees. Grease and flour the cups of muffin tins. For the muffins, mix the sugar, egg, vanilla, oil, and buttermilk. In a large bowl mix the flour, baking soda, and salt. Stir the sugar mixture into the flour mixture and blend until evenly moistened. Fold in the rhubarb and nuts. Spoon into the prepared muffin tins.

For the topping, stir together the brown sugar, nuts, and ground cinnamon, and sprinkle evenly over the top of each muffin. Bake for about 20 minutes, or until the center springs back when touched.

ANNABELLE THARALDSON | DAZEY, NORTH DAKOTA

Tips From Our Test Kitchen:

These muffins are good for breakfast, with a cup of mid-morning coffee, or even as a dessert.

The nation's largest beet sugar producer, American Crystal Sugar Company, operates processing plants at Drayton (pop. 913) and Hillsboro (pop. 1,563), North Dakota, and at sites in Minnesota and Montana. Sugar beets are grown on about 500,000 acres in the Red River Valley.

Scones with Clotted Cream

Yield: 10 to 12 scones and 11/2 cups cream

"Last year my husband and I hosted a party in honor of our favorite British author, C. S. Lewis. I developed these recipes for the occasion."

Scones:

2	cups all-purpose flour
1/4	cup granulated sugar
1/2	teaspoon salt
2	teaspoons baking powder
6	tablespoons butter, softened
2	eggs
1/2	cup sour cream
1	teaspoon vanilla extract

Clotted cream:

1	(8-ounce) package cream cheese, softened
1/2	cup sour cream
2	tablespoons confectioners' sugar
1	teaspoon vanilla extract

Preheat the oven to 375 degrees. Combine the flour, granulated sugar, salt, and baking powder in a mixing bowl. Add the butter and stir until the mixture resembles coarse meal. Combine the eggs, sour cream, and vanilla in a separate bowl. Add this mixture to the dry ingredients and stir until just moistened. Roll out the dough on a well-floured surface to a 1-inch thickness and cut into 2-to-3-inch circles. Bake on a lightly greased baking sheet for 20 minutes, or until light golden brown. Cool slightly.

For the cream, combine the cream cheese, sour cream, sugar, and vanilla and stir until well mixed. It will be slightly lumpy. Refrigerate until ready to serve.

ESTHER BALL | RINCON, GEORGIA

Saturday Bean Soup

Yield: 6 to 8 servings

"I cook this soup in a slow cooker so it is ready by lunchtime and stays hot throughout the day. Folks can help themselves as they come into the kitchen from various activities. It makes a nice hot pick-me-up or a sit-down meal. Serve with cornmeal muffins and fresh fruit."

1	pound dry navy beans, sorted and soaked	1	medium onion, finely chopped
2	quarts water	1/2	teaspoon black pepper
1	pound meaty ham bones or chunks	1	teaspoon salt, or to taste
1	celery stalk with leaves, finely chopped	1	bay leaf
1	large carrot, finely chopped		

Drain the soaked beans, rinse, and put them in a slow cooker. Add the water, ham bones, celery, carrot, and onion. Season the beans with the pepper, salt, and bay leaf. Cover and cook for 5 to 6 hours on high. Lower the temperature, remove the bay leaf, and let the soup remain in the slow cooker for serving throughout the day.

ROSALIND HESS | STORY CITY, IOWA

Creamy Broccoli Cheese Soup

Yield: 6 to 8 servings

"I've served several Hometown Recipes to my friends. When I served this soup, they asked me which issue of American Profile *had featured it. This one happens to be my own. It only seemed right to share it with your readers."*

2	cups diced potatoes	1/2	cup chopped onion
2	(14-ounce) cans chicken broth	2	(10 3/4-ounce) cans condensed cream
3	(10-ounce) packages frozen chopped		of chicken soup
	broccoli	12	ounces Cheddar cheese, cubed

Parboil the potatoes in water for about 10 minutes. Drain the water and add the chicken broth, broccoli, and onion. Cook for 20 minutes. Reduce to a simmer and add the chicken soup and Cheddar cheese. Stir to prevent the cheese from sticking to the pan. When heated through, serve immediately.

ALFRED LEES | CALLICOON, NEW YORK

Cabbage-Bean Soup

Yield: 8 to 10 servings

"This favorite standby makes a quick and satisfying meal on a cold night."

1	to 2 tablespoons vegetable oil	2	cups canned tomatoes with juice
1/2	cup diced onion	1	teaspoon chili powder
2	cups water	1/4	teaspoon black pepper
6	ounces precooked ham, diced	1	(16-ounce) can great Northern beans, drained
2	cups shredded cabbage		

In a large saucepan heat the oil over medium-high heat and sauté the onion until tender. Add the water, ham, cabbage, and tomatoes. Season with the chili powder and black pepper. Bring the mixture to a boil and then lower the heat. Cover and simmer for 15 minutes. Add the beans. Continue simmering for 20 minutes, or until the cabbage is tender.

FLO BURTNETT | GAGE, OKLAHOMA

Potluck Black-Eyed-Pea Soup

Yield: 10 to 12 servings

2	tablespoons vegetable oil	1	(15-ounce) can Italian-style stewed tomatoes
2	pounds ham or turkey ham		
2	cups chopped celery	1	(10-ounce) can tomatoes with green chiles (Ro-tel)
2	cups chopped green pepper		
2	cups chopped onions	3	(15-ounce) cans black-eyed peas

In a large stockpot heat the vegetable oil and sauté the ham, celery, green pepper, and onions until soft. Add the stewed tomatoes, tomatoes with green chiles, and black-eyed peas. Add 1 to 2 cups water if the soup is too thick. Simmer, stirring occasionally, for 30 to 40 minutes.

EDITH PERATTA | DURANT, OKLAHOMA

Tips From Our Test Kitchen:

Smoked turkey makes a tasty alternative to the ham. A cup of diced carrots is a nice addition too. They can be sautéed with the onions.

Tips From Our Test Kitchen:

This stew-like soup is great with cornbread. It's an economical way to use leftover ham, and it freezes beautifully.

Fall Potato Soup

Yield: 6 servings

"I don't know anyone else who makes potato soup like this. It is a favorite at our house—pretty and so good."

10	to 12 small red new potatoes or 4 to 5 medium-size red potatoes	1	tablespoon bacon grease
2	tablespoons margarine	1	(14-ounce) can chicken broth
1	carrot, grated	1	cup milk
1	celery stalk, finely chopped		Salt and pepper
1/4	onion, finely chopped		Grated Cheddar cheese
1	teaspoon all-purpose flour		Chopped green onions

Steam the potatoes until very tender. Peel and cut into bite-size pieces when cool. Melt the margarine and sauté the carrot, celery, and onion until crisp-tender. Stir in the flour and bacon grease. Pour in the chicken broth and milk and stir until smooth. Add the potatoes and stir until well mixed. Season with the salt and pepper to taste. Heat until ready to boil but not boiling. Serve topped with grated Cheddar cheese and chopped green onions.

GWEN COX | CANYON, TEXAS

Tips From Our Test Kitchen:

For a decadent treat, top with crisply fried and crumbled bacon.

Zucchini-Cream Cheese Soup

Yield: 4 to 6 servings

"This soup is good served hot or cold. It freezes well too."

4	tablespoons butter	4	chicken bouillon cubes
1/2	cup chopped onion	8	ounces cream cheese
3	cups unpeeled chopped zucchini	2	cups water
1	teaspoon garlic powder		

Melt the butter in a large skillet. Sauté the onion and zucchini in the butter until soft. Blend or process the onion and zucchini with the garlic powder, bouillon cubes, and cream cheese. When the mixture is very smooth, stir in the water. To serve hot, pour the mixture into a saucepan and heat through. To serve cold, refrigerate the soup for 3 hours.

JOANN WILCOX | CANON CITY, COLORADO

Tips From Our Test Kitchen:

This soup offers a great way to use up some of that zucchini crop. Add a teaspoon of freshly ground black pepper or fresh lemon zest for extra zip.

French Three-Onion Soup

Yield: 4 servings

"This soup is out of this world. It goes with everything from chicken and chops to meatloaf. It's very hearty."

1/4	cup (1/2 stick) butter or margarine
2	large yellow onions, thinly sliced (about 4 cups)
1	medium red onion, thinly sliced (1 1/2 to 2 cups)
2	tablespoons sugar
1/2	cup red wine
2	garlic cloves, minced
2	(14 1/2-ounce) cans beef broth
2	scallions, thinly sliced
1/4	teaspoon salt
1/2	teaspoon pepper
4	slices toasted French bread about 1/2-inch thick
4	ounces Gruyère cheese, shredded

In a large pot melt the butter over medium heat. Cook the yellow and red onions, sugar, red wine, and garlic until the onions are just softened, stirring occasionally. Reduce the heat to low, and cook this mixture for 20 to 25 minutes, or until the onions are golden and the wine is absorbed. Add the broth, scallions, salt, and pepper and heat through for 3 to 4 minutes.

Preheat the oven broiler. Ladle the soup into four ovenproof bowls. Place a piece of French bread on each soup serving. Top the bread with the cheese. Broil for about 5 minutes, or until the cheese is light brown and bubbly. Serve immediately.

ALICE CHARITY | FREDERICK, MARYLAND

Peanut Butter Soup

Yield: 8 servings

"While attending a Kiwanis convention with my husband, I fell into conversation with another Kiwanis wife at a luncheon. She wrote this recipe for me on a paper napkin."

1/4	cup (1/2 stick) butter
1	cup thinly sliced celery
1	medium onion, chopped
2	to 3 tablespoons all-purpose flour
2	quarts chicken broth
1	cup creamy peanut butter
1	cup light cream or half-and-half
	Salt and pepper

Heat the butter in a large saucepan and sauté the celery and onion until tender but not browned. Add the flour and whisk until smooth. Gradually add the chicken broth, and bring the mixture to a boil. Stir in the peanut butter until all the lumps are blended. Simmer for 10 to 15 minutes over medium-low heat, stirring occasionally. Just before serving, add the cream and the salt and pepper to taste.

JOYCE O'LAUGHLIN | JACKSONVILLE, NORTH CAROLINA

Potato Soup

Yield: 8 to 10 servings

"One day a friend told me she added cream of chicken soup and sour cream to her potato soup to make it a richer, creamier dish. I worked with my own recipe and came up with this one and feel it is delicious enough to share with others. It is one dish the entire family agrees on."

1/2 cup finely chopped celery	1 (10 3/4-ounce) can condensed cream
1/2 cup finely chopped carrots	of chicken soup
1/2 cup finely chopped onion	1 cup sour cream
2 to 4 bay leaves	1 cup milk
Salt and pepper	Finely chopped chives (optional)
Chicken broth (or water)	
6 cups peeled and diced potatoes	
(smaller than 1-inch-square)	

Tips From Our Test Kitchen:

Substitute a sour-cream-based ranch or onion dip for the sour cream. This recipe also is very good when served cold like vichyssoise.

Combine the celery, carrots, onion, bay leaves, and salt and pepper to taste in a large stockpot. Cover with the broth and cook over medium-high heat until soft. Add the potatoes and more broth to cover. Boil until the potatoes are soft but not mushy (about 25 minutes). Whisk the chicken soup and sour cream in a bowl until smooth. Add to the potatoes. Add the milk a little at a time until you reach the desired consistency. Stir lightly so as not to break the potatoes. Garnish with chives, if desired.

VARIATIONS:

Add 2 to 4 links of cooked sausage, cut into small pieces, or small pieces of cooked ham. Garnish with paprika or crisply fried and crumbled bacon.

DONNA VIOLA | MCPHERSON, KANSAS

Gilroy's Great Garlic Gathering

Residents of Gilroy, California (pop. 41,464), know garlic. They should, considering that they live in the "Garlic Capital of the World," where local companies process truckloads of the crop and more than two tons of fresh garlic cloves flavor food during a summer celebration paying tribute to the pungent plant.

Each July, 120,000 people attend the three-day Gilroy Garlic Festival, which features a cooking contest, entertainment, and sixty-five food booths that tempt the palate with garlic fries, garlic ice cream, garlic kettle corn, deep-fried garlic pickles, and garlic chocolate.

"Garlic is easy to grow here in the Santa Clara Valley," says third-generation farmer Don Christopher. "It likes a long growing season—very little moisture, and lots of sunshine."

Christopher, who owns the Christopher Ranch in Gilroy, began growing garlic in the mid-1950s with just ten acres. Today, he has 800 full-time employees who process the garlic he grows in the Santa Clara, Salinas, and San Joaquin valleys. Sixty million pounds of fresh garlic are processed and shipped annually from his ranch.

As one of the creators of the annual festival, Christopher has provided truckloads of garlic for the event. In 1978 Dr. Rudy Melone, then president of the town's Gavilan College, contacted area garlic farmers to ask for help in planning the festival as a community fund-raiser. They scheduled the event to coincide with the end of the garlic harvest and estimated that about 5,000 visitors would attend. When 10,000 garlic lovers showed up, they ran into a few problems. Tickets collected at the gate had to be given to runners who took them back to the ticket booth to re-use. Then they ran out of pesto for their garlic.

"You should have seen my kitchen," Christopher says. "There were people chopping and people blending and still more people running back and forth between here and the festival. It was a lot of hard work, but it was also a lot of fun."

After all the bills were paid, the fund-raiser netted $19,000, and a nonprofit corporation, the Garlic Festival Association, was created to distribute the funds.

The festival has since taken on a life of its own and become a communitywide event, enlisting the help of four thousand volunteers. For their participation, volunteers are "paid" according to the number of hours they help. That money is then donated to the charitable group or service organization of their choice. Since 1979 the association has distributed nearly $7 million to causes such as school sports teams, church groups, senior centers, and service organizations.

The Gilroy Garlic Festival Cook-Off is one of the event's highlights, in which eight cooks work onstage for up to three hours to create their favorite garlic dishes. Judges look for preparation, flavor, texture, creativity, appearance, and, of course, the use of garlic. The 2004 winner, Ginger Moreno of Rancho Palos Verdes, California (pop. 41,145), won for her garlic seafood soup.

The onion-like plant, which thrives in Gilroy's Mediterranean-like climate, was first introduced to California by the Spaniards in the late 1700s. It wasn't until Japanese farmers arrived in Gilroy following World War I, however, that the crop became synonymous with the area. Although today less than 1 percent of the state's garlic is grown in Gilroy, Gilroy Foods and Christopher Ranch are among the nation's largest processors and shippers of garlic.

"At one point, the town was one of the largest garlic growing areas on the West Coast," says Susan Voss, a museum assistant at the Gilroy Museum. "Today, garlic and garlic products are still very much a part of the community and economy, and I expect that'll always be the case."

For more information, log on to www.gilroygarlicfestival.com or call (408) 842-1625.

Laura Harris is a freelance writer in Salinas, California.

Grandma's Prune Soup

Yield: 8 to 10 servings

"When I was a little girl, my grandmother used to serve this soup along with homemade bread. It brings back fond memories for me."

2	pounds beef chuck roast		1	medium onion, chopped
	Salt and pepper		1	cup quartered prunes
	Canned beef broth		1	cup raisins
4	potatoes, peeled and diced			Cider vinegar

Wash the beef and place it in a 4-quart saucepan, generously covering it with water. Add the salt and pepper to taste. Over high heat bring the water to a boil. Cover and reduce the heat. Simmer for 2 hours, or until the beef is tender. Remove the beef from the broth and place it on a platter to cool. Skim the fat from the top of the broth. Reserve 11/2 quarts of broth. (If there isn't enough, add canned beef broth.) Trim and chop the beef into bite-size pieces. Discard any bone.

Place the beef back in the pot with the potatoes, onion, prunes, and raisins. Add extra beef broth if needed to keep the liquid level to at least 11/2 quarts. Cover and simmer for 1 hour, or until the vegetables and beef are very tender. Adjust the seasonings. Serve in bowls with hearty bread. Use the vinegar as a condiment.

Tips From Our Test Kitchen:

This outstanding German stew should be called Grandma's Delight. The seasonings can be adjusted by adding a bit of garlic or more salt and pepper. Experiment with different vinegars. Pear and balsamic are good choices.

MERNA HANSON | JUNIATA, NEBRASKA

Pumpkin Soup

Yield: 6 servings

"My friend Natalie Hartman introduced me to this soup. I make it in the fall and winter months. It's easy to make and good for you."

6	tablespoons butter	1	(15-ounce) can solid packed pumpkin
1/2	small yellow onion, diced	1/2	cup apple juice
1/2	cup all-purpose flour		Dash of salt and pepper
4	cups chicken or vegetable broth	1 1/2	cups heavy cream

Melt the butter and sauté the onion over medium heat until translucent. Do not allow the onion to burn. Add the flour and continue to cook for about 10 minutes, stirring often. This cooks the flour and gives it a roasted, rather than floury, taste. Slowly stir in the broth. Add the pumpkin, apple juice, and salt and pepper and heat thoroughly. Working in small batches, purée the soup in a blender. Return it to the saucepan. Add the cream and heat.

CAROLYN BATEMAN | NEW BRAUNFELS, TEXAS

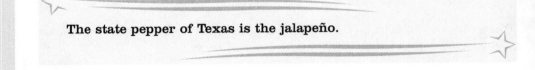
Ginger Pumpkin-Tomato Soup

Yield: 6 servings

"I had extra canned pumpkin when making a pie the night before Thanksgiving. I invented this soup to make certain it didn't go to waste. It's so rich that it seems like it has cream in it. The flavors blend flawlessly. Making this soup is now a tradition."

2	to 4 tablespoons butter	1	(15-ounce) can pumpkin purée
1 1/2	cups minced yellow onion		Freshly ground black pepper
1	cup minced celery		Sour cream
3/4	teaspoon dried ginger		Chopped flat leaf parsley
2	cups chicken broth (more if needed)		
1	(14-ounce) can Mexican-style stewed tomatoes		

Melt the butter in a Dutch oven or heavy skillet over medium heat. Add the onion and celery. Cook for about 10 minutes, or until the vegetables are soft. Sprinkle the dried ginger on top and sauté for 30 seconds. Add the chicken broth and bring to a low boil. Purée the canned tomatoes with their juice in a blender or food processor. Stir the tomatoes and the pumpkin into the broth mixture and simmer for about 20 minutes. If the soup is too thick, add more broth. Season with the pepper to taste and garnish with sour cream and parsley.

ERIN RENOUF MYLROIE | ST. GEORGE, UTAH

Ravioli Soup

Yield: 8 servings

"We like all kinds of soup. This one is very good served with focaccia or hot pepper bread."

8	ounces sweet Italian sausage, casing removed	1	(14-ounce) can diced tomatoes
1	teaspoon garlic powder	1	(15-ounce) can garbanzo beans
4	cups water	1/4	cup brown mustard
2	to 4 tablespoons chicken bouillon granules (or 6 to 8 cubes)	1/2	teaspoon chopped fresh oregano leaves
9	ounces frozen miniature cheese ravioli	1/4	teaspoon pepper
3	tablespoons all-purpose flour	11/2	cups chopped fresh spinach
			Grated Parmesan cheese

Brown the sausage. Add the garlic powder and cook for 1 minute with the sausage. Crumble the sausage and drain the grease. Heat the water with the chicken bouillon. When it boils, add the ravioli and cook for 4 to 5 minutes, or until tender. Combine the flour and the diced tomatoes and whisk until the lumps are gone. Add the tomato mixture, beans, mustard, oregano, and pepper to the broth. Heat through until thick. Stir in the spinach and cook just until wilted, about 1 minute. Serve immediately, topped with lots of Parmesan cheese.

JANET HARPST | GREENVILLE, PENNSYLVANIA

Albondiga Soup

*"When asked what my family wanted on Christmas Eve, it was unanimous—
Mom's Albondiga Soup. It's a holiday tradition—delicious, warm, and filling."*

Meatballs:

4 ounces ground pork
1 pound lean ground beef
1 egg, lightly beaten
1/8 cup finely chopped celery
1/8 cup finely chopped cilantro
3/4 cup fine breadcrumbs
1/2 cup finely chopped onion
1/4 cup uncooked rice
1/4 teaspoon cumin powder
1/4 teaspoon cayenne pepper
1/4 teaspoon seasoned salt
1/4 teaspoon chili powder
1/4 teaspoon black pepper

Soup:

2 tablespoons vegetable oil
2 celery stalks, chopped
1 large onion, chopped
1 garlic clove, minced
3 (10 1/2-ounce) cans condensed beef broth
3 cans water
1 (28-ounce) can diced tomatoes with juice
2 large potatoes, peeled and cut into small chunks
1 1/2 cups sliced carrots
Salt and black pepper
1/2 teaspoon ground cumin
Dash of cayenne pepper
1/4 cup chopped cilantro
1 medium zucchini, sliced
Cheddar cheese for garnish
Chopped cilantro for garnish
Avocado slices for garnish

For the meatballs, combine the pork, beef, egg, celery, cilantro, breadcrumbs, onion, and rice. Add the cumin, cayenne pepper, seasoned salt, chili powder, and black pepper and stir until very well mixed. Form into small meatballs. Cook, covered, in a skillet or microwave for about 6 minutes, or until the centers are no longer pink.

For the soup, heat the oil in a large soup pot, and sauté the celery, onion, and garlic. Add the broth, water, tomatoes, meatballs, potatoes, and carrots. Stir in the salt and black pepper to taste, cumin, cayenne pepper, and cilantro. Simmer for 25 to 30 minutes. Add the zucchini during the last 10 minutes of cooking. Serve hot with Cheddar cheese, cilantro, or avocado as garnishes.

KATHY HOWARD | TEHACHAPI, CALIFORNIA

Wild Rice Soup

Yield: 8 to 10 servings

"We like this soup. It's a big hit wherever we take it."

2/3	cup uncooked wild rice, rinsed		11/4	teaspoons salt
2	cups water		1/4	teaspoon pepper
2	tablespoons butter		1	teaspoon parsley flakes
1	cup finely grated potatoes		8	ounces processed cheese (such as Velveeta)
1	onion, minced (or 1/4 cup dried onion flakes)		10	strips bacon, crisply cooked and crumbled
33/4	plus 1/4 cups milk			
2	tablespoons all-purpose flour			

Cook the wild rice in enough water to cover it well. Simmer over low heat until barely tender, taking care not to overcook it. Drain and set aside. Combine the water and butter in a soup pot. Then add the potatoes and onion, stirring often to avoid scorching. Stir 33/4 cups of the milk into the potato mixture. In a bowl combine the flour into the remaining 1/4 cup of milk and whisk together. Stir this milk mixture into the heated potato mixture until the soup is creamy and smooth. Season with the salt and pepper. Stir in the rice, parsley flakes, cheese, and bacon and heat until the cheese melts. Adjust the salt and pepper to taste.

ELAINE HAUSSLER | HOLBROOK, NEBRASKA

> *Tips From Our Test Kitchen:*
>
> Add 1/4 teaspoon cayenne pepper if you enjoy spicy dishes.

Greek Egg-Lemon Soup

Yield: 8 to 10 servings

6	cups chicken stock	Juice of 1 lemon
1/4	cup converted rice	Salt and pepper
2	eggs, beaten	

In a large saucepan bring the chicken stock to a simmer. Stir in the rice and simmer for 15 minutes, or until the rice is soft. Combine the eggs with the lemon juice. Drizzle the juice mixture into the simmering broth. The egg will cook instantly. Season with the salt and pepper to taste.

MARSHA MCCLOSKEY | LONG BEACH, INDIANA

Beef Soup

Yield: 6 to 8 servings

*Tips From Our
Test Kitchen:*

You could add almost
any vegetable you
like to this soup, or
add some pasta during
the last 7 minutes of
cooking.

*"To get an assortment of vegetables into our three sons, I experimented with
vegetable juice. This is the favorite recipe of all."*

1½	pounds lean ground beef
1	garlic clove, minced
1	large onion, chopped
1	quart vegetable juice
1	tablespoon firmly packed brown sugar
1	bay leaf

2	(10¾-ounce) cans condensed cream of celery soup
2	cups thinly sliced carrots
1	cup thinly sliced celery
	Salt and pepper

In a large skillet brown the ground beef with the garlic and onion. Drain and transfer to a large soup pot. Add the vegetable juice, sugar, bay leaf, and celery soup. Microwave the carrots and celery until tender. Add to the soup mixture. Simmer for 30 minutes. Season with the salt and pepper to taste.

KAYE BRECKENRIDGE | TINGLEY, IOWA

Cassoulet

Yield: 8 to 10 servings

*Tips From Our
Test Kitchen:*

The classic recipe for
this French bean dish
requires many more
hours of preparation.
This short-cut version
is delicious and easy to
make.

*"This recipe makes a lot of soup. It's delicious and freezes well. It's great on a
cold evening with French bread and a dessert."*

1	cup dried navy beans (see note below)
1	cup dried kidney beans
1	cup dried great Northern beans
2	quarts water
1½	teaspoons Bouquet Garni or other no-salt herb blend
½	teaspoon dried thyme
1	(28-ounce) can whole tomatoes, mashed
1	pound mild Italian sausage, cooked, drained, and crumbled

1½	cups diced ham
2	medium onions, diced
3	medium carrots, diced
2	celery stalks, diced
2	garlic cloves, minced
2	tablespoons chicken stock granules
	Tabasco

Place the dried beans in a large stockpot and cover with the water. Add the Bouquet Garni and thyme and simmer for 1 hour. Add the tomatoes, sausage, ham, onions, carrots, celery, garlic, chicken stock granules, and Tabasco to taste. Simmer for 1 to 2 hours, or until the vegetables and beans are tender.

Note: Substitute 2 (14½-ounce) cans of each of the dried bean varieties listed above. Add the remaining ingredients and simmer for 1 to 2 hours.

EDNA HARTER | MOHAVE VALLEY, ARIZONA

Canadian Cheese Soup

Yield: 8 to 10 servings

"My aunt never minded sharing her 'masterpieces' with us. This soup is one from over thirty years ago."

5	tablespoons butter	1/2	teaspoon dry mustard
2	medium carrots, finely chopped	1	quart (4 cups) milk
2	celery stalks, finely chopped	1/2	teaspoon paprika
1/2	cup finely chopped onion	1/4	teaspoon cayenne pepper
1/2	green bell pepper, finely chopped	1	pound sharp Cheddar cheese, grated
1/2	cup finely chopped cooked ham		Salt and pepper
1/2	cup all-purpose flour	1	(4-ounce) can mushrooms, drained
2	tablespoons cornstarch		(optional)
1	quart chicken broth		

In a large stockpot melt the butter and sauté the carrots, celery, onion, and green bell pepper. Cook over medium heat for about 10 minutes until the vegetables are crisp-tender, but not brown. Stir in the ham. Add the flour and cornstarch, and cook, stirring constantly, for 3 minutes. Add the broth, stirring constantly, until the soup thickens slightly. Add the mustard, milk, paprika, cayenne, cheese, salt and pepper to taste, and the mushrooms if using. Continue stirring until the soup is heated through and thick. Do not boil or the cheese will curdle. Remove from the heat and serve immediately.

DIANE HAMPTON | GAYLORD, MICHIGAN

> *Tips From Our Test Kitchen:*
>
> This hearty treat is perfect on a chilly day with a green salad and hot rolls. For quicker preparation, put the vegetables together in a food processor to chop finely.

Arenzville Cooks Don't Spoil the Burgoo

Q: How many cooks does it take to make a batch of burgoo?

A: In Arenzville, Illinois (pop. 419), about half the town.

"Burgoo?" you ask. To call it soup doesn't really do it justice. The bubbling vegetable and meat concoction served up steaming hot at the Arenzville Burgoo Festival is more like a stew. Its origins are clouded in local folklore, and its contents, though simple, have evolved over the last 100 years.

In the old days you could taste local game, such as venison or squirrel, added into the mix. Nowadays you'll taste chicken and beef cooked up with corn, potatoes, carrots, cabbage, onions, celery, and spices—nothing out of the ordinary.

Volunteers start chopping vegetables the day before the kettles are filled and stay up all night tending the wood-burning fires and cooking the burgoo for fourteen hours before it's ready. Then for two days, 4,000 to 5,000 people show up to eat more than 1,500 gallons of thick, chunky, almost chewy burgoo.

A handful of small towns in western Illinois are known for making burgoo each year, although Arenzville has the largest event. How the tradition got started, though, is a bit of a mystery.

Some suggest it simply grew out of a long-ago gathering of locals putting whatever food they had into a community pot for a shared meal. Another possibility is that German settlers who founded the town back in 1853 brought the tradition with them. Adding credence to that theory is the fact some towns in Kentucky founded by Germans also have a burgoo tradition.

Whatever the origin, the idea has stuck, and it's grown into much more than a simple community meal. The annual event, held on the Friday and Saturday after Labor Day, has developed into a major celebration that's part festival, part homecoming, and part community fundraiser, and includes everything from carnival rides to big-name country music entertainment. Festivalgoers mainly come from within a twenty-five-mile radius. Friends, relatives, and former residents from all over the country tend to drop in, helping to bring in as much as $40,000 each year. After costs, that translates into about $12,000 to be used for things such as youth baseball and recreation facilities.

Not bad for a town with 400 people. Maybe that's because half the town gets involved in putting on the event: at least 200 volunteers from Arenzville and the surrounding area show up and pitch in with everything from organizing to setup to the ever-important job of cooking and serving the burgoo. And those who have signed up to be on the volunteer list tend to come back year after year to do it all over again!

For more information, log on to www.burgoo.org or call (217) 997-5514.

Margaret Schroeder is a freelance writer in Springfield, Illinois.

Thai Chicken Soup

Yield: 6 servings

"My friends and I have hosted international dinners for the past twenty years. This soup was featured at our Thai dinner. We modified it with noodles and peanuts."

3	to 4 tablespoons peanut oil
2	garlic cloves, minced
	Meat and reserved stock from 1 small cooked roaster chicken
1/2	teaspoon ground turmeric
1/2	teaspoon ground coriander
1/4	teaspoon hot or regular chili powder
1	(48-ounce) can chicken broth or 33/4 cups reserved chicken stock
1/3	cup creamed coconut, unsweetened (not coconut milk in a can)
2	tablespoons fresh lime juice (no substitutes)
2	tablespoons chunky peanut butter
1/2	cup finely chopped green onions
1	cup fine egg noodles, broken into pieces
1/2	cup finely ground peanuts

Heat the oil in a medium-size stockpot and sauté the garlic until light golden. Add the chicken, turmeric, coriander, and chili powder. Stir-fry for 3 to 4 minutes. Remove from the pot.

Pour the chicken broth into the pot and heat to a simmer. Stir the coconut into the hot stock. Return the chicken and spices to the stockpot. Add the lime juice, peanut butter, and green onions. Simmer on low heat for 15 minutes. Add the noodles, cover, and simmer until they are tender. Do not boil. Serve in bowls sprinkled with the ground peanuts.

ARMIDA GEIGER | DURHAM, NEW HAMPSHIRE

Tips From Our Test Kitchen:

Use a precooked chicken to save time. If you can't find creamed coconut in the Asian section of your grocery store, blend 3 ounces unsweetened coconut with 1 to 2 teaspoons milk. Purée until the consistency is paste-like.

Hampshire Pewter Company in Wolfeboro, New Hampshire (pop. 2,979), uses sixteenth-century techniques to produce pewter table accessories. It's the only firm in the country to mix and use Queen's metal, an alloy of tin, antimony, copper, bismuth, and silver.

Vegetable Beef Soup

Yield: 4 to 6 servings

"I love homemade soups during the winter. I'm always willing to experiment with what I have on hand. This spicy, delicious soup is the result. It's fit for a king, or any Texan."

1/2	pound ground chuck, browned and drained	1	(15-ounce) can ranch-style beans or pinto beans
1	cup sliced carrots	3	to 4 cups water
1	large onion, sliced	1	teaspoon chili powder
4	celery stalks, sliced		Salt and pepper
1	(10-ounce) can tomatoes with green chiles (such as Ro-Tel)	1	(15 1/4-ounce) can corn

Add the cooked beef, carrots, onion, and celery to a 6-quart soup pot. Stir in the tomatoes with chiles, beans, water, chili powder, and salt and pepper to taste. Simmer over low heat until all of the vegetables are tender, about 1 hour. Add the corn and cook an additional 10 minutes. Adjust the seasonings to taste.

MARY JARRETT-ALLEN | MOUNT ENTERPRISE, TEXAS

Four-Bean Vegetarian Chili

Yield: 6 to 8 servings

"As a vegetarian, I'm always looking for quick and nutritious dishes. My mom and I concocted this easy, meatless chili recipe."

2	tablespoons olive oil	1	cup water
1	onion, chopped	2	tablespoons cornmeal
1	(15-ounce) can black beans	3	tablespoons chili powder
1	(15-ounce) can pinto beans	1	tablespoon ground cumin
1	(15-ounce) can great Northern beans	1	bunch fresh cilantro, chopped (optional)
1	(15-ounce) can kidney beans		
1	(16-ounce) jar salsa		

In a large saucepan heat the olive oil and sauté the onion until a light brown. Add the black beans, pinto beans, Northern beans, and kidney beans. Stir in the salsa, water, cornmeal, chili powder, cumin, and cilantro. Cook over medium heat, stirring gently until well blended and hot. Serve immediately.

SONJA T. CARTER | BOYNE CITY, MICHIGAN

Chicken Soup with Homemade Noodles

Yield: 10 servings

"I am the first in my family to write down the exact ingredients for this recipe. I tweaked it a bit from my mother's method. She adapted it from her grandmother who brought the recipe to America from Germany in the late 1800s."

Soup:

1	3-to 4-pound hen or broiler, halved
1	medium onion, chopped
3	to 4 celery stalks, chopped
1	teaspoon celery seed
2	to 3 carrots, chopped
2	bay leaves
1	tablespoon salt
1/2	tablespoon black pepper

2	tablespoons white wine vinegar
1	teaspoon sugar
2	chicken bouillon cubes

Noodles:

2	large eggs
4	tablespoons milk or cream
1/2	teaspoon salt
2	cups all-purpose flour

Place the chicken in a large stockpot or soup kettle. Cover with water, about 8 cups. Bring to a boil over medium heat. Remove the foam with a slotted spoon as it forms on top. Add the onion, celery, celery seed, carrots, bay leaves, salt, pepper, vinegar, sugar, and bouillon cubes. Reduce the temperature and simmer for 1 to 2 hours, or until the meat is tender. Adjust the seasonings to taste. Remove the chicken from the pot. Discard the bones and skin. Chop the meat when cool enough to handle. Reserve the stock for boiling the noodles.

For the noodles, beat the eggs with a fork in a medium bowl. Stir in the milk and salt. Add the flour and blend with the fork until the dough can be worked with your fingers. Separate the dough into two pieces. On a floured surface roll out each piece of dough with a rolling pin until thin, keeping the rolling surface floured to avoid sticking. Slice the dough into thin strips. Place on waxed paper and allow to dry for 20 to 30 minutes. Add the strips to the hot broth and cook for 10 minutes, or until tender. Stir in the meat and serve.

SUSAN BEZNER | LINDSAY, TEXAS

Tips From Our Test Kitchen:

This delicious labor of love is hearty and healing. The noodles can be rolled thicker to resemble dumplings. Kluski brand egg noodles can substitute as a time saver.

Karen's Fast Chili

Tips From Our Test Kitchen:

Experiment with different types of beans, like lima or black beans. Serve with a dollop of sour cream and a piece of cornbread.

"I found a chili recipe I liked over twenty years ago in a magazine. My kids and I love this recipe. I've changed it to suit us, and it continues to evolve each time I make it."

3	pounds lean ground beef	1	tablespoon ground cumin
2	cups chopped onion	1	tablespoon sugar
1	cup chopped green pepper	2	teaspoons salt
1	cup chopped red bell pepper or hot peppers	2	(16-ounce) cans whole tomatoes
3	garlic cloves, pressed or minced	1	(16-ounce) can chopped tomatoes (spicy style)
3	tablespoons chili powder	1	(16-ounce) can tomato sauce
1	tablespoon dried oregano	1	(6-ounce) can tomato paste
1	tablespoon dried basil	4	(15-ounce) cans red kidney beans
1/2	teaspoon crushed red pepper		

In a large kettle brown the beef over medium heat. Drain the excess fat. Add the onion, peppers, and garlic. Stir in the chili powder, oregano, basil, red pepper, and cumin and mix well. Cook until the onions are tender. Add the sugar and salt. Stir in the tomatoes, sauce, paste, and beans. Bring to a boil and simmer for 20 to 40 minutes.

KAREN ELLINGSON | ABERDEEN, WASHINGTON

The World's Champion Milk Cow Statue stands near Carnation, Washington (pop. 1,893), honoring a cow named Segis Pietertje Prospect, which produced a record 16,500 quarts of milk and 1,400 pounds of butter a year in the 1920s—roughly ten times the yield from an average cow.

Dr Pepper Stew

Yield: 8 to 10 servings

"I serve this family favorite with garlic bread."

3   pounds stew meat or flank steak, cut into bite-size pieces
3   teaspoons salt
1   teaspoon pepper
1/4   cup all-purpose flour
3   tablespoons vegetable oil
1 1/2   cups diced onion
1   cup diced celery

2   cups beef broth
2   cups Dr Pepper
2   cups sliced carrots
3   cups diced potatoes
3   garlic cloves, minced
1   (10-ounce) can tomatoes with green chiles (Ro-Tel)
1   cup English or sweet peas

Season the meat with the salt and pepper. Dredge the meat in the flour. Heat the oil in a skillet and brown the meat. In a large stockpot add the browned meat, onion, and celery. Cook until fork tender. Add the broth, Dr Pepper, carrots, potatoes, garlic, and tomatoes with green chiles and cook for 2 to 3 hours, or until the meat and vegetables are very tender. Add the peas toward the end of the cooking time so they don't become mushy. Season to taste.

BARRY BRASWELL | BRAGGADOCIO, MISSOURI

Tips From Our Test Kitchen:

Check the stockpot occasionally to make certain there is enough liquid. Add more broth or Dr Pepper if needed.

Taco Soup

Yield: 6 servings

1   pound ground beef
1   onion, chopped
1   package dry ranch-style dressing mix
1   package dry taco seasoning mix
1   cup water

2   (14 1/2-ounce) cans diced tomatoes with green chiles
2   (15-ounce) cans pinto beans
1   (15-ounce) can black beans
1   (14 3/4-ounce) can cream-style corn

Brown the beef with the onion in a medium-size soup pot. Drain the excess grease. Add the ranch dressing mix, taco seasoning mix, and water. Gently stir in the tomatoes and green chiles, pinto beans, black beans, and corn. Simmer for 20 minutes.

RUTH HULL | ALLARDT, TENNESSEE

Tips From Our Test Kitchen:

This quick and flavorful soup is good with 1/4 cup chopped fresh cilantro. You can make a batch of this recipe ahead of time and store it in individual containers in the freezer to heat in the microwave later.

Clarence Saunders established the country's first self-service grocery in Memphis, Tennessee, in 1916, calling it Piggly Wiggly. He never explained the name.

Red Beans and Rice

Yield: 6 to 8 servings

"I made up this recipe while living in the South. My husband takes a batch with him when he goes hunting. It's very hearty."

Cajun seasoning:
2 tablespoons dried basil
2 tablespoons dried oregano
2 tablespoons paprika
4 teaspoons dried thyme
2 tablespoons cayenne pepper
2 tablespoons garlic powder
2 teaspoons ground mace
2 bay leaves, crumbled

Beans:
1 pound dried red kidney beans
1/2 teaspoon Cajun seasoning
4 beef bouillon cubes
1/2 teaspoon cayenne pepper
1 garlic clove, minced
1 pound precooked smoked beef sausage, cut into bite-size pieces
Rice

For the seasoning, process the basil, oregano, paprika, thyme, cayenne pepper, garlic, mace, and bay leaves well in a food processor, or grind with a mortar and pestle. Store in a zip-lock bag to use later.

For the beans, rinse and cover the beans with water. Allow to sit overnight. Drain the beans and place them in a heavy saucepan or Dutch oven. Cover again with water and add 1/2 teaspoon of the Cajun seasoning along with the bouillon, cayenne pepper, garlic, and sausage. Bring to a boil. Reduce the heat to low and cook for about 11/2 hours, stirring occasionally and adding more water when necessary to prevent scorching. (Or you can transfer the beans to a slow cooker and cook them on high for 6 to 8 hours.) The liquid will turn into a red gravy, and the beans will be soft when done.

Prepare the rice according to the package directions for the number of servings desired. Serve the red beans over the rice.

NANCY RENS | PRESCOTT, ARIZONA

New Mexico-Style Posole

Yield: 8 to 10 servings

"This recipe is a family favorite that was made by experimenting. My recipe is easier than some of the more traditional methods. It takes only fifteen minutes to put it together."

3	tablespoons olive or vegetable oil		1	(16-ounce) can seasoned chili-style
3	pounds boneless pork, cubed			tomatoes
2	medium white onions, chopped		1	(4-ounce) can taco sauce
3	garlic cloves, minced		1	bay leaf
2	(29-ounce) cans white or yellow		1	teaspoon salt
	hominy, drained		1	teaspoon cumin
4	cups water		1/2	teaspoon black pepper
2	(4-ounce) cans diced green chiles,undrained		1/2	teaspoon oregano
1	(10-ounce) can red enchilada sauce, mild or hot			

Heat the olive oil in a 6-quart stockpot and brown the pork, onions, and garlic. Drain the excess grease. Add the hominy to the pot along with the water. Add the chiles, enchilada sauce, tomatoes, taco sauce, bay leaf, salt, cumin, pepper, and oregano. Cook over low to medium heat for about 2 hours, stirring occasionally. After 2 hours, add more water if needed. Adjust the seasonings if desired and continue to simmer for 2 to 3 hours longer.

WANDA TAYLOR | TRUTH OR CONSEQUENCES, NEW MEXICO

Tips From Our Test Kitchen:

Seasonings are easily adjusted to suit your taste, and the assembly is quick and easy. Serve hot with corn chips, warm flour tortillas, or cornbread.

The forty-seven-acre New Mexico Farm and Ranch Heritage Museum in Las Cruces, New Mexico (pop. 74,267), salutes 1,000 years of farming and ranching and features a working farm and ranch with live demonstrations of sheep shearing, blacksmithing, and butter churning. The museum has exhibits and illustrations ranging from replicas of Anasazi structures to antique tractors.

Circleville's Passion for Pumpkins

Growing giant pumpkins has evolved into a competitive passion in south-central Ohio, and entries at the annual Circleville Pumpkin Show just keep getting bigger.

During the 2004 show, the top three winners weighed in at more than 1,000 pounds each—with the first place winner tipping the scales at 1,353 pounds. That was 776 pounds heavier than the winning pumpkin just five years before.

Pumpkin growers within a twenty-mile radius of Circleville (pop. 13,485), the county seat of Pickaway County, are eligible to compete in the annual contest and have been doing so since 1903. That's when George R. Haswell, the town's mayor and water works superintendent, conceived the idea of holding a small agricultural exhibit and street fair in Circleville. Now the show, which took a brief hiatus during World War II, is a four-day event that brings 400,000 to 500,000 visitors to Circleville. The show always begins on the third Wednesday in October and runs through Saturday night.

Schools close for at least part of the festival, and business takes a decided upturn during this time. Churches and nonprofit organizations also take part in the event, raising money for activities throughout the year. Still, the heart and soul of the show is the display and sale of fall produce—pumpkins, squash, gourds, and Indian corn.

Pickaway County growers have turned pumpkin patches into scientific experiments—in 1939, the prizewinning pumpkin weighed a puny 62 pounds, but with careful seed selection, crossbreeding, and nurturing, top entries now routinely tip the scales at over 1,000 pounds.

Photo courtesy of Circleville Pumpkin Show. Used by permission.

To reach their goals, Circleville farmers trade growing tips, visit each other's fields, buy and sell seeds among themselves, and sympathize with one another when unfavorable weather, insects, or disease bring an untimely end to a champion in the making.

They find out if their hard work has paid off on the first day of the Pumpkin Show, when the official weigh-in is held at Court and Main at noon immediately after the opening ceremonies.

The show, which sprawls across eight city blocks, is an eclectic mix of carnival rides; food vendors hawking burgers, pancakes, fudge, and pizza all made from pumpkin; parades; craft demonstrations; and music. Festivalgoers try their hand at pumpkin tossing, learn how to make gourd art, spin wool, sculpt clay, and exercise their vocal cords in a hog-calling contest. And best of all, they cheer on the local farmers who bring their colossal crops to the show.

For more information, log on to www.pumpkinshow.com or call (740) 474-7000.

John B. Kachuba is a freelance writer in Athens, Ohio.

Grandma Gras' Soup

Yield: 6 servings

"*My grandma, Grace Weenum Gras of Borculo, Michigan, would make this soup for our family on Memorial Day. My dad, John Weenum, would march in the parade in his Navy uniform. I've never seen this soup or recipe anywhere else. It has a flavor all its own.*"

2	pounds carrots, cut into chunks to equal about 3 cups	1/2	cup diced onion
		1	cup diced celery
1	pound potatoes, cut into chunks to equal about 2 cups	1 1/2	cups finely shredded cabbage
			Salt and pepper
1	kielbasa sausage, sliced		Noodles (optional)

Put the carrots and potatoes in a blender to two-thirds full. Cover with water and blend until they are in small pieces. Pour the mixture into a large saucepan. Add the kielbasa, onion, celery, cabbage, salt and pepper to taste, and the noodles if using. Cook on low heat for at least 45 minutes.

ADELLE J. VAN DAALEN | ZEELAND, MICHIGAN

Tips From Our Test Kitchen:

Serve this hearty soup with hot rolls or cornbread and a fruit salad.

Tamale Soup

Yield: 6 to 8 servings

"A friend brought this soup to a Blue Bonnet Reading Council meeting about two years ago because we love eating as well as reading. Since then, I've made it for family and friends, and they all love it."

2	tablespoons vegetable oil	1	teaspoon cumin (optional)
1	pound ground beef	1	teaspoon salt
1	onion, chopped	1	(15-ounce) can diced tomatoes
1	green pepper, chopped	1	(15-ounce) can tomato sauce
1	(15-ounce) can corn, drained	1	(15-ounce) can pinto beans, drained
2	beef bouillon cubes	10	fresh tamales, frozen (see Tips)
2	cups water		Grated cheese
1	tablespoon chili powder		Tortilla chips

Heat the oil in a large skillet and brown the beef with the onion and pepper. Drain the excess grease. Add the corn. Dissolve the bouillon cubes in the water and stir into the soup. Season with the chili powder, cumin, and salt. Gently stir in the tomatoes, tomato sauce, and beans. Cook on low heat until the flavors are blended.

Thirty minutes before serving the soup, cut the frozen tamales into 1-inch pieces and add them to the soup. If the tamales are not frozen, they will fall apart after cooking a short time. Garnish with the cheese and serve with tortilla chips.

KATHLEEN KECHNIE | WEATHERFORD, TEXAS

Tips From Our Test Kitchen:

If fresh tamales are not available, use canned. Drain the tamales, remove the paper, and slice into 1-inch pieces. Add them to soup at the last minute just to heat through.

Ham Bone and Pea Soup

Yield: 4 servings

"One of the best times I recall growing up in New England during our cold and snowy winters was coming home from school to my mom's ham bone and pea soup. It's easy to prepare, and you get to use the bone from your baked ham dinner."

1	meaty ham bone	3	large potatoes, cut in small chunks
1	cup dried green or yellow split peas or 1/2 cup of each	1	bay leaf
1	small onion, thinly sliced		

Tips From Our Test Kitchen:

For additional flavor, add 1/2 cup finely chopped carrots and 1/2 cup finely chopped celery.

Put the ham bone, peas, and onion in a large soup pot and cover with water. Boil over medium heat until the ham is soft and falls off the bone. Remove the bone and the ham. Cut the ham into small pieces and return to the pot. Add the potatoes and bay leaf. Cook until the peas and potatoes are tender. Serve with hard rolls for dunking.

KATHERINE MIDDLEN | GARDNER, MASSACHUSETTS

Seafood Stew

Yield: 4 to 6 servings

"I like to doctor recipes to my own specifications by trying this and that. I also like using vegetables I grow in the garden."

1   tablespoon extra virgin olive oil
1   medium onion, chopped
2   garlic cloves, minced
2   (6 1/2-ounce) cans chopped clams, undrained
1   (6-ounce) can white crabmeat or imitation crab, drained and rinsed
1   (6-ounce) can shrimp, drained and rinsed
1   (10 3/4-ounce) can condensed tomato soup
1   (2-ounce) jar pimientos, undrained

1 1/2   cups hot water
1/4   teaspoon salt
      Black pepper
1/4   teaspoon dried basil
1/4   teaspoon dried oregano
1/4   cup chopped fresh parsley
      Parmesan cheese (optional)

Heat the oil in a large saucepan over low heat. Add the onion and garlic, cover, and cook for about 15 minutes. Stir in the clams and clam liquid, crab, shrimp, tomato soup, pimientos with liquid, water, salt, and pepper to taste. Add the basil, oregano, and parsley to the seafood mixture. Cover and cook over low heat for 10 minutes. Sprinkle with the Parmesan cheese if desired before serving.

DUANE KASTEN | LONG PRAIRIE, MINNESOTA

Tips From Our Test Kitchen:

This easy and tasty stew, which won first place during a competition at the 2000 Minnesota Renaissance Festival, can be easily doubled for a large group.

Tips From Our Test Kitchen:

A food processor with the shredding blade attached makes shredding cabbage a snap.

Martha's Cabbage Stew

Yield: 6 servings

"This is an easy recipe for a small group of friends on a cold day. It is delicious with cornbread muffins. All my friends love it."

1	pound ground beef	1	tablespoon sugar (or to taste)
3	medium onions, finely chopped	1	teaspoon salt
4	celery stalks, chopped	1/2	teaspoon pepper
1/2	head cabbage, shredded		Garlic powder
1	quart tomatoes		Soy sauce
1	(401/2-ounce) can kidney beans		Vinegar
1	cup water		

Brown the beef in a large heavy pot or skillet. Drain the excess grease. Add the onions, celery, and cabbage. Cook and stir over medium heat until the cabbage is light brown and glassy looking. Add the tomatoes, beans, and water. Stir in the sugar, salt, and pepper. Add the garlic powder, soy sauce, and vinegar to taste. Increase the heat and bring to a boil. Reduce the heat and simmer for 30 to 45 minutes.

MARTHA WATKINS | NATURAL BRIDGE STATION, VIRGINIA

Slow-Oven Beef Stew

Yield: 6 servings

"I found this recipe in 1960, and it's been a favorite of my family since I first made it—a very simple and delicious main dish."

2	pounds stew beef, cut in 11/2-inch pieces	1/3	cup quick-cooking tapioca
2	medium onions, cut in eighths	1	tablespoon sugar
3	celery stalks, cut in diagonal pieces	1	tablespoon salt (or to taste)
4	medium carrots, cut in half across and then lengthwise	1/4	teaspoon pepper
		1/2	teaspoon basil
1	cup tomato juice	2	medium potatoes, cut in 1/4-inch-thick slices

Preheat the oven to 300 degrees. Combine the meat, onions, celery, and carrots in a 21/2-quart casserole. Add the tomato juice, tapioca, sugar, salt, pepper, and basil. Cover and cook for 21/2 hours. Stir in the potatoes and continue cooking, covered, for 1 hour, or until the meat and vegetables are done, stirring occasionally.

MARY NEWELL | OSKALOOSA, KANSAS

Clutching skillets with pancakes, women in Liberal, Kansas (pop. 19,666), race against their "sisters" in Olney, England, during the International Pancake Race each Shrove Tuesday, the day before Ash Wednesday, the start of Lent. Since 1950, the cities have competed at 11:55 a.m. local time along a 415-yard course.

Winter Stew Delight

Yield: 8 servings

"This is a very good stew and is easy to make. It has been in my family for a long time."

4	medium onions, diced	1	cup tomato juice
4	medium potatoes, diced	1	(15-ounce) can beans (kidney, black, or pinto)
1	(28-ounce) can diced tomatoes		
1	pound carrots, peeled and sliced		Salt
2	pounds Italian sausage, fried and drained		Balsamic or red wine vinegar (optional)
4	cups beef or chicken broth		

Preheat the oven to 350 degrees. In a large ovenproof stew pot, combine the onions, potatoes, tomatoes, carrots, and sausage. Stir in the broth, tomato juice, and beans. Season with the salt to taste. Cover and bake for 11/2 to 2 hours, or until tender, stirring occasionally. If necessary, add more broth or tomato juice. Drizzle with vinegar, if desired. Serve with homemade bread or biscuits.

LEE R. SAUERS | MIFFLINBURG, PENNSYLVANIA

Tips From Our Test Kitchen:

You may also season with chopped basil, sage, or chives. This recipe freezes beautifully.

Hamburger Soup

"This soup is delicious and fun to eat. My family makes a game out of finding the peppercorns. We collect all ten in a small bowl to be certain that no one bites down on one."

3	tablespoons butter	2	consommé cans water
1	medium onion, chopped	1/2	teaspoon thyme
2	pounds ground beef	1	bay leaf
4	celery stalk tops	10	peppercorns
1	(28-ounce) can tomatoes	1/2	cup barley
4	carrots, diced	1	(15-ounce) can black beans, drained
3	(14 1/2-ounce) cans beef consommé		(optional)

Melt the butter in a large soup kettle and sauté the onion. Add the beef and cook until slightly browned. Add the celery tops, tomatoes, carrots, consommé, water, thyme, bay leaf, and peppercorns. Bring to a boil. Add the barley and cook over medium heat, stirring occasionally for about 1 hour. Add the beans, if using, and heat through. Remove the celery tops and peppercorns before serving.

JOAN CLARE | HARBOR SPRINGS, MICHIGAN

Company Salad

Yield: 8 to 10 servings

"This recipe is from a favorite niece. Everyone insists that I bring it to all of our family gatherings."

Dressing:

3/4	cup canola oil
1/4	cup lemon juice
2	garlic cloves, minced
1/2	teaspoon salt
1/2	teaspoon pepper

Salad:

2	bunches Romaine lettuce
2	cups chopped tomatoes
1	(3-ounce) jar real bacon bits or 6 strips bacon, crisply cooked and crumbled
1	cup grated Swiss cheese
1/2	cup grated Parmesan cheese
2/3	cup slivered almonds, toasted
1	cup Caesar-style croutons

Prepare the dressing by combining the oil, juice, garlic, salt, and pepper. Mix well and refrigerate until ready to use.

For the salad, rinse, dry, and tear the lettuce leaves into a large bowl. Add the tomatoes, bacon bits, cheeses, almonds, and croutons. Toss well. Add the dressing just before serving.

ARLENE RUHSTORFER | MAYVILLE, MICHIGAN

Tips From Our Test Kitchen:

This salad is also good with a mixture of Romaine lettuce and fresh baby spinach.

Terrific Broccoli Tree Salad

Yield: 8 servings

"The trees on my grandmother's lush property always reminded me of broccoli. She made up this summertime favorite as a way to celebrate my childhood imagination."

2	bunches broccoli, trimmed and chopped	1/2	cup slivered almonds
8	strips bacon, crisply cooked and crumbled	1	cup mayonnaise
1	cup raisins	2	teaspoons red wine vinegar
1/2	cup chopped onion	3	teaspoons sugar

Mix the broccoli with the bacon, raisins, onion, and almonds. Stir in the mayonnaise, vinegar, and sugar. Chill overnight before serving.

TERESA SITES | VICTORVILLE, CALIFORNIA

Tips From Our Test Kitchen:

For a lower-fat version of this tasty salad, use only four strips of bacon and substitute plain yogurt for the mayonnaise.

Twenty-Four-Hour Cabbage Salad

Yield: 8 to 10 servings

"My Aunt Loretta made this salad when I was a little girl visiting her home in New Jersey. I always think of her when I make it."

Salad:

1	medium head cabbage, thinly shredded
1	small onion, grated
1	green bell pepper, very finely diced
6	stuffed olives, thinly sliced
1/2	cup sugar

Dressing:

1	cup white vinegar
1	tablespoon celery seed
1	teaspoon prepared mustard
1/2	cup vegetable oil
1	teaspoon salt
1/8	teaspoon pepper
1	tablespoon mustard seed

For the salad, place the cabbage, onion, green pepper, olives, and sugar in a medium bowl.

For the dressing, boil the vinegar, celery seed, mustard, oil, salt, pepper, and mustard seed for 3 minutes over medium heat. Pour the hot dressing over the cabbage mixture and stir well. Cover and refrigerate for at least 8 to 10 hours. Stir again before serving.

Mary Louise Bishop | Waymart, Pennsylvania

Tips From Our Test Kitchen:

The key to preparing this tasty dish is to make certain that the cabbage is thinly sliced. This allows it to be more evenly coated with the dressing.

Cauliflower Cashew Salad

Yield: 10 to 12 servings

"This recipe is great for a big group because it makes a big salad. I use extra cashews because my family loves them so much."

Salad:

1	head iceberg lettuce, washed and torn into small pieces
1	head cauliflower, washed and cut into bite-size pieces
2	cups grated Cheddar cheese
1	box (about 2 cups) seasoned croutons
2	cups cashews

Dressing:

1	cup Miracle Whip or mayonnaise
1/2	cup sugar
1/4	cup grated Parmesan cheese

For the salad, combine the lettuce, cauliflower, cheese, croutons, and cashews.

Tips From Our Test Kitchen:

This dish is also good with 1/2 cup chopped green onions. Adjust the sugar to your taste. A lower-calorie dressing can be made by using plain yogurt instead of the Miracle Whip.

For the dressing, stir together the Miracle Whip, sugar, and Parmesan cheese. The dressing and salad can be made ahead, making this a great potluck dish. However, wait until just before serving to dress the salad.

PEG HOUSENGA | ZEELAND, MICHIGAN

With 13,500 acres of vineyards, Michigan is the fourth largest grape-growing state, behind California, New York, and Washington, according to the Michigan Grape and Wine Industry Council.

Balkan Cucumber Salad

Yield: 4 to 6 servings

"My mother's grandmother made this recipe, so it's been in the family for years. We enjoy it best during the hot, lazy days of summer."

2   cups plain yogurt
1/2 garlic clove, crushed
1   tablespoon white vinegar
11/2 teaspoons salt
1   tablespoon olive oil
1   tablespoon chopped chives

1   teaspoon chopped mint leaves or 1/2 teaspoon dried mint
11/2 cups peeled, seeded, and diced cucumbers
1   cup seedless green grape halves

Pour the yogurt into a large bowl. Beat with an electric mixer until very smooth. Add the garlic, vinegar, salt, olive oil, chives, and mint leaves and beat for 30 seconds. Fold in the cucumbers and grape halves. Chill for at least 1 hour before serving.

ALYCE ZURA | SUGAR RUN, PENNSYLVANIA

Tips From Our Test Kitchen:

Prepare this dish the day you plan to serve it to keep the cucumbers crunchy.

Fiesta Black Bean Salad

Yield: 6 servings

"As a Spanish teacher, I enjoy trying authentic cuisine from a variety of Hispanic cultures. This fiber-filled recipe pairs perfectly with grilled steak, chicken, or pork."

2	cups corn (canned, fresh, or frozen)		1/4	teaspoon garlic powder
1/2	purple onion, diced		1/8	teaspoon salt
1	red bell pepper, diced		2	tablespoons balsamic vinegar
2	(15-ounce) cans black beans, rinsed and drained		2	tablespoons lemon juice
3	teaspoons chili powder		1/2	cup minced fresh cilantro
2	tablespoons olive oil			Black pepper

Gently toss together the corn, onion, red pepper, and beans. Stir in the chili powder and allow to sit at room temperature. Whisk together the olive oil, garlic, salt, vinegar, and lemon juice. Pour this dressing over the vegetables. Stir in the cilantro and season with black pepper to taste. Chill for 2 hours before serving.

AMBER DOERING | KERKHOVEN, MINNESOTA

Marinated Bean Salad

Yield: 4 to 6 servings

"I got this recipe from my aunt many years ago. It's been ideal for family get-togethers, church suppers, and other special meals."

Salad:

1	(15-ounce) can English or sweet peas, drained		4	to 5 celery stalks, chopped
1	(11-ounce) can white shoepeg corn, drained		1	green bell pepper, diced
1	(15-ounce) can French-style green beans, drained			**Marinade:**
1	(2-ounce) jar pimientos, chopped and drained		1 1/2	teaspoons salt
1	medium onion, chopped		1/4	teaspoon black pepper
			1/2	cup vegetable oil
			1/2	cup water
			1	cup cider vinegar
			1 1/2	cups sugar

For the salad, combine the peas, corn, green beans, pimientos, onion, celery, and green pepper.

For the marinade, combine the salt, pepper, vegetable oil, water, vinegar, and sugar. Heat in the microwave until the sugar has dissolved. Allow the marinade to cool.

Pour the marinade over the vegetables. Refrigerate the salad for 24 hours. Before serving, drain the marinade. This salad keeps in the refrigerator for about one week.

ALICE POUNCEY | DECATUR, MISSISSIPPI

Vardaman, Mississippi (pop. 1,065), proclaims itself the "Sweet Potato Capital of the World."

Mediterranean Green Bean Salad

Yield: 6 to 8 servings

"I am a diabetic vegetarian. This recipe is perfect for my diet. It's especially good when served with garlic toast."

6	cups trimmed and halved green beans, cooked and cooled	25	black olives, halved
		4	ounces Feta cheese, crumbled
1/2	cup thinly sliced onion	3/4	cup Italian dressing
2	tomatoes, cut into 16 wedges	1/2	teaspoon salt (optional)
3	hard-cooked eggs, halved		

Gently mix the beans, onion, tomatoes, eggs, olives, and cheese. Stir in the Italian dressing and salt if using. Chill.

LINDA MEGGISON | STURGIS, MICHIGAN

Michigan leads the nation in the production of dry edible navy beans, black beans, and cranberry beans.

Tips From Our Test Kitchen:

Reduce the amount of dressing to 1/2 cup for a lower-fat version. You can also add more eggs or cheese if you wish.

Broccoli and Cauliflower Salad

Yield: 8 servings

"This makes a great lunch salad when served with a sandwich. It's great any time of year."

Salad:
1 cup broccoli florets
1 cup cauliflower florets
6 slices bacon, crisply cooked and crumbled
1 to 1 1/2 cups grated mild Cheddar cheese

1 small onion, diced
1 cup mushrooms (optional)

Dressing:
1/2 cup light sour cream
1/2 cup light Miracle Whip or mayonnaise
1/2 cup sugar

For the salad, cut the broccoli and cauliflower into bite-size pieces. Toss them together with the bacon, cheese, onion, and mushrooms.

For the dressing, mix together the sour cream, Miracle Whip, and sugar and pour over the vegetable mixture. Stir to evenly coat the vegetables. Refrigerate for 1 hour or overnight before serving.

MILDRED HUFFMAN | LEXINGTON, VIRGINIA

> **Tips From Our Test Kitchen:**
>
> Steam the broccoli and cauliflower until crisp-tender. This brings out the bright green color in the broccoli and makes the salad easier to eat.

Festive Carrot and Apple Salad

Yield: 8 to 10 servings

"We like this salad any time of the year. It's an easy one to take to 'dish to pass' and holiday gatherings because it's colorful and good."

2 to 3 cups grated carrots
3 cups diced unpeeled apple
1/2 cup crushed pineapple
1/2 cup raisins or red or green grapes

1 cup walnut or pecan pieces or sunflower seeds
8 ounces pineapple yogurt

Mix together the carrots, apple, pineapple, raisins, and nuts. Stir in the yogurt. Chill. This recipe can be made several hours before mealtime.

GRETCHEN KNOLL | CANISTEO, NEW YORK

> **Tips From Our Test Kitchen:**
>
> Lemon or vanilla yogurt makes a nice substitute if pineapple yogurt is hard to find.

Cabbage Salad

Yield: 8 servings

"My cabbage salad is always a hit at potlucks and picnics. Everyone asks for the recipe. I love this salad."

Salad:

1	package chicken-flavored Ramen noodles
1/2	cup slivered almonds
2	tablespoons sesame seeds
1/2	large head cabbage, chopped
1/2	bunch broccoli, chopped
1/2	head cauliflower, broken into florets
4	green onions, chopped

Dressing:

1/2	cup vegetable oil
3	tablespoons cider vinegar
2	tablespoons sugar
1	teaspoon salt
	Flavor pack from Ramen noodles

Preheat the oven to 350 degrees. For the salad, toast the noodles, almonds, and sesame seeds on a cookie sheet in the oven until golden. Combine the cabbage, broccoli, cauliflower, and onions in a large bowl. Toss in the toasted noodle mixture.

For the dressing, stir together the oil, vinegar, sugar, salt, and flavor pack. Pour over the salad and mix well. Refrigerate until ready to serve.

JULIANNE DORR | COLUMBIA CITY, OREGON

Tips From Our Test Kitchen:

This salad is ideal for picnics because the dressing is mayonnaise free. Toss in slices of sweet red pepper or shredded carrot for additional flavor and color.

Festive Corn Salad

Yield: 6 to 8 servings

"This recipe came through a friend who got it from a lady . . . you get the idea. It was served at a luncheon and was a big hit. I've adjusted it from the original."

2	(15¼-ounce) cans yellow or white whole kernel corn, drained
1/2	cup chopped red or white onion
1/2	cup chopped sweet red or green bell pepper

1/2	cup mayonnaise
1	cup grated Cheddar cheese,
1/2	(10-ounce) bag chili-flavored corn chips, crushed

Mix together the corn, onion, pepper, and mayonnaise in a medium salad bowl until well blended. Stir in the cheese and chips just before serving.

JAN GRUMMERT | JANSEN, NEBRASKA

Tips From Our Test Kitchen:

If you are unable to find chili-flavored chips, use traditional corn chips seasoned with 2 teaspoons chili powder.

Warrens Is Afloat in Cranberries

Farmers around Warrens, Wisconsin (pop. 286), have generations of experience growing cranberries, one of only three major fruits native to North America, and Wisconsin's number one fruit crop. Commercial production began in Wisconsin in 1860 when Edward Sacket arrived and began cultivating the cranberry marsh he found on his land near Berlin, sixty miles east of Warrens.

The tiny population of Warrens, the "Cranberry Capital of Wisconsin," swells to 100,000 during the annual Warrens Cranberry Festival, scheduled for three days in September. In addition to tours of marshes and receiving stations, festivalgoers find arts and crafts, a flea market, and fall produce at the Farmer's Market plus cranberry cream puffs, cranberry sundaes, and cranberries jubilee to sample. Also included are a parade, cranberry recipe contest, quilt and needlework contest, and pancake breakfasts.

Festivalgoers also tour the Wisconsin Cranberry Discovery Center. Established in 1989 as the Cranberry Expo Museum, the organization moved to the historic Union Cranberry Company Warehouse in downtown Warrens in 2004 and features an exhibit hall, ice cream parlor, bakery, and resource library.

The festival's dedicated volunteers raise funds for the community, and since the festival's beginnings in 1972, contributions have gone to the ballpark, fire station equipment, student scholarships, and tree planting throughout the town. The 2004 festival raised $40,000 for community projects.

The ruby-red berries grow in sandy peat soil on dry land but are harvested in September and October by flooding the beds with water, allowing the berries to float on the surface. Acidic soil, an abundant water supply, and sand make the area ideal for growing cranberries.

Special harvesting equipment employed today illustrates the ingenuity of the early growers who designed, shared, and improved on each other's creations for the benefit of all. Over the years, cranberry growers have planted their acreage with new hybrids that produce bigger, redder berries. Higher yields and good weather have created bumper crops in recent years.

Most growers sell their crops to large processors such as Northland and Ocean Spray. Most of the crop is used as ingredients in other products, ranging from juices, cereals, and mustards to teas, baking mixes, and sausages.

Cranberry growers in Warrens proudly carry on their community and family heritage of self-sufficiency and stewardship of the land, viewing today's bountiful crops as exciting opportunities for developing new products and marketing globally.

For more information, log on to www.cranfest.com or call (608) 378-4200.

Ann Hattes is a freelance writer and author in Hartland, Wisconsin.

Mexican Corn and Bean Salad

Yield: 4 to 6 servings

"When I told my aunt that I didn't have a good recipe to accompany Mexican food, she gave me this one. Everyone wants it."

1	(15 1/4-ounce) can whole kernel corn, drained	1/2	cup mayonnaise
1	(15-ounce) can red kidney beans, drained	1/4	cup minced green onions
1	(7-ounce) can pitted olives, drained	2	tablespoons chili sauce
2	cups shredded lettuce	2	teaspoons cider vinegar
		1/2	teaspoon chili powder

Combine the corn, beans, olives, and lettuce in a serving bowl. Stir together the mayonnaise, onions, chili sauce, vinegar, and chili powder. Add to the lettuce mixture and serve.

VIOLET CAMP | BROKEN BOW, OKLAHOMA

Tips From Our Test Kitchen:

This salad is great as a main dish too. Add shredded cheese and crushed tortilla chips to make it heartier.

Grilled Portobello Mushroom and Goat Cheese Arugula Salad

Yield: 5 servings

"Every summer we host a large picnic with family and friends. I was looking for something new in a salad, and my son gave me this recipe."

4	tablespoons red wine vinegar	4	ounces goat cheese, sliced into 5 rounds
1/2	cup olive oil	1	small bunch baby arugula, stems trimmed
	Salt		
2	teaspoons Dijon mustard	16	grape tomatoes, halved
5	large portobello mushroom caps		

Whisk together the vinegar, oil, salt to taste, and mustard. Place the mushroom caps (rounded side up) on a plate and drizzle them with half of the vinegar mixture. Broil the mushrooms in a shallow ovenproof pan for about 5 minutes. Turn the caps over and top with a piece of goat cheese. Return to the oven. When the cheese is slightly melted, remove from the oven and place the mushrooms back on the plate. In a medium bowl toss the arugula with the remaining vinegar mixture and the tomatoes. Spoon the arugula mixture into five serving bowls and top each one with a warm, cheese-topped mushroom.

ROSELL BOCCHIERI | LOVELAND, COLORADO

Tips From Our Test Kitchen:

The salad also is good with baby spinach.

Crunchy Pea Salad

Yield: 8 servings

"This salad is a family favorite. The recipe was given to me by my mother's friend in Sikeston, Missouri."

1	(10-ounce) package frozen peas, thawed	1	cup chopped cashews
1	cup diced celery	1/2	cup sour cream
1	cup cauliflower florets	1	cup ranch-style dressing
1/4	cup diced green onion	1/2	cup crisply cooked and crumbled bacon

Combine the peas, celery, cauliflower, onion, cashews, sour cream, and dressing in a salad bowl and mix well. Chill until ready to serve. Top each serving with the crumbled bacon.

JEANETTE BRINKER | WASHINGTON, MISSOURI

Pa's Pea Salad

Yield: 6 servings

"My father seldom did anything in the kitchen. This salad was about the only dish he ever prepared. He loved nuts. We loved his salad."

1	(10-ounce) package frozen snow peas or sugar snap peas	1	cup low-fat Miracle Whip
1	(10-ounce) package frozen English or sweet peas (thawed)	1/2	cup low-fat sour cream
1	cup cashews	1/3	cup diced red onion
1	cup chopped cauliflower	1/3	cup diced celery
		1/4	cup crisply cooked and crumbled bacon

Cook the snow peas in boiling water for 2 minutes. Cool. Mix the snow peas with the English peas, cashews, and cauliflower. Stir in the Miracle Whip and sour cream. Add the red onion and celery. Chill for at least 2 hours. Garnish with the bacon.

BETSY WEST | FULTON, KENTUCKY

Seven-Layer Pea Salad

Yield: 12 servings

"To me, this recipe is very special because it is so good. My neighbors and all my friends at church find this to be an excellent dish to carry to family reunions. They all love it. I can make a meal on it alone."

1	bunch leaf lettuce	2	tablespoons sugar
2	green bell peppers, chopped or sliced	1	cup Miracle Whip
2	red bell peppers, chopped or sliced	1	cup sour cream
1	red onion, chopped or sliced	2	cups grated Cheddar cheese
1	yellow onion, chopped or sliced	8	to 10 slices bacon, crisply cooked and crumbled
2	(15 1/2-ounce) cans English or sweet peas, drained		

Layer half the lettuce in a bowl or trifle dish. Add layers of the green and red bell peppers, red and yellow onion, and peas. Mix together the sugar, Miracle Whip, and sour cream and spread on top of the peas. Add a layer of the cheese and the bacon. Top with the remaining lettuce. Refrigerate until ready to serve. (The amounts of the ingredients can vary according to the size of your container.)

LILLIE DUNLAP | ROBBINS, NORTH CAROLINA

Pat's Summer Salad

Yield: 6 to 8 servings

"This salad is nutritious and colorful. You can substitute ingredients to suit your taste."

2	cups fresh spinach	1	red onion, quartered and sliced
1	large head iceberg lettuce	1 1/2	cups grape tomatoes
1	cucumber, peeled and sliced	1	cup mandarin orange sections
1	carrot, peeled and thinly sliced	1	cup poppy seed or other dressing
1	yellow squash, halved lengthwise and sliced	1 1/2	cups pecans
		1	cup crumbled blue cheese

Combine the spinach, lettuce, cucumber, carrot, squash, onion, tomatoes, and oranges in a large salad bowl. Add the dressing and toss until the vegetables are well coated. Sprinkle the pecans and blue cheese on top.

PAT LOGSDON | LEITCHFIELD, KENTUCKY

Tips From Our Test Kitchen:

Try toasting the pecans before adding them to the salad.

Dilly Potato Salad

Yield: 6 servings

"I learned about seasoning with herbs when I was old enough to help my mother make pickles. At that time, I developed a great fondness for dill's spicy fragrance and pretty lacy flowers. I have always included it in my herb garden."

6	medium potatoes, boiled, slightly cooled, and cubed	1/2	cup chopped fresh dill
1	medium sweet onion, very thinly sliced	1/4	cup chopped fresh parsley
1/2	cup chopped celery and celery leaves	1/2	cup mayonnaise or Miracle Whip
1/2	cup chopped sweet red pepper	1/4	teaspoon paprika
1	teaspoon lemon juice	1/2	cup chopped walnuts

While the potatoes are still warm, combine with the onion, celery, and pepper and gently mix. Add the lemon juice, dill, and parsley. Gently stir in the mayonnaise. Chill overnight. To serve, garnish with the paprika and walnuts.

PEGGY MARTIN | ROSEBURG, OREGON

Roasted Potato Salad

Yield: 6 to 8 servings

"This is a family reunion favorite and is popular at church fellowship meals."

4	cups red potatoes	2	hard-cooked eggs, chopped
	Vegetable oil or cooking spray	1/4	cup finely chopped onion
6	slices bacon, crisply cooked and crumbled	1/2	to 1 cup mayonnaise
			Salt and pepper

Preheat the oven to 325 degrees. Scrub the potatoes and cut them into bite-size pieces, leaving the skins on. Roast them on a lightly oiled cookie sheet until tender, about 25 minutes. Allow them to cool. Mix the potatoes with the bacon, eggs, onion, mayonnaise, and salt and pepper to taste. Chill thoroughly.

VESTA MCLEAN | GALAX, VIRGINIA

Left: Baked Custard on page 11
Bottom Left: Spiced Apple Pancakes on page 13
Below: Sour Cream Coffeecake on page 16

Above: Cheesy Black Bean and Artichoke Dip on page 32

Left: Spinach Triangles on page 40

Wonton Sausage Appetizers on page 44

Nutty Rhubarb Muffins
on page 73

Above: Saturday Bean Soup on page 77
Right: Winter Stew Delight on page 103

Above: Taco Soup on page 95

Right: Mediterranean Green Bean
Salad on page 111

Above: Old-Time Fruit Salad on page 122

Left: Seven-Layer Pea Salad on page 117

Right: Cornbread Salad
on page 126

Below: Supreme Chicken Salad
on page 127

Left: Lemon Asparagus on page 141

Below: Orange Jell-O Salad on page 135

Above: Pasta with Garbanzo Beans on page 171
Right: Hot Hominy Casserole on page 170

Above: Hamburger Pie on page 193
Right: Tomato Tart on page 169

Right: Chicken-Artichoke Pasta on page 207
Bottom Right: Oven-Fried Chicken on page 202
Below: Turketti Casserole on page 214

Above: Snapper Tropical on page 236
Right: Weiner and Kraut Casserole on page 217

Right: Blueberry Pound Cake on page 249
Bottom Right: Heavenly Cake on page 249
Below: French Almond Cake on page 274

Left: Moist Chocolate Brownies on page 281

Below: Chocolate-Zucchini Cake on page 265

Above: Banana Pudding on page 310
Left: Homemade Grape Ice Cream on page 313

Mama's Potato Salad

Yield: 12 servings

"Everyone liked the way Mother combined egg yolks with the seasonings in this recipe. It gives the salad such a good taste. When I take it to covered dish luncheons, people always ask me for the recipe. I get lots of compliments on the way it's put together."

3	to 3 1/2 pounds potatoes (about 10 medium-size potatoes)	2	tablespoons Dijon mustard
6	hard-cooked eggs	1/4	cup sugar
1	medium onion, finely chopped	1	teaspoon salt
1/2	cup mayonnaise	1/2	teaspoon pepper
1/2	cup evaporated milk		Paprika, for garnish
3	tablespoons balsamic vinegar		Additional hard-cooked eggs, sliced, for garnish

In a large pot cook the potatoes in boiling, salted water until tender. (Potatoes can be peeled and cubed before boiling to save cooking time.) Drain and transfer them to a bowl to cool. Separate the egg yolks from the whites. Set the yolks aside. Chop the whites and add them to the potatoes. Add the onion. In a separate bowl mash the egg yolks. Stir in the mayonnaise, milk, vinegar, mustard, sugar, salt, and pepper. Pour the egg mixture over the potatoes and toss well. Taste and adjust the seasonings if necessary.

Spoon potato mixture into a serving bowl. Garnish with the paprika and egg slices. Chill until serving time.

MILDRED SHERRER | BAY CITY, TEXAS

The original "Meals on Wheels," the cowboy chuck wagon, was invented in 1866 by prominent Texas cattleman Charles Goodnight. Goodnight, a veteran of cattle drives, built shelves, drawers, and cubbyholes behind a hinged lid in a wagon that lowered to become a worktable for a cook. The device was first used in 1866 on the inaugural cattle drive on what would become the "Goodnight-Loving Trail" from Texas to New Mexico and Colorado.

Summer Spinach Salad

Yield: 8 to 10 servings

"As a home economics teacher, I had the opportunity to prepare and test numerous recipes. This is a favorite that I've shared with friends and relatives over the years."

2	pounds fresh spinach	1/2	cup alfalfa sprouts
1	ripe avocado	2	green onions, chopped
1/4	ripe cantaloupe	1/2	cup vinaigrette dressing

Wash the spinach and pat dry. Tear into bite-size pieces (unless using baby spinach). Peel and cut the avocado into small chunks. Peel and scoop the melon into small balls. Toss the avocado, cantaloupe, sprouts, green onions, and spinach in a large salad bowl. Drizzle the dressing on top just before serving.

WadeDelle Moody | Bamberg, South Carolina

Strawberry Spinach Salad

Yield: 4 to 6 servings

"This is a family recipe that I've made for many years."

Salad:

1	large bunch fresh spinach, broken in pieces
1	pint strawberries, sliced
1/2	cup slivered almonds

Dressing:

1/4	cup sugar
2	tablespoons sesame seeds
1	tablespoon poppy seeds
11/2	teaspoons minced onion
1/2	teaspoon Worcestershire sauce
1/4	teaspoon paprika
1/4	cup vegetable oil

For the salad, wash the spinach and pat it dry. Add the strawberries and almonds to the spinach in a salad bowl and toss. Cover and refrigerate until ready to serve. If desired, toast the almonds before adding them to the spinach.

For the dressing, combine the sugar, sesame seeds, poppy seeds, onion, Worcestershire sauce, paprika, and oil in a jar with a fitted lid. Shake well. Pour over the salad and toss just before serving.

Marvel Lint | Reads Landing, Minnesota

Layered Spinach Salad

Yield: 6 servings

"This salad is awesome."

Salad:

6	ounces fresh baby spinach		1	red bell pepper, thinly sliced

6 ounces fresh baby spinach
1 plus 1 teaspoons sugar
6 hard-cooked eggs, sliced
1/2 pound deli-style roast turkey, sliced
2 cups chopped romaine lettuce
Salt and pepper
10 ounces frozen peas, thawed

1 red bell pepper, thinly sliced
1 small onion, thinly sliced
2 cups cubed Swiss cheese

Dressing:

1 ounce dry ranch-style dressing mix
1 cup sour cream
2 cups mayonnaise or nonfat yogurt

For the salad, rinse the spinach leaves and dry them very well. Place the spinach in the bottom of a deep, straight-sided glass bowl. Sprinkle with 1 teaspoon of the sugar. Add a layer of eggs, turkey, and romaine. Sprinkle with the remaining 1 teaspoon sugar and the salt and pepper to taste. Add a layer of peas, bell pepper, onion, and Swiss cheese.

For the dressing, in a small bowl mix together the ranch-style dressing mix, sour cream, and mayonnaise. Spread the dressing evenly over the entire salad. Cover and refrigerate overnight. Toss just before serving.

AUDREY MISNER | PRICE, UTAH

Tips From Our Test Kitchen:

Frozen peppers and onions can substitute for the fresh vegetables. Be certain to squeeze out the excess liquid from the frozen vegetables after thawing or the salad will be soggy.

Tomato Salad

Yield: 4 servings

"This is one of our family's favorite salads. It's so simple to prepare."

5 Roma tomatoes, quartered
2 garlic cloves, minced
1 tablespoon red wine vinegar

2 tablespoons olive oil
1 tablespoon finely chopped fresh basil
Salt and pepper

Place the tomatoes in a bowl and toss them well with the garlic, vinegar, oil, basil, and salt and pepper to taste. Serve chilled or at room temperature.

TINA STINSON | LOVELAND, COLORADO

Tips From Our Test Kitchen:

This quick salad is best when the tomatoes are at their peak of ripeness. Two cups of halved grape tomatoes can substitute when larger ripe tomatoes aren't available.

Cool Fruit Salad

Yield: 8 to 10 servings

"I am eighty-five years old, and the following recipe has been in my family for many years. My mother made it when I was very young. Now this salad is served at every family gathering."

1	pint whipping cream	2	chopped bananas
1	(8-ounce) can crushed pineapple, drained	3/4	cup small marshmallows
1	(6-ounce) jar maraschino cherries, drained and halved	1	tablespoon sifted confectioners' sugar
		2	tablespoons mayonnaise

Whip the cream until soft peaks form. Fold in the pineapple, cherries, bananas, and marshmallows. Mix the confectioners' sugar and mayonnaise, and add to the fruit mixture. Freeze in a flat 10 x 9-inch pan. Cut in squares and serve on lettuce leaves.

MARTHA LARSEN-VAN AUKEN | PENN YAN, NEW YORK

Old-Time Fruit Salad

Yield: 8 servings

"I first tasted this recipe at a card party. I was told it is a very old recipe. I have served it often and have passed it along to many friends and family."

3	eggs, beaten	1	bunch seedless green grapes
3/4	cup sugar	1	bunch seedless red grapes
3	tablespoons butter, softened	1	(20-ounce) can pineapple tidbits, drained
1/2	cup lemon juice		
3	Golden Delicious apples, peeled, cored, and chopped	1/2	cup chopped pecans or walnuts
3	Red Delicious apples, peeled, cored, and chopped	11/2	cups mini-marshmallows

Combine the eggs, sugar, and butter in a saucepan. Stir in the lemon juice. Cook over medium heat until thickened, stirring constantly. The dressing will thicken quickly. Refrigerate until cool. In a large serving bowl place the apples, grapes, pineapple, pecans, and marshmallows. Pour the dressing over the fruit mixture and mix well.

DORA LECHMAN | DERRY, PENNSYLVANIA

Tossed Salad with Apples and Cashews

Yield: 6 to 8 servings

"This recipe is from a missionary currently serving with her family in Africa. I make it often. It always sparks positive comments."

Dressing:

3/4	cup sugar
1	teaspoon dry mustard
1	teaspoon salt
1/3	cup cider vinegar
1	teaspoon chopped onion
1/2	cup water
1/2	cup vegetable oil
1 1/2	teaspoons poppy seeds

Salad:

1	small head lettuce
5	ounces fresh baby spinach (half a standard-size bag)
2	large Granny Smith apples, very thinly sliced
1/2	pound Swiss cheese, grated
1	(9 1/4-ounce) can cashews (halves or pieces)

For the dressing, heat the sugar, mustard, salt, vinegar, and onion until the sugar is dissolved. Do not boil. Add the water, oil, and poppy seeds. Chill slightly.

For the salad, toss together the lettuce, spinach, apples, cheese, and cashews. Serve with the dressing on the side.

ELIZABETH MANN | SWANTON, OHIO

Tips From Our Test Kitchen:

The dressing is good with up to 1/2 cup of chopped onion. Red onion makes a pretty dressing when served in a clear glass pitcher or cruet.

Raw Cranberry Salad

Yield: 8 to 10 servings

"My mother got this recipe from her friend Lucille in the 1940s. She passed it down to my sister and me. Someday we'll pass it on to our grandchildren."

1	pound raw cranberries
2	oranges
1 1/2	cups sugar
1	(8-ounce) can crushed pineapple, drained

1	cup chopped walnuts
1 1/2	cups whipped cream or topping
1	pound miniature marshmallows

Chop the cranberries in a food processor, but do not purée them. Peel the oranges and dice the sections. Stir together the cranberries, oranges, sugar, pineapple, and walnuts. Cover and refrigerate overnight. Stir in the whipped cream and marshmallows before serving.

SUSAN WELLS | APPLE VALLEY, CALIFORNIA

Tips From Our Test Kitchen:

This pretty pink salad is a fresh side item with ham or turkey. Omit the whipped cream and marshmallows to make a delicious cranberry sauce.

Crunchy California Sunshine Salad

Yield: 8 servings

*Tips From Our
Test Kitchen:*

If jicama is unavailable at your grocer, substitute a crisp apple.

"I made a similar version of this salad when I lived in Montana. When I moved to California, I updated it to include local ingredients."

Salad:

2	heads (about 4 cups) baby romaine lettuce
2	oranges
1	pound fresh bean sprouts
1	ripe avocado, peeled and diced
1	teaspoon lemon juice
1/3	cup diced jicama
1/3	cup golden raisins
1/3	cup dried cherries or cranberries
1/3	cup sunflower seeds

Dressing:

1	(8-ounce) container cream cheese
2	teaspoons grated orange zest
1/2	cup orange juice
1	tablespoon honey
1	tablespoon Dijon-style mustard
1	tablespoon flavored oil (walnut, hazelnut, or olive oil)
1	teaspoon sea salt
1	teaspoon dried mustard
1/2	teaspoon freshly ground black pepper

For the salad, wash and dry the lettuce and tear it into bite-size pieces. Place them in a large salad bowl. Grate the zest of 1 orange for the dressing. Peel both oranges, remove the pith, and cut small pieces into the salad bowl. Add the sprouts, avocado, lemon juice, jicama, raisins, cherries, and sunflower seeds. Cover and chill.

For the dressing, combine the cream cheese, orange zest, orange juice, honey, mustard, oil, sea salt, mustard, and pepper in a blender or food processor, or mix with a hand mixer. When creamy and smooth, pour the dressing over the prepared salad and toss to coat the salad well.

MICHAELA ROSENTHAL | WOODLAND HILLS, CALIFORNIA

With its annual avocado crop valued at $26 million, Fallbrook, California (pop. 29,100), is known as the world's avocado capital. A single avocado tree can produce up to 120 pieces of fruit a year. California is the top avocado growing state, producing 95 percent of the nation's crop.

Festive Cranberry Salad

Yield: 12 servings

"This dish is easy to fix ahead and store frozen afterward. It accompanies any entrée and adds color to a food plate. It makes a generous amount and can be cut into larger or smaller pieces to suit the number of diners, so I have never run out when serving it."

1	(14-ounce) can sweetened condensed milk	1	(16-ounce) can whole-berry cranberry sauce
3/4	cup lemon juice	1/2	cup pecans (or other nut)
1	(20-ounce) can crushed pineapple, drained	8	ounces whipped topping

Mix together the milk, lemon juice, pineapple, cranberry sauce, and pecans. Fold in the whipped topping. Pour into a 13 x 9-inch container and freeze. Remove from the freezer about 5 minutes before serving.

BARBARA DABUL | PASO ROBLES, CALIFORNIA

Tips From Our Test Kitchen:

Serve this sweet salad with colorful fresh fruit garnishes such as kiwi, mandarin oranges, cranberries, or strawberries.

Pear Romaine Salad

Yield: 2 servings

"This is a wonderful salad that pleases the palate. It's also quick and easy to prepare."

2 1/2	cups romaine lettuce	1	firm pear
1/2	teaspoon balsamic vinegar	1	tablespoon butter
1	teaspoon olive oil	8	to 10 pecan halves

Wash, dry, and slice the romaine lettuce into long, thin strips. Combine the vinegar and olive oil, mix well, and pour over the lettuce. Toss well. Arrange the lettuce on salad plates. Cut the pear into cubes or slices. Melt the butter and sauté the pears over medium heat until brown. Place the pear slices on top of the lettuce. Top with the pecan halves.

GLENNA HOFF | PRESCOTT, ARIZONA

Tips From Our Test Kitchen:

This salad also is delicious with blue cheese or Gorgonzola crumbles, which provide the perfect foil to the sweetness of the pears.

Cornbread Salad

Yield: 12 servings

"This recipe is a favorite. The longer it sits, the better it tastes. It's one of those recipes that everyone wants when they try it."

1	(8 1/2-ounce) package cornbread mix	1/2	cup chopped onion
1	(1-ounce) envelope dry ranch-style dressing mix	3	large tomatoes, chopped
1	cup sour cream	1	(16-ounce) can pinto beans, drained
1	cup mayonnaise	2	cups fresh or frozen corn
1/2	cup chopped green bell pepper	2	cups grated Cheddar cheese
1/2	cup chopped sweet red pepper	10	slices bacon, crisply cooked and crumbled (optional)

Bake the cornbread mix according to the package instructions and crumble the cornbread. Combine the dressing mix, sour cream, and mayonnaise in a small bowl. In another bowl mix together the bell pepper, sweet pepper, onion, tomatoes, pinto beans, and corn. In a 3-quart salad bowl, layer half the cornbread, half the vegetables, half the cheese, half the bacon if using, and half the dressing. Repeat the layers. Be careful not to mix the layers or the cornbread will become soggy. Cover and store in the refrigerator until ready to serve.

EVA MAE CLARK | EASTON, ILLINOIS

Zippy Egg Salad

Yield: 2 servings

"When I ran across this recipe for egg salad for two, it suited our lifestyle. Serve it on bread or crackers. It's especially good with Triscuits."

3	tablespoons mayonnaise	1/8	tablespoon lemon juice
1	tablespoon mustard	3	hard-cooked eggs
1/8	tablespoon salt	1	tablespoon minced green onion
1/8	tablespoon pepper		

In a small bowl combine the mayonnaise, mustard, salt, pepper, and lemon juice. Stir in the eggs with a fork, chopping them into bite-size pieces. Add the green onion.

NINA COOMBS | SALEM, INDIANA

Tips From Our Test Kitchen:

This tasty egg salad is especially good with fresh garden tomatoes. It's also great with alfalfa sprouts on a whole-wheat bagel.

Wild Rice Salad

Yield: 4 to 6 servings

"I store this salad in a large plastic bag and turn it occasionally to marinate it evenly. It's even better the second day."

6	ounces wild rice	1	(6-ounce) can sliced water chestnuts, drained
1/4	cup rice vinegar	1	(7-ounce) can sliced mushrooms, drained
1/4	cup olive oil	1/4	pound snow peas
1/4	cup soy sauce	3	cups bean sprouts
2	fresh garlic cloves, minced	1/4	cup chopped toasted cashews
3	tablespoons minced fresh gingerroot		

Cook the rice according to the package instructions. Drain and rinse. In a medium bowl whisk together the vinegar, oil, soy sauce, garlic, and gingerroot. Add the water chestnuts and mushrooms. Toss in the cooked rice, snow peas, and bean sprouts. Refrigerate. Top with the cashews at serving time.

JOAN LLOYD | LADY LAKE, FLORIDA

Supreme Chicken Salad

Yield: 4 to 6 servings

"This family recipe has been passed down through four generations. My great-grandmother brought it from Nova Scotia. It's a hit wherever it's served."

2	whole boneless chicken breasts	11/2	to 2 cups mayonnaise
1	celery stalk	2	tablespoons lemon juice
1	small onion, quartered		Salt and pepper
1	cup finely chopped celery		Romaine lettuce for serving

Place the chicken breasts in a saucepan and cover with water. Add the celery and onion and boil for about 20 minutes, or until the chicken is done. Cool. Drain and discard the vegetables. Chop the cooked chicken in a food processor or meat grinder. Combine the chopped celery, mayonnaise, and lemon juice with the chicken in a medium bowl. Season with the salt and pepper to taste. Chill and serve on Romaine lettuce.

BEVERLY COLGLAZIER | PHELAN, CALIFORNIA

Tips From Our Test Kitchen:

Toss in some cherry tomatoes with the snow peas for a red and green holiday accent. This delightful salad is ideal with roast turkey, ham, or roast beef.

Tips From Our Test Kitchen:

Add 1/2 cup chopped fresh herbs, such as dill, parsley, or tarragon or 1 tablespoon brown mustard for some extra zip. This recipe is excellent served with fresh tomatoes.

Craisin and Chicken Salad

Yield: 18 servings

"I bring this salad to group functions or family gatherings. It's always a big hit."

1	head red leaf lettuce	1/2	cup sliced almonds
1	head green leaf lettuce	6	chicken breast halves, cooked and diced
1	head iceberg lettuce	1/2	cup chopped sweet onion
8	ounces mozzarella cheese, shredded	1	cup sugar
6	ounces Parmesan cheese, shredded	2	teaspoons dry mustard
1	cup craisins (dried cranberries)	1/2	cup red wine vinegar
1	pound bacon, cooked and crumbled	1	cup canola oil

Wash the red and green leaf lettuces and the iceberg lettuce. Break into bite-size pieces in a large bowl. Add the mozzarella and Parmesan cheeses, craisins, bacon, almonds, and chicken. In a blender combine the onion, sugar, mustard, and red wine vinegar. Blend and slowly add the canola oil until well mixed. Pour the dressing on the salad and toss or serve the dressing on the side.

AUDREY MISNER | PRICE, UTAH

Wild Rice and Chicken Salad

Yield: 4 to 6 servings

"My mother-in-law gave me this recipe many years ago. I make it frequently."

1	cup mayonnaise	11/2	cups green grapes, halved
11/2	teaspoons seasoned salt	1	(8-ounce) can water chestnuts
2	cups cooked wild rice, chilled	1	cup cashews
1	cup cooked diced chicken		Romaine lettuce

Stir together the mayonnaise and seasoned salt. Add the rice, chicken, grapes, and water chestnuts. Chill until ready to serve. Stir in the cashews just before serving. Serve on a lettuce leaf with fresh fruit and muffins.

NANCY J. SHANER | SHOREVIEW, MINNESOTA

Rice-A-Roni Chicken Salad

Yield: 6 servings

"My wife has many wonderful traits but cooking is not one of them. If I want to hide something from her, I put it in the oven. I do the cooking. This recipe always gets high marks."

1	(7-ounce) box chicken-flavored Rice-A-Roni	2	cups chopped cooked chicken
1	(8-ounce) jar marinated artichoke hearts	1	(8-ounce) can sliced water chestnuts, drained
2	to 4 green onions, chopped	1/2	cup mayonnaise
1/2	green bell pepper, chopped	1	teaspoon curry powder
1	cup sliced black olives		Salt and pepper

Cook the Rice-A-Roni according to the package instructions. Drain the artichokes, reserving the marinade. Chop the artichokes and combine with the rice. Add the onions, pepper, olives, chicken, and water chestnuts. Mix together the mayonnaise, curry powder, and reserved marinade. Pour the mayonnaise mixture over the rice mixture, and stir until well mixed. Season with the salt and pepper to taste. Serve warm or cold.

ROBERT LONG | OXFORD, MISSISSIPPI

Tips From Our Test Kitchen:

This salad makes a perfect light lunch or dinner. Use low-salt Rice-A-Roni and reduce the quantity of olives if you're watching your sodium. Substitute plain yogurt for mayonnaise to reduce calories.

Seafood Salad

Yield: 4 to 6 servings

1	pound fresh shrimp	1/4	cup chopped olives
6	ounces crabmeat, canned or fresh crab-boil seasoning	1/2	cup mayonnaise
1/2	green bell pepper, chopped	1	bunch lettuce, rinsed
1/4	cup sliced celery	1/2	cup Good Seasons salad dressing, prepared according to package instructions
1	cup peeled and shredded carrots		
1/4	cup chopped onion		

Cook the shrimp and crab in the crab-boil seasoning until just done. Do not overcook. Set aside to cool. Mix the bell pepper, celery, carrots, onion, and olives with the mayonnaise. Stir in the seafood. Chill until ready to serve. Place about 1/2 cup salad on lettuce leaves on each plate, and top with the Good Seasons dressing to taste.

BONNIE SANDERS | OAKLAND, MISSISSIPPI

Tips From Our Test Kitchen:

Serve this quick salad with sliced tomatoes and hot rolls. It's perfect for a special first course or light luncheon.

Terrific Taco Salad

Yield: 4 servings

"I got this taco salad recipe from my sister. Many people around here have enjoyed it. Even the grandkids think it's the best."

1	pound ground beef	8	ounces Cheddar cheese, grated
1	package taco seasoning mix	2	medium tomatoes, diced
1/2	head lettuce, diced		French or ranch dressing
1	medium onion, diced	1	bag taco-flavored tortilla chips

Brown the ground beef. Add the taco seasoning as directed on package. Drain the excess liquid and cool. Mix together the lettuce, onion, cheese, tomatoes, and dressing in a large bowl. Add the beef. To serve, top with pieces of the tortilla chips.

GERMAINE STANK | POUND, WISCONSIN

Tips From Our Test Kitchen:

Ground turkey also works well in this dish. Try adding peppers, cucumbers, carrots, or other seasonal vegetables to this salad.

Turkey Salad

Yield: 12 to 14 servings

"This recipe was served at my son's wedding in 1970. Since then, I've prepared it for many church and family gatherings. It always goes over well."

12	cups cooked diced turkey	3	cups Miracle Whip
4	cups diced celery	1	tablespoon curry powder
1	medium onion, diced		Salt and pepper
3	(10-ounce) jars watermelon pickles, diced	4	cups chow mein noodles

In a very large bowl combine the turkey, celery, onion, and pickles. Stir in the Miracle Whip, curry, and salt and pepper to taste. Toss in the chow mein noodles just before serving to retain their crunch.

IRENE FABER | SHELL LAKE, WISCONSIN

Tips From Our Test Kitchen:

If watermelon pickles are hard to find, substitute 2 cups golden raisins. This recipe for leftover turkey can be halved or even quartered. Chicken can also replace the turkey.

Pistachio and Pasta Salad

Yield: 4 to 6 servings

"My children didn't like to eat pistachio nuts. I tried this secret recipe, and they really relished the nuts."

1	tablespoon olive oil	1	cup fresh baby spinach
1	tablespoon cider vinegar	1/2	cup chopped pistachios plus some
1	tablespoon dried oregano		for garnish
	Salt and pepper	1/2	cup grated Parmesan cheese
1	cup pasta, uncooked (rigatoni, gemelli,	8	cherry tomatoes
	or small shells)		Parmesan cheese, shaved
1	cup snow peas		

In a small bowl combine the oil, vinegar, oregano, and salt and pepper to taste. Cook the pasta according to the package instructions. Drain and set aside to cool. Blanch the snow peas and spinach by putting them in hot water and taking them out immediately. Quickly rinse them in cold water, drain well on paper towels, and pat dry. Mix the blanched snow peas and spinach with the pasta, pistachios, cheese, tomatoes, and marinade in a medium bowl. Garnish with additional pistachio nuts and shaved Parmesan cheese.

NEELAM TANEJA | WHITEVILLE, NORTH CAROLINA

Tips From Our Test Kitchen:

Sugar snap peas can replace the snow peas if desired.

Poppy Seed Pasta Salad

Yield: 6 to 8 servings

"I take this to all of the potlucks, and everyone asks for the recipe."

12	ounces bowtie pasta, cooked	1/4	cup chopped green onion
2	cups chopped cooked chicken	3	ounces slivered almonds
1	(6-ounce) package dried cranberries	8	ounces poppy seed dressing
1/2	cup finely chopped celery		Salt and pepper

Combine the pasta, chicken, cranberries, celery, onion, and almonds in a medium bowl. Stir in the dressing and season with the salt and pepper to taste. Serve chilled.

DELORIS OLESON | BUFFALO, MINNESOTA

Tips From Our Test Kitchen:

A teaspoon of garlic salt gives this salad a tangy taste. For a creamier dressing, add 1/2 cup plain yogurt. This salad also is good with a small can of mandarin oranges.

Horseradish Festival

Citizens of Collinsville, Illinois (pop. 24,707), go to their roots during their annual festival. The town, known as the "Horseradish Capital of the World," celebrates this distinction at the International Horseradish Festival. Usually held the second weekend in June, the festival features a root derby, root sacking contest, Bloody Mary contest, Little Miss Horseradish pageant, and bands with music ranging from western to blues. Continuing throughout the festival are a crafts village, petting zoo, and train and pony rides.

One of the major highlights is the horseradish recipe contest where fifteen to twenty participants cook up everything from appetizers and salads to meat dishes. Judges use taste, originality, and appearance as criteria, and first, second, and third place winners receive monetary prizes.

The International Horseradish Festival began in 1987 in the parking lot of the Collinsville Chamber of Commerce. Farmers brought machines to show the public what it took to grow the root, and they competed in a contest for the biggest, as well as the most unusually shaped, root. Today the festival draws 15,000 to 20,000 to Woodland Park for the two-day celebration. Funds raised go to the park, a scholarship fund for high school students, and other community projects.

Collinsville and the surrounding area are part of what is known as the American Bottoms, a Mississippi River basin across the river from St. Louis, Missouri. Carved by Ice Age glaciers, the soil is rich in potash, a chemical nutrient on which horseradish thrives. Winters provide temperatures cold enough for the root to go dormant, while the long, hot summers provide excellent conditions for it to grow. In addition, the horseradish plant is not bothered by pests that ravage other crops.

German immigrants moved to the area and began growing horseradish in the late 1800s and passed their growing method down from generation to generation. The Keller farm in Collinsville has been a successful horseradish farm for 110 years and is still in the same family, as are many other farms in the area. In addition the J. R. Kelly Company, in Collinsville, markets 7 to 8 million pounds of horseradish each year produced by twelve area growers.

A labor-intensive crop that must be planted by hand, horseradish is a member of the mustard family that includes kale, cauliflower, Brussels sprouts, and radish. About 24 million pounds are grown in the United States annually and processed into about 6 million gallons of prepared horseradish. Sixty percent of the world's supply of horseradish is grown in Collinsville.

For more information, log on to www.horseradishfestival.com or call (618) 346-5210.

Dawn Cordle is employed by the City of Collinsville and is chair of the Horseradish Festival.

Shrimp and Pasta Salad

Yield: 10 servings

"This is an easy recipe to prepare. It's great as an appetizer on a hot day, or as a light meal. I bring this to covered dish dinners and people love it."

1	pound sea shell pasta	2	tablespoons olive oil
1	small red onion, diced	1	pound peeled shrimp
1	red or yellow bell pepper, diced	2	to 3 garlic cloves, minced
1	ripe tomato, diced		Salt and pepper
1	(2 1/4-ounce) can sliced black olives	1	cup Italian dressing

Cook the pasta and when done rinse with cold water to stop the cooking. Drain the pasta and put it in a bowl. Combine the onion, bell pepper, and tomato and add them to the pasta. Drain the olives and add them to the pasta. Heat the olive oil in a skillet. Add the shrimp and minced garlic. Season with the salt and pepper to taste. Stir-fry until the shrimp turn pink, 3 to 5 minutes. Do not overcook. Remove the shrimp from the hot skillet and allow them to cool. Stir the cooled shrimp into the pasta mixture. Pour the Italian dressing over all and mix until well coated. Chill for 1 to 2 hours before serving.

HANS GRAY | DAPHNE, ALABAMA

Tips From Our Test Kitchen:

Serve this salad over a bed of spinach with warm garlic toast on the side.

Leroy Brown, a bass with personality and intelligence, escaped the skillet and lived famously at Tom Mann's Fish World in Eufaula, Alabama (pop. 13,908), until he died in 1981. More than 700 mourners attended his funeral, where the Eufaula High School band played "Bad Bad Leroy Brown." Fishing pros served as pallbearers. A marble statue honors the world's luckiest bass.

Overnight Spinach Pasta Salad

Yield: 4 to 6 servings

"For years our family has enjoyed a hot pasta dish with basil, garlic, Parmesan, and olive oil. I decided to use the same basic ingredients to create a cold pasta salad."

2	cups penne pasta, uncooked
1/3	cup olive oil
3	to 4 garlic cloves, crushed and minced
1	bunch fresh basil, chopped
1	teaspoon salt
1/4	teaspoon black pepper

1	(10-ounce) bag fresh spinach, coarsely sliced
1/2	cup chopped walnuts
3/4	cup grated Parmesan cheese
1/3	cup mayonnaise

Cook the pasta, rinse it, and drain. Put the pasta in a mixing bowl. Blend the olive oil, garlic, basil, salt, and pepper in a food processor. Add to the pasta and refrigerate 6 to 8 hours or overnight.

When ready to serve, toss the spinach, walnuts, Parmesan cheese, and mayonnaise into the pasta mixture until well blended. Adjust the mayonnaise, salt, and pepper to achieve the desired seasoning and consistency.

DONNA GALLI | GRAEAGLE, CALIFORNIA

California's wine country can thank Agoston Haraszthy de Mokcsa, a Hungarian-born immigrant, for introducing grape cultivation in the region. He planted a large vineyard in the Sonoma Valley, near Buena Vista (pop. 100), in 1858. In 1861, he traveled to grape-producing regions in Europe, returning with about 300 different types of vines to grow in California.

Apple Salad

Yield: 9 to 12 servings

"My friend Lucille gave me this recipe, and I have added a bit to it for more flavor. Sometimes I add lemon juice and a half package of peach Jell-O."

1	(20-ounce) can crushed pineapple, undrained	1	cup diced unpeeled apples
2/3	cup sugar	1/2	to 1 cup chopped nuts
1	(3-ounce) package lemon Jell-O	1	cup chopped celery
8	ounces cream cheese, softened	1	cup whipped topping

In a saucepan combine the pineapple and sugar. Boil for 3 minutes. Add the Jell-O and stir until dissolved. Add the cream cheese, stirring until the mixture is thoroughly combined. Cool. Fold in the apples, nuts, celery, and whipped topping. Pour into a 9-inch square pan. Chill until firm. Cut into squares and serve on lettuce leaves.

RUTH STAFFORD | LIMESTONE, TENNESSEE

Tips From Our Test Kitchen:

Use mini-Bundt pans or a decorative mold and serve over lettuce with apple slices.

Orange Jell-O Salad

Yield: 10 to 12 servings

"I make this salad for special family dinners and our church fellowship dinners. It's always a favorite dish. It makes a large salad and is really delicious."

1	(15 1/2-ounce) can crushed pineapple	2	cups buttermilk
1	(6-ounce) package orange Jell-O or any other gelatin	1	cup pecan pieces (optional)
1	cup flaked coconut	12	ounces whipped topping (Cool Whip)

Pour the pineapple and its juices into a saucepan and bring to a boil. Remove from the heat and stir in the Jell-O until dissolved. Cool. Mix in the coconut and buttermilk. Add the pecans if using. Fold in the whipped topping. Pour into a Bundt pan or ring mold that has been sprayed lightly with cooking spray. Refrigerate until congealed.

LOIS GOOCH | PRINCETON, WEST VIRGINIA

In Fayette County, West Virginia (pop. 48,000), Camp Washington-Carver was dedicated in 1942 as a 4-H camp for African-American youths. It now serves as the state's mountain cultural arts center.

Grenadine Salad

Yield: 8 to 10 servings

"I remember a wonderful salad that my mother made. It was unique because of the grenadine syrup."

Salad:

3	tablespoons unflavored gelatin
1/2	cup cold water
1	cup pineapple juice
1/2	cup fresh lemon juice
1/2	cup fresh orange juice
13/4	cups grenadine syrup
2	fresh grapefruits, peeled, white membrane removed, and sectioned

Dressing:

1	tablespoon sugar
1/3	teaspoon dry mustard
1/4	teaspoon salt
1	egg, lightly beaten
1	tablespoon cider vinegar
1	tablespoon lemon juice
2	tablespoons grenadine syrup
1	cup whipping cream, stiffly whipped

For the salad, soak the gelatin in the cold water in a bowl. Heat the pineapple juice to boiling, and add the gelatin to dissolve. Cool. Add the lemon juice, orange juice, and the grenadine syrup. Pour into a 51/2-cup ring mold or individual bowls, and chill in the refrigerator. When partially set, add the grapefruit. Return to the refrigerator and chill until firm.

For the dressing, mix the sugar, mustard, and salt. Add the egg and then the vinegar, lemon juice, and grenadine syrup. Cook and stir over medium heat until thick. Cool. Fold in the whipped cream.

When ready to serve, unmold the salad on a plate or tray and fill the center of the ring with the dressing.

JEANNE CRABB | APPLE VALLEY, CALIFORNIA

Strawberry and Pretzel Salad

Yield: 12 to 16 servings

"I got this recipe from my aunt who lived back East. Every summer we went to her place, and I made it all the time."

2½ to 3 cups crushed pretzels	1	(6-ounce) box strawberry Jell-O
1	cup plus 3 teaspoons sugar	2	cups boiling water
3/4	cup (1½ sticks) butter, melted	2	(16-ounce) packages frozen sliced
8	ounces cream cheese, softened		strawberries
12	ounces whipped topping (Cool Whip)		

Preheat the oven to 350 degrees (250 degrees if you're using a glass pan). Mix the crushed pretzels with 3 teaspoons of the sugar and the butter, and spread in a greased 13 x 9-inch pan. Bake for 10 minutes. Cool.

Mix the cream cheese and the remaining 1 cup sugar until smooth. Fold in the whipped topping. Spread on top of the pretzel layer to the edges of the dish.

In a medium bowl dissolve the Jell-O in the boiling water. Add the strawberries, mixing well. Refrigerate until slightly thickened. Pour over the cream cheese layer. Refrigerate until firm and ready to serve.

Note: Raspberry Jell-O and frozen raspberries may be substituted for strawberry Jell-O and frozen strawberries.

BETTY L. FREEMAN | BARSTOW, CALIFORNIA

California produces more than 350 different food and agricultural crops a year. The state leads all other areas worldwide in the production of almonds, artichokes, dates, pistachios, raisins, and walnuts.

Thousand Island Dressing

Yield: 2 cups

"We always use this dressing, and no other kind. We never tire of it. It's been a favorite for sixteen years."

1	cup mayonnaise		1	teaspoon paprika
1/2	cup vegetable oil		1	teaspoon Tabasco
1/4	cup ketchup		1	teaspoon red pepper
1	tablespoon Worcestershire sauce		1	garlic clove, crushed
1	tablespoon horseradish		1	small onion, grated
1	tablespoon cold water		1	teaspoon sugar (optional)
1	teaspoon mustard			

In a small bowl mix the mayonnaise, oil, ketchup, Worcestershire, and horseradish. Stir in the water, mustard, paprika, Tabasco, red pepper, garlic, onion, and sugar. Store in the refrigerator.

RUTH NOLLEY | NEW ALBANY, MISSISSIPPI

Lemon Asparagus

Yield: 6 to 8 servings

"My mom loves asparagus. I invented this recipe to offer her a new way to enjoy it."

1½	pounds fresh asparagus		Juice and zest of 1 lemon
3	to 5 tablespoons butter	1	teaspoon salt
1/4	cup water	1/4	teaspoon pepper

Cut the tough ends off the asparagus. Rinse and remove the scales with a vegetable peeler. Heat the butter, water, juice, and zest in a large skillet to boiling. Add the asparagus, salt, and pepper. Cover and simmer for 3 to 5 minutes, or until crisp-tender. Serve immediately.

CONNIE KELLY | HUALAPAI, ARIZONA

Barbecued Beans

Yield: 6 servings

"This bean recipe was my mother's. Whenever I need to take a covered dish, I always take these beans. They are easy to make and good for picnics or any party."

1/4	cup ketchup		Salt
3/4	cup water		Celery salt
1	teaspoon cider vinegar		Onion salt
1	teaspoon Worcestershire sauce	1	(28-ounce) can pork and beans, drained
4	tablespoons firmly packed brown sugar		

Preheat the oven to 300 degrees. Mix the ketchup, water, vinegar, Worcestershire sauce, and brown sugar. Season with salt, celery salt, and onion salt to taste. Stir in the beans. Pour into a casserole dish and bake for 1 hour.

MARY ANN REMALY | BATH, PENNSYLVANIA

Gene's Bean Medley

Yield: 6 to 8 servings

"This family favorite is nutritious and inexpensive. It's great served with cornbread."

1/2	pound bacon	1	(16-ounce) can garbanzo beans
2	tablespoons bacon grease	1/4	teaspoon ground cumin
1	medium red onion, chopped	1/4	teaspoon red pepper flakes
2	garlic cloves, minced	1/4	teaspoon dried thyme
2	celery stalks, diced	2	cups tomato sauce
1	(16-ounce) can pinto beans	1/2	cup water
1	(16-ounce) can kidney beans		

Fry the bacon until crisp, reserving 2 tablespoons bacon grease, and crumble when cool. In a heavy saucepan, heat the bacon grease and sauté the onion, garlic, and celery until crisp-tender. Rinse and drain the beans. To the onion mixture add the beans, crumbled bacon, cumin, pepper flakes, thyme, tomato sauce, and water. Cook, stirring occasionally, over medium heat for about 1 hour.

GENE HERZOG | GREEN VALLEY, ARIZONA

Tips From Our Test Kitchen:

This bean dish is delicious served over macaroni and topped with shredded sharp cheese. Add a dash of salsa with cilantro for a Southwestern flavor.

Slow Cooker Baked Beans

Yield: 10 to 12 servings

"I adapted this bean recipe from the oven to the slow cooker. I hope you enjoy these beans as much as my family, extended family, and friends do."

10	strips bacon	2	(16-ounce) cans kidney beans, drained
2	tablespoons bacon grease	1	(16-ounce) can lima beans, drained
4	medium onions, chopped	1	(16-ounce) can cannelloni beans, drained
1	(30-ounce) can pork and beans, undrained	1/2	cup ketchup
		1/2	cup firmly packed brown sugar

Fry the bacon until crisp and reserve 2 tablespoons grease. Crumble the bacon. Heat the grease over medium heat and sauté the onions until clear. Drain the excess fat. Stir the onions together with the pork and beans, kidney beans, lima beans, cannelloni beans, ketchup, crumbled bacon, and brown sugar in a large slow cooker. Cook on the low setting for 2 hours.

JOAN BARTON | BATAVIA, NEW YORK

Tips From Our Test Kitchen:

Adjust the amounts of the sugar, ketchup, and onions to suit your taste, and experiment with great Northern, butter beans, and fava beans. This recipe is even better the second day.

Old Settler Baked Beans

Yield: 10 to 12 servings

"This recipe has been a hit at potlucks over the past fifty years. People love this dish and always request the recipe."

1/2	pound bacon, crisply cooked and crumbled	2	tablespoons molasses
1/2	pound ground beef, browned and drained	1/2	teaspoon chili powder
1	medium onion, chopped	1	teaspoon salt
1/2	cup firmly packed brown sugar	1/2	teaspoon black pepper
1/4	cup ketchup	1	(16-ounce) can kidney beans
1/4	cup barbecue sauce	1	(16-ounce) can butter beans
2	tablespoons mustard	2	(16-ounce) cans pork and beans

Preheat the oven to 350 degrees. Combine the bacon, ground beef, and onion in a large bowl. Stir in the brown sugar, ketchup, barbecue sauce, mustard, and molasses. Season with the chili powder, salt, and pepper. Gently fold in the beans. Pour into a large, lightly greased casserole dish. Bake for 1 hour.

DARLENE BANDY | ALBUQUERQUE, NEW MEXICO

Tips From Our Test Kitchen:

Experiment to suit your taste by substituting great Northern, red beans, black beans, or even lima beans.

Green Beans and Shoepeg Corn

Yield: 8 servings

1	(15-ounce) can French green beans, drained	1	(10 3/4-ounce) can condensed cream of celery soup
1	(15-ounce) can shoepeg corn, drained	8	ounces sharp Cheddar cheese, grated
1	cup sour cream	1	sleeve Ritz crackers, crushed
1	medium onion, chopped	1/2	cup (1 stick) margarine, melted

Preheat the oven to 350 degrees. Lightly grease a 13 x 9-inch baking dish. Layer the green beans and corn in the baking dish. Mix together the sour cream, onion, and soup and spoon the mix over the beans and corn in an even layer. Top with the cheese and crushed crackers. Pour the margarine over all. Bake for 30 minutes.

PEGGY MCTHENIA | GLADE SPRING, VIRGINIA

Tips From Our Test Kitchen:

Sweet white corn can replace the shoepeg corn. Frozen 16-ounce bags of vegetables can be used instead of the canned vegetables but add 15 minutes to the cooking time if you use frozen vegetables.

Say Corn, and They're
All Ears in Olathe

Photo by Tim Sale. Used by permission.

Shelling out money for a sweet corn harvest festival didn't appeal to Olathe, Colorado (pop. 1,573), residents who were struggling with a poor market for their barley and sugar beet crops.

But in 1992 John Harold, a local business-man and farmer, convinced them a festival could boost the town and its new super-sweet strain of sweet corn. Today the festival, held on the first Saturday in August, draws about 20,000 people, and proceeds have already helped build a thirty-seven-acre events and recreation park.

Organizers say the corn festival has become known nationwide, and it's given people a sense of pride in their community—not to mention introducing Olathe Sweet to corn lovers all over the country. Patented and trademarked, the Olathe Sweet variety is so tender it has to be picked by hand and is shipped in an ice slurry mixture to keep it at maximum sugar content.

The farming community is north of the San Juan Mountains, where the towns of Ouray, Telluride, and Durango beckon skiiers and mountain climbers. But agriculture, not tourism, still drives the economy on the fertile farming flats of the Uncompahgre Valley. Crops include onions, pinto beans, alfalfa, apples, cherries, sugar beets, and wine grapes, but Olathe Sweet is king.

The strain was developed by corn geneticist David Galinat, who moved his Mesa Maize research and production headquarters to Olathe about the time markets for sugar beets and barley crops were shrinking and farmers were looking for a new cash crop. Olathe's sandy, loamy soil and cool nights and warm days are perfect for growing the sweet corn.

Nearly all the 35 million ears of the sweet corn handpicked each year are grown within a fifteen-mile radius of the town. The corn is shipped to Roanoke, Virginia, and Los Angeles, California, and all points in between. It's even made its way to the shelves of London's Harrods department store.

The festival, now a division of the town's government, is a major source of revenue for local nonprofit groups, whose members perform all the festival jobs. In 2004, nonprofit groups raised more than $50,000.

Throughout the one-day, family-oriented festival, there are old-fashioned contests such as ice-block sitting, corn husking, and a corn-kernel-spitting contest. By far the most popular aspect is the all-you-can-eat sweet corn. Most years, farmers donate 70,000 ears that are boiled and roasted to perfection by volunteers.

As a spectator sport, it's hard to top the corn-eating contest. Kernels fly when competitors line up on the stage, plowing through as many as twenty-eight ears in ten minutes. Techniques include the "typewriter" method—gnawing horizontally across the rows of corn—and the "rotary" method—twisting the ears along the teeth like a bandsaw blade.

Since the second festival in 1993, the finale of the event has featured a concert by a major recording artist, including the Nitty Gritty Dirt Band, The Mavericks, Three Dog Night, STYX, and Randy Travis.

These performers may shine during the evening finale, but it's corn that is the star in Olathe—a town that was saved by the sweet and juicy kernels.

For more information, log on to www.olathesweetcornfest.com or call (970) 323-6006.

Laurena Mayne Davis is a writer in western Colorado.

Lima Bean Casserole

Yield: 15 to 20 servings

"As the young bride of a lima bean farmer, I felt it my duty to find a dish to highlight our main crop."

2	(16-ounce) bags frozen baby lima beans
1/4	cup olive oil
1	large onion, chopped
1	medium green bell pepper, chopped
1	garlic clove, minced
1/2	cup sliced black olives

1/2	plus 1/2 cup grated sharp Cheddar cheese
1	rounded tablespoon cornstarch
1/4	cup cold water
1	teaspoon salt
1	rounded tablespoon chili powder
	Black pepper

Cover the beans with water and cook until tender. Preheat the oven to 375 degrees. Heat the oil in a deep skillet and sauté the onion, bell pepper, and garlic. Add the olives. Drain the beans, reserving 1 1/4 cups of the cooking liquid. Add the beans to the onion mixture. Stir in 1/2 cup of the cheese.

Dissolve the cornstarch in the cold water. In the pan used to cook the beans, add the dissolved cornstarch to the reserved cooking liquid. Stir in the salt and chili powder. Bring the liquid to a boil and stir until clear. Add more cornstarch if a thicker sauce is desired. Season with pepper to taste.

Lightly grease a 13 x 9-inch baking dish. Place the beans in the dish and pour the sauce evenly over the top. Bake, covered with foil, for about 45 minutes. Remove the foil and add the remaining 1/2 cup cheese. Return to the oven and bake until the cheese melts.

GLENNA SUE PETZ | TRACY, CALIFORNIA

Want to know more about those classic little Pez candy dispensers? The Museum of Pez Memorabilia in Burlingame, California (pop. 26,801), offers an in-depth look at the candy invented in 1927 by Austrian candy executive Eduard Haas. The original candies were peppermint, and Pez is a shorthand version of the German word for "peppermint"—*pfefferminz*.

Delicious Baked Beets

Yield: 4 to 6 servings

"Boiled beets lose a lot of their flavor. I created this easy recipe to keep them yummy."

4	to 6 whole beets, scrubbed	Salt	
	Butter	Black pepper	

Preheat the oven to 350 degrees. Cut the tops and root ends off the scrubbed beets. Wrap each beet tightly in foil, and bake for about 2 hours, or until soft. Slide the skins off the baked beets. Slice them, and serve with the butter, salt, and pepper to taste.

SHERRI FAGA | CARROLL, IOWA

Broccoli Casserole

Yield: 6 to 8 servings

"This recipe has been a favorite of my family's to take to a church supper or a family gathering. It is simple to make and receives many compliments."

1	egg, beaten	1	(10-ounce) box frozen broccoli pieces, thawed
1	onion, finely chopped, or 1/8 cup dehydrated onions	1	(8-ounce) package cornbread stuffing, divided
8	ounces fat-free sour cream	16	ounces grated Cheddar cheese, divided
1	(103/4-ounce) can condensed cream of broccoli soup, undiluted	2	tablespoons margarine, melted

Preheat the oven to 350 degrees. Spray a casserole dish with cooking spray. In a large bowl mix the egg, onion, sour cream, soup, broccoli, half of the stuffing, and half of the cheese. Pour into the casserole dish. Mix the remaining stuffing and cheese and add the margarine. Spread the stuffing over the top of the casserole. Bake for 30 minutes, or until lightly browned. Cooked yellow squash may be substituted for the broccoli.

ANITA BLANKENSHIP | HICKORY, NORTH CAROLINA

147

Cabbage Parmesan

Yield: 6 servings

"My family and I like sautéed cabbage any day of the week. We don't add much salt to our food, so I need to know how to use spices. Family and friends like this dish."

1/4	cup slivered almonds	1	teaspoon Italian herb seasoning
1	medium head green cabbage		Salt and pepper
1/4	cup (1/2 stick) butter or margarine	1/3	cup grated Parmesan cheese
1	garlic clove, minced		

Brown the almonds in a skillet over low heat, stirring occasionally to prevent burning. Cut the cabbage into 1/2-inch slices and discard the core. Separate the cabbage into strips. Layer the cabbage in a saucepan with the butter, garlic, seasoning, and salt and pepper to taste. Cook over medium-high heat until tender, stirring frequently. Garnish with the cheese and toasted almonds.

BARB JENNINGS | VILLA RIDGE, MISSOURI

Luscious Spicy Red Cabbage

Yield: 6 servings

"The cook at the hospital where I worked used to make this dish. The scent would 'attack' our senses. Just before she retired, she shared her secret recipe with me."

2	tablespoons butter or margarine	1/3	cup plus 1 tablespoon red wine vinegar
1	pound red cabbage, chopped	1/8	cup firmly packed brown sugar
1/2	cup chopped unpeeled apple		Salt and pepper
1/4	cup chopped onion		

Melt the butter in a saucepan, and sauté the cabbage, apples, and onion for 20 minutes, stirring occasionally. Add the vinegar and brown sugar. Cook for 20 minutes more, or until the vegetables are soft. Season with the salt and pepper to taste.

Lightly grease an ovenproof dish. Pour the vegetable mixture into the dish. Cover and refrigerate 6 to 8 hours or overnight. When ready to bake, preheat the oven to 325 degrees and bake for 45 minutes.

ALICE HAYES | SANBORN, NEW YORK

The American Maple Museum in Croghan, New York (pop. 3,161), founded in 1977, preserves the history and evolution of the maple syrup industry. Exhibits depict maple syrup-making techniques, from those used by American Indians to the plastic tubing and stainless steel evaporators used today.

Coleslaw and Dressing

Yield: 6 to 8 servings

"Everyone who has ever tasted this dressing over coleslaw tells me how much he or she likes it. Comments usually heard are, 'It is not too sweet. Not too tangy, unlike some commercial coleslaw dressings.' The good part is that it accompanies any kind of meat entrée—so light, yet so tasty. I like to make up the dressing and refrigerate it for future use."

Dressing:

3/4 cup mayonnaise

3 tablespoons sugar

1 1/2 tablespoons white wine vinegar

1/3 cup vegetable oil

1/8 teaspoon garlic powder

1/8 teaspoon onion powder

1/8 teaspoon dry mustard

1/8 teaspoon celery salt

Dash of black pepper

1 tablespoon lemon juice

1/2 cup half-and-half

1/4 teaspoon salt (or more to taste)

Coleslaw:

1 large green cabbage, finely shredded

Purple cabbage, finely shredded (optional)

Carrots, finely grated (optional)

For the dressing, blend together the mayonnaise, sugar, vinegar, and oil. Add the garlic powder, onion powder, mustard, celery salt, pepper, lemon juice, half-and-half, and salt to taste. Stir until smooth. Refrigerate until ready to use.

For the coleslaw, pour the dressing over the cabbage and carrots if using. Toss until the vegetables are well coated.

ESTHER PAYNE DAVIS | MOUNTAIN VIEW, CALIFORNIA

Martha's Slaw

Yield: 8 servings

*Tips From Our
Test Kitchen:*

Try substituting toasted almonds for the sunflower seeds.

"After a forty-year separation, I was able to rekindle a special relationship with my childhood friend Martha. This is her slaw recipe."

Slaw:
- 2 (3-ounce) packages chicken- or beef-flavored Ramen noodles
- 1 pound cabbage slaw mix
- 1 cup sunflower seeds
- 1 bunch green onions, chopped

Dressing:
- 3/4 cup peanut or sesame oil
- 1/3 cup sugar
- 2 flavor packets from Ramen noodles

For the slaw, in a medium bowl crush the Ramen noodles into bite-size pieces. Stir in the slaw mix, sunflower seeds, and green onions.

For the dressing, mix together the oil, sugar, and flavor packets from the Ramen noodles. Pour the dressing on top of the slaw mixture and refrigerate for at least 1 hour. Stir well before serving.

BRENDA COLINGER | FOREST, VIRGINIA

Slaw with Red Cabbage and Red Onions

Yield: 8 servings

*Tips From Our
Test Kitchen:*

Use the leftover marinated red onions as a relish for cooked peas or beans. They're also great as a sandwich relish.

"I found this old Southern recipe quite a few years ago. My husband likes it so much he requests that I make it often."

Marinated Red Onions:
- 1/2 cup apple cider vinegar
- 1 tablespoon chopped fresh tarragon or 1 teaspoon dried
- 1/4 teaspoon salt
  Black pepper
- 1/4 cup canola oil
- 1/2 pound red onions, peeled and sliced

Slaw:
- 4 cups shredded red cabbage
- 2 cups grated carrots
- 1/2 cup marinated red onion
- 3 tablespoons chopped sweet pickles
- 1/2 cup apple cider vinegar
- 3/4 cup canola oil
- 2 tablespoons sugar
- 1 teaspoon Creole or grainy mustard
  Salt and pepper

For the onions, mix the vinegar, tarragon, salt, and pepper to taste in a small bowl. Whisk in the oil and pour the mixture over the sliced onions. Refrigerate 6 to 8 hours or overnight. Makes about 2 cups.

For the slaw, toss the red cabbage, carrots, onion, and pickles together in a large bowl. Place the vinegar, oil, sugar, and mustard in a small saucepan and bring to a boil over high heat. Remove from the heat and pour the mix over the slaw while still hot. Refrigerate for several hours. Season with salt and pepper to taste. Serve cold.

DIANA C. HULT | CROCKETT, VIRGINIA

Canned Corn Casserole

Yield: 8 servings

"This dish is a real hit at family dinners and church carry-ins. The taste is just delicious."

1	(15 1/4-ounce) can whole-kernel corn, drained	1/2	cup sugar
1	(14 3/4-ounce) can cream-style corn	2	eggs, well beaten
1	(8 1/2-ounce) box Jiffy corn muffin mix	1/2	cup (1 stick) margarine, melted
		1	cup sour cream

Preheat the oven to 350 degrees. Generously grease a 13 x 9-inch baking dish. Mix together the kernel corn, cream-style corn, muffin mix, and sugar. Add the eggs, margarine, and sour cream. Pour into the prepared dish. Bake for 45 minutes to 1 hour, or until the center is firm.

SHEILA NESTOR | WINCHESTER, INDIANA

Tips From Our Test Kitchen:

The kernels from two large ears of fresh corn are a seasonal substitute for the canned whole-kernel corn. If you like a slightly less sweet dish, use only 1/4 cup sugar. Serve this casserole as a side dish with fried chicken and fresh tomatoes with basil.

The historic Log Inn, an eatery near Haubstadt, Indiana (pop. 1,529), is known for its family-style fried chicken dinners. It was built as a stagecoach stop in 1825. Abraham Lincoln reportedly visited there in 1844 on his way home to Illinois from Evansville, where he'd been campaigning for Henry Clay.

Corn Pudding

Yield: 6 to 8 servings

"I have never tasted another corn pudding that equals this recipe. It can be doubled easily. I try not to overbake it, since that will dry it out. This is a very old recipe—probably sixty years or more."

1	(14³/₄-ounce) can cream-style corn	2	teaspoons salt
1	(15¹/₄-ounce) can whole-kernel corn, drained	4	eggs
		1	medium green bell pepper, diced
4	tablespoons all-purpose flour	1	(2-ounce) jar chopped pimientos,
4	tablespoons sugar		drained
1/4	cup (1/2 stick) margarine	1/2	cup shredded Cheddar cheese

Preheat the oven to 325 degrees. Pour the cream-style and whole-kernel corn into a medium bowl. Blend the flour, sugar, margarine, salt, and eggs in a blender. Add to the corn. Stir in the green pepper, pimientos, and cheese. Pour into a casserole dish and bake for at least 1 hour. The pudding is done when a knife inserted in the center comes out clean.

JOAN NORENBERG | WAHOO, NEBRASKA

Spaghetti Corn

Yield: 4 to 6 servings

"My family loves this recipe. My mother made a similar dish using noodles instead of the spaghetti."

1	(14³/₄-ounce) can cream-style corn	1	cup shredded mozzarella cheese
1	(15¹/₄-ounce) can whole-kernel corn with liquid	1/2	cup (1 stick) butter, melted
1	cup broken spaghetti, uncooked (about 1/3 pound)	2	to 4 tablespoons chopped onion (optional)

Preheat the oven to 350 degrees. Butter a 13 x 9-inch baking dish. Stir together the cream-style corn, whole-kernel corn, spaghetti, cheese, butter, and onion if using. Pour the mixture into the prepared dish. Cover with foil and bake for 30 minutes. Remove the foil and bake for an additional 30 minutes.

MILDRED MAAS | SLEEPY EYE, MINNESOTA

Tips From Our Test Kitchen:

This mild side dish is popular with children. Try different shapes of pasta instead of the spaghetti.

South Carolina "Scalped" Corn

Yield: 10 to 12 servings

"A childhood mispronunciation of 'scalloped' by my sister Roxie lent its name to this family favorite."

3	(14³/₄-ounce) cans cream-style corn	2	(20-ounce) cans oysters or chopped clams
2	(10³/₄-ounce) cans condensed cream of mushroom soup	2	cups coarsely ground whole wheat crackers
3	large eggs, beaten	1/4	pound bacon, cooked and crumbled
1	tablespoon finely chopped garlic		Coarse ground black pepper
1	small onion, chopped		
1	teaspoon Tabasco (optional)		

Preheat the oven to 350 degrees. Lightly grease a 2-quart casserole dish. Combine the corn, soup, eggs, garlic, onion, and Tabasco if using, and mix well. Stir in the oysters and crackers. Spoon the mixture into the prepared dish. Sprinkle the bacon evenly over the top. Season with pepper to taste. Bake for 1 hour, or until a knife inserted in the center comes out clean.

IVAN KERSHNER | SALEM, SOUTH CAROLINA

Eggplant Casserole

Yield: 6 to 8 servings

"This recipe was a favorite at my church socials—the teens loved it. And my family loves it too."

2	medium eggplants	2	pounds processed cheese (Velveeta)
2	eggs, well beaten	1	(10-ounce) can tomatoes and green chiles (Ro-Tel)
	All-purpose flour		Dash of ground cumin
1	to 2 tablespoons oil		

Preheat the oven to 350 degrees. Wash and peel the eggplants and cut them into 1/4-inch slices. Dip the eggplant slices into the egg and then into flour. Heat the oil in a skillet over medium heat and brown the eggplant slices on both sides. In a separate saucepan melt the Velveeta and add the tomatoes and cumin. Mix until creamy. Layer the eggplant and Velveeta mixture in an 11 x 9-inch dish, or until all is used. You should make three layers of each. Bake for about 15 minutes. Sliced or shredded cooked chicken may be added for a complete meal.

PAT SIMMONS | BATESVILLE, ARKANSAS

Tips From Our Test Kitchen:

Serve this cheesy casserole with sliced fresh tomatoes.

Vidalia: How Sweet It Is

Heading into Vidalia, Georgia (pop. 10,491), the first thing you spot is the welcome sign, then below it, the distinct reminder that this is "the sweet onion city."

In fact, signs touting this distinction are visible throughout the town, because the vegetable—the Vidalia onion—is a source of great pride for Vidalia residents.

This is where, in 1931, a local farmer named Mose Coleman discovered the onions he had planted were not hot, as he'd intended, but were sweet instead—sweet enough, in fact, to eat like an apple. Coleman knew he'd found something special, but he didn't realize that his discovery would forever put the town of Vidalia on the map.

About 75,000 people from all over the nation come to celebrate the onion harvest at the annual Vidalia Onion Festival, held in April since 1978. Festivalgoers sample onions, take part in the onion-eating contest, and enter the Vidalia Onion Cook-Off, which has resulted in more than a few flavorful recipes. An air show (featuring the U.S. Navy's Blue Angels), arts and crafts fair, carnival, car show, soft-ball tournament, rodeo, children's costume parade, street dance, and one-mile, 5K, and 10K runs round out the festivities celebrating the famous crop.

The sweet onion hasn't always been so well known. Georgia gave it a boost by generating a little mass marketing. In the 1940s, the state built a Farmer's Market in Vidalia because it was the juncture of several major highways and tourists buying produce there began to spread the word about the sweet onions, which they called Vidalias. Through the next several decades, the onion steadily grew in popularity, and in 1986, the state legislature defined the twenty-county production area as the only land from which growers could legally call their product the Vidalia onion. In 1990, the legislature bestowed another honor and named the Vidalia onion Georgia's official state vegetable.

Vidalias are bigger and flatter in the middle, not round and bulb-shaped like hot onions. Some growers attribute the onion's sweetness to the mild climate and the sulfur content of the area's loamy soil. More than 100 growers raise Vidalias on 14,500 acres of land. Their harvest represents 40 percent of the total national spring onion production. During harvest time—from late April to mid-June—several area growers offer tours of the fields and packing sheds.

But Vidalia is not content to rest on its onions. Some growers are experimenting with other vegetables to see what crops up. Maybe the Vidalia carrot will come next.

For more information, log on to www.vidaliaonionfestival.com or call the Vidalia Area Convention and Visitors Bureau at (912) 538-8687.

Larry Perrault is a writer based in Avondale Estates, Georgia.

Onion Casserole

Yield: 6 to 8 small servings

"This dish was served at a Christmas party I attended several years ago. I asked the cook for the recipe and was told that it was made with 'a bit of this and a bit of that.' I had to come up with the recipe on my own, and this is it."

2	tablespoons butter or margarine	1	teaspoon black pepper
4	to 5 large onions, sliced	1/2	cup bread crumbs
1/2	teaspoon salt	1/2	cup grated Parmesan cheese

Preheat the oven to 350 degrees. Lightly grease an 8-inch square baking dish. Heat the butter over medium heat and sauté the onions until slightly brown. Season with the salt and pepper. Spoon into the prepared dish. Cover with the bread crumbs and top with the cheese. Bake for 20 to 30 minutes, or until the bread crumbs begin to brown.

PAT RAMSEY | STEPHENVILLE, TEXAS

Good Luck Black-Eyed Peas

Yield: 12 servings

"This dish is good any time of the year, not just at New Year's celebrations."

1	(16-ounce) package dried black-eyed peas	1	package dry Italian dressing mix
3	cups water	3	to 4 tablespoons canola or olive oil
1	(14-ounce) can chicken broth or 2 tablespoons granules dissolved in 2 cups water	2	tablespoons ground red pepper

Soak the peas in 6 to 8 cups of water for 1 to 2 hours. Drain, rinse, and sort them. Place the peas in a large saucepan with 3 cups of water, the broth, dressing mix, red pepper, and oil. Bring to a boil, reduce the heat, and simmer with the lid tilted for 1 to 2 hours, or until the peas are tender. Add more water or broth if needed. Serve over rice.

BARBARA RANDALL CLARK | ORANGEBURG, SOUTH CAROLINA

Tips From Our Test Kitchen:

This side dish is excellent when paired with meats and pastas. It also works well as a topping for hamburgers or bratwurst.

Tips From Our Test Kitchen:

This high-fiber dish is a healthful alternative to the traditional high-fat and high-salt versions. Serve with chow chow or pickled sweet peppers.

Devil's Laker Potatoes

Yield: 4 servings

"Every year my family camped at Devil's Lake in Wisconsin. These potatoes were prepared ahead so we could throw them on the grill when we got there."

4	baking potatoes, quartered		1	garlic clove, minced
1/4	cup (1/2 stick) butter			Seasoned salt
1	large onion, quartered			

Divide the potato quarters, butter, onion, and garlic equally in the center of four pieces of heavy-duty aluminum foil. Sprinkle with seasoned salt to taste. Wrap tightly and grill for about 1 hour, or until the potatoes are soft. These make-ahead potatoes can also be roasted in a 425 degree oven for about 1 hour.

RACHEL CZIPO | CRYSTAL LAKE, ILLINOIS

Tips From Our Test Kitchen:

This no-mess dish can also be prepared with red or green bell pepper slices. Sprinkle a little Parmesan cheese on top at serving time.

Blue Cheese Mashed Red Potatoes

Yield: 4 to 6 servings

"I had some blue cheese that I wanted to use. Company was coming for dinner. I put together this recipe, and everyone loved it."

8	to 10 medium red potatoes		1	tablespoon butter
5	garlic cloves, halved		1	cup milk or cream
2	tablespoons crumbled blue cheese			Salt and pepper
1	tablespoon mayonnaise			

Wash the potatoes, but do not peel. Boil them for about 20 minutes. Add the garlic cloves, and continue to cook until the potatoes are tender. Meanwhile, set out the measured amounts of cheese, mayonnaise, butter, and milk to bring these ingredients to room temperature. When the potatoes and garlic are soft enough to mash, remove from the heat and drain. Place in a large bowl, and blend with other ingredients, adding only 1/2 cup milk to start. Whip until fluffy. Adjust the amount of milk to achieve the desired consistency. Season with salt and pepper to taste.

LILLIAN MUISE | THE VILLAGES, FLORIDA

Tips From Our Test Kitchen:

Because there's no need to peel the potatoes, this side dish can be made in a flash. Pair it with any meat dish or vegetarian favorite.

The dining room walls of Florida's Cabbage Key Inn and Restaurant, near Pineland, Florida (pop. 444), are covered in dollar bills—more than $10,000 worth—held in place with masking tape. Each bill is signed by the tourist who put it there.

Festive Calico Potatoes

Yield: 8 to 10 servings

"These potatoes are a sure thing when you want your family to feel special. I like to prepare them on birthdays, holidays, or when someone needs a little extra TLC."

5	pounds potatoes, peeled and quartered	1/4	cup chopped fresh parsley
1/4	plus 1/4 cup (1 stick) butter	3/4	cup heavy cream
1/2	cup chopped green bell pepper	1/4	pound processed cheese (Velveeta), cubed
1/2	cup chopped roasted red pepper		
1/2	cup chopped onion		Salt and pepper
2	to 3 garlic cloves, minced		

In a large saucepan boil the potatoes until tender. Heat 4 tablespoons of the butter over medium heat and sauté the peppers and onions. Add the garlic and parsley after the onions and peppers are soft.

Preheat the oven to 350 degrees. Lightly grease a 13 x 9-inch baking dish. Drain the potatoes. Put them back into the saucepan and add the sautéed vegetables, the remaining 1/4 cup butter, cream, cheese, and salt and pepper to taste. Mash together until most of the lumps are gone. This dish is not meant to be creamed. Spoon into the prepared dish. Bake for about 45 minutes, or until the potatoes begin to turn golden.

CYNDE SONNIER | MONT BELVIEU, TEXAS

Tips From Our Test Kitchen:

Use milk instead of the cream and decrease the butter by half to reduce the fat content. It's the ideal side dish for beef, pork, chicken, or fish.

Cream Cheese Potatoes

Yield: 8 to 10 servings

"My family loves this recipe for cream cheese potatoes; they don't know what 'regular' mashed potatoes are. This is a recipe from my husband's mother."

10	medium red potatoes, skins on or off	1	tablespoon grated onion
1/2	cup (1 stick) butter	1	cup scalded milk
1	teaspoon salt (or more to taste)	8	ounces cream cheese
1/4	teaspoon pepper		

Boil the potatoes until tender. Drain the water. Preheat the oven to 350 degrees. Mash the potatoes and add the butter, salt, pepper, onion, milk, and cream cheese. Whip until fluffy. Spoon into a greased pan and bake for 30 minutes. If you are using a glass baking dish, bake at 325 degrees.

BARBARA DICK | PARIS, ILLINOIS

Tips From Our Test Kitchen:

We found it easy to drain the boiled potatoes and then add a cup of milk and scald. Then add the remaining ingredients and whip.

Raw Potato Pancakes (Latkes)

Yield: 8 to 10 latkes

"This old Jewish recipe was handed from my grandmother to my mother. I am now a great-grandfather. To this day I still make latkes for the family during Chanukah."

2	large potatoes, peeled and quartered	2	tablespoons butter, melted
1	small to medium onion, peeled and quartered	1/4	cup all-purpose flour
2	large eggs	1/2	teaspoon salt
2	to 4 tablespoons milk	1/8	teaspoon pepper
			Vegetable oil

Grate the potatoes and onions, using a food processor or hand grater. Press the potatoes and onions lightly in a dishtowel to remove the excess liquid. Whisk or process the eggs, milk, and butter together. Add the flour, salt, and pepper, and mix well. Fold this into the potato mixture in a medium-size bowl. Heat several tablespoons of oil in a heavy skillet over medium-high heat. Scoop the mixture, using 1/4 cup for each latke, onto the heated oil. Press to form the pancakes into 4-inch circles. Brown each side.

LEONARD A. GARDNER | PARKVILLE, MARYLAND

Tips From Our Test Kitchen:

Serve with sour cream or applesauce. This side dish is great with meat or fish.

Garden Bounty

"When my mother-in-law was a girl, it was hard to use up all the surplus garden veggies. She served this concoction with soda crackers and sat under a shade tree to eat. No bacon was added, but it was cooked in bacon grease. Since I don't keep bacon grease on hand as in the old days, I have to fry some bacon. It does add to the flavor."

6	slices bacon	1	to 2 banana peppers, chopped
3	large potatoes, chopped and boiled	6	eggs
4	tomatoes, diced, or 1 (14-ounce) can tomatoes with juice		Salt and pepper

Cook the bacon until crisp, reserving the grease. When cool, break the bacon into pieces. Add the potatoes to the grease in the skillet. Add the tomatoes, peppers, and bacon pieces. Beat the eggs and pour them on top of the potato mixture. Cook for 15 minutes on medium heat, or until heated through and the eggs are done. Season with salt and pepper to taste.

CATHY WILSON | MIDVALE, UTAH

Ro-Tel Potatoes

Yield: 8 servings

"When I take this to covered-dish events, I've learned to bring copies of the recipe."

1	(10-ounce) can tomatoes and green chiles (Ro-Tel)	1/2	can water
1	(10 3/4-ounce) can condensed Cheddar cheese soup	1	tablespoon onion flakes or chopped fresh onion
1	(10 3/4-ounce) can condensed cream of mushroom soup		Salt and pepper
		10	to 12 small potatoes, peeled and sliced
		1/4	cup (1/2 stick) margarine, cut in pieces

Preheat the oven to 350 degrees. In a bowl mix the tomatoes and green chiles, cheese soup, mushroom soup, water, onion, and salt and pepper to taste. Arrange the potato slices in a greased baking dish. Pour the tomato mixture over the potatoes. Dot the top with margarine pieces and bake for 1 hour, or until the potatoes are soft when pierced with a fork.

DEE MCDONALD | LAPORTE, TEXAS

Aunt Rita's Potatoes

Yield: 12 to 15 servings

"My husband's Aunt Rita always used to make these tasty potatoes when we went to her house for Christmas. We always went back for seconds if there were any left. They are a family favorite."

10	large potatoes	8	ounces shredded Cheddar cheese
1	(2-ounce) jar pimientos, drained and diced	1/2	cup (1 stick) butter, melted
1	tablespoon chopped onion	1	teaspoon salt
1	green bell pepper, diced	1/2	teaspoon black pepper
1	slice fresh white bread, cut into small pieces	1/2	cup milk
		3/4	cup cornflake crumbs

Preheat the oven to 325 degrees. Place the potatoes in a large pot and cover with water. Bring the water to a boil and then reduce the heat. Cover and cook until the potatoes are done. Peel and dice the potatoes. Place them in a 13 x 9-inch baking dish. Mix the pimientos, onion, green pepper, bread, Cheddar cheese, butter, salt, and pepper. Pour over the potatoes, mixing well. Drizzle the milk over the potato mixture and cover with the cornflake crumbs. Bake for 1 hour.

PATTY STROCK | LIBERTY CENTER, OHIO

Twice-Baked Potatoes

Yield: 4 servings

"This recipe is easy to prepare. It's good when served with roast pork, beef, or chicken. Serve corn or peas on the side."

4	large russet potatoes	1/2	teaspoon white pepper
1	cup milk	1/2	teaspoon paprika
1	cup diced sharp Cheddar cheese	1	cup chopped green onions
1	teaspoon salt		

Scrub the potatoes well. Puncture the tops of the potatoes with a knife, and cook on high in the microwave for 10 minutes. Check for doneness. Cook for 10 to 15 minutes longer if necessary, or until all the pulp is softened. (Remember, microwaves can have different levels of heat intensity.)

Preheat the conventional oven to 350 degrees. Peel off the skin from the top half of each potato. Carefully scoop the pulp out of the potatoes into a mixing bowl, allowing about 1/2-inch "wall" to remain on the sides and bottom of each potato. Mix the pulp with the milk, cheese, salt, and pepper. When well blended, spoon the mixture evenly into each potato skin. Sprinkle paprika over the tops. Bake in the conventional oven for 30 minutes. Sprinkle the green onions on top.

JAMES HAYES | RIDGECREST, CALIFORNIA

Mom's Creamed Spinach

Yield: 4 servings

"My mother's handwritten recipe card calls this 'Slovene or Hungarian-Style Spinach.' I remember it served with roast chicken or meatloaf for our Sunday family dinners."

1	bunch fresh spinach (about 1 pound)	Dash of garlic salt
1	tablespoon butter or bacon drippings	1/2 cup milk
1	tablespoon all-purpose flour	Salt and pepper

Remove the stems from the spinach and rinse the leaves well. Cook the spinach in water in a saucepan until just limp. Drain well in a colander and then finely chop. In the same pan melt the butter. Stir in the flour and garlic salt and cook until it's bubbly and begins to turn golden. Stir in the milk. Continue to cook, stirring constantly, until the sauce thickens. Add the spinach and season with salt and pepper to taste.

DOTTI HYDUE | MORRISTON, FLORIDA

Tips From Our Test Kitchen:

Consider adding sautéed onions or mushrooms. It's also good with 1/2 teaspoon ground nutmeg or a dash of hot sauce. It's an ideal omelet filling.

Dania, Florida (pop. 13,024), originally was settled by Danish farm families. The city was once hailed as the tomato center of the world because of the crops they produced. The town now is an attraction for tourists seeking antiques.

Zesty Spinach Casserole

Yield: 8 servings

"This recipe has been in my 'Among Favorites' box for over forty years. I first used it to get my children to eat spinach. Now my grandchildren request it."

32	ounces spinach, chopped, or 3 (10-ounce) boxes frozen spinach, thawed		Salt and pepper
8	ounces cream cheese, softened	1	tablespoon grated lemon rind
1/2	cup (1 stick) margarine	1	tablespoon minced onion
4	tablespoons sour cream	1/4	teaspoon prepared horseradish
		1	cup stuffing mix

Preheat the oven to 350 degrees. Cook the spinach and drain well. If using frozen spinach, thaw it well and squeeze out the liquid before cooking. Lightly grease an 8-inch square baking dish. In a large bowl stir together the cream cheese, margarine, and sour cream. Add the cooked spinach. Season with the salt and pepper to taste. Add the lemon rind, onion, and horseradish. Spoon into the prepared dish. Cover with the stuffing mix and bake about 20 minutes, or until the edges begin to bubble.

PATTY NEWTON | PRESCOTT, ARIZONA

Fresh Squash Casserole

Yield: 6 servings

"I am a retired school cafeteria worker. This dish was a favorite with teachers for twenty-nine years."

1/4	cup (1/2 stick) margarine	1/2	teaspoon salt
3	cups sliced zucchini or yellow squash	1/2	teaspoon black pepper
1/4	cup chopped onion	1	cup grated sharp Cheddar cheese
2	eggs, beaten	1	cup crushed Ritz crackers
1/4	cup milk		

Preheat the oven to 350 degrees. Heat the margarine over medium heat, and sauté the squash and onions until tender. Drain. Add the eggs, milk, salt, and pepper. Spoon the mixture into a 12 x 9-inch casserole dish, and top with the cheese and crackers. Bake for 20 minutes.

MILDRED BUNN | HUEYTOWN, ALABAMA

Tater Times in Blackfoot

"Free Taters for Out-of-Staters"—this catchy billboard lures hundreds of travelers every day to the small town of Blackfoot, Idaho (pop. 10,419), during the summer months. Just off Interstate 15, en route to the Grand Tetons and Yellowstone National Park, Blackfoot lays claim to one of only two museums in the world dedicated to the potato.

The world's largest potato chip, listed in the *Guinness Book of World Records* as a potato "crisp," is at the Idaho Potato Expo. Created for a Pringles promotion in the early 1990s, it's more than two feet long and outweighs a quarter pound hamburger. There's also a potato signed by former Vice President Dan Quayle, commemorating his infamous "potatoe" spelling-bee blooper.

Like most of the state, the Blackfoot area primarily grows the famous Idaho Russet potato. Blackfoot's 4,500-foot elevation provides the perfect combination of warm days and cool nights, while the light volcanic-ash soil makes a rich growing medium. The nearby Snake River provides irrigation water, essential in Blackfoot's high-desert climate. It allows moisture levels to be precisely regulated, a key to potato quality.

To the residents of Blackfoot, potatoes are serious business. Idaho produces one-quarter of the nation's potato crop—and southeast Idaho, where Blackfoot is located, produces half of Idaho's output. Not surprisingly, potato fields, fresh pack sheds, and dehydration processing facilities are major employers, and Blackfoot and Bingham County are referred to as the "Potato Capital of the World."

Housed in the old stone Oregon Short Line Railroad building, the Expo uses large mounted photos and simple explanations to illustrate every aspect of modern-day potato growing and processing. Other exhibits trace the history of the potato, from its origins in the Andes Mountains of Bolivia and Peru to the development of the famous Russet Burbank.

One large room devoted to antique farming equipment, much of it horse-drawn, explores everything from planting potato seed to digging bud-protruding potato tubers.

How many ways can you use a potato? The 25,000 annual visitors to the Expo come away with new ideas about this American carbohydrate staple. They can sample potato fudge and potato ice cream, made on the premises, and buy locally made potato hand lotion, "Tuber Humer" postcards, and potato-print gift-wrap. A potato-sack outfit made for a local rodeo queen is on display, as well as a sample of Teton Glacier Potato Vodka, distilled and bottled in Rigby, Idaho.

While Blackfoot residents enjoy a lovely two-mile greenbelt, a top-ranked golf course, and a skateboard park, it's the Potato Expo that pulls the majority of travelers into town.

For more information, log on to www.potatoexpo.com or call (208) 785-2517.

Joanne Hinkel is a freelance writer from Boise, Idaho.

Spinach & Rice Casserole

Yield: 8 servings

"This dish is my favorite, as well as the favorite of everyone in my family. My grandmother, Della Stansbury, got this recipe from her best friend, Linda Jensen, and then passed it on to me. I cannot thank her enough."

1	(10-ounce) package frozen spinach, cooked, drained, and cooled	3/4	pound Cheddar cheese, grated
3	cups cooked rice	4	eggs
1/4	cup (1/2 stick) butter or margarine, melted	1	cup milk
1	teaspoon onion flakes	1	teaspoon Worcestershire sauce
		2	teaspoons salt (optional)

Preheat the oven to 350 degrees. Grease a 2-quart baking dish. In a large bowl combine the spinach, rice, butter, and onion flakes. Add all but a handful of the cheese. In a separate bowl mix the eggs, milk, Worcestershire sauce, and salt if using. Add to the spinach mixture and mix well. Pour into the prepared dish. Sprinkle the reserved cheese on top. Bake for 35 to 40 minutes, or until the middle of the casserole is set.

KAREN COLLIGNON-FOLEY | ELLENSBURG, WASHINGTON

Kras Mapolski

Yield: 8 to 10 servings

"This dish looks terrible when you put it in the oven, but it's really good. And it's even better reheated the second day."

1	or 2 (10-ounce) packages frozen spinach, thawed	6	eggs, beaten
1	onion, chopped (optional)	16	ounces cottage cheese
2	garlic cloves, minced (optional)	2	tablespoons all-purpose flour
6	plus 2 tablespoons (1 stick) butter, melted	1	pound sharp Cheddar cheese, grated
			Salt and pepper

Preheat the oven to 350 degrees. Lightly grease a 13 x 9-inch baking dish. Drain the spinach well. If using onion and garlic, sauté them first in 2 tablespoons of the melted butter. Mix the spinach, eggs, the remaining 6 tablespoons melted butter, cottage cheese, flour, and cheese in a large mixing bowl. Add the onions and garlic if using. Season with the salt and pepper to taste. Pour the mixture into the prepared dish and bake for 1 hour.

LOIS THOMPSON | BIGFORK, MONTANA

Many businesses in Havre, Montana (pop. 10,201), went "underground" after a 1904 fire destroyed most of the downtown. Bakeries, bars, laundries, and pharmacies opened in the basements while the street-level buildings were rebuilt. When the downtown was restored, the basement entrances were covered. The business area beneath Havre has been partially restored and can be viewed in tours.

Squash Dressing

Yield: 6 servings

"This recipe from my mother-in-law is more than fifty-five years old. She lived on a farm and had plenty of vegetables, so she decided to use her yellow squash. My family loves this dressing, and it is very easy to make. Sometimes I make it a week ahead and put it in the freezer."

1 plus 2 tablespoons butter	2 cups cornbread crumbs
1 small onion, diced	3 eggs, beaten
3 large yellow squash, diced	2 tablespoons sage
1 teaspoon salt	Shredded Parmesan or Colby cheese
Dash of black pepper	

Preheat the oven to 350 degrees. Grease a 13 x 9-inch baking pan. In a saucepan melt 1 tablespoon of the butter and sauté the onion. Add the remaining 2 tablespoons butter along with the squash, salt, and pepper. Add enough water to cover and cook until the squash is tender. Mix the squash mixture with the cornbread crumbs, eggs, and sage. Spoon the dressing into the prepared pan and sprinkle the cheese on top. Bake for 25 to 30 minutes.

ANNIE COX | TERRELL, TEXAS

Stuffed Zucchini

Yield: 6 servings

"This recipe is a delicious alternative to the breads and cakes I usually prepare with zucchini."

3	medium zucchini	2	tablespoons all-purpose flour
1	tablespoon butter	2	tablespoons sour cream
2	tablespoons chopped onion	2	tablespoons grated Parmesan cheese
1	cup grated provolone or Monterey Jack cheese	1/2	teaspoon salt
4	ounces mushrooms, chopped	1/2	teaspoon dried basil

Preheat the oven to 350 degrees. Cut off the ends of the zucchini and cut the zucchini in half lengthwise. Cook the zucchini in 1-inch-deep, salted, boiling water for 5 to 10 minutes, or until crisp-tender. Drain. Scoop out the pulp, leaving a 1/4-inch-thick shell. Chop enough of the pulp to make about 3/4 cup.

Grease a 13 x 9-inch baking dish. Melt the butter in a skillet and sauté the onion. Add the onion to the pulp. Stir in the provolone cheese, mushrooms, flour, sour cream, Parmesan, salt, and basil. Spoon evenly into the zucchini shells. Place the shells into the prepared dish. Bake, uncovered, for 25 minutes.

TONI MONTON | CUSTER, MICHIGAN

Apricot Sweet Potatoes

Yield: 6 servings

"I don't know where I found this recipe, but it's been on a card in my recipe box for years. Everywhere I take this dish, I receive several requests for the recipe."

4	medium sweet potatoes	1/4	teaspoon salt
1	(15-ounce) can apricots in syrup	1/2	teaspoon ground cinnamon
1 1/4	cups firmly packed brown sugar	1	tablespoon butter
1 1/2	tablespoons cornstarch	1/2	cup chopped pecans

Bake or boil the sweet potatoes until tender, and set aside to cool. Grease an 8-inch square baking dish. Cut the potatoes into 1-inch-thick pieces and place them into the prepared dish.

Preheat the oven to 350 degrees. Pour about 1 cup of the juice from the canned apricots into a small saucepan. Add the brown sugar, cornstarch, salt, and cinnamon and stir together over medium-low heat until the mixture boils. Add the butter. Layer the apricots over the sweet potatoes. Pour the liquid over the top. Sprinkle the pecans evenly over the top. Bake for 30 minutes.

DOROTHY HUTCHINS | CARTHAGE, MISSOURI

Zucchini Patties

Yield: 5 to 6 servings

"We always have plenty of zucchini from my husband's garden. My grandson is learning how vegetables look, feel, and taste when they come directly from the earth."

1	cup Bisquick or other baking mix	2	eggs, beaten
1/2	cup shredded mozzarella or Cheddar cheese	2	cups grated zucchini
		2	tablespoons chopped onion (optional)
1/8	teaspoon salt	2	tablespoons butter

Combine the Bisquick, cheese, salt, eggs, zucchini, and onion in a mixing bowl. Blend well. Melt the butter in a large skillet over medium-high heat. Spoon heaping tablespoons of the zucchini mixture onto the melted butter. Fry for 3 to 5 minutes per side, or until golden brown. Place the browned patties on a paper towel. Add more butter to the skillet when necessary for additional batches.

SHERRY McCARTY | GLENWOOD HILLS, NEW MEXICO

Tips From Our Test Kitchen:

For an Italian flair, try dipping these morsels in marinara sauce. They're also great with grated Parmesan cheese sprinkled on top.

Hatch, New Mexico (pop. 1,136), is the self-proclaimed "Chile Capital of the World." More than a dozen varieties of chile peppers are grown in the Hatch Valley.

Sweet Potato Purée with Cranberry-Pecan Topping

Yield: 6 servings

"This recipe, which I created last Thanksgiving, was such a hit that I ended up making it all winter long."

11/2	pounds sweet potatoes, peeled		1/4	cup mango chutney
1	large Granny Smith apple, peeled		1/3	cup orange juice
1	large onion		1/2	cup dried cranberries
1	cup chopped carrots (2-inch pieces)		2	tablespoons firmly packed brown sugar
4	large garlic cloves			Salt and pepper
2	teaspoons chopped fresh thyme		3	tablespoons unsalted butter, melted
11/3	cups vegetable broth		2/3	cup toasted pecans

Preheat the oven to 375 degrees. Lightly grease a 13 x 9-inch baking pan. Cut the sweet potatoes, apple, and onion into wedges. Arrange them in the prepared dish along with the carrots and garlic cloves. Toss in the thyme. Sprinkle with several tablespoons of the broth. Cover with foil and bake for about 30 minutes. If the vegetables are not yet soft, remove the foil and bake for an additional 10 minutes. In a saucepan combine the chutney, juice, cranberries, brown sugar, salt, and pepper. Heat through, just until the chutney melts. Purée the vegetables with the remaining broth and the butter. Place them back into the baking dish. Spoon the chutney mixture evenly over all. Sprinkle the pecans on top. Return to the oven for about 15 minutes, or until heated through.

MARGEE BERRY | WHITE SALMON, WASHINGTON

The tasty Dungeness crab is named for a Washington town northwest of Seattle from which it was first harvested commercially in the late 1800s. The crab can grow to ten inches across and is found from Alaska's Aleutian Islands to northern California, usually in shallow water.

Garden Tomato Pie

Yield: 6 to 8 servings

"I was looking through some of my late mother's recipes and remembered that she made this tomato pie for my dad when he was alive. Hope you enjoy."

1   (9-inch) frozen deep-dish pie shell, baked and cooled

2   large red or green tomatoes (or enough to fill the pie shell), peeled and thickly sliced

Salt and pepper

1   teaspoon dried sweet basil or 1 tablespoon fresh chopped basil

1   tablespoon fresh chopped chives

1   slice bacon, crisply cooked and crumbled

1   cup mayonnaise

1   cup grated Cheddar cheese

Preheat the oven to 350 degrees. Fill the pie shell with the tomato slices, and sprinkle with the salt and pepper to taste, the basil, chives, and bacon. Mix the mayonnaise with the cheese, and spread the mixture over the tomatoes. Bake for 30 minutes, or until lightly browned.

Betty Thompson | La Porte, Texas

Tomato Tart

Yield: 6 to 8 servings

"This recipe is from a sweet, young teacher. She was a good friend to my daughter and son-in-law. It's always a hit."

1   (9-inch) piecrust

1   tablespoon butter

1/2   cup chopped onion

1/2   cup chopped mushrooms

3/4   cup grated Parmesan cheese

1   cup grated mozzarella cheese

1/2   cup mayonnaise

1   garlic clove, minced

1/4   cup fresh chopped basil

6   fresh medium tomatoes, cut into wedges

1   tablespoon chopped parsley

Black pepper

Preheat the oven to 350 degrees. Bake the piecrust for about 15 minutes. Remove from the oven. Melt the butter over medium-high heat and sauté the onions and mushrooms until the onions are translucent. Mix together the Parmesan and mozzarella cheeses, mayonnaise, garlic, and basil. Stir in the cooled mushrooms and onions. Place the tomato wedges, skin side down, into the piecrust. Spoon the cheese mixture evenly over the tomatoes. Sprinkle the parsley and pepper on top. Bake for about 30 minutes, or until brown and bubbly.

Kay McMahan | Rockport, Texas

Tips From Our Test Kitchen:

This dish is good served hot or cold.

Hot Hominy Casserole

Yield: 6 to 8 servings

"This recipe makes a great side dish for steak, ribs, chicken, or fish. It's a nice change from potatoes and pasta. It's a favorite in my community. It is also popular as a complement to Mexican dishes."

2	(15 1/2-ounce) cans yellow or white hominy, drained	6	strips bacon, crisply cooked and crumbled (optional)
1	(4-ounce) can green chiles		Salt and pepper
1/2	cup grated onion	1 1/2	cups grated sharp Cheddar cheese
8	ounces low-fat sour cream		

Preheat the oven to 350 degrees. Lightly grease an 8-inch square casserole dish. Combine the hominy, chiles, and onion. Stir in the sour cream, bacon, salt, and pepper. Spoon into the prepared dish. Sprinkle the cheese evenly over the top. Cover with foil and bake for 20 minutes. Remove the foil and bake for an additional 10 minutes, or until golden and bubbly.

GAYLA LEECH | ALBANY, TEXAS

Baked Macaroni and Cheese

Yield: 8 to 10 servings

"This is the easiest and most delicious macaroni and cheese. I take it to picnic suppers, and I'm always asked for the recipe. It also is an attractive dish."

2	cups uncooked elbow macaroni	4	ounces grated mozzarella cheese
1/2	cup (1 stick) butter or margarine, sliced into several pats	5	cups milk
			Salt and pepper
12	ounces grated Cheddar cheese		

Preheat the oven to 350 degrees. Layer the macaroni, butter slices, Cheddar, and mozzarella cheese in the order given in a 13 x 9-inch dish. Pour the milk over the top. Bake, uncovered, for 1 hour.

SUE MALONEY | WAVERLY, NEW YORK

Mom's Noodles

Yield: 4 to 6 servings

"My mother was a small woman, just four feet, nine inches tall. She raised eight children. She made Christmas dinner for her grown children and our families until she was ninety-one years old."

12	egg yolks	3/4	cup cream or evaporated milk
32/3	plus 1/3 cups all-purpose flour	11/2	teaspoons salt
2	tablespoons lard	11/2	teaspoons baking powder

Mix the egg yolks with 32/3 cups of the flour. Add the lard, cream, salt, and baking powder. Roll this very elastic dough as thin as you desire for noodles on a board sprinkled with the remaining 1/3 cup flour. Allow the dough to dry for a few hours and then cut it into strips of the desired width. Boil until just done. The cooking time will depend on the size of the noodles.

JENNIE DITTY | RIMERSBURG, PENNSYLVANIA

Tips From Our Test Kitchen:

These delicious noodles are perfect with any sauce. Try tossing them in a bit of olive oil, Parmesan cheese, garlic, and basil, and serve them with just a bit of butter, salt, and pepper.

Pasta with Garbanzo Beans

Yield: 4 to 6 servings

"This recipe is nutritious and easy to put together for a quick dinner or holiday buffet. Because it pairs beans with pasta, it's a great complete protein dish for vegetarian diets."

1	pound fusilli or gemelli pasta	1	(16-ounce) can garbanzo beans, drained
1/2	cup olive oil		
2	garlic cloves, minced	1/2	cup grated Parmesan cheese
1	(15-ounce) can diced tomatoes	2	to 3 tablespoons fresh chopped basil

Prepare the pasta according to the package instructions, making sure not to overcook it. When the pasta is almost done, heat the olive oil in a separate saucepan and sauté the garlic. Stir in the tomatoes and beans and heat through. The pasta should be done by the time the other ingredients are hot. Toss the pasta and the bean mixture together with the cheese and basil. Season to taste.

TERESA MOURAD | ANN ARBOR, MICHIGAN

Tips From Our Test Kitchen:

Great Northern or black beans can be used instead of the garbanzos. Add sliced red and green peppers to the vegetable mixture for a colorful flair.

Caraway Rice Special

Yield: 4 servings

"My husband and I like this Caraway Rice Special so much that we make the full recipe as a side dish for one meal; then the next day or two, we add chopped cooked chicken or pork for a main dish. When my nephew, Keith, first tried it, he asked for seconds, then thirds."

1	teaspoon vegetable oil	21/4	teaspoons caraway seeds
1	cup thinly sliced celery	1/4	teaspoon salt
1/2	cup chopped onion	2	teaspoons Mrs. Dash seasoning blend
11/4	cups long-grain rice	1/2	cup sliced fresh mushrooms
21/2	cups water	1/4	cup chopped green bell pepper
2	teaspoons chicken bouillon	1	teaspoon lemon juice

In a large kettle heat the vegetable oil, and sauté the celery and onion for about 2 minutes, or until crisp-tender. Stir in the rice, water, bouillon, caraway seeds, salt, and Mrs. Dash. Bring the mixture to a boil, reduce the heat, and simmer, covered, for 10 minutes. Add the mushrooms and bell pepper. Cover and simmer for 10 minutes. Stir in the lemon juice and fluff with a fork.

CARMELLA BRINK | HARRISON, SOUTH DAKOTA

Tips From Our Test Kitchen:

Use a combination of green and red bell pepper for a colorful dish. If you prefer brown rice, increase the cooking time from 20 minutes to about 40 minutes, or until all the liquid is absorbed.

Italian Stuffing

Yield: 8 to 10 servings

"This stuffing is my family's answer to our mixed heritage and love of Italian food. It began in the 1940s, when my father was in the U.S. Army and my mother made friends with our Italian neighbors in California."

2	standard-size loaves French bread (not sour dough), cut into 1-inch cubes	1	cup grated Romano cheese
1	cup chopped fresh parsley	1/2	teaspoon black pepper
1/2	cup chopped onion	1	tablespoon salt
1/2	cup chopped celery	4	teaspoons dried oregano
2	garlic cloves, minced	3	cups chicken broth
1/3	cup chopped green bell pepper	1	cup (2 sticks) margarine

Tips From Our Test Kitchen:

It is safer to cook stuffing outside the turkey. This side dish is also good when served with pork, chicken, or beef.

Preheat the oven to 350 degrees. Lightly grease a 2-quart ovenproof dish or two 8-inch square baking dishes. Mix the bread cubes, parsley, onion, celery, garlic, and bell pepper in a large bowl. In another bowl combine the cheese, pepper, salt, and oregano, and stir the cheese into the bread mixture. Heat the broth and margarine together until the margarine is melted. Pour over the bread mixture and stir just until evenly moistened. Spoon into the prepared dish. Cover with foil. Bake for 45 minutes. Remove the foil for the last 15 minutes if a golden brown stuffing is desired.

GEORGIA CAVANAUGH | FALLON, NEVADA

Mushroom and Cashew Stuffing

Yield: 6 to 8 servings

"I love original and homemade dishes where you add the special ingredients yourself. This is definitely one of my favorites."

8	cups 1/2-inch cubes white sandwich bread		Salt and pepper
1/4	cup (1/2 stick) butter	11/2	cups roasted, unsalted cashews (halves and pieces)
1	large red onion, chopped	2	tablespoons dried rosemary
1	large red pepper, chopped	1/4	teaspoon ground nutmeg
3	celery stalks, chopped	3/4	cup chicken broth
1/2	pound button mushrooms, sliced	3	eggs, beaten

Preheat the oven to 400 degrees. Toast the bread cubes on a cookie sheet for about 20 minutes, or until evenly golden, turning once. Transfer the bread cubes to a large mixing bowl. Reduce the oven temperature to 350 degrees.

Lightly grease a 13 x 9-inch baking dish. Melt the butter in a heavy skillet over medium-high heat. Sauté the onion, red pepper, celery, and mushrooms. Add the salt and pepper to taste. When the vegetables are tender, add them to the bread cubes. In a separate bowl stir together the cashews, rosemary, nutmeg, broth, and eggs. Add the nut mixture to the bread mixture. When well mixed, transfer the mixture to the baking dish. Bake, covered, for about 1 hour. If you desire a browned top, remove the cover for the final 15 to 20 minutes of baking.

JOYCE JAMESON | MINDEN, NEBRASKA

Tips From Our Test Kitchen:

For a more intense chicken flavor, dissolve 2 chicken bouillon cubes in the broth. Add about 2 cups chopped chicken to make this a very hearty dish.

Asparagus Is King in Shelby and Hart

The moderate breezes along Lake Michigan's eastern coast combine with the rolling terrain and sandy soil of Oceana County to produce the perfect growing conditions for the region's first commercial crop of the year—asparagus.

Each spring between late April and late June, farmers around Shelby (pop. 1,914) and Hart (pop. 1,950), Michigan, harvest asparagus from more than 10,000 acres of land.

Residents of Shelby and Hart celebrate the harvest at the National Asparagus Festival, which has been held in Oceana County since 1974. The festival alternates between Shelby and Hart and is held the second full weekend in June. It features an asparagus smorgasbord with appetizers, casseroles, and desserts made from the local vegetable, as well as parades, a 5K run or walk, square dancing, quilt show, golf tournament, arts and crafts fair, and tours of local asparagus farms. Festivalgoers also enjoy a Saturday night rodeo and a fly-in breakfast at the airport.

Each year, a local woman is chosen Mrs. Asparagus to preside over the event and to promote the crop. One recent winner traveled around the state, riding in parades and visiting schools to educate people about this tasty vegetable that has been cultivated for more than 2,000 years.

A member of the lily family, asparagus has been grown in Oceana County for nearly a century. The tender green spears grow from a crown planted about a foot deep in sandy soil. Michigan's crop, more than 25 million pounds annually, ranks third in asparagus production behind California and Washington, and much of the state's harvest is grown on Oceana County farms. Average yield is 1,700 pounds per acre.

Harvesting techniques used by Michigan asparagus growers differ from those used in other parts of the country. In Michigan, asparagus shoots, which can grow as much as an inch an hour when weather conditions are ideal, are "snapped" by hand rather than cut, ensuring that only the most tender portion of the plant is processed for market.

About 85 percent of the local asparagus crop is frozen or canned. The rest is sold fresh.

While festivalgoers learn these facts and more, it's the food and fun that keep them coming back to celebrate the state's delectable crop.

For more information, log on to www.nationalasparagusfestival.org or call (231) 861-8110.

Judith Karns is a freelance writer in Clio, Michigan.

Pear Relish

Yield: 12 pints

"This delicious recipe was given to me by a retired school-teacher friend. It's great on pinto beans. I like to add some to my barbecue sauce too."

1	peck pears, peeled and cored (1 peck equals 2 gallons, or 1/4 bushel)	4	hot peppers
5	medium onions	2	pounds sugar
4	green bell peppers	5	cups cider vinegar
4	red bell peppers	1	tablespoon salt

Process or finely chop the pears, onions, and the green, red, and hot peppers. Place in a large kettle and add the sugar, vinegar, and salt. Boil for 40 minutes over medium heat, stirring occasionally to avoid burning.

Carefully follow the canning directions supplied with your jars to guarantee sterile jars, well-sealed flavor, and a long shelf life.

RACHEL LEWIS STROUTH | ELON, NORTH CAROLINA

Tips From Our Test Kitchen:

For a chutney-style relish, add 1 tablespoon each of dry mustard, cumin, cinnamon, and allspice and 1 teaspoon cloves. When the relish is cooked, add 2 cups golden raisins, if desired. This relish is delicious with East Indian food.

At Louise's Famous Rockhouse Restaurant in Linville Falls, near Marion, North Carolina (pop. 4,943), diners order pie in one county and it's baked in another. The restaurant straddles three counties: Burke, McDowell, and Avery.

Main Dishes

Sunday Pot Roast

Yield: 6 to 8 servings

"For forty-six years, we have had special food for Sunday and Sunday company. It was always something that could be left in the oven so our meal would be ready when we returned home from church."

Roast:

6   slices peppered bacon
3   tablespoons all-purpose flour
     Salt and pepper
3   to 4 pound beef or pork roast

Vegetables:

2   to 3 celery stalks, cut in 2-inch pieces (about 1 cup)
3   to 4 potatoes, peeled and cubed

2   to 3 carrots, cut in 2-inch pieces (about 1 cup)
1   onion, quartered

Gravy:

1/4   cup all-purpose flour
1/3   cup milk
2   cups meat drippings (add water if necessary)
     Salt and pepper

For the roast, preheat the oven to 450 degrees. Fry the bacon until crisp in the bottom of a large roasting pan in the oven. Remove the bacon and crumble it into small pieces, reserving the bacon grease in the bottom of the pan. Mix the flour and the salt and pepper to taste, and coat the roast, pressing the flour firmly into the meat. Place the meat in the bacon drippings and brown in the oven on all sides. Reduce the oven temperature to 325 degrees. Pour in enough water to have about 1 inch of liquid. Place the lid on the roaster and cook for about 11/2 hours.

For the vegetables, place the celery, potatoes, carrots, and onion on top of the roast. Add water, if necessary, to maintain a depth of 1 inch. Cook for another 1 to 11/2 hours, or until the meat and vegetables are very tender. Remove the roast and vegetables and top with the reserved bacon pieces.

For the gravy, mix the flour and milk until smooth. In a medium-size saucepan, whisk together the milk mixture and 2 cups of the meat drippings. Season with salt and pepper to taste.

DELORES FIELDS | TEXAS CITY, TEXAS

Barbecued Pot Roast

Yield: 6 to 8 servings

*"The following recipe has been a favorite dish for company, or to take on a
sympathy visit, for at least thirty years."*

2	tablespoons vegetable oil		1	to 1 1/2 cups water
3	to 5 pounds beef brisket		4	tablespoons firmly packed brown sugar
3	cups sliced yellow onions		1/4	cup chili sauce
3	to 4 garlic cloves, minced		1/4	cup cider vinegar
1	(8-ounce) can tomato sauce		2	tablespoons Worcestershire sauce

Heat the oil in a large, heavy skillet and brown the meat in the oil. When lightly browned on
both sides, add the onions and garlic. When the onions begin to brown, add the tomato sauce
and 1/4 cup of the water. Cover and cook over low heat for 45 minutes. Check occasionally to
be sure the water has not evaporated. Add another 1/4 cup water if necessary. Turn the meat
about every 20 minutes to keep it from becoming too brown or sticking to the pan.

Add the brown sugar, chili sauce, vinegar, and Worcestershire sauce and cook, covered, for
1 1/2 hours. As before, turn the meat occasionally, and add more water, if needed, in small incre-
ments to avoid making the barbecue too soupy. At this point, the meat should be tender. Remove
the meat from the skillet and slice very thinly. Continue to cook the sauce until it is thick. Return
the meat to the sauce, and cook until the meat is well coated and warm enough to serve.

FRAN ROSENBERG | WEST DOVER, VERMONT

Gwen's Special Occasion Chuck Roast

Yield: 6 to 8 servings

*"When I want to gather a crowd, I ask family and friends to guess what I'm
cooking: chuck roast in wine sauce, rice, steamed cabbage, candied yams,
and cornbread."*

3	pounds chuck roast		1/2	plus 1/2 cup Worcestershire sauce
1	plus 1 plus 1/2 cups red cooking wine		9	bay leaves
	Water to almost cover roast		1	large bell pepper, chopped, divided
6	medium onions, sliced, divided		1	teaspoon black pepper
1/2	plus 1/2 cup soy sauce		1/2	teaspoon crushed basil leaves

In a large glass bowl marinate the roast for 1 hour in 1 cup of the wine, turning the roast once. Drain the marinade and place the roast in a heavy, deep skillet that is large enough for it to lie flat. Fill the skillet with enough water to almost cover the meat. Add half the onions, 1 cup of the wine, 1/2 cup of the soy sauce, 1/2 cup of the Worcestershire sauce, 4 of the bay leaves, and half the chopped bell pepper. Cook over medium heat for 40 minutes. Turn the meat and cook for an additional 20 minutes. When the liquid gets low, add up to 2 cups of additional water. Add the remaining onions, remaining 5 bay leaves, the remaining 1/2 cup wine, 1/2 cup soy sauce, and 1/2 cup Worcestershire sauce, and the remaining half chopped bell pepper. Add the black pepper and crushed basil leaves. Cook for about 1 hour and 30 minutes longer, or until the meat is tender. Check to make sure the liquid is always several inches deep to ensure there is enough gravy for the meat and for a side dish of rice.

GWENDOLYN MCNEILL | DUNN, NORTH CAROLINA

Italian Beef Pot Roast

Yield: 6 to 8 servings

"As a young bride, I searched for tasty and dependable recipes. The compliments for this dish have been unceasing throughout the years of my marriage."

1	(3 to 4-pound) beef chuck roast		2	medium onions, sliced
1/2	cup all-purpose flour		1/2	teaspoon dried oregano
1/2	teaspoon salt		1	beef bouillon cube
1/4	teaspoon black pepper		1	cup hot water
2	tablespoons olive oil			

Cut the beef into bite-size pieces. Season the flour with the salt and pepper and dredge the meat pieces in it. Heat the olive oil in a medium-size pot and brown the meat. Add the onions and oregano. Dissolve the bouillon cube in the hot water, and pour half the bouillon into the pot. Cover and simmer for 2 hours, or until tender, adding the remaining bouillon as needed. Serve over garlic-buttered noodles.

RUTH AUGUSTIN | HIGHLAND, ILLINOIS

Tips From Our Test Kitchen:

For a more intense Italian flavor, add more oregano and several cloves of minced garlic. Sprinkle with grated Parmesan cheese before serving.

Never-Fail Pot Roast

Yield: 8 to 10 servings

"I have cooked all my life as a hobby, because I like to eat good food. I invite several couples to Sunday dinner, and this roast is their favorite. The secret ingredient is chili powder."

1	to 2 teaspoons salt	4	to 5-pound chuck roast
1	to 2 teaspoons black pepper	1	large onion, cut in half
1	to 2 teaspoons garlic powder	2	heaping tablespoons cornstarch
1	to 2 teaspoons seasoned salt	1	cup water
2	to 3 teaspoons chili powder		Salt and pepper

Mix together the salt, pepper, garlic powder, seasoned salt, and chili powder. Sprinkle the seasonings on both sides of the roast. Heat a heavy cooking pan on medium heat. (Do not add oil.) Sear the roast on both sides until dark brown. Add enough water to cover the top of the roast. Dice half the onion. Slice the other half of the onion. Add the diced onion to the roast. Bring to a boil, cover, and reduce the heat, simmering slowly for about 4 hours, or until tender. Add additional water as needed until the last 30 minutes. During the last 30 minutes of cooking, let the liquid cook down to the drippings. Add the onion slices on top of the roast. Allow the roast to cool and place it in the refrigerator 6 to 8 hours or overnight.

To serve, preheat the oven to 350 degrees. Remove all the solid fat from the drippings. Heat the roast with the drippings in the oven, adding more water if needed. When heated through, about 20 minutes, remove the roast to a platter and make the gravy.

Stir the cornstarch into the water until blended. Add to the drippings, stirring well. Boil slowly and continue stirring until the gravy is clear and thickened. Add salt and pepper to taste.

BILL CARLTON | RUIDOSO, NEW MEXICO

Country-Fried Steak

Yield: 4 to 6 servings

"My mom is a very good cook. After church on Sunday, she would always make a big dinner and serve country-fried steak. I make it now, and it has become a family favorite."

4	to 6 large cube steaks	1/4	cup (1/2 stick) butter
1/2	cup all-purpose flour		Water to cover steaks
	Salt and pepper	1/2	package onion soup mix (Lipton)

Dredge the steaks in the flour, shaking off the excess, and add the salt and pepper to taste. Melt the butter over medium heat in a large skillet. Brown the steaks well on both sides. Add enough water to cover the steaks completely. Sprinkle the soup mix evenly in the water. Cover and simmer for 40 minutes.

KELLY HATCH | NAVARRE, FLORIDA

Chili Flank Steak

Yield: 4 to 6 servings

"I found a recipe similar to this one and decided to change it. I added the chili sauce and a dash of allspice. It's fork-tender when ready to eat. Our family of farmers loves it."

2/3	cup firmly packed brown sugar	2	tablespoons chili powder
2/3	cup V-8 juice or other brand vegetable juice	1/4	teaspoon ground cumin
2/3	cup soy sauce	1/2	cup chili sauce
1/2	cup olive oil	1/4	teaspoon ground allspice
4	garlic cloves, chopped	1	(3-pound) beef flank steak

In a large bowl combine the brown sugar, V-8 juice, soy sauce, oil, garlic, chili powder, cumin, chili sauce, and allspice. Whisk together until very well blended. Pour half the mixture into a large, sturdy, zip-lock-style bag. Add the steak, seal the bag, and turn to coat well. Marinate in the refrigerator for at least 8 hours. Cover and refrigerate the remaining marinade.

Drain and discard the marinade from the steak. Heat the grill to 400 to 500 degrees. Grill the steak for about 8 minutes on each side. Slice the steak very thinly. Heat the reserved marinade to serve with the steak.

LINDA BIER | HANNIBAL, MISSOURI

Tips From Our Test Kitchen:

This is great with any type of potato and green salad. Be sure not to overcook the meat or it will become tough.

In 1946, Orla Watson of Kansas City, Missouri, invented the telescoping grocery cart with hinged basket so the carts could nest for storage.

Grandma's Swiss Steak

Yield: 6 servings

"My mother came from a family with fifteen children. My father was in the navy. They traveled the world together. She learned how to make some of the best meals with the simplest ingredients. When visiting her with my own children, we were greeted with the aroma of this dish."

4	pounds round steak, well tenderized		1	(12-ounce) can tomato paste
1/2	cup all-purpose flour		2	teaspoons seasoning (Accent or other favorite)
1/3	cup vegetable oil			
6	carrots, peeled and sliced		1	teaspoon salt
3	celery stalks, chopped		1	teaspoon black pepper
1	medium onion, chopped into 1/2-inch pieces			

Cut the tenderized steak into 2-inch pieces. Dredge in the flour. Heat the oil in a large skillet and brown the meat, turning once to brown both sides.

Preheat the oven to 350 degrees. Lightly grease a large casserole dish. Place the meat in the prepared dish. Layer the carrots, celery, and onion evenly over the meat. In a separate bowl mix the tomato paste with 1 tomato paste can of water. Add the seasoning, salt, and pepper. Pour the tomato paste mixture over the meat and vegetables. Cover with foil and bake for 1 hour. If the meat is not tender enough, add another 1/2 cup water and continue baking, covered, for 30 minutes.

NANCY MILLER | APEX, NORTH CAROLINA

Beef Stroganoff

Yield: 8 servings

"This recipe was a favorite of my granddaughter and her friends when they were young, and it remains a family favorite. It is so easy and delicious. It can be prepared for an elegant dinner or for every day. I have been asked for the recipe many times."

2	pounds round steak		1	(10 3/4-ounce) can condensed golden mushroom soup
	Butter or olive oil			
1	(10 3/4-ounce) can French onion soup			Salt and pepper
1	(10 3/4-ounce) can condensed cream of mushroom soup		1/2	pint sour cream
			1	(4 1/2-ounce) jar sliced mushrooms

Cube the steak. Melt the butter in an electric skillet or in a large skillet on the stove, and brown the steak cubes. Mix the French onion, cream of mushroom, and golden mushroom soups (undiluted) and the salt and pepper to taste. Pour over the beef and simmer covered for 1 1/2 hours. When the meat is tender, add the sour cream and mushrooms. Serve over noodles or rice.

BEVERLY GEORGE | CLEBURNE, TEXAS

Short Ribs of Beef Braised with Burgundy

Yield: 6 to 8 servings

"My mother made this dish for our family of six. We were poor, but she found a way to make an elegant, yet economical, dish with this inexpensive cut of beef."

6	pounds beef short ribs, cut into serving-size pieces	1	carrot, finely chopped
1/2	cup all-purpose flour	1	celery stalk, finely chopped
1/3	cup bacon fat or vegetable oil	1/4	teaspoon dried savory
	Salt and pepper	1/2	cup beef broth
		1 1/4	cups red cooking wine or Burgundy

Preheat the oven to 300 degrees. Dredge the short ribs in the flour. Heat the fat or oil in a large skillet and lightly brown the meat. Season with the salt and pepper taste. Spread the carrot and celery over the bottom of a large, ovenproof dish and sprinkle with the savory. Place the short ribs over the vegetables in a single layer. Combine the broth and wine in a medium-size saucepan, heat until warm, and then pour the mixture over the ribs. Cover with foil and cook for 3 hours, or until the beef is tender.

CLARA SVEDA | ASHLAND, WISCONSIN

Tips From Our Test Kitchen:

This dish is great with buttered egg noodles. Dried thyme can be substituted for the savory. Extra carrots and celery can be placed in the bottom of the pan if desired and served as a side vegetable when the meat is done.

Each March since 1996, the world's largest weenie roast has taken place on the ice of Lake Namakagon, northeast of Hayward, Wisconsin (pop. 2,161), with 700 people standing shoulder-to-shoulder near a flaming trench cooking hot dogs.

Beef in Beer

Yield: 6 to 8 servings

"Our pastor was a chaplain in Germany after World War II. His wife was given this recipe while there. It's become a favorite with many of us."

2	pounds round steak	1	(14-ounce) can beef broth
1	teaspoon salt	1	tablespoon cider vinegar
1	teaspoon pepper	1	teaspoon sugar
1	plus 1 tablespoons bacon fat, solid vegetable shortening, or lard	1	sprig parsley, chopped
		1/8	teaspoon ground thyme
1	medium onion, minced	1	celery stalk, chopped
2	tablespoons all-purpose flour	2	bay leaves
1	(12-ounce) can beer		

Preheat the oven to 400 degrees. Cut the meat into 12 thin slices. Season with the salt and pepper. Tenderize slightly with a meat cleaver. Heat 1 tablespoon of the fat in a large skillet and sauté the meat on both sides. Place the meat in a casserole dish or Dutch oven and cover with the minced onion. Add the flour to the skillet with the remaining 1 tablespoon fat. Stir it until the flour turns brown. Add the beer, broth, vinegar, and sugar to the flour and cook until the gravy is smooth. Pour the gravy over the meat. Add the parsley, thyme, celery, and bay leaves. Cover and bake for 11/2 hours. Remove the bay leaves before serving.

Lois Stoelting | Niagara Falls, New York

Beef Rollups

Yield: 4 to 6 servings

"This dish is great with a baby spinach salad and hot rolls. I've been making this dish for thirty years. My daughter-in-law now makes it for my son."

11/2	pounds tenderized round steak	1	(103/4-ounce) can water
11/2	cups prepared stuffing (Stove Top)	1	teaspoon Kitchen Bouquet
1	tablespoon vegetable oil		
2	(103/4-ounce) cans condensed cream of mushroom soup		

Cut the steak into six portions. Spoon 1/4 cup of the stuffing into the center of each piece of steak. Roll up the steaks and secure with toothpicks. Heat the oil in a heavy skillet. Brown both sides of the steak rolls in the oil. Remove from the heat and drain the oil. Blend the soup, water, and Kitchen Bouquet. Pour evenly over the steaks and return the skillet to the stove. Cover and simmer for 1 1/2 hours, turning the steaks several times to prevent burning. Spoon the gravy over the top when ready to serve.

CAROL LOSER | CHILLICOTHE, ILLINOIS

Copper Country Hot Pasties

Yield: 4 very large or 6 medium-size pasties

"This recipe has been in my family since the early 1940s. My mother made pasties for my father to eat when he worked in an underground mine in the Upper Peninsula of Michigan. They're very tasty."

Crust:

3	cups all-purpose flour
1	teaspoon salt
1	cup solid vegetable shortening
1/4	to 1/2 cup water

Filling:

1	pound boneless round steak
1/4	pound boneless pork steak
1/2	cup chopped parsley
2	large onions, chopped
5	medium potatoes, cubed
1/2	medium-size yellow turnip, grated
1	teaspoon salt
1	teaspoon black pepper
4	to 6 teaspoons butter
4	to 6 teaspoons water

For the crust, blend the flour and salt in a medium bowl until well mixed. Cut in the shortening until evenly distributed. Add just enough water to form the dough into a ball.

Preheat the oven to 375 degrees.

For the filling, cut the round steak and pork steak into bite-size pieces. In a large bowl mix the meat with the parsley, onions, potatoes, grated turnip, salt, and pepper.

Roll the dough into four to six 10- to 12-inch circles. Measure about 1 1/2 cups of the filling onto half of each circle. Fold the other half of the dough over the filling. Pinch the edges to seal, making a half-moon shape. Place the filled pasties on a baking sheet with sides. Bake for about 1 hour , or until the meat is cooked and the vegetables are soft. Remove from the oven and cut a small slit in the top of each pasty. Put 1 teaspoon butter and 1 teaspoon water in each slit, return to the oven, and bake an additional 10 minutes. Serve hot with ketchup if desired.

HAROLD ERICKSON | BULLHEAD CITY, ARIZONA

Tips From Our Test Kitchen:

This rib-sticking dish is also good with 2 to 3 cloves minced garlic cooked in the filling. Pasties were designed to satisfy hard workers with a full meal that could be eaten like a sandwich.

Company Meatloaf

Yield: 8 to 10 servings

"When having guests for dinner, it seems I invariably prepare this favorite family recipe for meatloaf. It feeds eight to ten people and is easy to make, moist, and delicious. This recipe was given to me by an aunt and is one I would not want to do without. The meatloaf is very good served with pinto beans, salad, and cornbread."

1 1/2	pounds ground chuck	1 1/2	cups crushed Ritz (or similar) crackers
1 1/2	cups milk, scalded	1	tablespoon garlic salt
1	egg, slightly beaten	1	large onion, chopped
1/4	teaspoon baking powder	1	(10 3/4-ounce) can condensed tomato soup
1	small green bell pepper, chopped	1	(10 3/4-ounce) can water

Preheat the oven to 425 degrees. Spray a 13 x 9-inch baking dish with cooking spray. With your hands, mix together the ground chuck, milk, egg, baking powder, bell pepper, crackers, garlic salt, and onion. Form the meat mixture into a loaf and place it in the dish. Heat the soup and water to boiling in a saucepan. Pour over the meatloaf. Bake for 10 minutes at 425 degrees and then for 1 1/2 hours at 350 degrees. Baste the meatloaf three times during the baking.

PEGGY W. BARKER | SAN SABA, TEXAS

Herbed Meatloaf

Yield: 8 servings

"My family says this is the best meatloaf they've ever eaten. I found the recipe years ago and have made it many times."

2	beef bouillon cubes	1/2	teaspoon dried basil
1	cup boiling water	1/2	teaspoon dried thyme
2	pounds ground beef	1/4	cup ketchup, plus additional ketchup to coat loaf or loaves
1/2	cup finely chopped celery		
1/2	cup finely chopped onion	2	teaspoons mustard
1	egg	1	cup shredded Cheddar cheese
1/4	teaspoon black pepper	1 1/2	cups bread crumbs
2	teaspoons Accent		

Preheat the oven to 375 degrees. Dissolve the bouillon cubes in the boiling water. In a large bowl mix together the beef, celery, onion, egg, pepper, Accent, basil, and thyme. Mix in 1/4 cup of the ketchup, the mustard, cheese, crumbs, and bouillon with your hands. Shape into one large or two small loaves. Place in loaf pan(s), and coat with the additional ketchup. Bake for 1 hour. If making two small loaves, reduce the cooking time to 50 minutes.

MARY COLVIN | ROLLA, MISSOURI

Sweet-and-Sour Meatloaf

Yield: 4 to 6 servings

"This meatloaf is very simple to make and tastes delicious."

Meatloaf:
- 1 pound ground beef
- 1 1/2 teaspoons Worcestershire sauce
- 1 teaspoon salt
- 2 tablespoons minced onions
- 1/2 cup uncooked quick oats
- 2/3 cup milk

Sauce:
- 1/2 cup ketchup
- 2 tablespoons cider vinegar
- 4 tablespoons firmly packed brown sugar
- 2 tablespoons minced onion
- 6 tablespoons water

For the meatloaf, preheat the oven to 450 degrees. Combine the ground beef, Worcestershire sauce, salt, minced onions, oats, and milk. Place the meat mixture in a loaf pan. Bake for 20 minutes.

For the sauce, combine the ketchup, vinegar, brown sugar, onion, and water. Pour the sauce over the meatloaf after it has cooked for 20 minutes. Reduce the oven temperature to 375 degrees, and bake the loaf for an additional 40 minutes.

CHARLOTTE GRAVES | FORT PAYNE, ALABAMA

Tips From Our Test Kitchen:

This tasty small meatloaf is great with mashed potatoes and steamed green beans.

In Daphne, Alabama (pop. 16,581), locals scoop up crabs, shrimp, and other seafood by the basketful at a phenomenon called a "jubilee" in late summer along Mobile Bay's eastern shore. Oxygen-depleted water causes marine life to swim ashore, where locals shout "jubilee" and harvest the bounty.

Barnesville Takes Pride in the Potato

The entire downtown of Barnesville, Minnesota (pop. 2,173), is turned over to the Potato Days Festival the last weekend in August to celebrate the area's potato heritage and the state's farmers, who raise more than 2.2 billion pounds of potatoes annually in the rich black loamy soil of the Red River Valley.

Potatoes were first grown in Clay County in 1908, and by 1938, they had become so important to the local economy that civic leaders decided to celebrate the crop with a potato-picking contest. The next year the organizers added a peeling contest. The festival continued, with a gap during the war years, until 1957. Then in 1991, die-hard potato-heads decided it was time to revive the celebration.

Today more than 14,000 spud enthusiasts from across the United States flock to the festival. In addition to the potato-picking and potato-peeling contests, events include a potato soup feed, potato pancake breakfast, and the "Eyes of Fashion" fashion show featuring designs made from potato sacks.

Other activities are wagon rides, a classic car show, street fair, stage entertainment, whist and pinochle tournaments, the Miss Tater Tot Pageant for five- and six-year-olds, the Mr. and Mrs. Potato Head Contest, a parade with more than 150 entries, dances, demolition derby, Golden Potato scavenger hunt, and mashed potato wrestling, sculpting, and eating contests. Area cooks enter their best potato and *lefse* (Scandinavian flatbread) recipes in cook-offs.

Festivalgoers learn about potato growing by touring a display of antique farm equipment, most owned by area farmers, used in planting and harvesting potatoes—a potato planter, walking potato plow, potato digger, and a Red River Potato Duster, manufactured in Sabin, Minnesota, in the early 1890s. The oldest piece is a potato sorter made out of rods.

During a popular contest, two-man teams are timed as they sew and stack ten 100-pound burlap bags of potatoes. So far the record time is 2 minutes and 55 seconds. Then during the Potato Strong Man Contest, each contestant has three chances to throw a 100-pound sack of potatoes as high as possible.

During the Potato Sculpture Contest, entrants are supplied with cold mashed potatoes and given thirty minutes to create their works of art. They can decorate their masterpieces with other materials such as feathers, buttons, lace, nuts, and bolts.

These events and the Food Court—which serves up lefse, potato pancakes, French fries, sausage, soup, and dumplings, plus pork and beef sandwiches, fry-bread tacos, corn on the cob, and more—make for a "spudrific" family festival!

For more information, log on to www.potatodays.com or call (800) 525-4901.

Elaine Austin is the director of the Potato Days Festival.

One-Dish-Meal Casserole

Yield: 12 servings

"I prepare this recipe often. It's good when you're feeding a large family or going to a potluck supper."

1	pound ground beef	1/2	teaspoon chili powder
2	tablespoons vegetable oil	11/2	teaspoons salt
1/2	cup chopped onion	1/4	teaspoon black pepper
1	(8-ounce) can tomato sauce	2	teaspoons Worcestershire sauce
21/2	cups hot water	1	cup grated sharp Cheddar cheese
2	cups egg noodles, uncooked	1	(15-ounce) can cream-style corn

Preheat the oven to 350 degrees. Brown the ground beef in the oil. Stir together the onion, tomato sauce, hot water, noodles, chili powder, salt, pepper, Worcestershire sauce, cheese, and corn. Add this mixture to the ground beef. Spoon into a 13 x 9-inch pan. Bake for 40 to 50 minutes, or until the noodles are tender.

ANNICE MILSTEAD | TAYLORSVILLE, NORTH CAROLINA

Super Casserole

Yield: 4 servings

"This recipe is a favorite of mine. I was given it by a friend, who said it's for dieters, but her father-in-law said he couldn't tell it because it is so good. I have another friend who told me she adds corn and celery for extra flavor."

1	(8-ounce) package corkscrew pasta	1/2	cup chopped onion
1	pound lean ground beef or turkey	1	(15-ounce) can chopped tomatoes
1/4	cup chopped bell pepper	1/4	cup Cheddar cheese

Preheat the oven to 300 degrees. Cook the pasta as directed on the package and drain. Brown the meat, pepper, and onion in a skillet. Pour off the excess fat. Mix in the pasta and tomatoes. Pour into a casserole dish and top with the cheese. Cover and bake for 20 minutes.

GOLDEN RAY MALONE | AFTON, TENNESSEE

Tips From Our Test Kitchen:

Season this dish with sautéed garlic, lots of black pepper, a teaspoon of anise seed, crushed red pepper, basil, or oregano.

191

Wild Rice and Beef Casserole

Yield: 6 servings

"This recipe is delicious and easy. The ingredients can be doubled for larger amounts."

3	tablespoons vegetable oil	1	(4-ounce) can sliced mushrooms, drained
3	tablespoons chopped onion	1/2	cup water
1	pound lean ground beef	3/4	teaspoon celery salt
	Salt	3/4	teaspoon minced garlic
1	(103/4-ounce) can condensed cream of celery, chicken, or mushroom soup	3/4	cup wild rice, cooked according to package directions without salt
1	(8-ounce) can sliced water chestnuts, drained		

Preheat the oven to 375 degrees. Heat the oil in a large skillet and sauté the onion in the oil. Add the ground beef and salt to taste and brown the beef. Drain the grease. Stir in the soup, water chestnuts, mushrooms, water, celery salt, garlic, and cooked wild rice. Pour into a buttered casserole dish. Cover and bake for 30 minutes.

BETTY MAITHONIS | NEWHALL, CALIFORNIA

Mexican Casserole

Yield: 4 servings

"I came up with this recipe when I was dieting and looking for something that was simple, filling, low-fat, and, most of all, tasted good."

1/2	cup cooked brown rice	1/2	medium onion, chopped
1	(11-ounce) can sweet corn, drained	1	celery stalk, chopped
1	(141/2-ounce) can stewed tomatoes	1/2	pound lean ground beef, cooked
1	(4-ounce) can diced green chiles	2	tablespoons chili powder
1	(16-ounce) can pinto beans, drained		Tabasco
1/2	green bell pepper, chopped		Salt
1/2	red bell pepper, chopped		Low-fat shredded cheese
1	garlic clove, chopped		Reduced fat sour cream (optional)

Tips From Our Test Kitchen:

Try adding 11/2 teaspoons of ground cumin to the ground beef as it's browning. You may prefer to sauté the vegetables before adding them to the mixture.

Preheat the oven to 350 degrees. Mix together the rice, corn, tomatoes, chiles, and pinto beans. Add the green bell pepper, red bell pepper, garlic, onion, celery, cooked ground beef, chili powder, and Tabasco and salt to taste. Spoon this mixture into a 13 x 9-inch casserole dish. Top with the cheese. Bake about 10 minutes, or until the cheese is melted. The vegetables will still be crunchy. When serving, top with the reduced-fat sour cream, if desired.

KAREN BURMESCH | PLAINFIELD, ILLINOIS

Hamburger Pie

Yield: 6 to 8 servings

"A friend gave me this recipe years ago, back when our husbands were serving on the USS Wiseman. *It's economical and is still a treat."*

4	medium potatoes, boiled in skins until soft	1	pound ground beef
1/4	cup (1/2 stick) margarine	1/2	onion, chopped
1	teaspoon salt	1	(103/4-ounce) can condensed tomato soup
1/2	teaspoon black pepper	1	(15-ounce) can green beans, drained

Preheat the oven to 350 degrees. Lightly grease a 2-quart casserole dish. Slide the skins off the cooked potatoes. Whip the potatoes with the margarine, salt, and pepper. Brown the ground beef with the onion. Drain the excess grease. Stir in the tomato soup and beans. Spoon the mixture into the casserole dish. Top with the whipped potatoes. Bake for 35 minutes, or until the top is browned.

BARBARA BIRD | NEW BRAUNFELS, TEXAS

> *Tips From Our Test Kitchen:*
>
> This dish is also good with grated cheese sprinkled on top.

The spicy stew known as chili is believed to have originated in Texas in the 1880s. While seasoning meat with chili peppers was common, many accounts trace the development of modern chili to a seasoned soup sold on the streets of San Antonio from carts by women who prepared the dish at home.

Chinese Hamburger

Yield: 4 to 6 servings

"I'm the only sibling left in a big family. Last year, thirty-five nieces and nephews joined me at a family reunion, where many looked forward to my Chinese Hamburger dish."

1	pound ground beef	1/4	cup soy sauce
2	teaspoons vegetable oil	11/2	cups water
2	medium onions, chopped	1	(103/4-ounce) can condensed cream
1	cup diced celery		of mushroom soup
1	cup uncooked rice	1	(103/4-ounce) can condensed cream
1	(4-ounce) can mushrooms		of chicken soup
1	(28-ounce) can Chinese vegetables		Chinese noodles

Preheat the oven to 350 degrees. Heat the oil in a large skillet and brown the beef and onions in the oil. Drain the grease. Add the celery, uncooked rice, mushrooms, Chinese vegetables, and soy sauce. Stir in the water, mushroom soup, and chicken soup. Mix well and pour into a casserole dish. Cover and bake for 30 minutes. Top with the Chinese noodles to taste. Bake for another 30 minutes.

MYRNA GLASS | ST. MARYS, OHIO

Chile Relleno Bake

Yield: 8 servings

"My dear sister gave me this recipe back in 1973 in Glendale, California. It is simple but always gets many compliments."

4	(4-ounce) cans whole chiles	4	eggs, beaten
1/2	pound ground pork	1/4	cup all-purpose flour
1/2	pound ground beef	11/2	cups milk
1	onion, chopped	1	teaspoon salt
1	garlic clove, minced	1/4	teaspoon Tabasco or other hot sauce
3	cups grated Cheddar cheese	1	cup grated Monterey Jack cheese

Preheat the oven to 350 degrees. Lightly grease a 13 x 9-inch deep casserole dish. Remove the seeds from the chiles. Lay the chiles from one can flat on the bottom of the prepared dish. In a

Tips From Our Test Kitchen:

This comfort food with a Southwestern twist is great served with your favorite salsa.

skillet cook the pork, beef, onion, and garlic until the meat is well browned. Drain the grease. Spoon the meat mixture onto the chiles in the casserole dish. Add the Cheddar cheese in an even layer on top of the meat. Place the remaining chiles evenly over the cheese. Whisk together the eggs, flour, milk, salt, and Tabasco. Pour this over the second layer of chiles. Sprinkle the Monterey Jack cheese on top. Cover and bake for 25 minutes. Remove the cover and continue baking for an additional 15 minutes, or until lightly browned.

ROSEMARY RENO | POWELL, WYOMING

Red Enchiladas

Yield: 12 enchiladas

"I've been tweaking this recipe for thirty-five years. The cream makes it very mild and rich."

1	pound ground beef	1	(20-ounce) can red chili sauce, divided
2	garlic cloves, minced	1/4	cup olive oil
1	small onion, chopped	1/4	cup all-purpose flour
2	tablespoons salsa, any kind	1/4	cup whipping cream
3/4	teaspoon salt	1/2	teaspoon ground cumin
1	plus 11/2 cups shredded Cheddar cheese	24	(6-inch) corn tortillas, fried for a few seconds in oil until limp

Cook the ground beef until almost completely done, and then add the garlic and onion. Cook for a few minutes together. Drain the fat. Add the salsa, salt, 1 cup of the cheese, and 2 tablespoons of the chili sauce. Mix well.

In a saucepan heat the olive oil and add the flour. Mix well and cook until bubbly, about 3 minutes. Add the remaining chili sauce, the whipping cream, and cumin. Cook for about 5 minutes, or until thick. Pour 1 cup of this sauce over the bottom of a 13 x 9-inch baking dish.

Preheat the oven to 350 degrees. Use two limp tortillas (slightly overlapped) for each enchilada. Fill each enchilada with 2 to 3 tablespoons meat filling. Roll into a long cylinder. Place the rolled, filled tortillas in a snug row, lining the bottom of the baking dish. Spoon the remaining sauce evenly over the top. Cover with foil and bake for 40 minutes. Uncover and sprinkle with the remaining 11/2 cups of the cheese. Bake for 5 minutes longer.

AMY THOMPSON | SANDIA HEIGHTS, NEW MEXICO

Tips From Our Test Kitchen:

Garnish with sour cream. This hearty dish is great with rice and refried beans.

195

Tips From Our Test Kitchen:

This recipe is quick to make and tasty. Try adding a 12-ounce can of kidney or black beans to add fiber and more flavor. One table-spoon each of cumin and chili powder may be substituted for the taco seasoning. Also, several tablespoons of fresh chopped cilantro add more flavor.

Cornbread Taco Bake

Yield: 6 servings

"When I need a fast meal for unexpected guests, I always use this recipe. I usually have the ingredients on hand. All I need to complete the meal is a big salad. It is enjoyed by all."

1	pound ground beef	1	(8-ounce) can tomato sauce
1	(1 1/4-ounce) package taco seasoning	1	(8 1/2-ounce) package corn muffin mix
1/2	cup water	1	(2 3/4-ounce) can fried onions, divided
1	(12-ounce) can whole kernel corn, drained	1/3	cup shredded sharp cheese
1/2	cup chopped green bell pepper		

Preheat the oven to 400 degrees. Brown the beef in a skillet and drain. Stir in the taco season-ing, water, corn, pepper, and tomato sauce. Pour into a 12 x 7-inch glass dish or a 2-quart casse-role dish. In a bowl mix the corn muffin mix according to the package directions. Then stir in half the onions. Spoon the corn muffin mixture around the outer edge of the casserole. Bake uncovered for 20 minutes. Remove from the oven and sprinkle the cheese and remaining onions on the corn muffin topping. Bake 2 to 3 minutes more.

BETTIE WEDLOCK | MARYVILLE, MISSOURI

Tips From Our Test Kitchen:

This great dish is even better the second day. Add 1/2 cup of chopped cilantro to the salsa if desired.

Mexican Lasagna

Yield: 6 to 8 servings

"I've been asked to prepare this dish whenever we have company and when our children visit. It's really good."

2	pounds ground chuck	1	(16-ounce) jar chunky mild salsa
3/4	teaspoon minced garlic	2	cups water (or 1 salsa jar full)
2	teaspoons oregano	2	cups sour cream
1	teaspoon ground cumin	1	(6-ounce) can sliced black olives
1	(16-ounce) can refried beans	3/4	cup chopped green onions
5	plus 5 plus 5 lasagna noodles, uncooked	8	ounces shredded Monterey Jack cheese

Preheat the oven to 350 degrees. Lightly grease a 13 x 9-inch baking dish. Brown the beef in a large skillet. Drain the meat and return it to the pan. Add the garlic, oregano, and cumin. Mix well and stir in the beans. Layer 5 lasagna noodles over the bottom of the prepared dish. Spread one-third of the meat mixture over the noodles. Add 5 more noodles and another one-third of the meat mixture. Repeat the layers with the remaining noodles and meat mixture. Pour the salsa evenly over all. Fill the empty salsa jar with water, and pour it over the top. Cover the lasagna with foil and bake for 1 hour, or until the noodles are tender. Mix the sour cream, olives, and green onions together. Spoon this evenly over the lasagna. Top with the cheese. Return to the oven and bake until the cheese is melted.

EDNA HARTER | MOHAVE VALLEY, ARIZONA

Smith's Barbecued Meatballs

Yield: 40 meatballs with sauce

"The best story behind this recipe is when my son and his fiancée asked me to cater their rehearsal dinner. When I asked what they would like me to prepare, my son replied, 'I want your barbecued meatballs. There isn't a restaurant around that can beat those.'"

Meatballs:

2   pounds ground beef
1   cup Italian seasoned bread crumbs
2   eggs
1/2 teaspoon garlic salt

Sauce:

11/3 cups ketchup
4   tablespoons sugar
2   tablespoons Worcestershire sauce
4   tablespoons white vinegar
1   teaspoon chili powder
     Tabasco

For the meatballs, preheat the oven to 350 degrees. Mix the ground beef, bread crumbs, eggs, and garlic salt, and knead together in a mixing bowl. Shape into about 40 small meatballs. Place them on an ungreased cookie sheet. Bake for 20 minutes, or until browned. While the meatballs are baking, prepare the sauce.

For the sauce, mix together the ketchup, sugar, Worcestershire, vinegar, chili powder, and Tabasco to taste in a large saucepan. Add the browned meatballs to the sauce. Cover and simmer over low heat for about 30 minutes. Check occasionally to prevent scorching. Serve hot with your favorite potato dish.

CAROL SMITH | GREENVILLE, PENNSYLVANIA

Tips From Our Test Kitchen:

This main dish can also serve as an appetizer when the meatballs are rolled small and kept warm in a chafing dish.

Sloppy Joes

Yield: 20 sandwiches

4	pounds ground beef
1	medium onion, chopped
6	tablespoons chili powder
4	cups ketchup

1½	cups tomato juice
1	sleeve (¼ pound) saltine crackers, crumbled

Brown the ground beef and onion in a large pot. Drain the excess grease. Stir in the chili powder, ketchup, tomato juice, and crackers. Simmer until thick. If the sauce is too thick, add another 1/2 cup of tomato juice or water. Serve on hamburger buns.

VI SWISHER | PIEDMONT, KANSAS

Special Chicken and Mushrooms

Yield: 8 servings

"I prepared this chicken dish for our son's wedding rehearsal dinner in 1978. I experimented with some favorite flavors until I got it just right."

8	large bone-in chicken breasts with skin
	Salt and pepper
1/4	teaspoon garlic powder (or to taste)
6	tablespoons butter or margarine
1	plus 1/4 cups white wine

2	tablespoons minced onion
1	cup sliced fresh mushrooms
1	cup sour cream
1/2	cup slivered toasted almonds

Preheat the oven to 400 degrees. Sprinkle the chicken on both sides with the salt and pepper to taste and the garlic powder. Melt the butter in a large baking dish. Roll the seasoned chicken in the melted butter until coated on both sides. Bake skin side up for about 20 minutes, or until brown. Turn the chicken and reduce the temperature to 300 degrees. Pour 1 cup wine on top. Spoon the minced onion over the chicken. Return to the oven and bake until tender, about 1 hour.

While the chicken is baking, sauté the mushrooms in the remaining 1/4 cup of wine. Mix the sour cream into the sautéed mushrooms, and heat slowly until thoroughly blended. Place the hot chicken on a serving platter, pour the sauce on top, and sprinkle with the toasted almonds.

POLLY HOLMES | FALKVILLE, ALABAMA

Baked Chicken

Yield: 4 servings

"All of my brothers and sisters come by my house to see what I'm cooking. This chicken is a favorite."

1	(3-pound) broiler/fryer chicken, cut into serving-size pieces	2	tablespoons lemon juice
1	tablespoon all-purpose flour	2	tablespoons Worcestershire sauce
1/4	cup water	1	small onion, chopped
1/4	cup firmly packed brown sugar	1	teaspoon ground mustard
1/4	cup ketchup	1	teaspoon paprika
2	tablespoons white vinegar	1	teaspoon chili powder
			Salt and pepper

Place the chicken in a lightly greased 13 x 9-inch baking dish. In a saucepan over medium heat, whisk together the flour and water until smooth. Add the brown sugar, ketchup, vinegar, lemon juice, and Worcestershire sauce. Stir until the mixture begins to boil. Continue stirring for 2 minutes, or until thick. Add the onion, mustard, paprika, chili powder, and salt and pepper to taste. Pour the sauce over the chicken. Refrigerate for 2 to 4 hours.

Remove the chicken from the refrigerator 30 minutes before baking. Preheat the oven to 350 degrees. Bake uncovered for 35 to 45 minutes, or until the chicken juices run clear.

GERALD FRANCINE JONES | WILSON, NORTH CAROLINA

Tips From Our Test Kitchen:

This super moist chicken is also good served cold. For extra spice, add a dash of garlic powder and cayenne pepper.

Cranberry Chicken

Yield: 4 servings

"This sounds horrible, but tastes fabulous and is a snap to whip together with small kids around (I have twins). It goes great with chicken-flavored rice."

4	medium skinless, boneless chicken breast halves	1	packet dry onion soup mix
8	ounces Catalina dressing	1	(16-ounce) can whole berry cranberry sauce

Preheat the oven to 350 degrees. Spray a 13 x 9-inch glass baking dish with cooking spray. Place the chicken in the pan. In a medium bowl mix the Catalina dressing, soup mix, and cranberry sauce. Pour over the chicken and bake for 1 hour.

ANGELA LEPPER | LIVONIA, MICHIGAN

Tips From Our Test Kitchen:

Try marinating the chicken in the sauce for 1 hour before baking. This sauce also would be great with pork tenderloin.

Chicken Cacciatore

Yield: 6 to 8 servings

"My godmother gave me this recipe when I got married twenty-four years ago. I've been using it ever since. I make the dish the night before, and my family just loves it. Leftovers may be frozen."

1/2	cup olive or vegetable oil	2	large celery stalks, sliced into 1/4-inch strips
4	skinless, boneless chicken breasts		
1	tablespoon minced garlic	2	(28-ounce) cans crushed tomatoes
1	large red or Vidalia onion, sliced	1	(28-ounce) can diced tomatoes
1/2	pound fresh mushrooms, sliced	2	tablespoons Italian seasoning
2	large red peppers, sliced into 1/2-inch strips	1	teaspoon fresh cracked pepper
		1	cup white vinegar

In a large Dutch oven warm the oil over low-to-medium heat. Add the chicken breasts and cook for 6 to 8 minutes. Add the garlic, onion, mushrooms, peppers, and celery. Stir in the crushed tomatoes and diced tomatoes. Season with the Italian seasoning and pepper. Cover and cook over low-to-medium heat for 21/2 to 3 hours, stirring every 30 minutes. During the last 30 minutes, add the vinegar. Serve over white rice or linguine.

JANET TERCHILA | RIO RANCHO, NEW MEXICO

Magical Mustard Chicken

Yield: 8 servings

"I love this dish. It's simple, delicious, and low-fat."

8	boneless chicken breasts	1	cup grated Parmesan cheese
1	cup mustard	2	tablespoons butter or margarine
1	cup seasoned bread crumbs	2	tablespoons vegetable oil

Coat the chicken with a generous amount of mustard. Mix the bread crumbs and Parmesan cheese. Roll the chicken in the crumb mixture. Refrigerate for 15 to 20 minutes.

Preheat the oven to 375 degrees. Melt the margarine in a baking dish coated with cooking spray. Add the oil to the baking dish, tipping the dish to coat. Place the chicken in the dish and bake for 30 to 35 minutes, turning the chicken once.

MARGIE SPARKS | BRENTWOOD, TENNESSEE

Mystic Seaport's Lobsterfest and Sea Harvest

Located on seventeen acres along the Mystic River, Mystic Seaport—The Museum of America and the Sea—in Mystic, Connecticut (pop. 4,001), is the nation's leading maritime museum. Visitors can explore American maritime history as they climb aboard historic tall ships, stroll through a recreated nineteenth-century seafaring village, or watch a working preservation shipyard in action. Founded in 1929, the museum includes more than 2 million maritime artifacts, including 500 watercraft and 1 million photographs. In addition to education programs and a maritime library, the museum offers festivals throughout the year. Two of the more popular events are Lobsterfest and Sea Harvest.

At Lobsterfest, festivalgoers crack their first lobster claw of the season during Memorial Day Weekend. This butter-dribbling, shell-sucking, quintessentially New England event features lobsters in the rough served picnic-style under Mystic Seaport's open-air Boat Shed where diners can watch boats cruising on the Mystic River.

In addition to regular museum activities, attendees can learn about lobstering in "What a Catch!" and gain a cultural perspective on lobster as food at "The 'Rough' Stuff." Additionally, kids can "Create a Claw" with a lobster-themed craft activity. Musical entertainment is provided. Lobsterfest is a fund-raising activity of the Rotary Club of Mystic.

During Columbus Day weekend, visitors can celebrate the changing seasons by enjoying an afternoon of cool sea air and steaming hot "chowda." At Mystic Seaport's Sea Harvest, visitors taste a variety of chowders and other seasonal cuisine, peep at fall foliage along the Mystic River, and listen to the songs of the sea. But chowder is not the only thing served up at Mystic Seaport. Visitors can stroll through the village and enjoy live music by Finest Kind and the Mystic Seaport Chanteymen, and children can enjoy a "clammy" art project and story time in the Children's Museum. Programs on late summer stars under the Planetarium dome and the chance to climb aboard the 1908 steamboat *Sabino* for a closer look at the area's colorful foliage round out the event's offerings.

On the menu are a variety of chowders, additional seafood specialties, seasonal desserts, and beer, wine, and apple cider. The cost of food is in addition to museum admission.

For more information, log on to www.mysticseaport.org or call (888) 973-2767.

Michael O'Farrell is the publicist at Mystic Seaport—The Museum of America and the Sea—in Mystic, Connecticut.

Chicken Kerali

Yield: 6 servings

*Tips From Our
Test Kitchen:*

Like many Indian
dishes, this is delicious
with condiments such
as chutney and yogurt
with cucumber and
mint. Serve with rice
and a tossed salad to
complete your meal.

"This special recipe came to us through my daughter's dear childhood friend Joyce. While living in America for a year, she and my daughter became good friends. As a grown woman, Joyce made a return visit from her native Kerali, India, and prepared this chicken."

2	teaspoons lemon juice	2	tablespoons water
1/2	teaspoon curry powder	21/2	to 3 pounds boneless chicken breasts
1/2	teaspoon red pepper	1/4	cup vegetable oil
1/4	teaspoon turmeric	1	large onion, sliced
1/2	teaspoon black pepper	3	medium potatoes, peeled and cubed in 2-inch pieces
1/8	teaspoon ground cinnamon		
1/8	teaspoon ground cloves	1	large carrot, sliced
1/2	teaspoon salt	4	tablespoons tomato sauce

Combine the juice, curry, red pepper, turmeric, black pepper, cinnamon, cloves, salt, and water in a shallow pan. Cut the chicken into 1-inch strips. Place the chicken in the marinade for 20 minutes, turning at least once.

In a heavy skillet or Dutch oven, heat the oil and sauté the onion for 2 to 3 minutes. Add the potatoes and carrot and brown them slightly, stirring constantly for about 4 minutes. Add the tomato sauce, chicken, and marinade. Simmer for 45 minutes to 1 hour, stirring frequently.

BETTE KILLION | REELSVILLE, INDIANA

Oven-Fried Chicken

Yield: 4 servings

*Tips From Our
Test Kitchen:*

If you like spicier
chicken, add 1/2 tea-
spoon cayenne pepper,
1 teaspoon black pep-
per, and 2 cloves
minced garlic to the
bread crumb mixture.

"This is simple to make, but is so good. A good friend gave this recipe to me awhile ago, and I've made it many times."

4	skinless, boneless chicken breasts	1/2	cup seasoned dry bread crumbs
1/3	cup mayonnaise		

Preheat the oven to 350 degrees. Brush the chicken evenly with a thin coating of mayonnaise on both sides. Coat the chicken with the bread crumbs. Place in a shallow roasting pan. Bake for 30 to 40 minutes, or until fork tender.

LINDA T. BIGGS | SOMERSET, KENTUCKY

Angie's Pepper Chicken

Yield: 6 servings

"This recipe was created by combining elements from a couple of different restaurant dishes. It's very popular with my family and coworkers."

6	skinless, boneless chicken breasts	1	red bell pepper, chopped
2	tablespoons vegetable oil	1	green bell pepper, chopped
	Lemon pepper	1½	cups shredded Cheddar/Monterey
6	slices bacon		Jack blend cheese

Preheat the oven to 400 degrees. Lightly grease a 13 x 9-inch baking dish. Brush both sides of the chicken with the oil. Sprinkle both sides generously with the lemon pepper. Place in the baking dish. Bake until juicy and no longer pink, about 25 to 30 minutes. While the chicken is baking, fry the bacon until crisp. Drain, reserving 2 tablespoons of the grease. Sauté the peppers in the reserved grease until tender and remove from pan. Crumble the bacon and add to the peppers. Layer the pepper mixture and the cheese on top of the chicken after it is cooked through. Return to the oven just long enough to melt the cheese.

ANGIE SILCOX | CROSSVILLE, TENNESSEE

Tips From Our Test Kitchen:

Slice the chicken into in thin medallions and serve with rice and vegetables.

Vinegar Chicken

Yield: 5 servings

"I got this recipe from my mother many years ago. We all loved her chicken. It always turns out great."

5	chicken leg quarters	1/8	teaspoon salt
1/4	cup white or cider vinegar	1/8	teaspoon black pepper
1/4	cup soy sauce	1/8	teaspoon garlic powder
2	tablespoons Worcestershire sauce	1/8	teaspoon onion powder

Preheat the oven to 425 degrees. Lightly grease a 13 x 9-inch pan. Place the chicken in the pan. In a small bowl combine the vinegar, soy sauce, and Worcestershire sauce. Sprinkle one-third of this mixture over the chicken. Season with the salt, pepper, garlic powder, and onion powder. Bake for 30 minutes. Remove the chicken from the oven, and baste with another one-third of the vinegar mixture. Bake 15 minutes longer. Baste again with the remaining vinegar mixture. Return to the oven and continue baking for 15 minutes, or until the skin is golden brown and crispy.

TECHLER CLARK | GREENBRIER, ARKANSAS

Tips From Our Test Kitchen:

This recipe also works with chicken breasts with the skin on. A disposable pan is strongly suggested, because this basting sauce bakes on and blackens. Serve this chicken with green beans and mashed potatoes.

Chicken Piccata

Yield: 4 servings

"When I was very young, I watched and helped my grandmother cook. Since then, I've had a passion for cooking. This is one of my creations."

4	skinless, boneless chicken breasts	1/4	teaspoon garlic powder
1	egg	1/4	teaspoon paprika
1	plus 2 tablespoons fresh lemon juice	1/4	cup butter
1/2	cup chicken stock	1	tablespoon chopped fresh parsley
1/2	cup all-purpose flour	1	lemon, cut into 1/8-inch slices

Pound the chicken breasts between sheets of wax paper until very thin, about 1/4-inch thick. In a medium bowl whisk the egg with 1 tablespoon of the lemon juice. Stir the remaining 2 tablespoons lemon juice together with the chicken stock. In another bowl sift together the flour, garlic powder, and paprika. Melt the butter in a large, heavy skillet. Adjust the heat to avoid burning the butter. Dip the chicken into the egg mixture, and then coat it well with the flour mixture. Brown over medium-high heat for about 1 minute on each side. Pour the chicken stock mixture over the chicken breasts. Reduce the heat to medium-low, cover, and cook for 10 to 15 minutes, or until the chicken is very tender. Place the cooked chicken breasts on individual plates when done. Quickly stir the sauce in the pan and spoon some over each portion. Sprinkle with the parsley and garnish with the lemon slices. Serve immediately.

PETER QUAGLIA | STOVER, MISSOURI

Phony Abalone

Yield: 4 servings

"This is one of my favorite ways to prepare chicken, and it makes a real surprise. Don't tell your friends it isn't fish. (Note that you must prepare it well in advance.)"

2	skinless, boneless chicken breasts	3/4	cup plain bread crumbs
1	(8-ounce) bottle clam juice	1	egg, beaten
1	fresh garlic clove, minced (or more if you love garlic)		Lemon wedges, parsley, and tarter sauce for serving (optional)
3/4	cup all-purpose flour		

Slice each chicken breast into two steak-like slabs. Place them between wax paper and pound until thin. Combine the chicken and clam juice. Add the garlic, cover, and refrigerate for 36 hours.

Mix together the flour and bread crumbs. Drain the chicken. Dip the chicken in the beaten egg, roll it in the crumb mixture, and fry quickly. Serve with lemon wedges, a sprig of parsley, and tartar sauce, if desired.

WAUNIETA H. DUFFY | CAMERON PARK, CALIFORNIA

Curried Chicken

Yield: 6 servings

"My mother-in-law gave me this recipe shortly after I became a new bride. Twenty-six years later, it is still one of my family's favorite dishes. Whenever I take it to social gatherings, friends and coworkers ask me to share the recipe. It can be prepared ahead and refrigerated before cooking."

2	(10-ounce) packages frozen broccoli, cooked	1	cup mayonnaise
2	cups cooked bite-size chicken pieces	1	teaspoon lemon juice
2	(10 3/4-ounce) cans condensed cream of chicken soup	1	teaspoon curry powder
		1/2	cup shredded Cheddar cheese
		1	cup croutons

Preheat the oven to 350 degrees. Arrange the broccoli in the bottom of a 13 x 9-inch casserole dish. Place the chicken on top. Combine the soup, mayonnaise, lemon juice, and curry powder in a bowl. Pour over the chicken. Sprinkle with the cheese and top with the croutons. Bake, uncovered, for 25 to 30 minutes.

FRAN TUCKER | CANISTEO, NEW YORK

Tips From Our Test Kitchen:

Use garlic-flavored croutons for a tasty crunch in this dish. Substitute low-fat soup and use less mayonnaise to reduce the calories and fat.

The first public brewery in America was established by Peter Minuit (1580-1638) at the Market (Marckvelt) field in lower Manhattan, New York.

Chicken Salad Tacos

Yield: 2 to 4 servings

"Though when first married, I said that I would never get into a 'cooking rut,' I make these tacos almost every week. They are delicious."

1/3	cup mayonnaise	2	teaspoons taco seasoning
1/3	cup sour cream	1	cooked chicken breast, chopped
2	tablespoons chopped fresh cilantro	6	taco shells
1	tablespoon lime juice		

Combine the mayonnaise, sour cream, cilantro, lime juice, and taco seasoning. Stir in the chicken. Chill up to 24 hours. Serve in warm taco shells.

BETH MCCULLOUGH | HOOD RIVER, OREGON

Hot Chicken Brunch Casserole

Yield: 8 to 10 servings

"This recipe was given to me by my aunt. Though it's hot and hearty, the vegetables give it a nice crunch. Everyone loves it and requests the recipe."

4	chicken breasts	1/2	(103/4-ounce) can condensed cream
1	bay leaf		of chicken soup
5	celery leaves	1	cup mayonnaise
1	cup water	1	cup sour cream
2	cups chopped celery	2	tablespoons lemon juice
1	cup sliced water chestnuts		Salt and pepper
1/2	cup sliced mushrooms	1	cup shredded Cheddar cheese
1/2	cup slivered almonds	1	cup French's fried onions
2	tablespoons minced onions		

Simmer together the chicken, bay leaf, and celery leaves in the water for 30 minutes. Set aside to cool. Chop the chicken into bite-size pieces.

Preheat the oven to 350 degrees. Mix together the celery, water chestnuts, mushrooms, almonds, and onion. Stir in the chicken soup, mayonnaise, sour cream, and lemon juice. Season with the salt and pepper to taste. Add the chicken to the mixture. Spread in a 13 x 9-inch baking dish. Top with the Cheddar cheese and onion rings. Bake for 30 minutes.

ZEE ANNE REISHUS | WOOD LAKE, MINNESOTA

Fiesta Chicken Bake

Yield: 8 to 10 servings

5	boneless chicken breasts, cooked	1	cup grated Cheddar cheese
2	(10 3/4-ounce) cans condensed cream of chicken soup	1	cup grated Monterey Jack cheese
		2	tablespoons ground cumin
1	(4-ounce) can green chiles	8	ounces sour cream
1	large onion, chopped (sauté, if desired)	1	(13-ounce) bag tortilla chips

Cut the cooked chicken into cubes. Preheat the oven to 350 degrees. Generously grease a 13 x 9-inch baking dish. Mix the chicken with the soup, chiles, onion, Cheddar cheese, Monterey Jack cheese, cumin, and sour cream. Crumble the bag of chips. Stir three-fourths of the crumbled chips into the chicken mixture. Spoon the chicken mixture into the prepared dish. Sprinkle the remaining chips over all. Bake for 40 minutes.

PAM SMITH | TULSA, OKLAHOMA

Chicken-Artichoke Pasta

Yield: 4 servings

"This delicious dish was eliminated from the menu at a favorite restaurant. I had no choice but to find a way to make it myself. It tastes great."

1	pound skinless, boneless chicken breasts	12	ounces artichoke hearts
	Olive oil	1	cup manzanilla or other green olives, cut in half
	Salt and pepper	1/2	cup black olives, cut in half
2	to 4 garlic cloves, minced	8	ounces corkscrew pasta, cooked
1	medium onion, diced	1	cup Alfredo sauce or Italian dressing
2	zucchini squash, sliced		

Cut the chicken into bite-size pieces. Heat a small amount of oil in a skillet, and pan fry the chicken until cooked through. Season with the salt and pepper to taste. Remove from the skillet. Sauté the garlic, onion, squash, artichoke hearts, and olives in the same skillet. Mix the cooked chicken with the sautéed ingredients. Serve over the cooked pasta with the Alfredo sauce, or toss with the prepared pasta and Italian dressing for a delicious salad.

JODIE HUGHES | CORNING, CALIFORNIA

Chicken Dumplings

Yield: 6 to 8 servings

"I remember visiting my maternal grandmother in Fort Worth and being served these dumplings. We never fail to think of that sweet lady when we use her recipe."

Chicken:

1   (3 to 4-pound) chicken
2   celery stalks, unchopped
1   medium onion, quartered
    Salt and pepper

Dumplings:

3   cups all-purpose flour
1   teaspoon salt
1   teaspoon baking powder
3   tablespoons solid vegetable shortening
3/4 cup milk
    Reserved chicken broth

For the chicken, simmer it in a large pot with the celery, onion, and salt and pepper to taste in water deep enough to cover the chicken. Cook the chicken until tender enough to be gently pulled off the bone (about 2 hours). Remove the chicken from the broth, shred the chicken from the bones, and reserve the broth.

For the dumplings, combine the flour, salt, and baking powder in a medium mixing bowl. Cut in the shortening, combining the mixture with your hands until it resembles coarse meal. Add the milk and roll the dough into a large ball. On a well-floured surface, roll the dough into a paper-thin pastry. Slice into 1 1/2-inch squares. Heat the chicken broth in a large saucepan. Drop the dough slices into the broth, and cook on low for about 15 minutes, or until done. Stir occasionally to prevent sticking. Add the chicken pieces to the broth and heat through. Season to taste. Serve in soup bowls.

Marilyn Sommer | Brenham, Texas

State lawmakers declared Lockhart, Texas (pop. 11,615), "The Barbecue Capital of Texas" in 1999, thanks to the city's four barbecue restaurants, which report that 5,000 people visit them every week. One of the four, Black's Barbecue, was established in 1932 and claims to be the state's oldest barbecue restaurant owned and operated continuously by the same family.

Chicken-Broccoli Alfredo

Yield: 4 to 6 servings

"After eating in too many mediocre Italian restaurants and paying good money for jar sauce and overcooked pasta, I decided that I could do better. So I did."

Tips From Our Test Kitchen:

Timing is the key to success in this recipe. Cook the items in the order listed so that all of the items are hot and ready to eat at once.

1/3	cup fresh lemon juice	2	tablespoons olive oil
2	to 3 tablespoons mixed Italian herbs	3	plus 1 garlic cloves, minced
	Salt and pepper	2	cups broccoli tops
3	to 4 boneless chicken breasts, cut into bite-size pieces	1	pound pasta (spaghetti, penne, fettuccine, etc.)
1/3	cup all-purpose flour	2	tablespoons butter
1/4	cup grated Parmesan cheese plus more for serving	2	cups milk
			Freshly ground black pepper

In medium bowl combine the lemon juice, herbs, and salt and pepper to taste. Coat the chicken pieces in the lemon juice mixture. In a small bowl combine the flour and Parmesan cheese. Sprinkle two-thirds of the cheese mixture over the chicken. Heat the oil and 2 cloves minced garlic in a skillet. Add the chicken pieces. Brown them for 20 to 25 minutes, turning during cooking.

While the chicken is browning, steam the broccoli until crisp-tender. Boil the pasta until just done. Do not overcook. Allow the pasta to drain while making the Alfredo sauce.

Remove the browned chicken from the skillet. Using the same skillet, melt the butter and sauté the remaining 1 clove minced garlic. Stir in the remaining one-third of the flour mixture to make a roux. Stir constantly to avoid burning. When the flour is bubbly, stir in the milk. Heat through until thick and creamy. Add the chicken pieces and broccoli to the hot sauce. Stir to cover the pieces. Serve over the hot pasta. Top with freshly ground black pepper and grated Parmesan.

Tara Messersmith | Peoria, Illinois

In 1965, the New Mexico Legislature adopted the pinto bean, or frijol, and the chili as the state's vegetables.

Hungarian Chicken (Paprikash) with Spaetzle

Yield: 6 servings

"My maternal grandparents came to this country from Budapest, Hungary, in the late 1800s. My grandmother made Sunday dinner feasts from scratch. This was a favorite."

Chicken:

1/3	cup plus 3 tablespoons all-purpose flour
1	(3-pound) fryer, cut into serving-size pieces
1	plus 1 tablespoons oil
2	medium onions, thinly sliced
11/2	cups chicken broth
1	teaspoon salt
1	tablespoon Hungarian paprika
1/8	teaspoon black pepper
1/2	cup sour cream

Spaetzle (egg noodles):

4	plus 1/2 cups water
2	cups all-purpose flour
3	eggs, beaten
1/2	teaspoon salt
	Chopped parsley

For the chicken, place 1/3 cup of the flour in a large plastic bag. Place the chicken pieces in the bag and shake to coat them. Heat 1 tablespoon of the oil in a large, heavy skillet, and fry the chicken until light brown. Remove the chicken. Add the remaining 1 tablespoon oil to the skillet along with the onions and the remaining 3 tablespoons flour. Fry the onions until golden. Stir in the broth, salt, paprika, and pepper. Add the chicken, and cover. Cook, turning once, over medium heat for 25 to 30 minutes, or until the chicken is tender.

For the spaetzle, bring 4 cups of the water to a boil in a large saucepan while the chicken is cooking. In a bowl combine the flour and the remaining 1/2 cup water with the eggs and salt until smooth. The dough will be heavy and gluey. Reduce the heat to maintain a steady boil, and drop small pieces of dough into the water. (The dough can also be forced through the slits or holes in a colander or spaetzle maker.) Boil the noodles, which look like small dumplings, for 5 minutes, or until tender but firm. Stir occasionally to prevent sticking. Rinse the cooked noodles with very hot water. Serve immediately.

Place the hot chicken on a serving platter. Whisk the sour cream into the gravy, and pour the gravy over the chicken. Serve with the hot spaetzle. Garnish with the chopped parsley.

MARGARET VONDERWERTH | MORAN, MICHIGAN

Mom's Mafia Chicken

Yield: 4 servings

"When I visit my daughters in their city, they like me to make 'home food' for them. They recently asked if I'd make an Italian dish that we could eat together during their favorite Italian television show. They loved the result and named the dish after me."

4	skinless, boneless chicken breast halves	1/2	cup chicken broth
1/2	teaspoon chili powder	1	cup heavy cream
1/2	teaspoon salt	2	tablespoons capers
1/4	teaspoon black pepper	1/2	cup canned artichokes, sliced
3	tablespoons olive oil	1	pound angel hair pasta
3	tablespoons butter	10	ounces fresh spinach, chopped
4	tablespoons oil-packed, sun-dried tomatoes		

Pound the chicken breasts between sheets of wax paper until about 1/4-inch thick. Sprinkle the chicken with the chili powder, salt, and pepper. In a large skillet heat the oil with the butter over medium heat. Add the chicken and cook for about 8 minutes, turning once, or until the center is cooked. Remove the chicken from the skillet and keep it in a warm oven. Slice the sun-dried tomatoes into very thin pieces. Pour the broth into the skillet, and add the sun-dried tomatoes. Cook for about 3 minutes, or until the liquid is slightly reduced.

Start heating the water to cook the pasta.

Add the cream to the broth mixture, and cook for 3 to 4 minutes, or until thickened. Add the capers and artichokes. Cook until heated through.

Cook the pasta according to package instructions while the sauce is heating. Drain. Place a serving of pasta on each plate. Top with about 1/3 cup of the chopped spinach. Slice the chicken into strips and place them on the spinach. Ladle the sauce over all and serve immediately.

POLLY KRAUS | FORT SMITH, ARKANSAS

Tips From Our Test Kitchen:

This creamy and tasty dish can be seasoned with garlic, if desired. It's also good with chopped fresh basil.

Bradley County's Pink Tomato Festival in Warren, Arkansas (pop. 6,442), started more than forty years ago when citizens decided to promote the county's chief resource, the Bradley Pink tomato, a staple there since the 1920s.

Spicy Chicken in Sauce

Yield: 4 servings

"I was given this recipe by my mother-in-law. The seasonings give it just the right taste."

1/3	cup ketchup
1/4	cup applesauce
1 1/2	teaspoons curry powder
1/2	teaspoon salt
	Dash of black pepper
1/4	teaspoon crushed dried thyme
1/3	cup raisins
1	plus 1 tablespoons vegetable oil
1	medium onion, cut into eighths
1	medium green bell pepper, cut into thin strips
1	medium red bell pepper, cut into thin strips
1	garlic clove, minced
1	pound skinless, boneless chicken breasts, cut into 1/2-inch-wide strips
1/4	cup peanuts

Combine the ketchup, applesauce, curry powder, salt, pepper, thyme, and raisins in a bowl. In a large skillet heat 1 tablespoon of the oil, and sauté the onion, red and green peppers, and garlic until the peppers are crisp-tender. Remove the vegetables from the skillet. Sauté the chicken in the remaining 1 tablespoon oil until just cooked (about 2 to 3 minutes per side). Stir the ketchup mixture into the cooked chicken. Cook until the sauce is bubbly. Add the sautéed vegetables, and stir until they are coated with sauce. Garnish with the peanuts.

KENNETH ZURA | SUGAR RUN, PENNSYLVANIA

Chicken Spaghetti

Yield: 8 to 10 servings

"When I was a grill cook for a restaurant in Crawford, Texas, I was asked to make this recipe for Crown Prince Abdullah of Saudi Arabia, who was a guest of President George W. Bush at his Crawford ranch. This dish was one of the daily specials at the restaurant."

4	skinless, boneless chicken breasts
1	(12-ounce) package thin spaghetti
3	tablespoons butter or margarine
1/2	cup chopped celery
1/2	cup chopped onion
1	tablespoon chopped pimiento
1	(26-ounce) can condensed cream of chicken soup
1	cup milk
1 1/2	cups cubed Velveeta or similar cheese product
	Salt and pepper
	Grated Cheddar cheese

In a large saucepan cook the chicken in boiling water until done. Drain, saving the water. Chop the chicken into small pieces.

Preheat the oven to 350 degrees. Add the spaghetti to the chicken water and cook until done, following the directions on the package. In another pan melt the butter, and sauté the celery and onion. Stir in the pimiento. Add the chicken, soup, milk, Velveeta, and salt and pepper to taste. Drain the spaghetti and add it to the chicken mixture. Pour into a greased 13 x 9-inch baking dish. Sprinkle the Cheddar on top. Bake for 20 minutes.

CHERYL POMERENKE | MCGREGOR, TEXAS

Roasted Turkey with Herbs
Yield: 20 servings or more

"This is my own turkey dish. Folks who complain that turkey is too dry love this bird."

1	head (bulb) garlic	4	tablespoons chopped fresh thyme
1	pound unsalted butter at room temperature	1	tablespoon coarse salt
			Freshly ground black pepper
4	tablespoons chopped fresh rosemary	1	(14 to 16-pound) fresh or completely
4	tablespoons chopped fresh sage		thawed turkey
4	tablespoons chopped fresh parsley	1	cup water

Preheat the oven to 350 degrees. Wrap the garlic in foil and bake for 1 hour, or until very soft. This can be done a day or two ahead.

In a small bowl mix the butter with the rosemary, sage, parsley, and thyme. Squeeze the cooled, softened garlic head into the bowl. Stir together until smooth. Add the salt and the pepper to taste.

Preheat the oven to 400 degrees. Rinse the turkey and pat it dry with paper towels. Tuck the wing tips under the bird. Place the turkey on a roasting rack in a large roasting pan. Add the water to the pan. Using your fingers, gently separate the skin from the flesh. Smear about one-third of the butter mixture under the skin. Pat the remaining butter mixture on the exterior and in the cavity. Roast for 40 to 50 minutes. Place a foil tent over the turkey, and reduce the temperature to 350 degrees. Baste with the juices or additional butter while roasting the turkey for an additional 2 to 3 hours, or until it reaches an internal temperature of 180 degrees. The legs should rotate easily at the joint. Allow the turkey to rest for 30 minutes before carving. Save the juices to make a delicious gravy.

ILA CLEMENTS | BATESVILLE, ARKANSAS

Tips From Our Test Kitchen:

This recipe also works for a large roasting hen. Decrease the butter, herbs, and garlic by half if using a smaller bird.

Turketti Casserole

Yield: 4 to 6 servings

"This recipe has been in our family for about forty years. It is good for a gathering or covered-dish affair. You can make it ahead and refrigerate until ready to bake. It also freezes well."

11/4	cups (2-inch) spaghetti pieces	1/2	cup grated onion
1/4	cup minced pimiento	1	(103/4-ounce) can condensed
1/4	cup diced green bell pepper		cream of mushroom soup
1/2	cup turkey or chicken broth	1/8	teaspoon celery salt
1/8	teaspoon black pepper	1/2	cup grated Cheddar cheese
11/2	to 2 cups cooked, diced turkey or		Parmesan cheese (optional)
	chicken (1-inch chunks)		

Preheat the oven to 350 degrees. Cook the spaghetti until barely tender, following the instructions on the package. Drain and rinse with hot water. Drain well. Mix together the pimiento, green pepper, turkey broth, black pepper, turkey, onion, soup, and celery salt. Add the cooked and drained spaghetti, and toss lightly. Pour the mixture into 11/2-quart casserole dish. Sprinkle with the Cheddar cheese and Parmesan cheese, if using. Bake 45 minutes to 1 hour.

Ann M. Duerr | Mount Wolf, Pennsylvania

Cajun Turkey Meatloaf

Yield: 8 servings

"This recipe is hearty and healthy."

1/4	cup (1/2 stick) butter	1	tablespoon hot pepper sauce
1	large onion, chopped	1	tablespoon Worcestershire sauce
1/2	cup chopped celery	2	pounds ground turkey
1/2	green bell pepper, chopped	1	cup quick oats, uncooked
1/4	cup chopped green onion with tops	1	to 2 eggs, beaten
2	garlic cloves, minced	1/4	to 1/2 cup milk
2	tablespoons Tony Chachere's seasoning	1/2	cup ketchup
	(or other Cajun seasoning blend)		

Tips From Our Test Kitchen:

Serve this delicious meatloaf hot with your favorite side dishes, or chilled and sliced in a meatloaf sandwich. It's great with tangy mustard on whole wheat bread.

Preheat the oven to 350 degrees. In a medium-size saucepan melt the butter, and sauté the onion, celery, green pepper, green onion, and garlic for 5 minutes. Stir in the Cajun seasoning, hot pepper sauce, and Worcestershire sauce. When completely heated, set aside to cool.

Place the turkey in a large mixing bowl. Add the cooled, seasoned vegetable mixture and the oats, 1 egg, 1/4 cup milk, and the ketchup. Mix with your hands until well blended. Add a second egg and an additional 1/4 cup milk if the mixture needs more moisture. It should be firm enough to hold a loaf shape. Shape the mixture into a large loaf, and place the loaf in a 13 x 9-inch baking dish. Bake until the center is well cooked, about 1 hour.

SHARON SHANKS | RAYWOOD, TEXAS

Unstuffed Cabbage with Turkey

Yield: 4 to 6 servings

"This is my favorite cabbage recipe. I'd like to share it with all American Profile readers."

1	pound ground turkey	1	small cabbage
1/2	cup chopped onion	2	(103/4-ounce) cans condensed tomato soup
3/4	cup instant rice	2	cups water
1	teaspoon salt	1/2	cup grated Parmesan cheese
1	teaspoon black pepper		

Preheat the oven to 350 degrees. Grease a 13 x 9-inch baking dish. Brown the turkey with the onion in a large skillet. Stir in the rice, salt, and pepper. Finely chop the cabbage and layer it over the bottom of the baking dish. Spoon the turkey mixture over the cabbage. Mix the soup and water together and pour it evenly over the top. Sprinkle a generous layer of the Parmesan cheese over all. Cover lightly with heavy-duty aluminum foil. Bake for 11/2 hours.

LETTIE PATTERSON | ELLINGTON, CONNECTICUT

Tips From Our Test Kitchen:

This dish is much easier to prepare than stuffed cabbage. Try using your favorite marinara sauce instead of the tomato soup for a spicier result.

Grilled Turkey Cheeseburger with Sun-Dried-Tomato Mayonnaise

Yield: 4 servings

"This burger is great with greens such as lettuce, sprouts, and spinach."

Burgers:

1	plus 1 tablespoons olive oil
1	large shallot or 6 green onions, chopped
1/2	teaspoon poultry seasoning
1/2	teaspoon salt
1/2	teaspoon black pepper
1/4	cup bread crumbs made from day-old bread
11/2	pounds ground turkey
5	ounces extra sharp Cheddar cheese, sliced
4	deluxe burger buns or Kaiser rolls

Mayonnaise:

1/4	cup sun-dried tomatoes packed in oil
2	teaspoons cider vinegar
1	tablespoon water
1/4	cup light mayonnaise
1	strip bacon, cooked and crumbled

For the burgers, heat 1 tablespoon oil and sauté the shallot until lightly golden. Stir in the poultry seasoning, salt, and pepper. In a large bowl combine the shallot with the bread crumbs and turkey. Divide the meat mixture into eight equal portions and shape into flat patties. Place cheese slices on top of four patties. Cover with the remaining four patties. Pinch the edges to secure the cheese inside the meat. Heat the remaining 1 tablespoon oil in a skillet, and gently cook the burgers until the centers are no longer pink (about 4 minutes per side over medium-high heat).

For the mayonnaise, purée the tomatoes, vinegar, and water in a food processor or blender. Stir in the mayonnaise and crumbled bacon. Refrigerate until ready to serve.

When ready to serve, place the burgers on toasted buns with the tomato-mayonnaise and your favorite greens.

WILL NIST | COTTONWOOD, ARIZONA

Yuma Lettuce Days, an annual January event, promotes Yuma's lettuce industry and Arizona-grown products. Yuma (pop. 77,515), the "Winter Lettuce Capital of the World," and its surrounding area produce more than 90 percent of the nation's winter vegetable crops. Lettuce is the leading crop in Yuma County's agricultural industry.

Wiener and Kraut Casserole

Yield: 4 to 6 servings

"This recipe is a favorite from the old Depression days. I'm eighty-five-years old and live in northern Wisconsin, but I was a teenager during those years. This casserole was supper for many families because a lot of folks made their own kraut and wieners were reasonably priced."

1	(28-ounce) can sauerkraut	1	bay leaf
1	large onion, chopped	5	to 6 wieners, cut into 1/2-inch pieces
2	garlic cloves, crushed	4	potatoes, peeled and cut into
3/4	cup firmly packed brown sugar		1-inch cubes

Preheat the oven to 350 degrees. Drain and rinse the sauerkraut in a colander. Mix the sauerkraut with the onion, garlic, and sugar. Add the bay leaf, wieners, and potatoes, and pour into a large casserole dish. Cover and bake for 11/4 to 11/2 hours.

TOM R. BUICK | HAYWARD, WISCONSIN

Tips From Our Test Kitchen:

Smoked sausage or bratwurst is a nice option for people who don't eat wieners. To add color and texture, try substituting 1/2 cup applesauce and 1/2 cup diced apple for the brown sugar.

Zucchini-Pepperoni Casserole

Yield: 8 servings

"Surprise your family with this spicy dish."

2	tablespoons olive oil	1	teaspoon dried oregano
2	medium zucchini, diced	1/2	pound spaghetti, cooked
1/2	pound bacon, crisply cooked and crumbled	1	cup sliced onion
		4	ounces pepperoni slices
1	teaspoon salt	1	(26-ounce) jar marinara sauce
1/2	teaspoon black pepper	8	ounces mozzarella cheese
1	teaspoon dried basil	1/2	cup grated Parmesan cheese

Preheat the oven to 350 degrees. Grease a 13 x 9-inch baking dish with the olive oil. Layer the zucchini on the bottom of the dish. Sprinkle the bacon, salt, pepper, basil, and oregano evenly over the top. Follow with a layer of the cooked spaghetti, onion slices, and pepperoni. Next, spread the marinara sauce and then both types of cheese evenly over all. Bake for 30 to 40 minutes. Serve with garlic toast.

LEE SAUERS | MIFFLINBURG, PENNSYLVANIA

Tips From Our Test Kitchen:

This dish is also good with a layer of red or green bell peppers or a layer of sliced black olives.

Italian Peppers

Yield: 4 servings

"This is a special recipe. My husband's family came from Italy, and this recipe was a change from rice. It makes a delicious meal with corn and applesauce."

3	cups salted water		1½	cups tomato juice
4	ounces elbow macaroni		2	teaspoons to 1 tablespoon Italian seasoning, depending on taste
2	green or red bell peppers		1	teaspoon sugar
½	pound sausage			
½	cup chopped onions		¼	cup bread crumbs
2	tablespoons all-purpose flour		¼	cup Parmesan cheese
½	teaspoon salt		2	tablespoons butter, melted

Bring the water to a boil. Cook the macaroni in the boiling water. Boil rapidly, stirring constantly, for 2 minutes. Cover, remove from the heat, and let stand for 10 minutes. Rinse the macaroni with warm water and drain well. Wash the peppers and cut in half. Parboil the peppers in salted water for 10 minutes. Remove from the water.

Preheat the oven to 350 degrees. Brown the sausage in a large, heavy skillet. Drain the excess fat. Add the onions and brown lightly. Stir in the flour and salt. Add the tomato juice, Italian seasoning, and sugar. Cook until thickened, stirring constantly. Fold in the macaroni.

Fill the peppers with the sausage mixture. Pour the leftover mixture into a 1-quart casserole dish, and arrange the filled peppers on top. Combine the bread crumbs, cheese, and butter, and sprinkle over the peppers. Bake for about 30 minutes.

LORRAINE ELLINGSON | SAINT DAVID, ARIZONA

The Hayden Flour Mill in Tempe, Arizona, ran for well over a century and was the earliest important local industry during the city's development. After Tempe founder Charles Trumbull Hayden built the mill in the early 1870s, it burned down twice before being replaced by a concrete structure that operated until the late 1990s.

Bratwurst-Potato Skillet Dinner

Yield: 2 servings

"This skillet dinner is an old family recipe passed down from my husband's German grandmother."

2	teaspoons vegetable oil	2	tablespoons soy sauce
2	medium potatoes, sliced	1	tablespoon orange juice
2	fully cooked bratwurst links	1/2	teaspoon dried basil
1	small onion, chopped	1/4	teaspoon salt
1/3	cup chopped green bell pepper	1/8	teaspoon black pepper

In a heavy skillet heat the oil over medium heat. Cook the potatoes until they are lightly browned and crisp-tender, about 6 minutes. Add the bratwurst, onion, and green bell pepper. Stirring occasionally, cook until the vegetables are crisp-tender and heated through, 5 to 10 minutes. Combine the soy sauce, orange juice, basil, salt, and pepper in a small bowl. Stir the sauce mixture into the meat and vegetables, and heat through.

LUCY BRADSHAW | NEW BERN, NORTH CAROLINA

Tips From Our Test Kitchen:

This dish is good with almost any type of cooked smoked sausage or bratwurst. Serve it with rye bread and mustard.

Mamma Fossa's Northern Italian Risotto with Italian Sausage

Yield: 6 to 8 servings

"I hope you enjoy my mamma's recipe for risotto."

1	pound Italian sausage	1/8	teaspoon ground nutmeg
1/4	cup (1/2 stick) butter	1	cup white cooking wine
1/2	cup olive oil	11/2	cups instant rice (risotto or orzo)
3	garlic cloves	1	(4-ounce) can mushroom pieces
1	medium onion, finely chopped	1	(8-ounce) can tomato sauce
41/2	cups chicken stock	6	ounces grated Parmesan cheese

Remove the sausage from its casings. Brown the sausage and drain the grease. In a Dutch oven heat the butter and olive oil, and sauté the garlic and onion until golden. In the same pot add the chicken stock, nutmeg, wine, sausage, rice, and mushrooms. Stir constantly to keep the rice from sticking. Add the tomato sauce and cheese near the end of cooking (when the rice softens). The tomato sauce will turn the rice a light pink. Add more cheese if desired.

TOM FOSSA | CLAREMORE, OKLAHOMA

Tips From Our Test Kitchen:

Remember to stir constantly or the rice will stick. This makes a great meal when served with a salad and garlic bread.

Ham It Up in Marion County

Marion County, located in the geographic center of Kentucky, is home to one of the oldest and most successful community festivals in Kentucky.

First celebrated in 1969 with six hams and a handful of visitors, Marion County Country Ham Days now needs more than 6,000 pounds of country ham for the nearly 50,000 festivalgoers each year. Celebrated in Lebanon (pop. 5,718) during the last full weekend in September, Ham Days features the PIGasus Parade; free street dance with live entertainment; free musical entertainment all weekend; carnival rides; a car, truck, and motorcycle show; arts and crafts; a flea market; exhibits of antique tractors and gas and steam engines; the 5K Pokey Pig Fun Run; a climbing wall; and much more.

Children attending the festival find ample opportunity for fun during several contests and activities just for them: basketball free throw, bubble-gum blowing, jump rope, paper airplane flying, spelling bee, sack races, hula hoop, pedal pull, and hay bale toss.

Cured in sugar and salt and aged for up to a year, Kentucky country hams are some of the South's finest, and festivalgoers can get their fill of the smoky flavored meat. A country ham breakfast with apples, eggs, biscuits, red-eye gravy, and all the fixins opens the day for visitors, who also can partake of pinto beans and cornbread, ham and biscuits, pork chops, baked ham sandwiches, Polish sausage with green peppers and onions, and rib-eye steaks throughout the rest of the festival.

The Pokey Pig 5K Run, which attracts more than 125 runners, winds its way through Lebanon early Saturday morning. The PIGasus Parade draws more than 100 entries and takes almost two hours from start to finish.

Selected as a Top Ten Fall Festival for 2003 and 2004 in Kentucky by the Kentucky Tourism Council and a Top 20 Event in the Southeast by the Southeast Tourism Society in 2000 and 2001, the Marion County Country Ham Days pulls together volunteers from the whole community. Funds raised from the festival go to the Lebanon-Marion County Chamber of Commerce, which uses the money for next year's Ham Days and other events, such as the Heart of Kentucky Farm, Home and Garden Show, Dickens' Christmas on Main, and business seminars for members.

For more information, log on to www.hamdays.com or call (270) 692-9594.

Missy Spalding is administrative assistant at the Lebanon-Marion County Chamber of Commerce.

Italian Sausage Bread

Yield: 12 to 16 servings

"I watched my mother cook when I was a young girl and have added my own touch to her Italian recipes. I made this dish every Christmas Eve while raising my seven children."

2	(1-pound) packages frozen loaf-bread dough	1/4	cup grated Romano cheese
2	pounds Italian sausage	1/4	cup grated Parmesan cheese
6	plus 1 eggs	1/2	pound mozzarella cheese, shredded
2	pounds ricotta cheese	1	(8-ounce) can tomato sauce
2	tablespoons Italian seasonings (any combination of oregano, basil, rosemary, garlic, red or black pepper, celery, and salt)	1/2	cup sliced black olives (optional)
		10	ounces frozen spinach, thawed, chopped, and patted dry (optional)
2	tablespoons bread crumbs	1/2	pound provolone cheese, sliced Olive oil

Thaw the bread dough according to the package instructions. Allow it to complete its first rising.

Lightly grease a deep 13 x 9-inch casserole dish. While the dough is rising, cook and crumble the Italian sausage. Hard-cook 6 of the eggs. Slightly beat the remaining 1 egg. In a large bowl mix the ricotta, Italian seasonings, beaten egg, bread crumbs, Romano cheese, and Parmesan cheese. Add the cooked sausage, mozzarella, and tomato sauce to the ricotta mixture. Chop the hard-cooked eggs and fold them in. Add the olives and spinach if using. Place half the bread dough into the prepared dish. Press the dough evenly on the bottom of the pan with about 2 inches of extra dough rising up the sides. Spoon the sausage filling into this shell. Cover the filling with the provolone slices. Roll the second piece of dough out flat enough to cover the top of the provolone slices. Pinch the edges of the dough all around to seal. Punch holes in the top with the tines of a fork. Baste with a thin coat of olive oil, and let the dough rise in a warm place for 30 minutes covered with plastic wrap. While the bread is rising this second time, preheat the oven to 350 degrees. After the second rising, bake the stuffed bread for 45 minutes, or until lightly browned and well cooked in the center.

ANGELINE GREEN | SEBRING, FLORIDA

Maybe it's obvious, but it's still special. Florida's official state beverage, adopted in 1967, is orange juice.

Good 'n' Fillin' Sausage Casserole

Yield: 4 to 6 servings

*"This recipe was thrown together one weekend when I needed something for
my husband and son, who were coming home from an all-day fishing trip.
They liked it so much it has become a requested favorite."*

2	plus 1 tablespoons vegetable oil	2	(16-ounce) cans black-eyed peas,
1	pound smoked sausage, sliced		drained
1	large onion, cut into short, thin strips	1	cup corn muffin mix
2	large green bell peppers, cut into short,	1/4	teaspoon ground cayenne pepper
	thin strips	2/3	cup milk
1	(16-ounce) can tomatoes and green	1	egg, beaten
	chiles		

Preheat the oven to 400 degrees. Lightly grease a 13 x 9-inch baking dish with cooking spray. In
a large skillet heat 1 tablespoon of the oil over medium heat, and cook the sausage, onion, and
green pepper until the vegetables are tender and the sausage is done. Stir in the tomatoes and
green chiles and the peas. Reduce the heat and simmer for 5 to 10 minutes. Pour the sausage
mixture into the prepared dish.

In a small bowl combine the muffin mix, cayenne pepper, milk, egg, and the remaining 2
tablespoons oil. Stir until smooth. Pour over the sausage mixture. Bake 25 to 30 minutes, or
until golden brown.

PAM HUDENAK | WHARTON, TEXAS

Spaghetti Pie

Yield: 12 to 16 servings

*"My minister's wife shared this recipe with me many years ago. It has become
a popular and cherished favorite. Everyone who tries it wants the recipe."*

11/2	pounds bulk pork or turkey sausage	3	eggs, beaten
1	large onion, chopped	8	ounces grated Parmesan cheese
1	(32-ounce) jar spaghetti sauce	8	plus 8 ounces shredded mozzarella
1	cup water		cheese
1	pound spaghetti, cooked and rinsed	16	ounces cottage cheese
1/4	cup (1/2 stick) butter		

Preheat the oven to 350 degrees. Grease a deep 13 x 11-inch casserole dish. Brown the sausage and onion in a large saucepan. Drain the grease. Add the spaghetti sauce and water, and simmer until thick. Toss the cooked spaghetti with the butter, eggs, Parmesan, and 8 ounces of the mozzarella until well mixed. Spoon the spaghetti mixture into the casserole dish and press down. Cover evenly with the cottage cheese. Spoon the sauce on top. When smooth, poke holes with the handle of a wooden spoon randomly over the entire surface. Bake for 20 minutes.

Remove the dish from the oven and sprinkle the remaining 8 ounces mozzarella on top. Return to the oven and bake for 10 to 15 minutes longer, or until golden and bubbly. Cool 10 minutes before serving.

BEVERLY STOOPS | BARSTOW, CALIFORNIA

Stuffed Pork Roast

Yield: 6 to 8 servings

"My family is currently eating a high-protein diet, so I came up with this healthful and delicious recipe to satisfy three generations."

3	pounds pork tenderloin roast	2	to 3 tablespoons white cooking wine
2	tablespoons olive oil	1	(10-ounce) package frozen chopped spinach, thawed and squeezed dry
1/2	medium onion, chopped		
6	to 8 mushrooms, chopped	1	(15-ounce) can black beans
1/2	teaspoon fines herbes or a favorite herb blend	1/2	cup sliced almonds
		1/4	cup grated Parmesan cheese

Preheat the oven to 325 degrees. Cut a long pocket deeply into the tenderloin without slicing through and leaving about 3/4 inch uncut at each end. Heat the olive oil in a skillet and sauté the onion for about 5 minutes. Add the mushrooms, herbs, and wine. Sauté until most of the liquid is absorbed, for about 10 minutes. Add the spinach, beans, almonds, and cheese. Spoon this filling into the pork pockets. The meat is very elastic and will expand to allow room for the filling. Tie the roast snugly with twine. Place the meat in a roasting pan and bake for 2 to 3 hours, or until the internal meat temperature reaches 170 degrees. (Cover the roast loosely with foil after the first 45 minutes of cooking.) Allow to sit for 15 minutes before slicing.

GLORIA SMITH | NIXA, MISSOURI

Grilled Pork Tenderloin with Gingered Jezebel Sauce

Yield: 6 servings

"Jezebel sauce traditionally has dry mustard in the recipe. This sauce is different because it calls for fresh ginger instead."

Marinade and meat:

1/2	cup light soy sauce
2	tablespoons firmly packed dark brown sugar
2	green onions, chopped
2	tablespoons sherry (optional)
	Fresh rosemary (optional)
3	pounds pork tenderloin

Jezebel sauce:

2/3	cup pineapple preserves
1/3	cup apple jelly
2	tablespoons prepared horseradish
1	tablespoon grated fresh ginger

For the marinade, combine the soy sauce, brown sugar, onions, sherry, and rosemary in a shallow dish or a zip-lock bag. Add the pork and marinate it in the refrigerator for at least 20 minutes.

For the sauce, while the pork is marinating microwave the preserves and jelly until melted, or melt them over low heat in a saucepan. Stir in the horseradish and ginger.

Remove the meat from the refrigerator and discard the marinade. Grill the pork with the grill lid closed over medium-high heat (350 to 400 degrees) for 25 minutes, or until the internal temperature reaches 155 degrees. Turn once, basting with 1/2 cup of the sauce. Grill for another 5 to 10 minutes, or until the center temperature reaches 160 degrees. Slice and serve with the remaining sauce and fresh rosemary.

JANEY STUBBS | STARKVILLE, MISSISSIPPI

African Barbecued Pork

Yield: 6 to 8 servings

"I've had this recipe for over fifty years. It's delicious."

2	cups boiling water	1/2	teaspoon curry powder
1/2	cup dried apricots	2	teaspoons salt
2	tablespoons vegetable oil	1	tablespoon firmly packed brown sugar
1	cup thinly sliced onion	1/2	garlic clove, minced
1	teaspoon brown cooking sauce (like Kitchen Bouquet)	1/4	cup white vinegar
		2	pounds lean boneless pork

In a medium-size saucepan pour the boiling water over the apricots. Allow them to soak for 30 minutes and then cook until tender. Heat the oil and sauté the onion for 10 minutes, or until they are golden. When the apricots are done, mash them with a potato masher. Add the onion, brown sauce, curry powder, salt, brown sugar, garlic, and vinegar to the apricots in the saucepan. Bring the mixture to a boil and remove from the heat. Preheat the oven to 350 degrees. Cut the pork into 1-inch cubes. Place the pork evenly in a 13 x 9-inch baking dish. Pour the sauce over the pork. Cook, uncovered, for 11/4 hours, basting the meat several times with the sauce.

DORE C. SUTTA | PRESCOTT, ARIZONA

Hungarian Pork Chops

Yield: 4 to 5 servings

"This dish is a crowd pleaser. It's particularly good when served over mashed potatoes. You won't have to worry about leftovers."

3	tablespoons vegetable oil	1	medium onion, sliced
5	thick center-cut pork chops	1	(28-ounce) can diced tomatoes
2	banana peppers, sliced in rings (fresh or canned)	1	cup water
			Salt and pepper

In a heavy skillet heat the oil and brown the pork chops. They will not be cooked through. Add the peppers, onions, tomatoes, water, and salt and pepper to taste. Cover and simmer on low heat for about 11/2 hours, or until half the liquid has evaporated.

SHIRLEY STOTTS | BELEN, NEW MEXICO

Tips From Our Test Kitchen:

This dish also is delicious served with pasta and grated Parmesan cheese. A clove of minced garlic adds a nice flavor.

The FOOD Museum in Albuquerque, New Mexico, features dozens of exhibits on food from around the world, as well as the role played by food in entertainment and in corporate logos, and the development of different foods and drinks.

Barbecued Pork Roast

Yield: 12 to 16 servings

"I've been making this recipe since 1965, when I first tasted it at a PTA carnival at my sons' grammar school. As the ninth of thirteen children, I am accustomed to serving large groups."

4	to 6-pound lean Boston butt or other pork roast
1/2	cup ketchup
1/2	cup Worcestershire sauce
1	cup white vinegar
1 1/2	cups water
3	tablespoons firmly packed brown sugar
3	tablespoons mustard
1	teaspoon salt

1/2	teaspoon black pepper
1	teaspoon cayenne pepper
2	large onions, chopped

Sauce:

1/2	cup ketchup
1/4	cup Worcestershire sauce
1/2	cup favorite barbecue sauce
	Texas Pete (or favorite seasoning)

Place the pork roast in a large Dutch oven. Combine the ketchup, Worcestershire sauce, vinegar, water, brown sugar, mustard, salt, pepper, cayenne, and onions in a mixing bowl. Stir well and pour over the roast. Cover and cook over medium-low heat for 3 1/2 to 4 hours, or until tender enough to pull apart easily with two forks. Turn the roast every 45 minutes and check the liquid level. Add more water if needed to avoid scorching. Set the pork aside to cool slightly. Drain the excess liquid. Remove the bone and excess fat, but keep the onions. The pork can be chopped or pulled apart.

For the sauce, mix the ketchup, Worcestershire, barbecue sauce, and Texas Pete to taste together until well blended while the pork is cooking. Pour over the chopped or pulled pork, and serve the barbecued pork on buns.

PEGGY BARTHOLOMEW | IRON STATION, NORTH CAROLINA

Go Whole Hog in Newport

More than eighty cooks compete for the top prize in the annual Pig Cookin' Contest in Newport, North Carolina (pop. 3,349).

Proclaimed by organizers as the "Largest Whole Hog contest" in the country, the event features a whole pig split down the middle (without head and feet), roasted with a special sauce on a large grill. Organizers say they have always cooked whole hogs, which differentiates this event from contests that use pork shoulders only. While propane gas usually is used to cook the pigs now, during the first years cooks used blackjack oak, burned down to coals, under the pig. But with wood, the cooks had to stay up all night to keep replenishing the coals.

In addition to the cook-off, arts and crafts, carnival rides and games, live musical entertainment, and food are offered for the 15,000 annual festivalgoers in Newport Community Park.

The contest got its start in 1978 when Doris Oglesby, the director of the Newport Developmental Center, asked Mayor Derryl Garner to help her raise funds for furniture for a new wing she was adding to her school for handicapped children. Garner contacted eighteen Newport-area churches and organizations requesting their ideas to raise the money.

As luck would have it, some Newport residents had participated in a pig-cooking contest the previous weekend in Jacksonville, North Carolina. Out of that group, Larry Howard and Lionel Garner contacted the mayor with the suggestion that Newport could have a contest, too. It was decided to try it—with the goal of cooking fifteen pigs to raise the needed $5,000.

The contest was held in early 1979, and with the help of about everybody in town plus their good neighbors at the Marine Corps Air Station, forty-two pigs were cooked and $15,000 was raised and donated to the Developmental Center.

Incorporated in 1985, the festival organization has grown over the years and now has its own building filled with warmers, pots, and pans, along with a ticket booth, canteens, and souvenir trailer. Many of these supplies were donated by businesses and community groups. More than 100 volunteers work each year to organize and run the festival, which is usually held the first weekend in April.

The contest has provided more than $500,000 for the community. Recipients include sports teams, school booster groups, churches, scout groups, and community groups such as Meals-on-Wheels and the 4-H Club.

For more information, log on to www.newportpigcooking.com or call (252) 223-7447.

Gary Roberson handles public relations for the Newport Pig Cookin' Contest.

Breaded Pork Chops

Yield: 4 to 6 servings

"I've enjoyed this recipe for over fifty years. My mother made it often, and I always looked forward to it. It was one of the recipes I learned to make as a new bride."

2	eggs	1	cup bread crumbs
2	tablespoons water	6	to 8 pork chops, cut 1/2-inch thick
1/2	plus 1/2 teaspoon salt	2	plus 2 tablespoons vegetable oil
1/2	plus 1/2 teaspoon black pepper	1/2	cup cider or apple juice

Preheat the oven to 350 degrees. Break the eggs in a shallow bowl. Whisk in the water, 1/2 teaspoon salt, and 1/2 teaspoon pepper. Pour the bread crumbs in another shallow bowl, and season with the remaining 1/2 teaspoon salt and 1/2 teaspoon pepper. Wipe each pork chop with a paper towel. Dip each chop in the egg mixture, and then coat each well with the bread crumbs. Heat 2 tablespoons of the oil in a heavy skillet. Fry half the pork chops until brown on both sides. Place in a shallow baking dish. Repeat with the remaining chops in the remaining 2 tablespoons oil. When all the chops are placed in the dish, pour the cider into the baking dish. Cover with foil and bake for 30 to 40 minutes. Uncover and bake for 10 to 15 minutes longer to brown the chops. Serve hot with applesauce, potatoes, and a green vegetable.

ANGELA M. LEPITRE | CLAREMONT, NEW HAMPSHIRE

Tourtière (Pork Pie)

Yield: 8 servings

"This French pie was a special part of my childhood's Christmas Eve celebration. We ate it with all of the trimmings, exchanged gifts, listened to carols, and attended midnight mass. Those were the good old days."

3	pounds ground pork	1	teaspoon ground cinnamon
2 1/2	teaspoons salt	2/3	cup chopped onion
1/4	teaspoon black pepper		Water
1/4	teaspoon allspice	3	medium potatoes
1/2	teaspoon dried sage		Pastry for 2 double-crust pies
1	teaspoon poultry seasoning		Milk

In a large skillet combine the pork, salt, pepper, allspice, sage, poultry seasoning, cinnamon, and onion. Add enough water to cover. Simmer uncovered for 21/2 to 3 hours, mashing often with a fork during the first hour to separate the meat. The liquid will dissipate during cooking, leaving a very moist meat filling. Strain the cooked meat to remove the excess fat. Boil the potatoes until they are soft. Mash them and stir them into the meat mixture.

Preheat the oven to 450 degrees. Divide the filling into two unbaked pie shells. Place the top crusts over the pies, and brush them lightly with milk. Bake at 450 degrees for 10 minutes. Reduce the oven temperature to 350 degrees, and continue baking for 30 to 40 minutes, or until the crusts are golden.

ANITA DOUCETTE | ROLLINSFORD, NEW HAMPSHIRE

Truck Driver's Favorite Pork Chops
Yield: 4 to 6 servings

"My husband was a truck driver for thirty years. He got this recipe from a cook somewhere between Burlington, North Carolina, and Atlanta, Georgia. It became a family favorite."

3	tablespoons cooking oil	1	cup ketchup
1	cup minced onion	1/2	cup cold water
1/3	cup cider vinegar	1	tablespoon mayonnaise
2	tablespoons brown sugar	1/3	teaspoon salt
2	tablespoons mustard		Dash of Tabasco
1	tablespoon Worcestershire sauce	6	thick pork chops, well trimmed

Heat the oil in a medium saucepan, and sauté the onion until tender, but not brown. Add the vinegar, brown sugar, mustard, Worcestershire, ketchup, water, mayonnaise, salt, and Tabasco to the onions and simmer for 10 to 15 minutes. Place the pork chops in a shallow baking dish. Pour the sauce evenly over the top. Cover and refrigerate for 1 hour. Preheat the oven to 350 degrees. Uncover the dish and bake the pork chops for 1 hour, or until the meat is very tender.

ELLEN WILLIAMS | SNOW CAMP, NORTH CAROLINA

Tips From Our Test Kitchen:

Serve these chops with mashed potatoes and your favorite green vegetable.

Pork Chop and Potato Bake

Yield: 4 to 6 servings

"I took this to a sick neighbor, and he especially liked the potatoes. His wife called me the next day for the recipe."

6	thin-cut pork chops with bone	1/2	cup milk
1/2	teaspoon salt	1	(24-ounce) package frozen hash
1/8	teaspoon black pepper		browns, thawed
1	(10 3/4-ounce) can condensed cream	1/2	plus 1/2 cup shredded Cheddar cheese
	of celery soup	1/2	plus 1/2 cup French's-fried onions
1/2	cup sour cream		

Preheat the oven to 350 degrees. Lightly grease a 13 x 9-inch baking dish. Brown the pork chops in a lightly greased skillet. Season with the salt and pepper. Combine the soup, sour cream, milk, and hash browns with 1/2 cup of the cheese and 1/2 cup of the onions. Spoon the mixture into the baking dish. Layer the pork chops over the hash browns. Cover and bake for 40 minutes. Uncover, top with the remaining 1/2 cup cheese and 1/2 cup onions, and bake 8 minutes longer.

MARION KRUGER | ADRIAN, MINNESOTA

Smothered Pork Chops

Yield: 4 servings

3	to 4 pork chops	1/2	cup diced onion (optional)
	Favorite spices (such as salt, pepper,	1	(10 3/4-ounce) can condensed cream
	rosemary, basil, or Italian seasoning)		of mushroom soup
1/2	cup water (or more as needed)	1/2	cup red wine (or more to taste)

Remove the excess fat from the chops. Spread the spices and herbs over the chops, and using a meat tenderizer mallet, beat them into the meat. Brown the chops on one side in a skillet over medium heat. Pour the water in the skillet, turn the chops over, and brown the opposite side. If the water evaporates, add 1/2 to 1 cup water. Stir in the onion if using. Add the soup and wine. Cover the skillet, lower the heat, and simmer for 1 hour. As the chops cook, add water if needed to maintain gravy consistency.

MARY FORREST | HEARNE, TEXAS

Sauerkraut and Ribs

Yield: 6 to 8 servings

"My husband told me about this favorite family recipe when we first married. We had both been picky eaters, but this recipe taught us to love sauerkraut."

2	quarts sauerkraut	1	large apple (skin on), cored and diced
2	cups firmly packed brown sugar		Water (enough to cover the sauerkraut)
1	large onion, diced	2	pounds country pork ribs

Preheat the oven to 350 degrees. In a large roaster combine the sauerkraut, brown sugar, onion, and apple. Add enough water to reach the top of the sauerkraut. Place the ribs on top. Cover and cook for 4 hours. Check occasionally to be sure the water has not evaporated, and add more water, 1 cup at a time, if needed. Uncover the ribs and cook for an additional hour.

DEBRA BRALEY | GLADWIN, MICHIGAN

Tips From Our Test Kitchen:

It is important to maintain the water level so that the sauerkraut is not overcooked. This dish is very simple to prepare and is excellent with potatoes.

Sweet-and-Sour Spareribs

Yield: 6 to 8 servings

"Everyone says that my ribs are really good and better than those served at a famous rib restaurant. They make an excellent 'warm-up' dinner and an easy guest meal."

1/2	cup firmly packed brown sugar	1/2	cup barbecue sauce
1/2	cup granulated sugar	1/2	cup chopped onion
2	tablespoons cornstarch	4	teaspoons chili powder
1	cup ketchup	5	to 6 pounds boneless pork ribs
2/3	cup white vinegar		

Preheat the oven to 350 degrees. Mix the brown and granulated sugars, cornstarch, ketchup, vinegar, sauce, onion, and chili powder in a medium-size saucepan. Stir over low heat until well mixed, thick, and clear.

Place the ribs in a shallow roasting pan. Cover with foil and bake for 1 hour, or until the fat is cooked out. Discard the liquids. Pour the sauce over the ribs and bake, uncovered, for 45 minutes to 1 hour.

JANET HARPST | GREENVILLE, PENNSYLVANIA

Tips From Our Test Kitchen:

Serve these tasty and filling ribs with mashed potatoes, a green vegetable, and rolls for a great company meal. The sugar in the sauce can be decreased by half if desired.

Skillet Ham Barbecue

Yield: 4 servings

"I started making this recipe in the 1960s as a new bride trying to stretch the food budget. We like to entertain. This dish pleases everyone."

2	tablespoons butter or margarine
1/2	cup chopped onion
1/4	cup firmly packed brown sugar
2	tablespoons white or cider vinegar
1	tablespoon mustard
1	cup ketchup
1	tablespoon Worcestershire sauce
1/2	cup pineapple chunks (strain and reserve 1/3 cup juice)
12	ounces ham or canned luncheon meat, cut into 1/2-inch strips
1/2	cup (1/2-inch) green bell pepper strips
	Cooked rice, noodles, or hamburger buns

In a large skillet melt the butter, and cook the onion until soft but not browned. Stir in the brown sugar, vinegar, mustard, ketchup, Worcestershire sauce, and the reserved pineapple juice. Add the ham, pineapple, and bell pepper strips. Simmer, uncovered, for 15 minutes. Serve over cooked rice, noodles, or toasted hamburger buns.

EDNA McCALLION | TEHACHAPI, CALIFORNIA

Tips From Our Test Kitchen:

Drain the excess juice before serving this dish on buns. This is an excellent use for left-over ham and is also good on flour tortillas.

Lamb and Green Beans over Rice

Yield: 6 servings

"My grandmother used to make this dish for her family. My aunt and I have carried on the tradition of making it for the entire extended family. The spices make it unique."

1	(28-ounce) can diced tomatoes
1 1/2	(28-ounce) cans water
	Salt and pepper
1	pound green beans, cut in 1-inch pieces, uncooked
3/4	teaspoon ground cinnamon
3/4	teaspoon allspice
1	medium eggplant, peeled and cut into 1-inch cubes
2	tablespoons margarine or olive oil
1	pound boneless lamb stew meat
1	cup sliced onion
1	medium potato, cut into 1-inch cubes

Place the tomatoes into a large kettle. Add the water. Bring to a boil, and reduce the heat. Season with the salt and pepper to taste. Add the green beans, cinnamon, and allspice. Cover loosely, and

Tips From Our Test Kitchen:

The longer this tasty dish cooks, the more tender the lamb will be. Add 2 cloves of minced garlic when browning the meat if desired. Chopped fresh mint makes a nice garnish.

boil slowly until the beans are slightly cooked. Stir in the eggplant, and continue cooking, still covered loosely, at a slow boil. In another pan, melt the margarine, and brown the lamb and onion. Add the lamb, onion, and potato to the large kettle. Cook until the vegetables and meat are tender, about 1 hour, stirring occasionally to prevent burning. Allow the liquids to cook down and become thick enough to make a sauce. Adjust the seasonings to taste and serve over rice.

JAN HUGHES | NIAGARA FALLS, NEW YORK

Dairy farming is New York's most important agricultural activity, with more than 18,000 cattle and calving farms.

Chinese-Style Rice

Yield: 4 servings

"I recall my mother's teaching me how to make this recipe when I was a girl. It is fairly simple and versatile. I've added celery and other meats besides pork to fit my family's tastes. It was served with biscuits and sometimes with salad or soup as a side dish, depending on how many people were eating."

4	eggs	2	cups cooked meat (pork, chicken, beef,
	Vegetable oil		and/or shrimp), cut into strips
1	small onion, chopped		Thyme (or favorite Asian seasonings)
2	celery stalks, chopped		Soy sauce
4	cups cold, cooked rice		Salt

Beat the eggs with a small amount of water, and cook them, omelet style, in a greased or nonstick frying pan. Cut the cooked eggs into strips. Heat a small amount of the oil, and sauté the onion and celery. Add the rice, eggs, meat, and the thyme, soy sauce, and salt to taste. Heat thoroughly.

Note: To stretch this dish for more than 4 servings, add 1 egg and 1/2 cup cooked meat for each additional serving.

AMIE A. CONANT | LOVELAND, COLORADO

Tips From Our Test Kitchen:

For additional color and flavor, add some snow peas, baby corn, or strips of red bell pepper.

233

*Tips From Our
Test Kitchen:*

Boiled new potatoes or
rice make ideal side
dishes.

Baked Seasoned Salmon

Yield: 4 servings

"Salmon is especially good when prepared this way. It's a quick and healthful dish. By the time I fix a salad and set the table, dinner is ready."

1	pound salmon fillets or steaks, thawed	1	teaspoon prepared mustard
1	tablespoon cider vinegar	1/8	teaspoon black pepper
1	tablespoon Worcestershire sauce	1/2	cup (1 stick) butter, melted
1	tablespoon lemon juice		Paprika
1	teaspoon salt		Chopped parsley

Preheat the oven to 450 degrees. Arrange a single layer of the fish in a shallow baking dish. Combine the vinegar, Worcestershire, lemon juice, salt, mustard, pepper, and butter. Pour half of the sauce over the fish. Bake for 20 minutes, basting occasionally with the remaining sauce. Sprinkle with paprika and chopped parsley.

FRANKIE ROLAND | COFFEYVILLE, KANSAS

Honey-Pecan Salmon

Yield: 4 servings

"I was tired of preparing salmon the same way all the time. I put together some of my favorite foods to prepare this mouth-watering recipe."

1/4	cup extra virgin olive oil	1 1/2	cups well-chopped pecans
3	tablespoons honey, plus additional for drizzling	1/2	tablespoon dried parsley or 1 1/2 table- spoons chopped fresh parsley
4	(4-to 6-ounce) salmon fillets		Salt and pepper

Preheat the oven to 425 degrees. Lightly grease a 13 x 9-inch baking dish. Mix the olive oil with 3 tablespoons of the honey in a medium bowl. Dip each fillet in the honey mixture, and then roll and press it in the pecans. Place in the prepared baking dish. Sprinkle with the parsley and salt and pepper to taste. Drizzle a bit more honey over each fillet. Bake for 10 minutes, or until the fish flakes with a fork.

SHANNON ALEXANDER | HEBRON, MARYLAND

Catch the Shrimp Festival in Sneads Ferry

The Sneads Ferry Shrimp Festival, begun in 1971, celebrates the North Carolina town's main industry—shrimping and fishing—and the men and women who earn their living from the sea.

A dedicated group of volunteers known as the Sneads Ferry Shrimp Festival Committee works all year long to ensure a fun-filled festival for the Onslow County community and beyond.

Every year during the second weekend in August, the small fishing town of 2,248 swells to more than 16,000 for the two-day festival held at the Sneads Ferry Community Center on Park Avenue.

The kickoff of the festival actually begins months before with a pageant to crown the three shrimp queens for the year, who represent the town throughout North Carolina for the next year. The eight- to eleven-year-olds compete for Little Miss Shrimp, the twelve- to fourteen-year-olds for Miss Shrimp, and the fifteen- to eighteen-year-olds vie for Shrimp Festival Queen. Prospective contestants are interviewed, and those chosen go on to the next stage of the competition: Little Miss Shrimp and Miss Shrimp contestants don their fancy dresses for the event, while the Shrimp Festival Queen contestants compete in evening gowns.

On the first day of the festival, the annual parade winds through the streets and down along the waterfront. The parade grounds open with more than 100 artists and craftspeople from all parts of the Southeast selling everything from handcrafted woodwork to high-quality artwork, sculpture, jewelry, and beadwork. Food vendors have something to satisfy the most discriminating palettes. Skills of the locals are highlighted in the shrimp-heading and shrimp-peeling contest, and children enjoy pony rides, a train ride, and other activities.

Food is plentiful at the festival, but the main food attraction is the Shrimperoo Dinner, which serves up a fried or boiled shrimp dinner with all the fixin's. In 2005 the Shrimp Cook-off was added to the slate of events, to feature the culinary talents of local residents.

Two stages showcase live entertainment ranging from country and rock 'n' roll to gospel and bluegrass music. On Saturday night, fireworks light up the sky, and festivalgoers enjoy a street dance. Sunday features shag dance and karaoke singing contests.

Throughout the festival, there are reminders of the area's reliance on the sea and a steady focus on Sneads Ferry's annual harvest—385 tons of shrimp, 25 tons of flounder, and about 493 tons of clams, scallops, oysters, grouper, mullet, and other fish.

For more information, log on to www.sneadsferryshrimpfestival.com or call the community center at (910) 327-3335.

Irene Lambert is the Sneads Ferry Shrimp Festival secretary.

*Tips From Our
Test Kitchen:*

This quick main dish is
great with a crispy
green salad.

Salmon Rice au Gratin

Yield: 4 to 6 servings

"I really like making casseroles and have made this for years, passing it on to family and friends."

1/4	cup (1/2 stick) butter or margarine, plus more for dotting on top
1/2	cup chopped celery
2	tablespoons minced onion
2	tablespoons all-purpose flour
1	teaspoon salt
	Dash of black pepper
1	cup milk

1	(10¾-ounce) can condensed cream of mushroom soup
2	cups cooked rice
1	(16-ounce) can salmon, drained, boned, and flaked
8	ounces shredded American cheese
	Bread crumbs or cracker crumbs

Preheat the oven to 350 degrees. Grease a 2-quart casserole dish. Melt 1/4 cup butter in a saucepan. Add the celery and onion and cook until the onion is transparent. Add the flour, salt, and pepper. Mix in the milk and soup, stirring until the sauce is smooth. Stir in the rice, salmon, and cheese, and pour the mixture into the prepared dish. Top with bread crumbs or cracker crumbs and dot with butter. Bake for 25 to 30 minutes.

LILLIAN C. SCHMIDT | GREEN VALLEY, ARIZONA

Snapper Tropical

Yield: 4 to 6 servings

"This recipe reminds my husband and me of the tropics every time we make it. We use red snapper, but salmon or any white fish can be used."

1	cup frozen raspberries, thawed
2	tablespoons sugar
1	teaspoon lemon juice
1/4	cup vegetable oil
4	red snapper fillets (about 8 ounces each)
4	tablespoons all-purpose flour
1/2	cup fish stock or unsalted chicken broth

1/2	cup sherry
4	fresh basil leaves, chopped
1/4	cup frozen orange juice concentrate
1	tablespoon butter
2	cups diced fresh fruit (bananas, oranges, or strawberries)
	Salt and pepper

Combine the raspberries, sugar, and lemon juice in a saucepan, and cook until thickened, 6 to 8 minutes. Strain the sauce through a sieve. Cool in the refrigerator.

Preheat the oven to 350 degrees. Heat the vegetable oil in an ovenproof pan. Dredge the snapper in the flour and shake off the excess. Sauté both sides of the snapper in the oil until lightly brown. Remove the fish fillets and discard the oil. Deglaze the pan using the fish stock and sherry; cook for 2 to 3 minutes. Add the basil, orange juice concentrate, and butter to thicken the sauce. Add the fresh fruit and the salt and pepper to taste. Place the pan in the oven for 4 to 5 minutes. To serve, spoon the fruit over the snapper, and drizzle the raspberry sauce on top.

CATHERINE PAWELEK | LITTLETON, NEW HAMPSHIRE

> **The first potato known to have been planted in New Hampshire was on the common at Londonderry (pop. 800) in 1719.**

Crunchy Coated Walleye

Yield: 4 to 6 servings

"My husband and I live on the St. Mary's River. I'm always looking for new ways to prepare our daily catch. The potato flakes give this recipe an extra crunch."

2/3	cup all-purpose flour	1/2	teaspoon garlic powder
2	teaspoons paprika	4	eggs
1	teaspoon seasoned salt	3	cups dry mashed potato flakes
1/2	teaspoon black pepper	3	pounds walleye, perch, or pike
1/2	teaspoon onion powder	2/3	cup vegetable oil for frying

Combine the flour, paprika, salt, pepper, onion powder, and garlic powder in a medium bowl. In a separate bowl beat the eggs. Pour the potato flakes into a third bowl. Dip the pieces of fish in the eggs. Then dip them into the flour mixture, coating both sides. Next dip the floured fish into the egg wash again. Finally, dip the pieces into the potato flakes until well coated. Heat the oil in a skillet over medium-high heat, and fry the fish for about 5 minutes, turning once, or until cooked through. Serve hot.

BRENDA EAGLE-RANSOM | SAULT STE. MARIE, MICHIGAN

Hot Seafood Casserole

Tips From Our Test Kitchen:

This special dish is ideal for a brunch or a ladies luncheon. It's also good with 1/4 cup cooking sherry added to the seafood mixture before baking.

"This time-tested favorite was given to me in a recipe box as a wedding shower gift thirty-eight years ago. Just add a fruit salad and a green vegetable."

1	green bell pepper, chopped	1/2	teaspoon salt
1	medium onion, chopped	1/8	teaspoon black pepper
1	cup chopped celery	1	teaspoon Worcestershire sauce
1	(6-ounce) can crabmeat, flaked	1	cup mayonnaise
1	pound shrimp, cleaned, cooked, and cut in small pieces	1	cup buttery cracker crumbs

Preheat the oven to 350 degrees. Combine the green pepper, onion, celery, crabmeat, and shrimp in a medium bowl. Season with the salt and pepper. Stir in the Worcestershire sauce and mayonnaise. Mix gently. Spoon the crabmeat mix into an 8-inch square baking dish or individual ramekins. Sprinkle with the buttery cracker crumbs. Bake for 30 minutes.

NANCY FLORES | RUIDOSO, NEW MEXICO

Tuna-Chip Casserole

"This recipe was handed down from my mother, who made it for us (five) kids. We used to beg for it and would scrape the pot when it was gone. It's not too eye-appealing, but the more you eat, the more you want."

1	(10 3/4-ounce) can condensed cream of mushroom soup	1	(6-ounce) can drained tuna fish (packed in water, preferably)
1/2	(10 3/4-ounce) can water	1	(6-ounce) bag regular potato chips
1/2	(10 3/4-ounce) can milk		Shredded Cheddar cheese

Mix the soup with the water and milk in a large saucepan. Flake in the drained tuna. Mix thoroughly while heating over low to medium heat. Crunch the bag of potato chips into bits, and add to the soup-tuna mixture. Stir until all the chips are soaked. Remove from the heat and let sit a few minutes. Stir and serve, garnished with the shredded cheese. Green peas are a good complement to the casserole. The recipe is readily doubled or tripled.

JOE REIN | MIDLOTHIAN, VIRGINIA

Creole Jambalaya

Yield: 6 to 8 servings

"I am not a native of Louisiana, but I was married to one for fifty-eight years. My husband's sister made this dish for all family reunions because it's what everyone likes."

2	tablespoons butter or margarine	1	(10½-ounce) can beef broth
3/4	cup chopped onion	1	(10½-ounce) soup can water
1/2	cup chopped celery	1	cup uncooked long grain rice
1/4	cup chopped green bell pepper	1	teaspoon sugar
1	tablespoon chopped parsley	1/2	teaspoon dried crushed thyme leaves
1	garlic clove, minced	1/2	teaspoon chili powder
2	cups cubed fully cooked ham,	1/2	teaspoon black pepper
1	(28-ounce) can diced tomatoes, undrained	1½	pounds raw shrimp, peeled and deveined

Melt the butter in a Dutch oven. Add the onion, celery, green pepper, parsley, and garlic. Cover and cook until tender. Add the ham, tomatoes, broth, water, rice, sugar, thyme, chili powder, and pepper. Cover and simmer until the rice is tender, about 25 minutes. Add the shrimp and simmer until the shrimp are cooked through, about 10 minutes.

RUBY WILLIAMS | BOGALUSA, LOUISIANA

Tips From Our Test Kitchen:

This recipe can be seasoned according to taste. Hot sauce can be added to make it fiery. Smoked sausage can substitute for the ham if desired.

Italian Pasta

Yield: 6 to 8 servings

"My mother was born in Italy, and she always served this dish hot with Italian sausage or diced chicken. I serve it cold as a pasta salad."

1	cup olive oil	3	cloves garlic, diced
1	teaspoon dried basil	3	Roma tomatoes, sliced
1	teaspoon dried oregano	2	ounces Romano cheese, grated
1	teaspoon salt	1	pound bow-tie pasta
1	teaspoon black pepper		

Mix the oil, basil, oregano, salt, pepper, garlic, tomatoes, and cheese in large bowl. Cook the pasta according to package directions. Drain the pasta, add to the dressing, and serve or allow the pasta to cool, mix with the dressing, and refrigerate until cold.

MARINA DEEB | SANTA CLARITA, CALIFORNIA

Tips From Our Test Kitchen:

When fresh Roma tomatoes are out of season, use sweet grape tomatoes. Garnish this dish with fresh basil and parsley and grated Romano or Parmesan cheese. If you aren't used to fresh garlic, sauté it in a small amount of olive oil.

Baked Manicotti

Yield: 6 servings

"I became chief cook and bottle washer when my wife became disabled in 1995. She was always a great cook. I've co-opted some of her recipes. This is one of our favorites."

1	(8-ounce) box manicotti shells (14 shells)	4	large garlic cloves, minced
8	plus 4 ounces shredded mozzarella cheese	2	small, or 1 large, eggs
4	plus 4 ounces shredded Parmesan cheese	1	pound ricotta cheese
		1	teaspoon dried oregano
1	(10-ounce) box frozen spinach, thawed and drained	1	teaspoon dried basil
		1	(26-ounce) jar spaghetti sauce with basil
		1	(4-ounce) can chopped black olives

Cook the pasta according to the package instructions, drain, and rinse. Preheat the oven to 350 degrees. In a medium mixing bowl, combine 8 ounces of the mozzarella cheese, 4 ounces of the Parmesan cheese, the spinach, garlic, eggs, ricotta cheese, oregano, and basil. Mix well. Lightly grease a 13 x 9-inch baking dish. Spoon the cheese mixture into the pasta shells, and place them side-by-side in the baking dish. Spread the spaghetti sauce evenly over the shells. Sprinkle the black olives and the remaining 4 ounces mozzarella and 4 ounces Parmesan cheeses over the sauce. Bake for 50 minutes.

DUANE GROSHART | WORLAND, WYOMING

Angelo's Dish

Yield: 3 to 4 servings

"This recipe was given to me by a Greek neighbor in 1966. I've never found anyone who doesn't like it."

1/4	cup plus 3 tablespoons extra virgin olive oil	1	tablespoon garlic salt (or to taste)
1	pound lamb, beef, or pork, cut into 1-inch cubes	1/2	tablespoon black pepper (or to taste)
		4	cups cooked rice
1/2	medium onion, diced	1/2	cup Parmesan cheese

Tips From Our Test Kitchen:

This dish is so good that you'll want to make a double batch. The leftovers are great.

Heat 3 tablespoons of the oil in a heavy skillet, and brown the meat until no longer red. Add the onions, and sauté for 1 minute longer. Add the garlic salt and enough water to cover the meat. Add the pepper according to taste. Cook over low heat for 2 hours, or until the meat is very tender. Check the water level occasionally to prevent scorching the meat. When the meat is almost ready, shape the cooked rice into a ring on a platter. Sprinkle the cheese evenly over the rice. Heat the remaining 1/4 cup of oil quickly in a skillet. Spoon the meat into the center of the ring. Pour the hot oil over the rice. Pour the pan juices into a gravy boat, and serve alongside the meat dish.

JUDY PIERCE | PAHRUMP, NEVADA

Baked Ziti Pasta

Yield: 5 to 7 servings

"I was tired of trying ziti recipes that didn't taste good, so I made up my own. My family loves it. My dad says it is his favorite."

Cheese mixture:
15 ounces ricotta cheese
2 eggs, beaten
1/2 teaspoon dried basil
1/2 teaspoon dried oregano
1/2 teaspoon parsley flakes
1/2 teaspoon black pepper
1/4 teaspoon garlic powder

Filling:
12 ounces spaghetti sauce
12 ounces ziti pasta, cooked
1 pound Italian sausage, cooked
1/2 pound mozzarella cheese, shredded
1/4 cup grated Parmesan cheese

Preheat the oven to 375 degrees. Grease a 13 x 9-inch baking dish with olive oil.

For the cheese mixture, combine the ricotta cheese with the eggs, basil, oregano, parsley flakes, pepper, and garlic powder.

For the filling, layer the spaghetti sauce, pasta, Italian sausage, ricotta cheese mixture, and mozzarella cheese in the baking dish. Sprinkle the Parmesan cheese on top. Cover and bake for 20 minutes. Uncover and bake for an additional 20 minutes. Serve with breadsticks and salad.

CARRIE LEE | TAHLEQUAH, OKLAHOMA

Tips From Our Test Kitchen:

Use fresh herbs and fresh garlic in the dish when available. To achieve the same flavors with fresh herbs, use three times the amount of dried herbs called for in the recipe.

Belzoni: Where Catfish Rule

It used to be known as "Greasy Row" back in the 1800s, when it was little more than a short stretch of hardscrabble saloons along the banks of the Yazoo River. Others called it "the Dark Corner of Washington County," a place with no official name, no local government, and no law enforcement.

By the time it became the seat of newly formed Humphreys County (the last to be formed in Mississippi) in 1918, it finally had a name—Belzoni—bestowed on it by a local plantation owner, Alvarez Fisk. Fisk was a great admirer of Giovanni Belzoni (1778-1823), an Italian engineer, circus performer, and explorer of Egyptian antiquities.

Today, Belzoni, Mississippi (pop. 2,663), and Humphreys County also are known as the "Catfish Capital of the World."

Each year in April, about 20,000 people visit Belzoni to pay tribute to the whiskered fish at the World Catfish Festival. The annual day of celebration includes a catfish-eating contest, talent showcase, arts and crafts, entertainment, and the crowning of the Catfish Queen.

Visitors also have an opportunity to learn about the thriving catfish business in the area. Humphreys County has more than 40,000 acres in use for this aquacultural commodity. Catfish in this case are a crop like any other, farm-raised under stringent conditions in shallow, man-made ponds, then processed and shipped across the nation and around the world.

Catfish farming is a relatively new phenomenon to Belzoni, where for decades farmers had tried their hands at such crops as cotton and soybeans in the clay-heavy soil that makes up much of the Mississippi Delta land. Farmers were looking for a better use for these soils that made traditional crops difficult to grow. All this available acreage, plus a deep aquifer descending at 150 to 180 feet across much of the area, and a warm growing season of 180 to 220 days made Humphreys County ideal for catfish farming, which began there in the 1960s.

The fish are fed high-protein floating pellets, made predominately from soybeans, to give them a mild flavor with no "fishy" undertaste. The ponds are monitored constantly for water quality and dissolved oxygen levels during the warmer months of the year—if the oxygen level gets low, farmers can easily lose all their fish in a night.

The catfish business has spawned a catfish museum, The Catfish Capitol, in Belzoni, showcasing the industry and its practices and featuring outdoor sculpture made from spawning tanks, hatchery tanks, and seining nets. The Catfish Institute, a national trade organization, makes its home in Belzoni as well, establishing catfish-raising standards and sending recipes and pro-catfish messages across the globe.

For more information, log on to www.catfishcapitalonline.com or call (800) 408-4838.

Michael Depp is writer from New Orleans, Louisiana.

Stuffed Shells with Pumpkin

Yield: 6 to 8 servings

"I developed this recipe after I tasted some squash-stuffed ravioli in a restaurant. I raise a lot of squash and pumpkin. This is a great way to prepare it."

1	(12-ounce) package jumbo pasta shells	2	cups cooked pumpkin or squash
1/2	cup (1 stick) butter or margarine	2	cups ricotta cheese
1/4	cup plus 2 tablespoons all-purpose flour	1	cup chopped raw spinach
11/2	cups milk or more		Salt and pepper
1	plus 1/2 cups grated Parmesan or Romano cheese	1	garlic clove, crushed
		1	cup shredded mozzarella cheese

Preheat the oven to 350 degrees. Boil the pasta shells until done and rinse in cold water. Do not overcook, or the shells will tear when being stuffed. Prepare the sauce while the pasta is boiling.

Melt the butter in a medium-size saucepan. Stir in the flour. Continue stirring while adding the milk. When the sauce thickens, stir in 1/2 cup of the Parmesan cheese. If the sauce is too thick, add another 1/2 cup milk. Season to taste.

Lightly grease a 2-quart baking dish. Combine the pumpkin, ricotta, the remaining 1 cup Parmesan cheese, the spinach, salt and pepper to taste, and garlic. Stuff the shells with the filling. Place them in the baking dish. There should be about 30 shells. Cover the shells with the sauce. Sprinkle the mozzarella evenly over the top. Bake for 30 to 35 minutes, or until golden and bubbly. Allow to rest for 10 minutes before serving.

SELENDA GIRARDIN | NEWBURY, VERMONT

Tips From Our Test Kitchen:

Gruyère is a nice substitute for the mozzarella. Add a teaspoon of ground nutmeg to the filling or sauce for a mellow flavor.

In 2000, Vermont became the first state to receive a federal grant for farm-based tourism. A survey by the Vermont Agritourism Initiative indicates that a third of Vermont farms offer some type of agritourism, generating $10.5 million annually.

Lazy Pierogi

Yield: 8 servings

"This recipe was shared with me many years ago. My family has been enjoying it ever since."

15	lasagna noodles	1/4	teaspoon salt
2	cups cottage cheese or ricotta cheese	1/4	teaspoon garlic powder
1	egg, slightly beaten	1/8	teaspoon black pepper
1/4	teaspoon onion salt	1	cup (2 sticks) butter or margarine
1	cup grated Cheddar cheese	1	cup diced onion
2	cups mashed potatoes		

Cook the noodles according to the package instructions. Drain and rinse.

Preheat the oven to 350 degrees. Lightly grease a 13 x 9-inch baking dish. Place a layer of noodles on the bottom of the prepared dish. In a medium bowl mix the cottage cheese with the egg and onion salt. Pour the mixture over the noodles and spread evenly. Cover with another layer of noodles. Mix the Cheddar cheese, potatoes, salt, garlic powder, and pepper until well blended. Spread over the second layer of noodles. Top with a third layer of noodles. Melt the butter in a skillet and sauté the onion. Pour this evenly over the noodles. Cover with foil and bake for 30 minutes.

KATHLEEN KECHNIE | WEATHERFORD, TEXAS

Cynthia's Spinach Quiche

Yield: 6 servings

"This quiche has always been popular with my family of ten. It's delicious and easy to prepare."

4	to 6 large eggs	1/2	cup grated Romano cheese
1	teaspoon salt	1	(10-ounce) package frozen spinach, thawed and very well drained
1/2	teaspoon black pepper		
8	ounces mozzarella cheese, cut into cubes	1	unbaked piecrust Pepperoni (optional)

Preheat the oven to 350 degrees. Beat the eggs with the salt and pepper in a medium mixing bowl. Stir in the mozzarella, Romano, and spinach. Add the pepperoni, if using. Pour the mixture into the piecrust and bake for 35 to 45 minutes, or until the center is set.

CYNTHIA CLARK | MANASSAS, VIRGINIA

Vegetable Pizza

Yield: 8 slices

"I am eleven years old and have been interested in cooking for most of my life. This recipe is for people who like vegetable pizza and don't like pepperoni."

1	(16¼-ounce) can extra large biscuits	1/2	cup sliced purple onion
1/2	cup pizza or spaghetti sauce	1/2	cup diced green bell pepper
8	ounces mozzarella cheese, shredded	1	cup sliced mushrooms
1	(2½-ounce) can black olives	1/2	cup sliced tomatoes (optional)

Preheat the oven to 375 degrees. Separate each biscuit into two or three layers. Pat them out, and spread them evenly over a lightly greased 12-inch pizza pan or cookie sheet. Bake for about 8 minutes, or until lightly browned. Remove from the oven and cover with the sauce. Spread half the cheese evenly over the sauce, and add the olives, onion, pepper, mushrooms, and the tomatoes, if using. Sprinkle on the remaining cheese, and bake for 8 to 10 minutes, or until the cheese melts.

AUSTIN BOYS | GREENEVILLE, TENNESSEE

Tips From Our Test Kitchen:

Sprinkle 1 tablespoon dried oregano on top for a traditional pizza flavor. Experiment with your own favorite vegetables.

One-Pot Noodle Stroganoff

Yield: 2 to 4 servings

"I have modified this recipe to lower the fat and salt content. It's full of nourishment and flavor and has been a favorite for many years."

1	tablespoon olive oil	6	ounces whole wheat noodles, uncooked
1	pound mushrooms, sliced		
1	cup chopped onion	1	cup low-fat, or no-fat, sour cream
1	quart low-salt tomato juice	1	teaspoon dried dill weed or
	Black pepper		3 teaspoons fresh
2	teaspoons Worcestershire sauce		

Heat the olive oil in a large pan, and sauté the mushrooms and onion until just browned. Stir in the tomato juice, pepper to taste, and Worcestershire sauce. Bring to a low boil. Add the noodles. Reduce the heat, cover, and simmer for about 10 minutes, stirring occasionally until the noodles are tender. Stir in the sour cream and dill weed and heat through. Adjust the seasonings to taste.

MARY ELLEN BAKER | KEUKA PARK, NEW YORK

Tips From Our Test Kitchen:

For variety, toss in 6 to 8 ounces of baby spinach, 1 cup of shoestring carrots, or 1/2 cup of diced sweet peppers or fresh asparagus. Garnish with fresh sliced tomatoes, chopped parsley, and fresh dill.

Desserts

Blueberry Pound Cake

Yield: 12 servings

"We live on a blueberry farm. My daughter gave me this recipe several years ago. We've shared it with many of our blueberry customers."

1	(18¼-ounce) box butter flavored cake mix	1/2	cup vegetable oil
8	ounces cream cheese, softened	3	eggs
		2	cups blueberries

Preheat the oven to 325 degrees. Lightly grease and flour a 10-inch tube pan. Combine the cake mix, cream cheese, oil, and eggs. Beat until very smooth. Gently fold in the berries. Spoon into the prepared tube pan, and bake for about 1 hour, or until a toothpick inserted in the center comes out clean.

DONNA ROANE | ABERDEEN, MISSISSIPPI

Tips From Our Test Kitchen:

This cake is so easy to prepare. Serve it with whipped cream that has been flavored with 1/2 teaspoon almond extract.

Heavenly Cake

Yield: 12 servings

"I tried a recipe for chocolate cake. It was very good, but some of my friends and family cannot eat chocolate. I took out the chocolate and made 'heavenly' cake. I love both of them."

1	(18¼-ounce) box white cake mix	1/4	cup (1/2 stick) margarine
1	cup chopped walnuts or pecans	8	ounces cream cheese, softened
1	(3½-ounce) can sweetened flaked coconut	1	(16-ounce) box confectioners' sugar

Preheat the oven to 350 degrees. Grease a 13 x 9-inch baking pan. Prepare the cake batter according to the package instructions. Cover the bottom of the pan with the nuts and coconut. Pour the cake batter evenly over the top. Melt the margarine in a bowl or medium-size saucepan. Add the cream cheese and sugar. Mix well. Spoon the cream cheese mixture over the batter and bake for 40 to 42 minutes. You can't test this cake for doneness because it is so gooey.

LINDA VENTURA | ALLIANCE, OHIO

Tips From Our Test Kitchen:

Experiment by substituting your favorite cake mix, such as strawberry or cherry.

Apple Cake

Yield: 12 to 14 servings

"The following recipe has been in my family since I was eight years old. I am now seventy-seven. I buy tart apples—they are the best. I make twelve cakes at a time, freeze them in aluminum foil, and have them all year. The cakes actually taste better after they are frozen. I thaw a cake and put it in a 350-degree oven for 10 minutes and serve."

6	to 8 tart apples, depending on size of apples	2	teaspoons baking powder
2	eggs	2	cups all-purpose flour
1	cup sugar		Sugar
1	cup milk		Ground cinnamon
1/2	teaspoon salt		Butter

Preheat the oven to 350 degrees. Grease two 9-inch cake pans or one 13 x 9-inch pan. Peel and chop the apples. Beat the eggs in a large bowl. Add the sugar and milk and beat again. In a separate bowl combine the salt, baking powder, and flour, and add to the egg mixture. Beat all together. Pour into the prepared cake pans. Cover the batter with the apples. Sprinkle with the sugar and cinnamon and dot with the butter. Bake for about 30 minutes.

DORIS ELFLEIN | CALICOON, NEW YORK

Fresh Apple Cake with Caramel Glaze

Yield: 14 to 16 servings

"I wanted the taste of caramel apples and added the glaze to a recipe I had used before. It was a brilliant idea, and I would never serve it 'plain' again."

Cake:

1/4	cup cinnamon sugar	1/2	teaspoon baking soda
4	apples, chopped small (may leave on peel)	1	teaspoon ground cinnamon
3	eggs		**Glaze:**
1	cup vegetable oil	2	tablespoons butter
2	cups all-purpose flour	1/2	cup firmly packed light brown sugar
2	cups sugar	2	tablespoons milk

Tips From Our Test Kitchen:

This cake is delicious served with only the glaze, but it is also good with a dollop of whipped cream or scoop of vanilla ice cream. Nut lovers can add 1 cup chopped walnuts or pecans to the cake batter.

For the cake, preheat the oven to 350 degrees. Grease a Bundt or tube pan, and coat it well with the cinnamon sugar. Mix the apples, eggs, and oil with an electric mixer. Add the flour, sugar, baking soda, and cinnamon and mix well. Pour into the prepared pan and bake for about 1 hour, or until a toothpick inserted in the center comes out clean. Allow the cake to rest in the pan for at least 10 minutes, and then invert it onto a cake plate.

For the glaze, combine the butter, brown sugar, and milk in a medium-size saucepan. Bring to a boil and cook for 1 minute. Spoon the glaze over the cake. Allow the cake to cool before serving.

DIANE NEMITZ | LUDINGTON, MICHIGAN

Apple Grunt with Gravy

Yield: 12 to 14 servings

"This recipe has been in my family for years. For reasons unknown my children always have called it 'grunt and gravy.' My son-in-law and grandson always make sure ingredients for this dessert are on hand when I visit."

Filling (grunt):

4	to 5 apples, peeled and sliced
1/4	cup (1/2 stick) butter, softened
1	teaspoon ground cinnamon
1	teaspoon ground nutmeg
1	cup sugar

Shortcake crust:

2	cups all-purpose flour
3	teaspoons baking powder
1	teaspoon salt

1	teaspoon sugar
1/3	cup vegetable oil
2/3	cup milk

Vanilla sauce (gravy):

1	cup sugar
2	to 3 tablespoons cornstarch
2	cups water (or milk)
1/4	cup (1/2 stick) butter
2	teaspoons vanilla extract

Preheat the oven to 375 degrees.

For the filling, generously grease an 8-inch-square baking dish. Stir the apples, butter, cinnamon, nutmeg, and sugar together in a bowl, and spoon the mixture into the prepared dish.

For the crust, mix the flour, baking powder, salt, sugar, vegetable oil, and milk. Spoon over the apples. Bake for 35 to 40 minutes, or until golden. Cool slightly and serve with the vanilla sauce.

While the cake is cooling, prepare the sauce. Stir the sugar, cornstarch, and water over medium heat in a small saucepan until thick. Add the butter and vanilla. Stir until creamy. To serve, pour the "gravy" over each serving of "grunt."

HAZEL HYDEMAN | PRESCOTT, ARIZONA

Tips From Our Test Kitchen:

This tasty apple treat is easier to prepare than apple pie. Serve it warm with vanilla ice cream.

Peach Times in Chilton County

A 150-foot-tall water tank in the shape of a peach marks the spot—Clanton, Alabama (pop. 7,800), is the site of the week-long Chilton County Peach Festival that attracts as many as 20,000 festivalgoers each June. Festivities include the Peach Queen Pageants, Peach Festival Cook-Off, Peach Fashion Show, Peach Art Show, Peach Jam Jubilee, Peach Classic Car Show, Peach Run, Rotary Club Peach Fishing Tournament, Peach Parade, and the Peach Auction.

The Peach Jam Jubilee, which kicks off the week's events on Friday, features music, food, arts, crafts, and entertainment. The Peach Pageants currently award prizes and scholarships for four different age groups: Miss Peach (ages fifteen to eighteen), Junior Miss Peach (ages twelve to fourteen), Young Miss Peach (ages eight to eleven), and Little Miss Peach (ages five to seven).

Sponsored each year by Peoples Southern Bank of Clanton, the Peach Art Show awards prizes in the junior and adult categories to Chilton County artists.

Recipes for appetizers, main dishes, and desserts are judged at the Peach Festival Cook-Off Contest for adults and youth. All participants are encouraged to use their imaginations; the only requirement is they have to use fresh Chilton County peaches. Prizes provided by the Clanton Lions Club are awarded to the winning entries.

On Saturday morning, after the pageants are over and the queens have been crowned, festivalgoers are entertained at the Peach Parade, featuring bands and floats and cars carrying the queens, local dignitaries, and state and federal officials.

Immediately after the parade, peach growers show off their produce at the Peach Auction at the Clanton City Park Complex. They bring their finest peaches for judging on size, color, quality, and taste. The top ten growers are awarded cash prizes, and then the baskets of peaches are auctioned to the highest bidder. The money raised funds for programs serving underprivileged children in Chilton County and scholarships for the Miss Peach Pageant.

Billed as "a fitting tribute to Chilton's rapid progress as a peach-producing district, ranking in the forefront of an agricultural Southland," the county's first peach festival was held on Wednesday, July 16, 1947, and was the brainchild of J. Archie Ogburn, a former cashier at the Bank of Thorsby in Thorsby, Alabama (pop. 1,820).

Chilton County's mild winters and warm summers make it a good location for growing the sweet fruit, and the peach industry has become a mainstay of its economy. At its peak as many as 10,000 acres were filled with peach orchards, and today peaches bring in about $13 million in revenue to the area.

For more information, log on to www.aces.edu/Chilton/pages/peachfest.tmpl or call (202) 755-6740.

Tiffany Cannon is a writer for The Clanton Advertiser *in Clanton, Alabama.*

Cherry Coffeecake

Yield: 12 to 14 servings

"This recipe was given to me by my mother-in-law when I first married more than forty-four years ago. I've made it many times—it's so easy. Now my daughter makes it. It must be good because all three of us, through the years, have won local contests with this recipe."

Cake:

1   egg
     Milk
1   cup sugar
2   cups all-purpose flour
2   teaspoons baking powder
1/2   cup (1 stick) margarine, softened
2   (21-ounce) cans cherry pie filling

Topping:

1   cup all-purpose flour
1   cup sugar
1/2   cup (1 stick) margarine, softened
1/2   cup chopped nuts (optional)

Preheat the oven to 350 degrees. For the cake, break the egg into a measuring cup, and add enough milk to make 1 cup. In a mixing bowl combine the sugar, flour, and baking powder, and mix in the margarine. Combine the sugar mixture with the milk mixture. Pour into a 13 x 9-inch pan. Pour the cherry pie filling on top of the batter.

For the topping, mix the flour, sugar, and margarine until crumbly. Add the nuts if using. Spread the crumbs over the top of the cherries and bake for 40 minutes, or until lightly browned. Serve warm or cold.

Lorraine Kruse | Louisville, Illinois

In 1914, Bayard and Everett Heath opened a confectionery and ice cream shop in Robinson, Illinois (pop. 6,822), and by 1928 had perfected their recipe for Heath English toffee bars.

Orange Cake

Yield: 12 to 14 servings

"My mother made this cake back in the 1930s when I was growing up in Wisconsin. It's best served with whipped cream or ice cream on top. My mom is looking down from heaven saying, 'Enjoy.'"

1	small orange	1	cup buttermilk
1	plus 1/2 cups sugar	1/2	teaspoon salt
1/2	cup solid vegetable shortening or margarine	2	cups all-purpose flour
2	large eggs	1	cup ground raisins
1	teaspoon baking soda	1	cup chopped walnuts (optional)

Preheat the oven to 350 degrees. Grease and flour a 13 x 9-inch baking pan. Grate the orange and reserve the zest. Squeeze the orange and reserve the juice. With an electric mixer blend 1 cup of the sugar with the shortening and eggs. Mix well. Stir the baking soda into the buttermilk. Add the salt to the flour. Add the flour and buttermilk mixtures alternately to the creamed ingredients, and mix well. Fold in the orange zest, raisins, and walnuts if using. Spoon the mixture into the prepared pan. Bake for 35 to 40 minutes, or until a toothpick inserted in the center comes out clean.

While the cake is baking, stir the remaining 1/2 cup sugar into the reserved orange juice. When the cake is done and still warm, poke holes with a dinner fork over the entire top of the cake. Pour the orange juice mixture evenly over the cake.

FRANCES CHASE | VACAVILLE, CALIFORNIA

Tips From Our Test Kitchen:

This cake is a great basic. Add candy sprinkles (jimmies) to the batter for a festive touch. It's also nice with a light glaze, ice cream, fruit, or chocolate sauce.

Gary's Sponge Cake

Yield: 12 to 14 servings

"My husband, Gary, discovered this recipe when we were newlyweds in 1954. It's been our traditional family birthday cake for the past fifty years."

6	eggs, separated (room temperature)	1/4	teaspoon salt
1 1/2	teaspoons baking powder	1/2	cup cold water
1 1/2	cups sugar	1	teaspoon vanilla extract
1 1/2	cups all-purpose flour		

Preheat the oven to 325 degrees. Beat the egg whites until foamy. Add the baking powder and beat until the egg whites are stiff and hold peaks. In a separate bowl beat the egg yolks until thick and lemon colored. Add the sugar to the egg yolks, 1/2 cup at a time. Combine the flour and salt, and add alternately with the water and vanilla extract to the egg yolks. Blend well. Fold the egg whites into the egg yolk mixture. Spoon carefully into an ungreased angel food cake pan. Bake for about 1 hour. Turn upside down to cool for 1 hour.

MARGE MANKE | JEFFERSON, WISCONSIN

Peach Pound Cake

Yield: 12 to 14 servings

"I have served this several times at small dinner parties. Everyone loves it. They ask to take a slice home if there are any leftovers."

1	cup (2 sticks) butter, softened (no substitutes)	1/4	teaspoon baking soda
2	cups granulated sugar	1/4	teaspoon salt
6	eggs	1/2	cup sour cream
1	teaspoon almond extract	2	cups diced peaches (fresh or frozen, thawed and drained)
1	teaspoon vanilla extract		Confectioners' sugar
3	cups all-purpose flour		

Preheat the oven to 350 degrees. Grease and flour a 10-inch fluted tube pan. Beat together the butter and granulated sugar in a large bowl. When light and fluffy, add the eggs one at a time, beating after adding each addition. Stir in the almond and vanilla extracts. In a separate bowl combine the flour, baking soda, and salt. Add the flour mixture to the creamed butter mixture alternately with the sour cream. Fold in the peaches. Do not overstir. Spoon the peach mix into the prepared pan. Bake for 1 hour to 1 hour and 10 minutes, or until a toothpick inserted in the center comes out clean. Dust with confectioners' sugar.

DOROTHY DRONEBURG | FREDERICK, MARYLAND

Tips From Our Test Kitchen:

This taste-of-summer dessert is also good with a light lemon glaze.

Maple Cheesecake

Yield: 12 servings

"I've been preparing this cheesecake recipe with our award-winning Vermont Grade A Dark Syrup for a long time. It's fun to make—just six ingredients."

Crust:
2 cups honey graham cracker crumbs
1/4 cup (1/2 stick) butter, melted
1/4 cup maple sugar (or substitute 1/4 cup granulated sugar and 1/2 teaspoon maple flavoring)

Filling:
4 eggs, beaten
1 cup real maple syrup
24 ounces cream cheese, softened

Preheat the oven to 350 degrees. For the crust, combine the graham cracker crumbs, butter, and maple sugar. Press into a 9-inch springform pan to form the crust.

For the filling, in a mixing bowl combine the eggs, maple syrup, and cream cheese, and beat until very smooth. Pour the filling mixture over the crust. Bake for 1 hour. Cool and serve.

PAULINE COUTURE | WESTFIELD, VERMONT

Raspberry Cheesecake

Yield: 8 to 10 servings

"All the summers I picked raspberries along the fencerows and creeks, I would take them home and freeze them. Then I came up with this recipe. At our family get-togethers, my grandchildren always want this dessert."

Crust:
11/2 cups graham cracker crumbs
1/3 cup butter, melted
3 tablespoons granulated sugar

Filling:
8 ounces cream cheese, softened
3/4 cup sifted confectioners' sugar
1 teaspoon vanilla extract (optional)
11/2 cups whipped topping

Sauce:
1 cup granulated sugar
1 cup water
3 tablespoons cornstarch
3 tablespoons raspberry gelatin
2 cups fresh or frozen raspberries

Preheat the oven to 350 degrees. For the crust, mix the graham cracker crumbs, butter, and granulated sugar together, and press into the bottom of an 11 x 7-inch baking dish. Bake for 8 to 10 minutes and cool.

For the filling, whip the cream cheese in a bowl using an electric mixer. Mix in the sugar and vanilla if using. Fold in the whipped topping. Spread on top of the cooled crust. Put the cheesecake in the refrigerator.

For the sauce, combine the granulated sugar, water, and cornstarch in a medium-size saucepan, and cook over low heat until thick and clear. Remove from the heat, add the gelatin, and stir until dissolved. Allow to cool, and then add the fresh raspberries. (If the raspberries are frozen, add to the sauce before it cools.) Spread the raspberry mixture on top of the cream cheese layer, and refrigerate until the raspberry layer is thick.

GLADYS FLEDDERJOHANN | ST. MARY'S, OHIO

Pig Eatin' Cake

Yield: 16 to 18 servings

"Begin with a box, end with a beauty, and eat like a pig. This is an easy and excellent cake to take to parties, and I've used it on many occasions."

Cake:

1 (18 1/4-ounce) box Duncan Hines Golden Butter Recipe cake mix
1 (15-ounce) can mandarin oranges with juice
3 eggs
1/2 cup vegetable oil or 1 stick margarine

Frosting:

1 (16- ounce) container nondairy whipped topping
1 (3 1/2-ounce) box instant vanilla pudding
1 (16-ounce) can crushed pineapple, drained

Preheat the oven to 350 degrees. For the cake, grease three cake pans. Combine the cake mix, mandarin oranges, eggs, and oil. Beat on medium speed for 4 minutes. Pour into the prepared pans. Bake for 20 to 25 minutes. Allow to cool.

For the frosting, mix the whipped topping, pudding mix, and crushed pineapple together. Spread between each layer and frost the top of the assembled cake.

NANCY CHOP | LADY LAKE, FLORIDA

Tips From Our Test Kitchen:

You don't need to frost the sides of this cake. Garnish with extra mandarin oranges and fresh strawberries.

Miss Grace's Carrot Cake

Yield: 12 servings

"My grandmother baked this for so many celebrations and special family times. We all loved it and will continue her baking tradition."

Cake:
13/4 cups granulated sugar
4 eggs
11/4 cups vegetable oil
2 cups all-purpose flour
2 teaspoons baking powder
2 teaspoons ground cinnamon
1 teaspoon salt
1 teaspoon baking soda

3 cups grated carrots
1/2 cup chopped pecans

Frosting:
12 ounces cream cheese, softened
5 tablespoons margarine
11/2 (1-pound) boxes confectioners' sugar
11/2 cups chopped pecans

Preheat the oven to 350 degrees. For the cake, grease and flour three 8-inch round cake pans. Beat together the granulated sugar, eggs, and oil. In a separate bowl sift together the flour, baking powder, cinnamon, salt, and baking soda, and stir until blended. Combine the creamed mixture with the dry mixture, and stir until blended. Gently stir in the carrots and pecans until evenly distributed. Pour into the cake pans and bake for about 20 minutes, or until a toothpick inserted in the center comes out clean. Cool before frosting.

For the frosting, mix the cream cheese and margarine. Stir in the confectioners' sugar, and blend until creamy. Add the pecans. Frost the cooled cakes.

KELSI MCCOOL | COLUMBUS, GEOGIA

W. S. and Ethel Stuckey opened their first Stuckey's pecan shop in Eastman, Georgia (pop. 5,440), in 1937, and business took off like Ethel's pecan log rolls. By 1964, more than 100 Stuckey's stops sweetened highway travelers.

A Taste of the Apple in Springville

The Springville Apple Festival, which began with a few food and crafts booths along the main street of town in 1980, boasts more than 200 booths today and draws 25,000 to 30,000 visitors to the small California town. The two-day festival takes place the third weekend of October and was originally organized in Springville (pop. 1,109) by a group of women seeking to create a fund-raiser for the Springville Community Club.

The apple theme seemed appropriate since apple orchards were an early and important feature in Tulare County, dating back to the late 1800s of the Southern Sierra Nevada foothills where Springville is located. Community club-women first began baking pies in their homes, freezing them, and bringing them to sell at a booth during the apple festival. Today, everyone comes together at the Veteran's Memorial Building's state-certified kitchen, where cooks put on their gloves, set up an assembly line, and make 1,000 apple pies over a week's time. Some women have the special touch to make and roll out crusts; others measure the spices and assemble the pies; still others are excellent crust crimpers. While the ladies make the pies, the men from the Lion's Club do the baking; this is truly a cooperative effort. The pies are stored in a huge cold room until the day of the Apple Festival. Pie sales account for a large part of the club's annual budget, and all proceeds are used to support community programs.

Taking in hundreds of vendor applications, the Apple Festival Committee carefully selects only those with the finest arts and crafts and best food. Over the years, many other features have been added to the festival. Besides traditional pie-eating contests and a bake-off, the festival hosts the annual Fat Tire Classic, a mountain bike race along a challenging and scenic route with several competitive tiers for children and adults of varying skill levels. The Apple Run includes 5K, 10K, and children's races, plus a two-mile walk. Festivalgoers also enjoy live entertainment.

The whole town gears up for the apple festival. Because the crowds are large and the town is small, guests are asked to park in the rodeo grounds just west of town, and they are shuttled to and from town in buses that depart every twenty minutes throughout the day.

For more information, log on to www.springville.ca.us/applefest/index.html or call (559) 539-0619.

Sandy Whaling is publicity chair for the Springville Apple Festival and Springville Community Club.

Prune Cake

Yield: 10 to 12 servings

"In 1966 my mother-in-law gave me a jar of prune preserves along with a recipe. I've made a few changes over the years. Friends, neighbors, and family love this cake."

Cake:

4	eggs
2	cups sugar
1	cup vegetable oil
1/2	teaspoon salt
1	teaspoon baking soda
1	cup buttermilk
2	cups all-purpose flour
1	teaspoon ground nutmeg
1	teaspoon cloves
1	teaspoon ground cinnamon
1	cup bite-size pieces pitted prunes

Frosting:

1	cup sugar
1/4	teaspoon baking soda
1/2	cup buttermilk
2	tablespoons butter
1/4	teaspoon salt
1	teaspoon vanilla extract

Preheat the oven to 350 degrees. For the cake, grease and flour a 10-inch tube pan. Beat the eggs in a medium bowl. Add the sugar and beat well. Mix in the oil. In a small bowl dissolve the baking soda in the buttermilk. Sift the flour, nutmeg, cloves, and cinnamon. Add the flour mixture alternately with the buttermilk mixture to the egg mixture. Fold in the prunes. Pour the batter into the prepared pan, and bake for about 1 hour or until a toothpick inserted in the center comes out clean.

When the cake is almost ready to be removed from the oven, prepare the frosting. Combine the sugar, baking soda, buttermilk, butter, and salt in a medium saucepan. Bring to a boil over high heat. Remove from the heat and stir in the vanilla. Pour the frosting over the cake while both are still warm. Poke holes into the cake with a fork or long toothpick so the cake will soak up this thin icing.

MARY PRIETO | LOS LUNAS, NEW MEXICO

Tips From Our Test Kitchen:

The prunes tear apart easily when soaked briefly in boiling water. After draining, they can be torn by hand. The baking powder causes the icing to foam up while cooking.

Biscochito (biz-co-cheeto) is the official New Mexico state cookie, adopted in 1989 as a sweet tribute to the early Spaniards. The anise-flavored shortbread cookie is popular at weddings, baptisms, and on holidays.

The South Arkansas Vine Ripe Pink tomato was adopted in 1987 as the official state fruit—and vegetable.

Pumpkin Roll

Yield: 12 servings

"I enjoy baking Pumpkin Roll because it's quick. It makes an attractive dessert, and everyone seems to like it."

Cake:

1	cup granulated sugar
3	eggs, beaten
2/3	cup canned pumpkin
3/4	cup all-purpose flour
1	teaspoon salt
1	teaspoon ground cinnamon
1	teaspoon baking soda
3/4	cup chopped pecans

Filling:

8	ounces cream cheese
1	teaspoon vanilla extract
2	tablespoons margarine
1	cup confectioners' sugar, sifted, plus extra for rolling the cake

Preheat the oven to 375 degrees. For the cake, mix the granulated sugar, eggs, and pumpkin in a bowl. Sift the flour, salt, cinnamon, and baking soda into another bowl. Combine the flour and pumpkin mixtures. Grease a rimmed baking sheet with oil, and line it with greased wax paper. Extend the paper over the sides of the baking sheet. Pour the batter in a rectangular shape on the wax paper, and sprinkle with the pecans. Bake for 15 minutes.

For the filling, beat the cream cheese, vanilla, margarine, and confectioners' sugar until smooth and creamy.

Sprinkle a clean dish towel with the extra confectioners' sugar and flip the cake top down onto the towel. Remove the wax paper. Loosely roll the cake and allow it to cool. Unroll the cake. Spread with the filling. Roll again without the dish towel. Wrap the cake in aluminum foil and freeze. To serve, remove the aluminum foil and slice the roll while frozen. Thaw the cake in the refrigerator. Serve chilled.

WANDA COWARD | PARAGOULD, ARKANSAS

Tunnel Cake

"My family has made this cake for special occasions over the years. My daughter and family carried on this tradition even while working as missionaries in Brazil."

Filling:

1/4 cup granulated sugar
1 teaspoon vanilla extract
8 ounces cream cheese, room temperature
1 egg
1/2 cup flaked coconut
1 cup chocolate chips

Batter:

2 cups granulated sugar
1 cup vegetable oil
2 eggs
3 cups all-purpose flour
3/4 cup cocoa powder
2 teaspoons baking soda
2 teaspoons baking powder
1 1/2 teaspoons salt
1 cup hot coffee or water
1 cup buttermilk or sour milk
1 teaspoon vanilla extract
1/2 cup chopped walnuts or pecans (optional)

Glaze:

3 tablespoons cocoa powder
1 cup confectioners' sugar
2 tablespoons butter
2 teaspoons vanilla extract
1 to 3 tablespoons water

For the filling, mix the sugar, vanilla, cream cheese, egg, coconut, and chocolate chips together in a small bowl until well blended.

Preheat the oven to 350 degrees. For the batter, grease and lightly flour a 10-inch tube or Bundt pan. Combine the sugar, oil, and eggs, and beat for 1 minute at high speed. Add the flour, cocoa, baking soda, baking powder, salt, coffee, buttermilk, and vanilla. Beat for 3 minutes at medium speed. Stir in the nuts by hand. Pour half the batter into the prepared pan. Carefully spoon the filling over the batter. Top with the remaining batter. Bake for 1 hour and 10 minutes to 1 hour and 15 minutes, or until the top springs back when touched. Cool upright in the pan for 15 minutes. Remove from the pan and cool completely.

For the glaze, stir together the cocoa, confectioners' sugar, butter, and vanilla while the cake is cooling. Add the water until the desired consistency is reached. Drizzle over the cooled cake.

LEONA PERRY | CARO, MICHIGAN

Grandmother Benton's Gold Cake

Yield: 16 to 18 servings

"This is one of the best pound cakes you'll ever eat. It's super when served warm out of the oven with berries, butter, or ice cream . . . if you must."

3	cups sugar	3	cups all-purpose flour
11/2	cups solid vegetable shortening	11/2	teaspoons vanilla extract
9	small eggs	11/2	teaspoons almond extract

Preheat the oven to 350 degrees. Generously grease and flour a large tube pan. Beat the sugar and shortening until fluffy. Add the eggs and flour alternately, beating well after each addition. Stir in the vanilla and almond extracts. Spoon the batter into the prepared pan. Place this pan on a cookie sheet or pizza pan in case the batter overflows during baking. Bake for 1 hour and 25 minutes. Check the cake after 1 hour. If it's already golden, place an aluminum foil tent over the top to prevent the cake from becoming too brown.

LINDA BENTON SMITH | MCKINNEY, TEXAS

Tips From Our Test Kitchen:

This is a very heavy, old-fashioned cake. It's ideal for a tea. It's also excellent for packing in lunches or for picnics.

Grady's Plain Cake

Yield: 12 to 14 servings

"I once worked with a lady whose mom made this cake for us to take in our lunch boxes. Since it isn't iced and is moist and dense, it is perfect to pack in a lunch."

6	large eggs	1/4	teaspoon ground cinnamon
1	cup vegetable oil	1/4	teaspoon ground nutmeg
1/4	teaspoon ground allspice	2	cups all-purpose flour
1/4	teaspoon ground cloves	13/4	cups sugar

Preheat the oven to 350 degrees. Generously grease and flour a tube pan. In a large bowl slightly mix the eggs and with the oil. Combine the egg mixture with the allspice, cloves, cinnamon, nutmeg, flour, and sugar. Mix well. The batter will be very thick. Spoon the mixture into the prepared pan. Bake for about 1 hour. The cake is done when a toothpick inserted in the center of the cake comes out clean. Remove the cake from the pan when cool.

RITA FLENER | CROMWELL, KENTUCKY

Tips From Our Test Kitchen:

This plain cake is moist and a bit spongy with a sweet and slightly crunchy crust. It also would be good with a teaspoon of your favorite extract, such as vanilla or almond, added to the batter.

Gypsy Round Layer Cake

Yield: 12 to 14 servings

"When I walk through the door on Christmas Day, I am overwhelmed with a sense of pride when everyone looks to see if I'm carrying the blue Tupperware filled with this special cake."

Cake:

3/4	cup solid vegetable shortening
1 1/2	cups granulated sugar
3	eggs, beaten
2	cups cake flour
1/2	teaspoon baking powder
1/2	teaspoon baking soda
1/2	teaspoon salt
3/4	teaspoon ground nutmeg
1	teaspoon ground cinnamon
2	tablespoons cocoa powder
1	cup buttermilk
1	teaspoon vanilla extract
1	teaspoon lemon extract
1/2	cup chopped walnuts or pecans

Mocha icing:

6	tablespoons butter, softened
1	egg yolk
3	cups confectioners' sugar
1 1/2	tablespoons cocoa powder
1	teaspoon ground cinnamon
1 1/2	tablespoons hot coffee

Preheat the oven to 350 degrees. For the cake, grease and flour two 8-inch round cake pans. In a medium mixing bowl, beat the shortening with the granulated sugar until fluffy. Add the eggs and blend.

In a separate bowl sift together the flour, baking powder, baking soda, salt, nutmeg, cinnamon, and cocoa. Add to the creamed sugar mixture alternately with the buttermilk. Stir in the vanilla extract, lemon extract, and nuts. Pour into the prepared pans and bake for 30 minutes, or until the center is set. Set aside to cool.

For the icing, cream together the butter, egg yolk, confectioners' sugar, cocoa, cinnamon, and coffee until smooth and fluffy. Add another tablespoon hot coffee or more sugar if needed to improve the texture. Frost the top of each layer of the cake when cooled, and then assemble the layers. Store this cake in the refrigerator.

OCTAVIA FLECK | MOREHEAD, KENTUCKY

Bybee Pottery near Richmond, Kentucky (pop. 27,152), is the oldest existing pottery west of the Allegheny Mountains. The Cornelison family has operated it since 1809.

Chocolate Morsel Cake

Yield: 14 to 16 servings

"This is always a hit with friends and family. My mother gave me the recipe many years ago."

1   (18¼-ounce) box devil's food cake mix
1   (3-ounce) box instant chocolate
    pudding mix
1   egg, beaten

1¾ cups milk
6   ounces chocolate morsels
1/3 cup confectioners' sugar

Preheat the oven to 350 degrees. Grease and flour a 13 x 9-inch baking pan. Stir together the cake mix, pudding mix, egg, and milk. (This will be very sticky.) Spoon the mixture into the prepared pan. Sprinkle the chocolate morsels evenly over the top. Bake for 30 to 35 minutes, or until the top springs back to the touch. Cool then sprinkle with the confectioners' sugar.

LISA ROWETT | MINERAL WELLS, TEXAS

> *Tips From Our Test Kitchen:*
>
> This quick cake also can be made with butterscotch pudding and butterscotch morsels.

Chocolate-Zucchini Cake

Yield: 12 to 16 servings

"This recipe is a family favorite. My daughter's coworkers make requests for it too."

1/2 cup (1 stick) margarine, softened
1/2 cup vegetable oil or applesauce
1¾   cups sugar
2   eggs, beaten
1   teaspoon vanilla extract
2½   cups all-purpose flour
4   tablespoons cocoa powder
1/2 teaspoon baking powder

1   teaspoon baking soda
1/2 teaspoon ground cloves
1/2 teaspoon ground cinnamon
1/2 cup sour milk
2   cups finely diced zucchini
1/4 cup chocolate chips plus extra
     for the top

Preheat the oven to 325 degrees. Grease and flour a 13 x 9-inch baking dish. Beat together the margarine, oil, and sugar. Stir in the eggs and vanilla. Combine the flour, cocoa powder, baking powder, baking soda, cloves, and cinnamon. Stir the flour mixture into the sugar mixture alternately with the milk. Add the zucchini and 1/4 cup chocolate chips. Pour into the baking dish. Sprinkle extra chocolate chips over the top. Bake for 40 to 45 minutes, or until a toothpick inserted in the center comes out clean.

BARBARA GRIBBEN | FLORENCE, COLORADO

> *Tips From Our Test Kitchen:*
>
> Chocolate lovers will be pleased when you add 1 whole cup chocolate chips to the batter and sprinkle another cup over the top.

Red Velvet Cake

Yield: 12 to 14 servings

"I baked many 'red velvet' cakes before this recipe. Some were hard, and others were awful. This one is moist and has become a family favorite."

Cake:

2 1/2	cups self-rising flour
1 1/2	cups granulated sugar
2	eggs
1 1/2	cups vegetable oil
1	tablespoon baking soda
1	tablespoon vanilla extract
1	ounce red food coloring
1	cup buttermilk
1	tablespoon cocoa powder
1	tablespoon white vinegar

Icing:

7	cups confectioners' sugar
16	ounces cream cheese, softened
3/4	cup (1 1/2 sticks) margarine
1	teaspoon vanilla extract

Preheat the oven to 350 degrees. For the cake, lightly grease and flour three 9-inch round pans. In a large bowl mix the flour, granulated sugar, eggs, oil, baking soda, vanilla, and food coloring. In another bowl combine the buttermilk, cocoa powder, and vinegar. Stir well. Pour the buttermilk mixture into the flour mixture and blend well. Pour the batter into the pans, and bake for 20 to 25 minutes, or until the center springs back to the touch. Allow to cool for about 10 minutes, and then turn the layers onto wax paper.

For the icing, mix together the confectioners' sugar, cream cheese, margarine, and vanilla until creamy and thick. Spread on the cooled cake layers.

CARLA CHAMPION | BUFFALO, SOUTH CAROLINA

Chocolate Earthquake Cake

Yield: 12 to 14 servings

"This cake looks like it's been through a disaster, but don't worry. It's so rich and delicious that no one will get a very long look at it."

1	box German chocolate cake mix
1	cup chopped walnuts or pecans
1	(3 1/2-ounce) can sweetened flaked coconut
1/4	cup (1/2 stick) margarine
8	ounces cream cheese, softened
16	ounces confectioners' sugar

Preheat the oven to 350 degrees. Grease a 13 x 9-inch baking pan. Prepare the cake batter according to package instructions. Cover the bottom of the pan with the nuts and coconut. Pour the cake batter on top. Melt the margarine in a bowl. Add the cream cheese and confectioners' sugar. Stir to blend. Spoon the cream cheese mixture over the unbaked batter, and bake for 40 to 42 minutes. You can't test for doneness with this sticky cake. The icing sinks to the bottom while baking and makes a gooey white ribbon throughout.

JEAN BEARRICK | CHANUTE, KANSAS

German Chocolate Cake

Yield: 16 servings

"This is my absolute favorite kind of cake. I have it every year on my birthday. The recipe came from my mom and has long been a family favorite."

Cake:

1/4 cup cocoa powder
1/2 cup boiling water
1 teaspoon vanilla extract
1 cup (2 sticks) butter
21/4 cups sugar
4 eggs
2 cups all-purpose flour
1 teaspoon baking soda
1/2 teaspoon salt
1 cup buttermilk

Frosting:

1 cup evaporated milk
1 cup sugar
1 egg, beaten
1/2 cup (1 stick) butter
1 teaspoon vanilla extract
11/3 cups flaked coconut
1 cup chopped pecans

> *Tips From Our Test Kitchen:*
>
> There is not a shortcut in preparing this frosting. Stir as directed until it thickens. It will become a light amber color and will thicken at just about 12 minutes.

Preheat the oven to 350 degrees. For the cake, grease and flour three 9-inch round cake pans. Mix the cocoa and boiling water in a measuring cup. When cool, add the vanilla to the cocoa mixture. Cream the butter and sugar until fluffy. Add the eggs one at a time. In a separate bowl combine the flour, baking soda, and salt. Alternately add the flour mixture and the buttermilk to the creamed mixture. Pour the batter into the cake pans and bake for 25 to 30 minutes. Cool on wire racks while making the frosting.

For the frosting, cook the milk, sugar, egg, and butter in a saucepan over medium heat. Stir constantly until thickened, about 12 minutes. Remove from the heat, and add the vanilla, coconut, and pecans. Allow the cake to cool before frosting. Frost only the top of each cake layer.

AMBER MCNAMEE | FARMINGTON, UTAH

Brunswick's Homegrown Pecan Pride

Diners always can find a slice of pecan pie at Sherry's Home Cookin' Cafe in Brunswick, Missouri. The pie's homemade, but, even better, the pecans are homegrown too.

This north-central Missouri river town of 925 is the nation's northernmost pecan producer. The 3 million pounds of pecans harvested each year in Chariton County are just a plunk in the bucket compared to Georgia's 100 million pounds, but the town couldn't be prouder of its annual nut crop. While southern pecans are larger, locals swear the meat from northern pecans is sweeter and tastier.

Brunswick's annual Pecan Festival, held in October, promotes the crop and its growers and draws 3,000 to 5,000 attendees each year. About 100 of the town's best bakers prepare pecan pies for judging during the bake-off. Other activities include a parade, pet show, talent contest, musical entertainment, a baby contest, softball game, crafts, and pecan treats aplenty.

Wild native pecans long have been a wild delicacy in Chariton County, but the pecan industry didn't boom around Brunswick until the late George James began experimenting with a thin-shell variety he discovered on his farm in 1947. Stark Brothers Nursery in Louisiana, Missouri, has offered the Starking Hardy Giant Pecan, or *Carya illinoinensis* 'James,' ever since.

New machinery makes pecan harvesting safer and faster than in the old days when farmers would climb the towering trees while wielding five-pound wooden clubs to whack the nuts from the branches. Today's mechanical shaker on a tractor grabs the tree trunk like a giant fist and shakes it hard enough to knock the nuts off their limbs. A pecan harvester vacuums up the nuts, removing twigs and other debris. Pecans are cracked individually as they roll along a conveyor belt through a mechanical cracker.

Modern conveniences aside, it's the tradition of pecan growing and harvesting that Brunswick's residents celebrate each fall. Older residents recall times when gleaning pecans off the forest floor saved them from starvation. Others remember watching their parents jump from tree to tree at harvest time. And everyone looks forward to freshly baked pecan pie!

For more information, log on to www.brunswickmo.com or call (660) 548-3028.

Marti Attoun is a freelance writer from Joplin, Missouri.

Coca-Cola Cake

Yield: 12 to 16 servings

"My mother used to bake Coca-Cola Cake for me when I was a child. It was a favorite in our home. In memory of my mother, I share this recipe with American Profile *readers."*

Cake:

2	cups all-purpose flour
2	cups granulated sugar
1/2	teaspoon baking soda
1	cup (2 sticks) margarine
1	cup Coca-Cola
3	tablespoons cocoa powder
1 1/2	cups miniature marshmallows
1/2	cup buttermilk
1	teaspoon vanilla extract
2	eggs, beaten

Icing:

4	cups confectioners' sugar
1/2	cup (1 stick) margarine
6	tablespoons Coca-Cola
3	tablespoons cocoa powder
1	teaspoon vanilla extract
1	cup chopped pecans

> *Tips From Our Test Kitchen:*
>
> This delicious, old-fashioned cake is a great take-along and is ideal for a crowd.

Preheat the oven to 350 degrees. For the cake, generously grease and flour a 15 x 10-inch pan. Combine the flour, granulated sugar, and baking soda in a mixing bowl. In a saucepan combine the margarine, Coca-Cola, and cocoa powder, and stir until boiling. Remove from the heat and stir into the flour mixture. Add the marshmallows, buttermilk, vanilla, and eggs and mix well. Pour into the prepared pan. Bake for 30 to 35 minutes, or until the center is set.

For the icing, measure the confectioners' sugar into a mixing bowl while the cake is baking. Melt the margarine in a saucepan. Add the Coca-Cola and cocoa and stir until boiling. Remove from the heat and pour the mixture over the confectioners' sugar. Add the vanilla and beat on high speed for 2 minutes. Stir in the pecans and pour over the hot cake.

LISA BROWN | ALBERTVILLE, ALABAMA

The National Peanut Festival is held each fall in Dothan, Alabama (pop. 57,737), to celebrate the harvest. Roughly half the peanuts grown in the United States are raised within 100 miles of Dothan.

Heath Bar Brunch Cake

Yield: 12 to 14 servings

*Tips From Our
Test Kitchen:*

You can substitute
8 ounces Heath Toffee
Bits for the Heath bars.

"I received this recipe forty-six years ago. I didn't realize at the time that it would become a family favorite. It goes to every family reunion and family gathering."

2	cups all-purpose flour	1	cup buttermilk
1	cup firmly packed brown sugar	1	egg
1/2	cup granulated sugar	1	teaspoon baking soda
1/2	cup (1 stick) butter or margarine, melted	4	to 5 Heath bars, chopped
1	teaspoon vanilla extract	1	cup chopped pecans
	Pinch of salt		

Preheat the oven to 350 degrees. Generously grease a 13 x 9-inch baking dish. Mix together the flour, brown sugar, granulated sugar, margarine, vanilla, and salt. Set aside 3/4 cup of this mixture to use for the topping. To the remaining flour mixture, add the buttermilk, egg, and baking soda. It will be lumpy, but do not use an electric mixer. Pour the batter into the prepared baking dish.

Add the Heath bars and pecans to the reserved flour mixture. Spread evenly over the top of the batter. Bake for 35 to 40 minutes, or until the center is done.

MILDRED BIELSER | MONMOUTH, ILLINOIS

Southern Sweet Chocolate

Yield: 9 servings

*Tips From Our
Test Kitchen:*

This dessert holds
together in a square,
but it is on the gooey
side. Fresh berries and
whipped cream on the
top round out the flavor
and texture.

"This is always a favorite with our family, especially at holiday times. I find the texture is unique because it is not a pudding or a cake."

1	(4-ounce) bar German sweet chocolate	2	eggs
1/4	cup (1/2 stick) butter or margarine	1	teaspoon vanilla extract
1	(12-ounce) can evaporated milk	1	cup flaked coconut
1 1/2	cups sugar	3/4	cup chopped pecans
3	tablespoons cornstarch		Whipped cream or whipped topping
1/4	teaspoon salt		

Preheat the oven to 375 degrees. Melt the chocolate and butter in a saucepan over low heat. Remove from the heat and add the evaporated milk. Mix the sugar, cornstarch, and salt in a bowl. Beat in the eggs and vanilla and add this to the chocolate mixture. Mix the coconut and pecans in a separate bowl. Pour the chocolate mixture into an 8-inch square pan. Sprinkle with the coconut and pecan mixture. Cover with aluminum foil and bake for 55 minutes. Cool in the refrigerator. When ready to serve, top with whipped cream or whipped topping.

ARLETTA SLOCUM | VENICE, FLORIDA

Schimpff's Confectionery has been producing fine handmade candies in downtown Jeffersonville, Indiana (pop. 25,787), since 1891.

Swedish Nut Cake

Yield: 12 to 15 servings

"As a pastor's wife, I often was given extra good recipes. This one was given to me several years ago. I have used it many times, and I'm usually asked for the recipe. It is simple and an excellent cake to take to dinners."

Cake:
2   cups granulated sugar
2   cups all-purpose flour
2   eggs
1/2 teaspoon baking soda
1   (20-ounce) can crushed pineapple
    with juice
1/2 cup chopped walnuts or pecans

Frosting:
1   cup firmly packed brown sugar
1/4 cup (1/2 stick) margarine, softened
8   ounces cream cheese, softened
    Chopped walnuts or pecans for topping

Preheat the oven to 350 degrees. For the cake, grease a 13 x 9-inch baking pan. Mix the granulated sugar, flour, eggs, baking soda, and pineapple with juice in a mixing bowl. Add the nuts and pour into the prepared pan. Bake for 40 minutes.

For the frosting, mix the brown sugar, margarine, and cream cheese in a bowl. Spread on the cake while it is hot. Sprinkle with the nuts.

HELEN DICKSON | PLYMOUTH, INDIANA

Tips From Our Test Kitchen:

For the frosting, make sure the margarine and cream cheese are at room temperature for easier mixing.

Cocoa Devil's Food Cake

Yield: 12 to 16 servings

"I created this recipe for a light chocolate cake when my husband gave me a Mixmaster for Christmas in 1946. You wouldn't believe how many of these cakes I've made since."

Cake:

11/4 cups granulated sugar
2/3 cup solid vegetable shortening
2 large eggs
11/2 cups sifted all-purpose flour
3 tablespoons cocoa powder
1/4 teaspoon salt
11/4 teaspoons baking soda
1 cup buttermilk
1 teaspoon vanilla extract

Frosting:

1/2 cup (1 stick) butter or margarine
4 tablespoons milk
1 teaspoon vanilla extract
16 ounces confectioners' sugar
2 tablespoons cocoa powder
1 cup chopped pecans (optional)

Preheat the oven to 350 degrees. For the cake, lightly grease and flour a 13 x 9-inch baking dish. Beat the granulated sugar and shortening in a mixer until creamy. Add the eggs one at a time. Beat well on medium speed. Sift the flour, cocoa, salt, and baking soda together in a separate bowl. Add the flour mixture to the creamed mixture alternately with the buttermilk until evenly blended. Stir in the vanilla and beat again for 2 minutes. Pour into the prepared pan and bake for about 25 minutes. Remove from the oven and prepare the frosting.

For the frosting, melt the butter and add the milk and vanilla. Stir in the confectioners' sugar and cocoa. Beat on high speed until creamy and ready to spread. Stir in the pecans and spread the frosting over the cake.

GRACE HUNTER | BIG SPRING, TEXAS

For more than 100 years, Collins Bakery in Corsicana, Texas (pop. 24,485), has been making and shipping one of the Christmas season's main delights. Since 1896, fruitcake has been sold at the bakery and is shipped by mail across America and to customers in 196 nations.

The first Dairy Queen opened in Joliet, Illinois, in 1940. About 6,000 of the restaurants are now open around the world.

Oatmeal Cake with Penuche Frosting

Yield: 10 to 12 servings

"This recipe was my mother's and has become a favorite of our son, Scott, who is an astronaut. When he visited us recently, I sent this cake home with him. It rode well in the T-38 plane for his quick trip back to Houston."

Cake:

1   cup old-fashioned rolled oats
1   cup boiling water
1/2   cup (1 stick) margarine
11/2   cups firmly packed brown sugar
2   eggs
1   cup all-purpose flour
1   teaspoon baking soda
1   teaspoon baking powder
1/4   teaspoon salt

1   teaspoon vanilla extract
1/2   cup chopped walnuts or pecans
     (optional)

Frosting:

1/4   cup (1/2 stick) butter or margarine
3/4   cup firmly packed brown sugar
1/4   cup cream or milk
21/2   to 3 cups confectioners' sugar, sifted
     Chopped walnuts or pecans (optional)

Preheat the oven to 350 degrees. For the cake, grease a 9-inch square cake pan or an 11 x 7-inch baking dish. Combine the oats and water, and let stand while mixing the rest of the cake. Using an electric mixer, cream the margarine and brown sugar in a large bowl. Add the eggs and beat well. Sift together the flour, baking soda, baking powder, and salt, and add to the creamed mixture. Add the vanilla, oat mixture, and nuts, if desired. Pour into the prepared pan and bake for 30 to 40 minutes. Cool and frost with penuche frosting.

For the frosting, melt the butter and brown sugar in a saucepan over medium heat, stirring constantly. Add the cream slowly, cooking and stirring until bubbly. Remove from the heat, and stir in the confectioners' sugar until the frosting is the right consistency to spread on the cake. Decorate with nuts, if desired.

Sharon Altman | Pekin, Illinois

Puddle Cake

Yield: 12 to 16 servings

"I was taught to make this cake back when I was a young wife in Horse Springs, New Mexico. That was fifty years ago."

Cake:

1 1/2	cups all-purpose flour
1	cup sugar
3	tablespoons cocoa powder
1	teaspoon baking soda
1/2	teaspoon salt
6	tablespoons vegetable oil
1	tablespoon white vinegar
1	teaspoon vanilla extract
1	cup water

Topping:

1	cup sugar
2	tablespoons cocoa powder
1/2	cup water
1	teaspoon vanilla extract
1	tablespoon margarine

Preheat the oven to 350 degrees. For the cake, grease and flour a 13 x 9-inch cake pan. Mix together the flour, sugar, cocoa, baking soda, and salt. Make three holes in the mixture. In one hole, pour the oil. In the next, add the vinegar. In the third, pour the vanilla. Pour the water over all. Mix with a spoon and pour the batter into the cake pan. Bake for 20 to 25 minutes, or until the top springs back when touched. Let the cake cool.

For the topping, bring the sugar, cocoa, water, and vanilla to a boil. Cook for 1 minute. Remove from heat and stir in the margarine. Pour this topping over the entire cake.

JEAN TUGWELL | DONALDSON, ARKANSAS

French Almond Cake

Yield: 12 to 16 servings

"I copied this recipe from the Julia Child television show years ago. This cake is simple to prepare. I thank Mrs. Child for the lovely recipe and pleasant memories."

3/4	cup blanched almonds
1/4	plus 1/2 cup granulated sugar
1/2	cup (1 stick) butter, softened
3	eggs
1	teaspoon baking powder

1	tablespoon rum, kirsch, or vanilla extract
1/8	teaspoon almond extract
1/2	cup sifted cake flour
	Confectioners' sugar

Preheat the oven to 350 degrees. Grease and flour an 81/2-inch square cake pan. Pulverize the almonds with 1/4 cup of the granulated sugar in a blender. Beat the butter and the remaining 1/2 cup of the granulated sugar together in a medium mixing bowl. Add the almonds and beat 1 minute. Add the eggs one at a time, mixing between each addition. Add the baking powder, rum, and almond extract. Gently fold in the flour 1 tablespoon at a time. Fold the batter into the pan. Bake for 40 to 45 minutes. Sprinkle with the confectioners' sugar when cool.

ELIZABETH MONSON | IDYLLWILD, CALIFORNIA

Pistachio Cake

Yield: 8 to 10 servings

"This is the first choice of any dessert I make for my children and grand-children. Wherever I take it, I know I'll be handing out recipes. Once you bake this cake, be prepared to make it over and over."

1	(181/4-ounce) box white cake mix	2	plus 1 (3-ounce) packages instant
4	eggs		pistachio pudding
1	cup water	1	(10-ounce) container of Cool Whip
1	cup vegetable oil		

Preheat the oven to 275 degrees. Combine the cake mix, eggs, water, oil, and 2 packages of the pudding mix, and blend well. Pour the batter into a non-stick or greased cake pan, and bake for 10 minutes at 275 degrees, another 10 minutes at 300 degrees, and then 35 minutes at 325 degrees. The cake is done when a knife inserted into the center comes out clean.

For the topping, gradually add the remaining 1 package pudding mix to the Cool Whip. Spread on the cooled cake and refrigerate.

DIANA KOWALSKI | DANVILLE, INDIANA

Tips From Our Test Kitchen:

For a fluffier cake, bring all the ingredients to room temperature, including the eggs (warm them in medium-hot water) before mixing.

The state's first cookbook, *Mrs. Collins' Table Receipts Adapted to Western Housewifery*, was published in 1851 by J. N. O. Nunemacher in New Albany, Indiana (pop. 37,603).

Great-Grandmother's Gingerbread
Yield: 12 to 15 servings

"This recipe was handed down from my Great-Grandmother Crawford. It's more than 150 years old. It's so moist. Everyone loves it."

1/4	cup (1/2 stick) butter	1/2	teaspoon salt
1/4	cup lard or butter	1	teaspoon ground cinnamon
1/2	cup sugar	1	teaspoon ground ginger
1	egg, beaten	1/2	teaspoon ground cloves
1	cup molasses	21/2	cups sifted all-purpose flour
11/2	teaspoons baking soda	1	cup hot water

Preheat the oven to 350 degrees. Grease and flour a 13 x 9-inch baking dish. Cream the butter, lard, and sugar together. Add the beaten egg and molasses. In a separate bowl mix the baking soda, salt, cinnamon, ginger, cloves, and flour together. Stir the flour mixture into the creamed mixture. Add the hot water last. Beat the batter until smooth. Pour into the prepared baking dish. Bake for 30 to 35 minutes.

CARLA CAIN | LEBANON, MISSOURI

Tips From Our Test Kitchen:

Serve this classic cake warm with real whipped cream. It's also delicious topped with a lemon sauce.

Autumn Pumpkin Doughnuts
Yield: 24 doughnuts

"These delicious fry-cakes are great when there's a nip of cold in the air. Serve them with hot cider. They're ideal at Halloween parties or anytime."

2	eggs, beaten	2	teaspoons salt
1	cup granulated sugar	1	teaspoon ground nutmeg
1	cup canned pumpkin	1/2	teaspoon ground cinnamon
1/3	cup buttermilk	1/4	teaspoon ground ginger
2	tablespoons vegetable oil		Vegetable oil for frying
4	cups sifted all-purpose flour	2	cups confectioners' sugar
2	teaspoons baking powder		

Combine the eggs and granulated sugar and beat until fluffy. Combine the pumpkin, buttermilk, and oil. Beat into the egg mixture. Stir in the flour, baking powder, salt, nutmeg, cinnamon, and ginger. When well mixed, refrigerate the dough for at least 1 hour. This very soft and wet batter can be made the night before cooking the doughnuts.

Tips From Our Test Kitchen:

For best results keep the oil temperature at a steady 375 degrees.

Turn the dough out onto a well-floured surface, roll to a 1/2-inch thickness and cut into rings with a doughnut or cookie cutter.

Pour the vegetable oil into a heavy skillet to a depth of about 4 inches. Heat the oil until it reaches 375 degrees. (You can use a candy thermometer to check the temperature.) Using a spatula, ease the doughnuts into the hot oil two at a time. When one side is golden and the doughnut floats to the surface of the hot oil, turn it with a spatula. When golden on both sides, turn the fried doughnuts onto absorbent paper towels. Coat with the confectioners' sugar and serve warm.

ANGIE MILDRED BIGGS | LYONS, ILLINOIS

Tiramisu Torte

Yield: 12 to 16 servings

"This is a great dessert for a special occasion. It will be the talk of the meal because it is scrumptious."

Cake:

1 (181/4-ounce) package white cake mix
1 cup strong-brewed coffee, at room temperature
4 egg whites
4 Heath candy bars, chopped

Frosting:

4   ounces cream cheese, softened
2/3 cup sugar
2   cups whipping cream
1/3 cup chocolate syrup
1/4 cup plus 6 tablespoons strong-brewed coffee, at room temperature
2   teaspoons vanilla extract
1   Heath candy bar, chopped

Tips From Our Test Kitchen:

Make this cake a day ahead to allow the flavors to blend overnight.

Preheat the oven to 350 degrees. For the cake, grease and flour two 9-inch round baking pans. Beat together the cake mix, coffee, and egg whites on low speed with an electric mixer until moistened. Beat on high for 2 minutes. Fold in the chopped candy bars. Pour the batter into the prepared pans and bake for 25 to 30 minutes, or until a toothpick inserted in the center comes out clean. Set aside to cool. When cool, remove the cakes from the pans and cut them horizontally to make four layers.

For the frosting, beat the cream cheese and sugar in a chilled bowl until smooth. Add the whipping cream, chocolate syrup, and coffee. Whip until thick and creamy. Stir in the vanilla and blend well. Spread the frosting equally over the cake layers. Garnish the top layer with the crumbled Heath bar.

GLENNA TUCKER | MILLWOOD, WEST VIRGINIA

Down Le Roy's Jell-O-Brick Road

For more than a century before Pearle Bixby Wait sat down in his kitchen in Le Roy, New York, in 1897, entrepreneurs had been trying to simplify the process of preparing a gelatin dessert. Wait had done it and made it mass producible, but he was stymied for a name. No one knows what transpired in that kitchen, but his wife, May, might have said, "Honey, why don't you call it Jell-O?"

With that, the "World's Most Popular Dessert" was born. In 1899, Jell-O went into production, and the first four flavors—strawberry, raspberry, orange, and lemon—rolled off the line. Over the next sixty-five years, Jell-O and Le Roy (pop. 4,462) became synonymous as the kitchen-table recipe conquered the world. But you can't help but feel sorry for Wait: he sold the Jell-O secret for $450 the year his product was launched.

Wait is still a hero in Le Roy, however, and his name is on the first of the 6,508 bricks laid on the Jell-O Brick Road leading from Main Street past the Le Roy Historical Society to the 1898 schoolhouse that's home to the Jell-O Gallery. Here, the collection of Jell-O memorabilia keeps growing.

At the dawn of the twentieth century, no one had heard of what would become the World's Most Popular Dessert. But in 1899 the Jell-O Company was bought by Genesee Pure Food, whose pioneering marketing, advertising, and name recognition campaigns are still studied and copied today.

In its first quarter century, Jell-O salesmen fanned out across the country. The distinctive horse-drawn Jell-O wagon would roll into town, boys were hired to slip fliers under every door in the morning, and the salesmen would hit the stores in the afternoon to help merchants meet the demand for this new dessert.

In Le Roy, recipes were created, molds were invented and sold, and new flavors were added. Artists were hired to create original oil paintings for magazine ads. The Jell-O Girl featured in them became every child's best friend, every mother's favorite daughter.

By 1924, 15,000 "Jell-O, Le Roy, NY" crates, each containing thirty-six cartons of flavored powder, were shipped each day, filling five railroad cars. The factory employed 300 Le Royans, and production continued through the Great Depression.

The line ran twenty-four hours a day, seven days a week. It ended in 1964, when the factory moved to Delaware.

But the heart and spirit of Jell-O are still in Le Roy. Residents never expected Jell-O to leave town. They had been proud to introduce themselves with "Hi. I'm from Le Roy. That's where we make Jell-O." So, just as they had built the Jell-O Company, they built the gallery to mark its history, with more that 200 volunteers and donations from Kraft Foods, which now owns the Jell-O brand.

Born to celebrate the 100th anniversary of

Wait's recipe, the Jell-O Museum began humbly. The former school had been boarded up for fifty years. Wainscoted ceilings and wood floors were a mess. There was no electricity, no plumbing, and the front steps were cinderblocks. A lot had to be done with little money.

Today, the museum is a point of pride for residents and a focus for the town's history, a reminder that the past is part of the present, and, in Le Roy at least, that "There's always room for Jell-O."

For more information, log on to www .jellomuseum.com or call (585) 768-7433.

Warren D. Jorgensen writes from his home in New York City.

Irresistible No-Bake Torte

Yield: 8 to 10 servings

"This torte is very pretty served on a footed cake plate. We enjoy it with 1/2 teaspoon mint added to the mousse mixture and then garnished with fresh mint."

12	ounces semi-sweet chocolate chips	1	(9-ounce) package chocolate wafer cookies (about 41)
11/3	plus 2/3 cups whipping cream		

Line a 9-inch springform pan with plastic wrap. Be sure the sides of the pan are covered, and allow enough overhang to cover the top of the torte after it is assembled.

In a microwave-safe bowl melt the chocolate chips with 2/3 cup of the whipping cream. Heat just until the chocolate looks shiny. Stir until smooth.

Crush about one-third of the chocolate wafers in a food processor or blender until the crumbs are very fine. Add 2 tablespoons of the remaining 11/3 cups cream to the wafers. Mix until just moistened. (Add another tablespoon of cream if necessary.) Press the crumb mixture evenly into the bottom of the springform pan. Beat the remaining whipping cream until soft peaks form. Add 1/2 cup of the chocolate chip mixture and stir until well blended. Fold in the whipped cream and the chocolate mixture to create a mousse. Spoon 1 cup of the mousse over the crust. Place a layer of cookies flat over the mousse. Repeat this twice, and then spread the remaining mousse on top. Cover with the plastic wrap and refrigerate for at least 12 hours. The cake will become firm enough to slice and the wafers will soften.

CONEY TATRO | BARNET, VERMONT

Tips From Our Test Kitchen:

This torte freezes well. If frozen, thaw it in the refrigerator for several hours before serving. Delicious with fresh berries, toasted nuts, and fruit sauces, the torte should be served in small portions.

Chocolate-Pecan Torte with Praline Crème Anglaise

Yield: 12 to 16 servings

"We have a huge, thirty-year-old pecan tree in our backyard. I've been experimenting with pecan recipes for years. I think I've developed an incredible chocolate pecan pie."

Crust:

11/4 cups all-purpose flour

1/4 teaspoon salt

1/2 cup butter-flavored shortening

1 egg, beaten

3 tablespoons chilled orange juice

1/4 teaspoon pear or cider vinegar

Filling:

3 tablespoons unsalted butter

2 ounces unsweetened chocolate

2 eggs, beaten

3/4 cup dark corn syrup

1/2 cup firmly packed dark brown sugar

1/2 teaspoon orange zest

1 teaspoon vanilla extract

1 tablespoon praline liqueur

11/3 cups chopped pecans

Crème Anglaise:

2 cups plus 2 to 4 teaspoons whole milk

1/2 cup (1 stick) unsalted butter

1/2 cup firmly packed light brown sugar

1/2 teaspoon ground cinnamon

1 teaspoon vanilla extract

1 tablespoon cornstarch

3 egg yolks

2 tablespoons praline liqueur

For the crust, mix the flour and salt. Cut in the shortening with a pastry cutter. Combine the egg, juice, and vinegar, and blend into the flour mixture. Lightly work the dough on a floured surface, and fit it into a 10-inch springform pan. Crimp the edges about 2 inches high all around. Chill for 20 minutes.

Preheat the oven to 325 degrees. For the filling, melt the butter and chocolate together over very low heat, stirring constantly to prevent burning. Set aside to cool. In a medium bowl combine the eggs, corn syrup, dark brown sugar, and zest. Add the vanilla, liqueur, pecans, and cooled chocolate mixture. Pour the filling into the crust and bake for 40 to 45 minutes, or until the center is set. Allow to cool.

For the Crème Anglaise, combine 2 cups of the milk with the butter, light brown sugar, and cinnamon in a medium saucepan. Stir over medium heat until hot. In a small bowl mix the vanilla, cornstarch, and the remaining (2 to 4 teaspoons) cold milk together. In another bowl whisk about 1/4 cup of the hot milk mixture with the egg yolks, and then pour all back into the hot milk mixture. Add the cornstarch mixture and then the liqueur. Whisk together until thick. Cool and serve over the filling.

MILTON SWEET | NORTHWOOD HILLS, TEXAS

Moist Chocolate Brownies

Yield: about 48 brownies

"I take these brownies to most family gatherings and picnics. My grandchildren really go for them."

Brownies:

2 1/2 cups all-purpose flour
2 cups granulated sugar
1/2 cup sour cream
1 teaspoon salt
1 teaspoon baking soda
2 eggs
1 cup (2 sticks) margarine
5 tablespoons cocoa powder
1 cup water

Frosting:

1/2 cup (1 stick) margarine
3 tablespoons cocoa powder
6 tablespoons milk
1 (16-ounce) box confectioners' sugar
1 teaspoon vanilla extract
1/2 cup well-chopped walnuts

Preheat the oven to 350 degrees. For the brownies, generously grease and flour a 20 x 12-inch jelly-roll pan. In a large bowl stir together the flour, granulated sugar, sour cream, salt, baking soda, and eggs. Bring the margarine, cocoa, and water to a boil in a saucepan over high heat. Stir into the flour mixture until smooth. Pour the brownie mixture into the prepared pan. Bake for 20 to 22 minutes.

For the frosting, bring the margarine, cocoa, and milk to a boil in a medium-size saucepan. Remove from the heat. Add the confectioners' sugar and vanilla and stir until smooth. Fold in the nuts and spread evenly over the cooled brownies.

MAXINE MCCARTHY | NAPER, NEBRASKA

Tips From Our Test Kitchen:

Be sure to cool the brownies completely before frosting.

In 1927, Edwin E. Perkins of Hastings, Nebraska (pop. 22,008). decided to change his popular "Fruit Smack" from a bottled soft drink syrup to a dry powder, which he packaged in envelopes and shipped at a lower price. He named the product Kool-Aid.

One-Pot Brownies

Yield: 12 to 15 brownies

"My friend Babs and I used to make this recipe after school all of the time. They are never dry and are sure to be a hit with everyone who tries them."

1	cup (2 sticks) margarine	1/4	teaspoon salt
4	ounces unsweetened chocolate	2	teaspoons vanilla extract
2	cups granulated sugar	1	cup chopped walnuts or pecans
1	cup all-purpose flour		(optional)
4	eggs, beaten		Confectioners' sugar

Preheat the oven to 350 degrees. Lightly grease and flour a 13 x 9-inch baking dish. In a large saucepan melt the margarine and chocolate together over low heat, stirring to prevent burning. Remove from the heat as soon as the chocolate is soft. Stir in the granulated sugar, flour, eggs, salt, vanilla, and nuts until well blended. This makes a velvety batter. Pour it into the prepared baking dish. Bake for 20 to 25 minutes. Sprinkle the brownies with the confectioners' sugar.

MAUREEN MAGUIRE | CARY, ILLINOIS

Butterscotch Brownies

Yield: 16 brownies

"I've made these brownies for many years. They are so quickly put together. My children love them."

1/4	cup (1/2 stick) butter, melted	1	teaspoon baking powder
1	cup firmly packed brown sugar	1/2	teaspoon salt
1	egg	1/2	teaspoon vanilla extract
3/4	cup all-purpose flour	1/2	cup chopped pecans

Preheat the oven to 350 degrees. Generously grease an 8-inch square pan. Cream the butter, brown sugar, and egg together in a medium bowl. In a separate bowl mix together the flour, baking powder, and salt. Add the flour mixture to the creamed mixture. Stir in the vanilla and pecans. Spoon the batter into the prepared pan. Bake for 25 minutes.

KATHY POUNDER | EL CAMPO, TEXAS

Pumpkin Brownies

Yield: 24 to 36 brownies

"This dessert was shared at a children's Halloween party. It was enjoyed by all, children and adults alike."

4	eggs	1	teaspoon baking soda
1	cup vegetable oil	1	teaspoon baking powder
1	(15-ounce) can pumpkin	1	teaspoon ground cinnamon
2	cups sugar	1/2	teaspoon salt
2	cups all-purpose flour		

Preheat the oven to 350 degrees. Grease and flour a 13 x 9-inch baking dish. Beat together the eggs, oil, pumpkin, and sugar. Add the flour, baking soda, baking powder, cinnamon, and salt, stirring until evenly mixed. Pour into the prepared dish. Bake for 30 minutes, or until the center springs back when touched.

MARSHA KONKEN | STERLING, COLORADO

Tips From Our Test Kitchen:

Serve with whipped topping or a cream cheese frosting. Chopped nuts can be tossed on top of the frosting.

German Chocolate Bars

Yield: 12 to 15 bars

"This recipe is simple enough for a child to make. When I bring it to a gathering, I never have leftovers."

1	(181/4-ounce) box German chocolate cake mix	1	(14-ounce) bag caramels
1/2	cup (1 stick) butter, melted	3/4	cup milk chocolate chips
1/3	plus 1/3 cup evaporated milk	3/4	cup chopped walnuts

Preheat the oven to 350 degrees. Lightly grease a 13 x 9-inch baking pan. Mix together the cake mix, butter, and 1/3 cup of the evaporated milk. Press half this dough into the prepared pan. Bake for 8 to 10 minutes.

Unwrap the caramels and place them in a saucepan. Add the remaining 1/3 cup of the evaporated milk, and stir constantly over low heat until the caramels are melted.

Remove the baked dough from the oven, and pour the melted caramels evenly over it. Sprinkle with the chocolate chips and nuts. Crumble the remaining dough over the caramel layer. Bake for 10 to 15 minutes longer.

JENNY KAUN | REEDSBURG, WISCONSIN

Tips From Our Test Kitchen:

Try substituting pecans or semi-sweet chocolate chips to suit your taste.

283

While living in Racine, Wisconsin, in 1883, Englishman William Horwick was granted a U.S. patent for malted milk. Initially, the powdered product was mixed with hot water to be fed to infants.

GiGi Oat and Chocolate Bars

Yield: 16 to 20 bars

"This dessert is from my mom. I grew up on GiGi Bars. I have been in the kitchen making my own recipes since I was about nine years old."

Batter:
1   cup (2 sticks) butter, softened
2   cups firmly packed brown sugar
2   eggs
2   teaspoons vanilla extract
2 1/2   cups all purpose flour
1   teaspoon salt
1   teaspoon baking soda
3   cups uncooked quick oats

Filling:
1   (12-ounce) package semi-sweet chocolate chips
1   (14-ounce) can sweetened condensed milk
2   tablespoons butter
1   teaspoon vanilla extract
1/2   teaspoon salt
1/2   cup chopped walnuts

Preheat the oven to 350 degrees. For the batter, lightly grease a 13 x 9-inch baking pan. Cream together the butter and brown sugar. Add the eggs and vanilla. Stir in the flour, salt, and baking soda. Add the oats and mix well. Press two-thirds of the batter into the prepared pan.

For the filling, melt the chocolate with the milk, butter, vanilla, and salt in a saucepan over medium heat, stirring constantly to avoid scorching. Remove from the heat as soon as the chocolate is melted. Pour the chocolate over the batter in the baking pan. Sprinkle the top with the nuts. Crumble the remaining batter over the filling. Bake for 25 to 30 minutes, or until the batter is golden brown. Cut into squares when cooled.

CARRIE WOURMS | CALUMET, MINNESOTA

Sour Cream Banana Bars

Yield: 24 bars

"A friend gave this recipe to me many years ago. I've since prepared these moist bars often for family and church events. They keep well and are very good chilled."

Bars:

1 1/2	cups granulated sugar
1	cup sour cream
1/2	cup (1 stick) margarine, softened
2	eggs
1 1/2	cups mashed bananas (about 3 large bananas)
2	teaspoons vanilla extract
2	cups all-purpose flour
1	teaspoon salt
1	teaspoon baking soda
1/2	cup chopped walnuts

Frosting:

1/4	cup (1/2 stick) margarine
2	cups confectioners' sugar
1	teaspoon vanilla extract
3	tablespoons milk

Tips From Our Test Kitchen:

Keep overripe bananas on hand in your freezer. Pull them out to thaw when the mood strikes to make these delicious bars.

Preheat the oven to 350 degrees. For the bars, grease and flour a 15 x 10-inch baking dish. Beat together the granulated sugar, sour cream, and margarine. Mix in the eggs one at a time on low speed. Beat in the bananas and vanilla, scraping the sides of the bowl occasionally. Add the flour, salt, and baking soda. Beat on medium speed for 1 minute. Stir in the nuts. Spread the batter evenly into the prepared pan. Bake for 20 to 25 minutes, or until the center is done. Set aside to cool.

For the frosting, lightly brown the margarine in a saucepan, stirring to prevent burning. When lightly browned, remove from the heat. Beat in the confectioners' sugar, vanilla, and milk. Pour the frosting over the bars.

PATRICIA DICKERSON | SUTHERLAND, NEBRASKA

Beatrice Foods was founded in Beatrice, Nebraska (pop. 12,496), in 1894 when George Haskell and William W. Bosworth purchased a small churn and began producing butter from milk provided by local farmers.

Date Matrimonial Bars

Yield: 24 to 36 bars

"Though I'm ninety-one years old, I still enjoy baking. This Swedish recipe was given to me by a friend many years ago."

Crumb mixture:

13/4 cups quick oats
13/4 cups sifted all-purpose flour
1 cup firmly packed brown sugar
1 teaspoon baking soda
1 cup (2 sticks) butter, softened

Filling:

8 ounces chopped dates
1/2 cup water
1 cup granulated sugar

Preheat the oven to 350 degrees. For the crumb mix, grease an 8-inch square baking dish. Mix together the oats, flour, brown sugar, baking soda, and butter until well blended. Press half the crumb mixture into the prepared dish.

For the filling, stir together the dates, water, and granulated sugar in a small saucepan. Cook and stir over medium heat until bubbly and smooth. Pour the date mixture evenly over the crumb mixture. Spread the remaining half of the crumb mixture over the filling. Bake for 25 to 30 minutes, or until golden brown. Cut into squares and serve when cool.

MILDRED HENNON | NEWTON, IOWA

Tips From Our Test Kitchen:

This rich bar cookie is also good with chopped walnuts or pecans added to the crumb mixture.

Hawaiian Bars

Yield: about 24 squares

"This is our favorite dessert. It can be prepared ahead. Cheesecake lovers usually really like it."

Crust:

2 cups all-purpose flour
1 cup sugar
1 cup (2 sticks) butter, softened

Filling:

16 ounces cream cheese, softened
6 tablespoons sugar
4 tablespoons milk

2 eggs
2 teaspoons vanilla extract
1 (16-ounce) can crushed pineapple, drained

Topping:

2 cups flaked coconut
2 tablespoons butter, melted

Tips From Our Test Kitchen:

This creamy dessert is great to freeze and keep on hand for last-minute guests.

Preheat the oven to 350 degrees. For the crust, mix together the flour, sugar, and butter until well blended. Press into an ungreased 13 x 9-inch baking dish. Bake for 10 minutes.

For the filling, combine the cream cheese, sugar, milk, eggs, and vanilla in a large mixing bowl, and beat together until very smooth. Stir in the pineapple until well blended. Spoon over the crust.

For the topping, sprinkle the coconut evenly over the filling. Drizzle the butter evenly over the coconut. Bake for about 25 minutes, or until the coconut is lightly browned. Cool and serve.

GLADYS TUPY | OWATONNA, MINNESOTA

The Minnesota town of Menahga (pop. 1,220) derives its name from a Chippewa Indian word for "blueberry." Wild blueberries are native to northern and central Minnesota and were a major food source for American Indians in the region.

Blueberry Dessert

Yield: 6 to 8 servings

"This is a family favorite. We had a preacher who called it 'huck-a-berry puddle' and liked it hot out of the oven. You can use any fruit pie filling you wish."

1 1/2 cups graham cracker crumbs	1 cup sugar
1/2 cup (1 stick) butter, melted	1 (21-ounce) can blueberry pie filling
8 ounces cream cheese, softened	1 (12-ounce) container whipped
2 eggs	topping (optional)

Preheat the oven to 350 degrees. Mix the graham cracker crumbs and butter together, and press them into an 11 x 7-inch ovenproof glass dish. Mix the cream cheese, eggs, and sugar until smooth, and pour over the crumb layer. Bake for about 20 minutes, or until brown around the edges. Cool. Spread the pie filling over the cream cheese layer. Top with whipped topping, if desired.

JANIE SIPPER | GEORGIANA, ALABAMA

Grandma's Peanut Butter Squares

Yield: 12 to 24 squares

"My mother's health has limited her ability to make her great peanut butter squares. Last summer, however, she spent a day supervising my thirteen-year-old daughter in making this favorite."

Squares:

1/2	cup solid vegetable shortening
1/2	cup (stick) margarine
2	cups all-purpose flour
1	cup firmly packed brown sugar
1	cup uncooked quick oats
1/2	teaspoon baking soda
1/2	teaspoon salt
1	heaping tablespoon chunky peanut butter
2	heaping tablespoons creamy peanut butter

Frosting:

6	tablespoons butter, softened
1 1/2	teaspoons vanilla extract
1/4	cup cocoa powder
1/2	teaspoon salt
16	ounces confectioners' sugar
1/4	cup milk

Preheat the oven to 350 degrees. For the squares, lightly grease a 13 x 9-inch baking dish. In a large bowl mix the shortening, margarine, flour, brown sugar, oats, baking soda, salt, and peanut butters until well blended and crumbly. Press into the prepared baking dish. Bake for 20 minutes. Turn off the heat and leave the pan in the oven for 5 minutes longer.

For the frosting, combine the butter, vanilla, cocoa, and salt in a medium bowl. When smooth, alternately add the sugar and milk. If the frosting is too thin, add a bit more sugar. For thinner frosting, add more milk, 1 tablespoon at a time. Stir until creamy. Frost the peanut butter squares while warm.

DONNA CACIC WISSBAUM | PARDEEVILLE, WISCONSIN

Dream Fudge

Yield: 36 to 48 pieces

"I actually got this recipe in a dream. I haven't met anyone who doesn't like it."

2	(11 1/2-ounce) bags Ghirardelli milk chocolate chips
8	ounces cream cheese
1/2	cup chopped walnuts

Tips From Our Test Kitchen:

Add 2 tablespoons peanut butter to the frosting if desired.

Tips From Our Test Kitchen:

This fudge recipe has far less sugar than most. If Ghirardelli chocolate is not stocked at your grocery, try mixing one bag semi-sweet and one bag milk chocolate chips of another brand.

Butter an 8-inch square pan. Melt the chocolate over simmering water in a double boiler. (It can also be melted on a very low microwave setting. If using this technique, be sure to stir the chips every minute to prevent burning.) Add the cream cheese to the melted chips and stir. The warm chips will soften the cream cheese and make it easy to form a smooth texture. Stir in the walnuts. Spoon the fudge into the prepared pan and let it sit until firm.

Jo Ann Wilcox | Canon City, Colorado

Peanut Butter Fudge

Yield: 24 to 36 pieces

"A friend gave me this great candy recipe thirty years ago, and I have been making it ever since. It is so easy and so delicious."

11/2 ounces light corn syrup	1 (18-ounce) jar peanut butter
61/2 ounces evaporated milk	1 (7-ounce) jar marshmallow crème
1 cup (2 sticks) butter	1 teaspoon vanilla extract
4 cups sugar	1/2 cup chopped pecans (optional)

Grease a 13 x 9-inch baking pan. Pour the corn syrup into a measuring cup. Add enough evaporated milk (about 61/2 ounces) to measure 1 cup. Melt the butter and sugar in a medium-size saucepan. Add the milk mixture. Bring to a boil and cook for 5 minutes. Remove from the heat. Add the peanut butter, marshmallow crème, vanilla, and pecans if using. Pour into the prepared pan. Cool and cut in squares.

Drema J. Holstine | Gay, West Virginia

Thomas Grimes discovered the apple variety that bears his name, Grimes Golden, in the early 1800s near Wellsburg, West Virginia (pop. 2,891).

Tips From Our Test Kitchen:

Put the peanut butter and marshmallow crème into separate bowls at the start to make it easier to add them at the same time after the sugar is cooked. Try lining the prepared pan with overlapping wax paper greased on both sides to make the fudge easier to remove. Just peel off the paper and cut. Since not everyone likes nuts, you may want to divide this recipe into two pans, using nuts in only one. Store the fudge in the refrigerator.

Frying-Pan Chocolate Fudge

Yield: 24 pieces

"I have been using this recipe for years. Many friends and acquaintances request it as a Christmas gift every year."

2 1/2 cups sugar	6 ounces semi-sweet chocolate chips
1/2 cup (1 stick) margarine, softened	1 cup chopped pecans or other nuts
6 ounces evaporated milk	1 teaspoon vanilla extract

Mix the sugar and margarine together in a heavy frying pan over medium heat. Stir in the milk and bring to a boil. Reduce the heat to low and cook 6 more minutes, stirring occasionally. Remove from the heat, and add the chocolate chips and chopped nuts. Stir until the fudge begins to form. Quickly add the vanilla flavoring. Drop the fudge by teaspoonfuls onto wax paper. Let cool and store in an airtight container.

SUSAN F. GILLELAND | ROSEBORO, NORTH CAROLINA

Ma Moore's Deluxe Peanut Butter Frosting

Yield: Icing for 1 cake

"Join the Moore family tradition from upstate New York. Ma developed her special frosting in 1968. Her seven children chose this frosting to top their birthday cakes."

> **Tips From Our Test Kitchen:**
>
> This icing is particularly good on brownies. It is so delicious that it would taste good straight out of the bowl.

5 tablespoons butter, softened	1 teaspoon vanilla extract
1 1/2 cups plus 2 tablespoons confectioners' sugar	1 cup smooth peanut butter
1/8 cup cocoa powder	1/2 cup skim milk (other types of milk can substitute)

In a large bowl mix the butter by hand with 1 1/2 cups of the confectioners' sugar and cocoa powder. Stir in the vanilla. Add the peanut butter and mix until the texture resembles small beads. Add the milk slowly, beating with a mixer until very creamy. Add the remaining 2 (and up to 3) additional tablespoons of confectioners' sugar if necessary to achieve the desired consistency.

DON MOORE | ROCHESTER, NEW YORK

Becky's Pumpkin Pie

Yield: 16 servings (2 pies)

"When I first made this recipe, it called for 2 cups of sugar, and I had only 1 cup. I substituted the second cup of sugar with honey. Everyone loved it."

4	eggs, beaten		2	teaspoons vanilla extract
1	cup milk		1/2	teaspoon salt
1	teaspoon ground cinnamon		1	cup sugar
3	cups pumpkin		1	cup honey
1	tablespoon all-purpose flour		2	(9-inch) unbaked piecrusts
1/2	teaspoon ground nutmeg			

Preheat the oven to 425 degrees. Mix the eggs, milk, cinnamon, pumpkin, flour, nutmeg, vanilla, salt, sugar, and honey in the order given. Pour into the piecrusts. Bake for 10 minutes. Reduce the oven temperature to 350 degrees, and then bake for 40 to 50 minutes, or until the pies are golden and well set.

BECKY CLARK | GREENWICH, OHIO

Tips From Our Test Kitchen:

For a more traditional, custard-style pie, add two more eggs. Serve with whipped cream.

Southern Sweet Potato Pie

Yield: 8 servings

"This very sweet pie is a tasty dessert for all occasions. I like to bake special pies and cakes for my family during the holidays."

1	cup cooked, mashed sweet potatoes		1/4	cup light corn syrup
2	eggs, beaten		3	tablespoons all-purpose flour
1 2/3	cups sugar		1/4	teaspoon ground nutmeg
3/4	cup evaporated milk			Pinch of salt
1/2	cup (1 stick) butter, melted		1	(9-inch) unbaked piecrust

Preheat the oven to 350 degrees. Mix together the sweet potatoes, eggs, sugar, milk, butter, corn syrup, flour, nutmeg, and salt in a large bowl until smooth. Pour into the piecrust and bake for 55 to 60 minutes.

MAGGIE GRAVES | FORT PAYNE, ALABAMA

Tips From Our Test Kitchen:

For a denser pie, increase the mashed sweet potatoes to 1 1/2 cups. Serve with a dollop of whipped cream and a dash of ground nutmeg or crystallized ginger.

Zucchini Mock-Apple Pie

Yield: 8 servings

"This recipe is a favorite because no one can believe it is made from zucchini. It is fun when people think it is apple pie, and then you tell them it is zucchini. When they taste it, they want the recipe. It almost tastes better than apple pie—in fact, I like it better."

6 cups peeled, seeded, and sliced (1/4-inch) zucchini	2 tablespoons cornstarch
1 cup granulated sugar	1/2 teaspoon salt
1/2 cup firmly packed brown sugar	Butter
11/2 teaspoons ground cinnamon	1 teaspoon cider vinegar
11/2 teaspoons cream of tartar	Pastry for two-crust pie

Preheat the oven to 475 degrees. Cook the zucchini slices in boiling water until barely tender, about 2 minutes. Remove from the heat, drain well, and cool (see Tips). In a bowl toss the zucchini with the granulated and brown sugars, cinnamon, cream of tartar, cornstarch, and salt until well coated. Place a pastry crust in a 9-inch, greased pie pan. Fill with the zucchini mixture. Dot with butter and drizzle with the vinegar. Place another crust on top. Bake for 12 minutes. Reduce the oven temperature to 350 degrees and bake for an additional 11/4 hours.

DOLLY MASSARO | THE VILLAGES, FLORIDA

Mom's Banana Cream Pie

Yield: 8 servings

"I truly enjoy making this pie, because it uses so few ingredients and takes so little time. Yet the result is what appears to be a creamy masterpiece."

Crust:

11/2 cups cinnamon graham cracker crumbs	1/2 teaspoon salt
3 tablespoons butter, softened	21/2 cups milk
3 tablespoons sugar	3 egg yolks
	1 tablespoon butter
	1 teaspoon vanilla extract
Filling:	2 bananas
1/4 cup cornstarch	
3/4 cup sugar	

Preheat the oven to 325 degrees. For the crust, combine the graham cracker crumbs, butter, and sugar, and press into a 9-inch pie pan. Bake for 5 minutes. Set aside to cool.

For the filling, mix the cornstarch, sugar, and salt together in a medium-size saucepan. Pour in the milk and stir over medium heat until it begins to thicken. Bring to a boil and stir at a low boil for 1 minute. Remove from the heat. Whisk one-half of the hot milk mixture into the egg yolks. Mix well. Pour this back into the remaining milk mixture in the saucepan. Stir constantly and boil again for 1 minute. Remove from the heat.

Stir in the butter and vanilla. Allow the filling to cool slightly. Pour half the filling into the prepared pie shell. Slice the bananas evenly over the top. Spoon the remaining filling over the bananas. Cool and top with whipped cream or a meringue made with the leftover egg whites.

JOY SHAFFER | MATTOON, ILLINOIS

Sour Cream Peach Pie

Yield: 8 servings

"This past summer we had a surprise sixty-fifth wedding anniversary party for my grandparents. We made six of Grandma's Sour Cream Peach Pies so that everyone would be sure to get a piece."

Filling:
2 1/2 cups fresh peeled and sliced peaches
1 egg, beaten
1/2 teaspoon salt
1/2 teaspoon vanilla extract
1 cup sour cream
3/4 cup sugar
2 tablespoons all-purpose flour
1 (9-inch) unbaked pie shell

Topping:
1/3 cup all-purpose flour
1/3 cup sugar
1 teaspoon ground cinnamon
1/4 cup (1/2 stick) butter

Tips From Our Test Kitchen:

This delicious pie sets up best when refrigerated. Use chilled butter to ensure the crumb topping is the right consistency.

Preheat the oven to 375 degrees. For the filling, mix the peaches, egg, salt, vanilla, sour cream, sugar, and flour together, and pour into the pie shell. Bake for about 30 minutes, or until the pie is slightly brown. While this bakes, prepare the topping.

For the topping, combine the flour, sugar, and cinnamon. Cut in the butter with a pastry cutter, until the pieces are the size of small peas. Sprinkle the topping evenly over the pie and bake an additional 15 minutes. Allow to cool completely before serving.

SHELLEY STOLTENBERG | SPEARFISH, SOUTH DAKOTA

Banana Split Festival Promises
a Rockin' Good Time in Wilmington

The nation's one and only Banana Split Festival had its humble beginnings in 1995 and has grown each year, now attracting some 17,000 people each June to Wilmington, Ohio (pop. 11,921), to celebrate the ice cream concoction.

Set to a 1950s and '60s theme, the festival offers free concerts by well-known bands who deliver the music of the early rock 'n' roll days. Round-the-clock activities include a classic car cruise-in, shopping for handcrafted items and collectibles, street fair games for both young and old alike, and special delights for children, such as pony rides and inflatable rides.

Food is abundant at the festival, with offerings ranging from cheeseburgers to a fried pastry called elephant ears—and everything in between. The number one attraction is the build-your-own banana split booth, where all the ice cream is hometown-made by a local ice cream shop, Gibson's Goodies. Festivalgoers have a choice of toppings—strawberry, pineapple, or chocolate sauce, nuts, whipped cream, or cherries. Or they can choose all of them.

Other special activities include the Banana Split Festival Talent Contest, the Banana Split Eating Contest, and the Banana Split Masters Contest featuring restaurant chefs from all over southwest Ohio who create their own special banana splits.

The organizer of the first Banana Split Festival, Judy Gano of Wilmington, planned the event to raise funds to purchase playground equipment for the J. W. Denver Williams Park, the site of the celebration. The Wilmington Rotary Club (now the Wilmington Noon Rotary and Wilmington AM Rotary Clubs) took over planning the festival the second year. Some of the profits still go toward improvements at the Wilmington City Parks.

Festival organizers chose the banana split as a theme because of a story, rooted in local lore, about the tasty concoction's invention in 1907:

Ernest Hazard, proprietor of Hazard's Restaurant, wanted to attract the students of Wilmington College to his restaurant. He decided to create a new dish that was so unique everyone would want to try it.

It was a very blustery winter in 1907, business was slow, and the employees didn't have a lot of work to do. Hazard offered unlimited ingredients to his employees to encourage a creative solution. Taking part in the search himself, he arranged a peeled banana and three scoops of ice cream in a long dessert dish, added a shot of chocolate syrup, a little strawberry jam, and a few bits of pineapple. On top, he sprinkled some ground nuts and garnished his invention with a mountain of whipped cream and two red cherries on its peak.

Naming the dish presented another challenge. When Hazard asked his cousin, Clifton, to take a taste test, he explained that he had a name in mind: Banana Split. Clifton opined that he didn't think that the name was one that would generate any publicity, and that no one would ever walk in and ask for something called a banana split. Fortunately, Hazard didn't follow his cousin's advice.

While some might dispute Wilmington's claim to being the banana split's birthplace, thousands of people flock to Wilmington to sample old-fashioned banana splits during the second weekend in June. And sometime during the Friday evening and all-day-Saturday event, they'll also hear the story that has endured through the years of how Ernest Hazard created the first banana split.

For more information, log on to www .bananasplitfestival.com or call 1-877-4-A-VISIT.

Debbie Stamper is executive director of the Clinton County Convention and Visitors Bureau in Wilmington, Ohio.

Lemon Chess Pie

Yield: 8 to 10 servings

"There are many chess pie recipes. When you taste the zest in this recipe, which most people don't expect, you'll never make a plain chess pie again."

1	(9-inch) deep-dish unbaked piecrust		3	eggs
1	egg white		3	tablespoons lemon juice
1 1/2	cups sugar		2	teaspoons lemon zest
2	tablespoons cornmeal		3	tablespoons butter, melted
1	tablespoon all-purpose flour		3	tablespoons milk

Preheat the oven to 400 degrees. Brush the piecrust with the egg white. Bake for 10 minutes and remove from the oven.

Lower the oven temperature to 350 degrees. In a mixing bowl combine the sugar, cornmeal, and flour. Add the eggs one at a time, beating well between each addition. Stir in the lemon juice, lemon zest, melted butter, and milk. Mix well and pour into the piecrust. Bake for 45 to 50 minutes, or until the center is set. Serve warm or cool.

BETTY MARTIN | SMITHVILLE, TENNESSEE

Tips From Our Test Kitchen:

Only fresh lemon juice and zest will do. Serve this elegant pie with whipped cream.

Rhubarb Cream Pie

Yield: 8 servings

"I got this recipe from a friend back in 1957. Even people who think they don't like rhubarb pie are pleasantly surprised by this dessert. I think the eggs make the difference."

1 1/2 cups sugar	3 cups diced rhubarb
3 tablespoons flour	1 tablespoon butter
1/2 teaspoon ground nutmeg	Pastry for two-crust pie
2 eggs, well beaten	

Preheat the oven to 450 degrees. Blend the sugar, flour, and nutmeg in a medium bowl. Add the eggs and mix well. Add the rhubarb. Spoon the filling into 1 unbaked piecrust. Cut the butter into small pieces and sprinkle over the rhubarb filling. Cover with the top crust. Bake for 10 minutes. Reduce the oven temperature to 350 degrees and bake for 30 minutes longer.

SUSAN BAKER | FERNDALE, WASHINGTON

Raspberry Cream Pie

Yield: 10 to 12 servings

"I wanted to make a raspberry dessert similar to one we had tried at a local restaurant. I started experimenting and came up with this."

Crust:
2 cups graham cracker crumbs
1/3 cup sugar
1/2 cup (1 stick) butter or margarine, melted

Raspberry filling:
1 1/3 cups sugar
6 tablespoons cornstarch
1/8 teaspoon salt
1 plus 1/2 cups water (if using fresh berries, increase water to 2 cups)

4 tablespoons corn syrup
12 ounces frozen raspberries, thawed, or 1 pint fresh

Cream filling:
4 ounces cream cheese, softened
1/2 cup sugar
5 ounces whipped topping or whipped cream

Preheat the oven to 375 degrees. For the crust, mix the graham cracker crumbs, sugar, and butter, and press into a deep-dish pie pan. Bake for about 6 minutes. Set aside to cool.

For the raspberry filling, mix the sugar, cornstarch, and salt. Add about 1/2 cup of the water and stir until smooth. Add the remaining 1 cup water, corn syrup, and berries. Cook over medium heat in a saucepan, stirring constantly until thick. Set aside to cool. While the raspberry filling is cooling, make the cream filling.

For the cream filling, fold the cream cheese, sugar, and whipped topping together gently until smooth. Spoon over the cooled crust. Then spoon the cooled berry filling over the cream filling. Allow to sit for at least 2 hours before serving.

SANDRA LIPPOWITHS | CARO, MICHIGAN

Apple Dumpling Pie

Yield: 10 to 12 servings

"My mother loved to bake. She baked love into her delicious apple dumplings, so I created a pie that combines her filling with an easy-to-make, no-roll piecrust from my sister."

Crust:
1 1/2 cups all-purpose flour
1 1/2 tablespoons sugar
1 teaspoon salt
1/2 cup vegetable oil
2 tablespoons milk

Filling:
8 cups thinly sliced, peeled, tart baking apples (about 7 apples)

1 cup sugar
2 tablespoons all-purpose flour
3 tablespoons butter or margarine

Topping:
1 cup all-purpose flour
1/2 cup sugar
1/2 cup (1 stick) butter

Tips From Our Test Kitchen:

This no-fail recipe is great served with a dollop of vanilla ice cream.

Preheat the oven to 425 degrees. For the crust, combine the flour, sugar, salt, oil, and milk. Press into an 8-inch, deep-dish pie pan.

For the filling, toss the apples in the sugar and flour. Place them in the piecrust and dot with the butter.

For the topping, combine the flour and sugar. Cut in the butter until the mixture resembles coarse meal. Spread evenly over the apples. Cover the pie lightly with foil and bake for 25 to 35 minutes. Remove the foil and continue baking for 15 minutes.

CHRISTINE MAUCH | AMERICAN FALLS, IDAHO

Rancher's Pie

Yield: 8 servings

"While living on a ranch for fifty years, I often made this pie for the guys and gals who helped us brand cattle. They loved it, and I still make it now and then."

1 1/2 cups sugar	1 cup flaked coconut
1 cup crushed pineapple (do not drain)	1/3 cup (3/4 stick) butter or margarine
3 eggs, lightly beaten	1 (9-inch) unbaked piecrust
3 tablespoons all-purpose flour	

Preheat the oven to 350 degrees. Stir together the sugar, pineapple, eggs, flour, and coconut in a bowl. Melt the butter and add it to the pineapple mixture. Pour the filling into the piecrust. Bake for 1 hour, or until the filling is set and browned.

RUTH WARREN | STEAMBOAT SPRINGS, COLORADO

Buttermilk Pie

Yield: 16 servings (2 pies)

"My grandmother served delicious buttermilk pie when I was growing up. I was devastated when I discovered that she had been buying it, rather than baking it herself. This recipe, however, is as good as the one Grandma bought."

3 3/4 cups sugar	1 cup (2 sticks) butter, melted
4 tablespoons all-purpose flour	2 teaspoons vanilla extract
6 eggs	2 (9-inch) unbaked piecrusts
1 cup buttermilk	

Preheat the oven to 450 degrees. Combine the sugar, flour, eggs, buttermilk, butter, and vanilla. Mix until well blended. Pour into the piecrusts. Bake for 10 minutes. Reduce the oven temperature to 350 degrees, and bake for an additional 40 to 50 minutes, or until the center is firm.

VICTORIA STRICKER | LAREDO, TEXAS

Tips From Our Test Kitchen:

If the crusts start to become too brown, place an aluminum foil ring around the edges. Do not cover the whole pie. The filling is loose and will adhere to the foil.

Macaroon-Brownie Cream Pie

Yield: 10 to 12 servings

"Though I am the worst cook in my family, I decided to show my sisters that I can bake too. My creation fits best in a 10-inch square pan and is nicknamed 'Pie Are Square.' The name is fitting since I am a math teacher."

Crust:

2	egg whites (reserve yolks for filling)
1/2	teaspoon vanilla extract
1/8	teaspoon salt
1/2	cup granulated sugar
1 1/2	cups flaked coconut

Brownie layer:

1/2	cup (1 stick) butter, melted
3/4	cup granulated sugar
2	whole eggs
1	teaspoon almond extract
3/4	cup all-purpose flour
3	tablespoons cocoa powder

Cream filling:

2/3	cup sugar
1/2	cup all-purpose flour
1/4	teaspoon salt
3	cups milk
4	egg yolks (2 reserved from crust, 2 from meringue)
1 1/2	tablespoons vanilla

Meringue:

2	egg whites (reserved)
1/4	teaspoon vanilla
1/8	teaspoon cream of tartar
3	tablespoons confectioners' sugar

Preheat the oven to 325 degrees. Generously grease a 10-inch square baking dish.

For the crust, beat the egg whites until stiff. Fold in the vanilla, salt, granulated sugar, and coconut. Spoon into the baking dish.

For the brownie layer, beat together the butter and granulated sugar. Add the whole eggs and almond extract. Stir in the flour and cocoa until smooth. Pour over the crust. Bake for 25 to 30 minutes, or until set. Cool.

While the brownie layer is cooking and cooling, prepare the cream filling. Stir the sugar, flour, and salt together in a large microwave-safe bowl. Whisk in the milk until there are no lumps. Microwave on high until the mixture just begins to thicken. Check and stir. Pour 1/2 cup of this hot liquid into the 4 egg yolks, whisking to prevent lumps. Pour the egg mixture back into the hot milk mixture. Whisk again. Microwave, stirring occasionally, until the eggs are cooked and the mixture is thick. Stir in the vanilla. Cool.

Preheat the oven to 350 degrees. For the meringue, beat the remaining two reserved egg whites, vanilla, and cream of tartar until peaks form. Whip in the confectioners' sugar until stiff.

Assemble the pie by spooning the cream filling over the brownie layer and topping with the meringue. Bake until the meringue peaks turn golden. Chill before serving.

KELLY SCHNEIDER | GRANBURY, TEXAS

Charleston Coconut Pie

Yield: 8 servings

"My mother always told me that there is no excuse not to have a nice dessert to serve when the minister calls. This easy-to-prepare pie will become a favorite. It's delicious and forms its own crust."

4	eggs, beaten	2	cups milk
1/2	cup self-rising flour	1	teaspoon vanilla extract
11/3	cups sugar	1	(8-ounce) can flaked coconut
1/4	cup (1/2 stick) butter or margarine, melted		

Preheat the oven to 350 degrees. Beat together the eggs, flour, sugar, butter, milk, vanilla, and coconut. Pour into a 10-inch pie pan. Bake for 45 to 55 minutes.

Though the filling seems unsettled, do not cook the pie any longer. Refrigerate it, and it will set without spoiling its creamy consistency.

EVELYN BOONE | BOWMAN, SOUTH CAROLINA

Shoo-Fly Pie

Yield: 8 servings

"I ran across a recipe in Ladies' Home Journal *back in the 1950s. I changed it to suit my taste by adding spices and an egg. My family is still enjoying this recipe after more than fifty years."*

Crumb mixture:

1	cup all-purpose flour
2/3	cup firmly packed brown sugar
2	tablespoon solid vegetable shortening
1/8	teaspoon ground cinnamon
1/8	teaspoon ginger
1/8	teaspoon cloves
1/8	teaspoon ground nutmeg
1/8	teaspoon salt

Filling:

1	cup dark corn syrup
3/4	cup boiling water
1	teaspoon baking soda
1	egg, beaten
1	(9-inch) unbaked piecrust

For the crumb mixture, stir together the flour, sugar, shortening, cinnamon, ginger, cloves, nutmeg, and salt in a medium bowl until well blended. Preheat the oven to 375 degrees.

For the filling, stir together the syrup, water, and baking soda. Combine all but 1/2 cup of the crumb mixture with the syrup mixture. Stir in the egg. When well mixed, pour into the piecrust. Sprinkle the top with the remaining 1/2 cup crumbs. Bake for 10 minutes. Reduce the temperature to 350 degrees and bake for an additional 30 minutes, or until the center of the pie rises. Cool and serve.

RUBY SCHOCH | MUNCY, PENNSYLVANIA

Crazy Cappuccino Pie

Yield: 8 servings

"When a friend introduced me to Pennsylvania shoo-fly pie, I liked it and decided to create some variations. This one has been a hit with all who have tried it."

1   (9-inch) unbaked piecrust

Filling:
1   cup all-purpose flour
2/3 cup firmly packed brown sugar
2   tablespoons butter, melted
1/4 plus 3/4 cup very strong hot coffee
1   teaspoon baking soda

1/2 cup chocolate syrup
1/2 cup corn syrup
1   egg, beaten

Topping:
1   teaspoon instant coffee granules
1   teaspoon hot water
2   cups whipped topping

Preheat the oven to 350 degrees. Fit the piecrust into a pie plate. Flute the edges.

For the filling, combine the flour, brown sugar, and butter in a small bowl. Mix well. Set aside 1/2 cup of this mixture to sprinkle on top of the pie. Mix together 1/4 cup of the coffee with the baking soda. In a separate bowl combine the chocolate syrup, corn syrup, and egg. Add the remaining 3/4 cup coffee and the soda mixture. Mix well. Add the crumb mixture (excluding the 1/2 cup reserved), and mix until well combined. Pour into the piecrust. Sprinkle the top with the reserved crumbs. Cover the pie loosely with foil to prevent the fluted edge from burning. Bake for 30 to 35 minutes, or until the center is done. Cool.

For the topping, stir the coffee granules into the hot water until dissolved. Add this to the whipped topping. Place a dollop on each slice of pie when serving.

MARY BISHOP | NORTH PLATTE, NEBRASKA

Tips From Our Test Kitchen:

Keep instant coffee crystals on hand for quick baking needs. They dissolve easily in cake and cookie batters for a nice mocha flavor.

Best Piecrust Ever

Yield: 2 crusts

"The secret to this crust is the egg and vinegar mixture. I've never found a better piecrust."

3	cups all-purpose flour	1	egg
1	teaspoon baking powder	6	tablespoons water
1	teaspoon salt	1	tablespoon white vinegar
1 1/4	cups solid vegetable shortening		

Mix the flour, baking powder, and salt. Cut in the shortening until the texture resembles peas. Beat the egg, water, and vinegar together. Add to the flour mixture. Don't handle the dough more than is needed. Roll it out and fill two pie plates. Bake according to the pie filling instructions.

CAROLEE GOEBEL | CHEBOYGAN, MICHIGAN

Peanut Butter Pie

Yield: 8 servings

"This is a delicious pie. Everywhere I take it, whether to reunions, church suppers, or picnics, everyone asks for the recipe."

1	(9-inch) unbaked piecrust	**Topping:**	
1	cup granulated sugar	6	ounces cream cheese, softened
1/4	cup cocoa powder	8	ounces whipped topping, thawed
2	tablespoons all-purpose flour	1/4	cup plus 2 tablespoons peanut butter
1/2	cup milk	1	cup confectioners' sugar
2	eggs, beaten	1	teaspoon vanilla extract
3	tablespoons butter or margarine, melted	2	tablespoons miniature semi-sweet
1	teaspoon vanilla extract		chocolate chips

Preheat the oven to 425 degrees. Prick the bottom and sides of the piecrust and bake for 10 minutes. Set aside to cool.

Reduce the oven temperature to 350 degrees. Combine the granulated sugar, cocoa, flour, milk, eggs, margarine, and vanilla, and beat until well blended. Pour the blended mixture into the piecrust and bake for 30 minutes.

While the pie cools, prepare the topping. Combine the cream cheese, whipped topping, peanut butter, confectioners' sugar, and vanilla. Beat until smooth. Spoon evenly over the cooled chocolate filling. Sprinkle with the chocolate chips and chill well before serving.

BONNIE SPITSER | LONDON, KENTUCKY

German Chocolate Pie

Yield: 8 servings

"I've made this pie for family and friends for thirty-six years. Many people say that they haven't heard of German Chocolate Pie. Once they try it, however, they usually want the recipe."

Filling:

4	ounces German chocolate
1/4	cup (1/2 stick) butter
11/2	cups sugar
3	tablespoons cornstarch
1/8	teaspoon salt
1	teaspoon vanilla extract

2	eggs, beaten
11/2	cups evaporated milk
1	(10-inch) unbaked piecrust

Topping:

11/3	cups shredded coconut
1/2	cup chopped pecans

Preheat the oven to 375 degrees. For the filling, put the chocolate and butter in a medium microwave-safe bowl and cook on a low setting in the microwave. Stir several times during the melting process to prevent burning. When the chocolate is melted, stir in the sugar, cornstarch, salt, vanilla, and eggs until well blended. Stir in the evaporated milk until smooth. Pour into the piecrust.

For the toppping, mix the coconut and pecans together. Sprinkle evenly over the chocolate mixture. Use a knife to cut through the coconut into the chocolate mixture in several places. Bake for 45 to 50 minutes, or until the center is set.

JANET CURTIS | NORTH PLATTE, NEBRASKA

Tips From Our Test Kitchen:

The pie center puffs slightly and the top begins to crack when it is done. If the crust becomes too brown, place a piece of aluminum foil over the top of the entire pie for the final 15 minutes of baking. A dollop of whipped cream can be added if desired.

Too Easy Peach Cobbler

Yield: 12 servings

"When my sister told me about this cobbler, I didn't think it would be good. But when she made it for our lunch, I could not believe how good it was. I have given this recipe to lots of people, and they think it's great. In loving memory, I send this to you in her name, Gussie Arledge."

1	(29-ounce) can sliced peaches, drained	2	tablespoons all-purpose flour
5	slices white bread	1	egg, beaten
1 1/2	cups sugar	1/2	cup (1 stick) margarine, melted

Preheat the oven to 350 degrees. Place the peaches in an 8-inch square baking dish (or larger). Remove the crust from the bread slices, and cut each slice into five strips. Place the strips over the peaches. Mix the sugar, flour, egg, and margarine. Blend well and pour the mixture over the bread strips. Bake for 35 to 45 minutes, or until golden brown.

ADDINE STRINGER | GILMER, TEXAS

Quick and Easy Cobbler

Yield: 6 servings

"I grew up in the South, where cobblers are made frequently. My mother made this many times. My family carries on the cobbler tradition to this day."

1	cup plus 2 tablespoons self-rising flour or favorite baking mix	1/2	cup milk
		1/2	cup (1 stick) butter or margarine
1	plus 2/3 cups sugar	3	cups fresh fruit or 1 (15-ounce) can

Stir together 1 cup of the flour, 1 cup of the sugar, and the milk for the batter.

Preheat the oven to 350 degrees. Melt the butter in a 13 x 9-inch baking dish. Toss together the fruit, the remaining 2/3 cup sugar, and the remaining 2 tablespoons flour. Pour the batter into the baking dish. Spoon the fruit mixture over the top. Do not stir. Bake for 30 to 40 minutes, or until the batter is golden and the fruit is bubbly. Serve warm with ice cream.

BILLIE TERWILLEGAR | VALENCIA, CALIFORNIA

Tips From Our Test Kitchen:

This juicy cobbler can be thickened by adding 1/2 cup baking mix to the batter. If you prefer a more cake-like cobbler, double the batter recipe. Use one of the seasonal fresh fruits available at the market, or consider picking your own at a local farm or orchard. This easy cobbler is delicious chilled or warm. It travels well when cooled and even makes a delicious breakfast.

Apple & Peanut Butter Crisp

Yield: 12 servings

"My mother made this wonderful recipe, sort of a cross between a pie and a cobbler. Mom thinks the original came from Ladies' Home Journal *in about 1951."*

6	to 8 green apples, pared and sliced	3/4	cup all-purpose flour
1/2	cup water	3/4	cup firmly packed brown sugar
2	tablespoons lemon juice	1/3	cup peanut butter
1	tablespoon ground cinnamon	1/4	cup (1/2 stick) margarine

Preheat the oven to 350 degrees. Lightly oil a 13 x 9-inch baking dish. Arrange the apple slices in the bottom of the dish. Mix the water and lemon juice and pour over the apples. Sprinkle the cinnamon on top. Mix the flour, brown sugar, peanut butter, and margarine until crumbly. Spread evenly over the apples. Bake for about 40 minutes, or until golden brown.

GAËL P. MUSTAPHA | GREEN VALLEY, ARIZONA

Tips From Our Test Kitchen:

Serve with a small scoop of vanilla ice cream or a dollop of whipped cream. Mix 2 tablespoons caramel sauce with 1 table-spoon peanut butter for a decadent sauce.

Bavarian Cream

Yield: 8 to 10 servings

"This was a favorite recipe of my mother. She would make it for special events and holidays. It is delicious, and we loved it."

2	(3-ounce) boxes strawberry Jell-O	1/2	pint whipping cream
1	(10-ounce) package frozen strawberries		

Prepare the Jell-O as directed on the box. Add the strawberries, which have been thawed enough to mix with the Jell-O, and allow the mixture to gel in the refrigerator until almost firm. Whip the whipping cream until stiff peaks form, fold into the Jell-O, and return to the refrigerator until set. As a variation, you can substitute lime Jell-O and 1 (8-ounce) can drained, crushed pineapple for the strawberry Jell-O and frozen strawberries.

ANGELA LEPITRE | CLAREMONT, NEW HAMPSHIRE

Tips From Our Test Kitchen:

Whipping cream performs best when your bowl and beaters are cold. Garnish this dish with fresh strawberries and a sprig of mint.

Almond Delight

"Every time I take this dish to a cookout or get-together, everyone wants the recipe. It always seems to be a hit."

Crumb mixture:
1/4	cup firmly packed brown sugar
1/2	cup (1 stick) margarine, melted
1/2	cup sliced almonds
1	cup flaked coconut
1	cup all-purpose flour

Filling:
2	(3-ounce) boxes instant coconut pudding mix
2	cups cold milk
1	(8-ounce) container whipped topping

Preheat the oven to 350 degrees. For the crumb mixture, stir together the brown sugar, margarine, almonds, coconut, and flour until well blended. Pour into a shallow baking pan, and bake for 30 minutes, stirring several times while baking. The mixture will resemble granola. Remove the crumb mixture from the oven to cool.

For the filling, combine the coconut pudding mixes, milk, and whipped topping in a bowl, and set the mixture in the refrigerator to thicken for about 10 minutes.

In a 9-inch square pan, sprinkle three-fourths of the crumb mixture. Cover with the thickened filling and top with the remaining crumbs. Refrigerate until serving time.

RITA POHLMAN | DELPHOS, OHIO

The 1938 Ohio State Grange Cookbook included a recipe for wallpaper cleaner containing vinegar, motor oil, ammonia, salt and flour and told readers how to determine temperatures in the new gas ovens by seeing how long it took to brown flour in the bottom of a pie pan.

Garden City's Raspberry Roots

Residents of Garden City, Utah, have been cultivating raspberries since early homesteaders planted the first canes nearly a century ago. From those roots, the town has grown into the "Raspberry Shake Capital of the West."

The cool nights and warm days make it a great location to grow raspberries. Situated between the mountains of the Cache National Forest and twenty-mile-long Bear Lake, Garden City sits midway along the western shores of the lake's Caribbean-blue waters. Mormon settlers built the town's first cabins, and many locals can trace their roots back to those nineteenth-century pioneers.

Residents used to raise dairy cattle and grow hay. Now most cater to Utah's vacationers, dishing up shakes and fries in the town's numerous drive-in restaurants and renting out boats and jet skis during the summer and snowmobiles during the winter.

Still, it's raspberries that gave Garden City its nickname. Despite a blight that hit the town's raspberry crop in recent years, residents have vigilantly continued celebrating their local fruit during the Raspberry Days Festival.

The celebration, which begins on the first Thursday in August each year, was created by the Bear Lake Rendezvous Chamber of Commerce in 1983 and is a mainstay for the town's 357 residents.

The celebration features a parade, Miss Berry Princess contest, raspberry bake-off, rodeo, handmade arts and crafts, pancake breakfast, dancing, lighted-boat parade, musical entertainment, fireworks, and growers selling freshly picked berries from roadside stands.

Dubbed the biggest little parade in the West, the parade draws as many as seventy-five entries and 15,000 to 20,000 visitors. The Bear Lake Monster, fashioned after a Loch Ness-type creature that some locals say inhabits the lake, even makes appearances at the parade. The parade highlight is the Miss Berry Princess Float. All the four- to six-year-old girls who compete are entitled to ride on the float with the Raspberry Princess.

In 1998, the town added the popular lighted-boat parade. That year, nearly sixty entries—with lights strung in the shape of the Stars and Stripes, Christmas trees, and Snoopy—streamed out of the harbor.

While the festival has evolved over the years—the original flea market has turned into a juried crafts fair and the buckaroo rodeo with mutton busters (kids riding sheep) is now a full-fledged rodeo—one thing remains constant: Summer in Garden City means raspberries.

For more information, log on to www.gardencityut.us or call (435) 946-2901.

Karen Karvonen is a freelance writer from Englewood, Colorado.

Blueberry Bread Pudding

Yield: 8 to 10 servings

"The name for this recipe, which I call 'Soooooo Delicious Blueberry Bread Pudding,' came to me one weekend while my daughter was visiting. I served this dish at Sunday breakfast. She ate a spoonful and exclaimed, 'That is so delicious!'"

2	eggs		1/4	teaspoon almond extract
21/2	cups milk		4	cups cubed day-old bread
3/4	cup sugar		1	pint blueberries

Preheat the oven to 350 degrees. Lightly grease an 8-inch square baking dish. Whisk the eggs in a medium bowl. Stir in the milk, sugar, and almond extract. Add the bread, and set aside for 15 minutes, allowing the cubes to absorb the egg mixture. Gently stir in the berries. Spoon into the baking dish and bake for 45 minutes.

HAZEL GROGAN CARTER | MADISON, NORTH CAROLINA

Custard Bread Pudding

Yield: 4 to 6 servings

"If you try this recipe, I am certain that you will agree it's one of the best ever."

Pudding:

2	cups whole milk
1	cup heavy cream
2	tablespoons butter (no substitutions)
5	eggs, slightly beaten
1	teaspoon vanilla extract
2/3	cup granulated sugar
1/4	teaspoon salt
3	cups dry bread cubes (5 to 6 slices)
1	teaspoon ground cinnamon
1	teaspoon ground nutmeg

Sauce:

2	tablespoons butter
1/2	cup granulated sugar
1/4	cup firmly packed brown sugar
1	tablespoon all-purpose flour
1/4	teaspoon salt
1	egg, beaten
1	teaspoon vanilla extract
11/2	cups heavy cream

Preheat the oven to 350 degrees. For the pudding, scald the milk and cream in a very heavy saucepan. Set aside to cool slightly. Stir in the butter until melted. Butter a 2-quart casserole dish. In a mixing bowl combine the eggs, vanilla, granulated sugar, and salt. Gradually stir the milk mixture into the egg mixture and add the bread cubes. Spoon into the prepared dish. Sprinkle the cinnamon and nutmeg evenly over the top. Place the dish into a larger pan with about 1 inch of water in the bottom. Place both pans carefully into the oven, and bake until the center of the custard is set, about 35 to 50 minutes. Remove from the oven and serve with the sauce.

While the pudding is baking, prepare the vanilla sauce. Combine the butter, granulated sugar, brown sugar, flour, salt, egg, vanilla, and cream in the order given in the top of a double boiler set over simmering water. Stir over medium-low heat until the sauce thickens to desired doneness. Serve the warm sauce over the pudding.

RUTH EYMAN | IOWA CITY, IOWA

Chocolate Bread Pudding
Yield: 6 to 8 servings

"When my daughter married a chocolate lover, she began making this dessert for him. It has been a great success with all and has graced many a holiday table."

1	plus 2 cups semi-sweet chocolate chips	1	teaspoon vanilla extract
4	eggs	1/4	cup Kahlúa or brandy
1	cup firmly packed light brown sugar	2	cups milk
1/2	teaspoon ground cinnamon	4	cups cubed crusty bread
1/8	teaspoon ground nutmeg		

Preheat the oven to 350 degrees. Grease an 81/2 x 41/2-inch (6-cup) loaf pan. Melt 1 cup chocolate chips and set aside to cool slightly. Whisk together the eggs, brown sugar, cinnamon, nutmeg, vanilla, melted chocolate, and Kahlúa in a large bowl. When very smooth, stir in the milk and mix well. Add the bread to this mixture, and allow it to rest for 30 minutes. Stir occasionally to make sure the bread is evenly soaked.

Ladle half of the bread mixture into the loaf pan. Spread the remaining 2 cups chocolate chips on top. Ladle the remaining bread mixture over the chocolate chips. Bake for about 55 minutes, or until the center is set. Cool.

SARA JONES | SAULT STE. MARIE, MICHIGAN

Tips From Our Test Kitchen:

Serve this treat warm with whipped cream or vanilla ice cream.

Banana Pudding

Yield: 6 to 8 servings

"This was my mother's recipe. All of us children thought her banana pudding was the best. My daughter, Elaine T. McGruder, made me a cookbook out of the recipes I've collected. She said when she looked through these recipes, she was reminded of the bumper sticker that says, 'Life is short, eat dessert first.'"

1	(12-ounce) box vanilla wafers	1/2	cup cornstarch or flour
4	large or 6 small ripe bananas, sliced	11/2	cups evaporated milk
3	egg yolks, well beaten	1	teaspoon vanilla extract
11/2	cups sugar (see "Tips")		

Layer the vanilla wafers and bananas in a serving bowl until it is almost full. Mix the egg yolks with the sugar, cornstarch, and milk in a saucepan. Cook on low heat until thick. Add the vanilla and pour the cooked mixture over the wafers and bananas.

STELLA THOMPSON | FORT PAYNE, ALABAMA

Tips From Our Test Kitchen:

This recipe is still sweet with only 1 cup sugar. Try substituting a non-fat version of evaporated milk for a lighter dessert. If desired, the pudding can be topped with meringue or whipped cream.

Banana Cheesecake Pudding

Yield: 8 to 10 servings

"I always get compliments on this pudding. It's very good, easy to make, and quick. My son asks me to make this for his birthday every year instead of cake."

1	(14-ounce) can sweetened condensed milk	2	cups whipping cream, whipped
2	cups cold water	1/4	cup sugar
2	(3-ounce) packages instant cheesecake pudding mix	1	teaspoon vanilla extract
		1	(12-ounce) box vanilla wafers
		3	or 4 bananas, sliced

In a large bowl combine the condensed milk and water. Add the pudding mixes and beat until well blended. Chill for 5 to 10 minutes, or until the pudding begins to set. Fold in the whipped cream, sugar, and vanilla. Spoon a layer of the pudding mixture into a large serving bowl. Follow with layers of vanilla wafers and banana slices. Repeat the layering process three times, ending with the pudding mixture on top. Chill.

ELSIE HANEY | HARDIN, TEXAS

Tips From Our Test Kitchen:

Try substituting raspberries, strawberries, or blackberries for the sliced bananas. Cookie-style cinnamon graham crackers can be used instead of the vanilla wafers.

Lemon Cake-Top Pudding

Yield: 4 to 6 servings

"This is an old recipe from my mother. She brought it to family reunions every year. There were never any leftovers."

3	tablespoons butter, at room temperature	1/4	teaspoon salt
1	cup sugar	3	tablespoons all-purpose flour
4	eggs, at room temperature	1	cup milk
1/3	cup fresh lemon juice		

Preheat the oven to 325 degrees. Lightly grease a 9 x 5-inch loaf pan. With an electric mixer cream together the butter and sugar in a large bowl until fluffy. It will be grainy at first. Separate the eggs yolks and whites. Add the yolks to the butter and sugar mixture and beat well. Add the lemon juice, salt, and flour. Mix well. Stir in the milk until well blended. In a separate bowl beat the egg whites until stiff. Fold them into the lemon mixture. Pour the batter into the prepared pan. Bake for 40 minutes. Increase the oven temperature to 350 degrees, and bake for about 10 additional minutes, or until brown. Cool and keep refrigerated.

GLENDA BARBER | ST. JAMES, MISSOURI

Tips From Our Test Kitchen:

This recipe yields a light cake layer over a rich lemon pudding. It is wonderful served with fresh berries.

Russian Cream

Yield: 8 servings

"Whenever there's a family gathering, this recipe takes center stage at our table. It looks beautiful and tastes even better than it looks."

2	tablespoons unflavored gelatin	16	ounces sour cream
1/2	cup cold water	1	teaspoon vanilla extract
1	pint half-and-half	2	cups strawberries, blueberries, or peaches
1	cup sugar		

Combine the gelatin with the cold water. Heat the half-and-half and sugar to the scalded stage over medium heat. Remove from the heat. Stir the gelatin into the half-and-half mixture. Add the sour cream and vanilla. Pour into a 5-cup mold and refrigerate overnight. When set, turn the mold onto a large plate. Garnish generously with the fruit.

JAN TOMCHO | HINCKLEY, OHIO

Tips From Our Test Kitchen:

For a variation, try almond extract instead of vanilla.

The first Wendy's Old-Fashioned Hamburgers restaurant opened in Columbus, Ohio, on November 15, 1969. The restaurant, decorated now as a museum of Wendy's history, continues to serve customers.

Chocolate Éclair Dessert

Yield: 8 to 10 servings

"This is a recipe that my grandchildren enjoy. My granddaughter served it while working at a ranch in Wyoming. It was a hit there too."

Pudding:
2   (3-ounce) packages instant French vanilla pudding mix
3   cups cold milk
1   (9-ounce) container whipped topping
1   (16-ounce) box graham crackers

Icing:
2   tablespoons butter
4   tablespoons cocoa powder
2   teaspoons corn syrup
1   teaspoon vanilla extract
3   tablespoons milk
1 1/2   cups confectioners' sugar

For the pudding, blend the pudding mixes with the milk with an electric mixer until thick. Fold in the whipped topping. Layer a 13 x 9-inch baking dish with one-third of the graham crackers. Spoon half the pudding mixture on top. Repeat the cracker and pudding layers, and then cover with a final layer of graham crackers.

For the icing, mix together the butter, cocoa powder, corn syrup, vanilla, milk, and confectioners' sugar in a saucepan, and heat until the sugar has dissolved. This takes just a few minutes. Pour the icing over the graham crackers in an even layer. Refrigerate for 24 hours.

JANE WRIGHT | MILLVILLE, PENNSYLVANIA

Easy Flan or Crème Caramel

Yield: 6 to 8 servings

"I've been making this style of flan for more than thirty-three years. I've tried others, but they have too many steps. I get more requests for this one."

4	large eggs	1	cup whipping cream
1	(14-ounce) can sweetened	1/2	cup whole milk
	condensed milk	3/4	cup granulated sugar

Preheat the oven to 350 degrees. Put the eggs, condensed milk, cream, and whole milk in a blender, but do not blend yet. Cook the sugar, without stirring, in a small, heavy skillet. The sugar will melt and turn amber. Cook it until it begins to "string" when a spoon or knife is dipped in. Pour the melted sugar into a 1 1/2-quart Pyrex or glass soufflé dish.

Now start the blender. When the ingredients are whipped, pour this over the melted sugar. Place the flan dish into a larger pan holding 1 inch of water. Bake the flan in the water bath for about 1 hour, or until the center is set. The top of the flan will have a golden and bubbly crust. Test by inserting the blade of a knife in the center. It should come out clean. This flan can be turned out onto a plate when it's still warm or can be served out of the dish.

NELL HULL | PARADISE, TEXAS

Homemade Grape Ice Cream

Yield: 10 to 12 servings

"This recipe is just a little different. It was always a great hit with our church kids."

2 1/2	cups sugar	1	pint light cream or half-and-half
1	(12-ounce) can frozen grape juice, thawed	1	(12-ounce) can evaporated milk
		2	cups milk
1/2	cup fresh lemon juice		

Dissolve the sugar in the thawed grape juice. Add the lemon juice. Combine the cream, evaporated milk, and milk. Pour both mixtures into a 1-gallon ice cream freezer, stir, and freeze according to the manufacturer's instructions.

FERNE TREMELLING | WILLS POINT, TEXAS

Buttermilk Ice Cream

Yield: 6 to 8 servings

"This frosty treat is delicious alone or when served with a sweet, tart accent like cherry preserves."

1	quart buttermilk	1	(12-ounce) can evaporated milk
1	cup sugar	1	teaspoon vanilla extract

Combine the buttermilk, sugar, evaporated milk, and vanilla in a bowl. Stir until the sugar dissolves. Pour into an ice cream freezer and freeze according to the manufacturer's directions.

ELOISE RILEY | EUPORA, MISSISSIPPI

Tips From Our Test Kitchen:

This lower-fat, frozen treat tastes much like frozen vanilla yogurt. It's a nice alternative to ice cream when you're watching calories.

New Mexico Biscochitos

Yield: 36 to 60, depending on size

"This is a traditional wedding and holiday dessert in New Mexico. My family has made them for generations. I will pass this part of my heritage on to my granddaughter."

1	pound lard or solid vegetable shortening	3	teaspoons vanilla extract
2	plus 1/2 cups sugar	6	cups all-purpose flour
5	eggs	4	teaspoons baking powder
1/4	cup anise seeds	4	teaspoons ground cinnamon

Preheat the oven to 375 degrees. Cream together the lard and 2 cups of the sugar in a large mixing bowl. Add the eggs, anise seeds, and vanilla. Mix well. Combine the flour and baking powder in a separate bowl, and add it to the creamed mixture. Form into a ball and knead until smooth. Roll about one-third of the dough at a time on a generously floured surface until it is about 1/4-inch thick. Cut the dough into squares. Mix together the remaining 1/2 cup sugar with the cinnamon. Sprinkle evenly over the top of each square. Bake for 7 to 8 minutes.

PATSY CRAINE | BARSTOW, CALIFORNIA

Tips From Our Test Kitchen:

This dough is a bit sticky to work with at first. If necessary, blend in a bit more flour to assist in rolling.

Angel Cookies

Yield: about 30 cookies

"This was my grandmother's recipe. It was a family favorite. My brother always asked Granny to make these cookies when we got together for holidays and birthdays."

4	egg whites	1	cup chopped dates
	Pinch of salt	1	cup chopped walnuts or pecans
2	cups confectioners' sugar		

Preheat the oven to 300 degrees. Grease and flour a cookie sheet. Beat the egg whites with the salt for 3 minutes. Add the confectioners' sugar and beat for 10 minutes. Fold in the dates and nuts. Drop the dough, 1 tablespoon at a time, onto the prepared cookie sheet. Bake for 25 minutes, but watch them closely. They burn easily.

B.J. Brown | Oxford, Mississippi

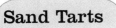

Sand Tarts

Yield: 24 tarts

"My mother prepared this recipe before I was born in 1931 and for many years after. She always made these cookies for her Pioneer Study Club teas. The tarts melt in your mouth."

1	cup butter (no substitutes)	1	cup finely chopped walnuts or pecans (optional)
3	tablespoons granulated sugar		Confectioners' sugar
1	teaspoon vanilla extract		
2	cups all-purpose flour		

Preheat the oven to 350 degrees. Cream the butter and sugar well. Add the vanilla. Stir in the flour and then the nuts, if using. This stiff dough can be mixed with your hands or a heavy-duty mixer. When blended, form the dough into 1 1/2-inch crescents. Bake on an ungreased cookie sheet for 10 to 12 minutes, or until light golden. When cool enough to handle, sprinkle generously with the confectioners' sugar.

Jan Edwards | McLean, Texas

Tips From Our Test Kitchen:

Be sure to add the dates and nuts at the last minute before baking, or the cookies will become flat rather than fluffy. Sprinkle colored sugar on top, if desired.

Tips From Our Test Kitchen:

These cookies freeze well. They are pretty when tinted with a bit of food coloring for a festive touch. The sandy texture is excellent.

*Tips From Our
Test Kitchen:*

These colorful cookies are dry but will remain fresh for a long time. Serve them with coffee, tea, or hot chocolate.

Biscotti

Yield: about 72 large cookies

"This Italian cookie has become a favorite down to the smallest grandchild. I make them for everyone."

1	pound (4 sticks) butter, softened	4	tablespoons anise seed
4	cups sugar	6	ounces almonds, chopped
8	eggs	8	cups all-purpose flour
1	tablespoon baking powder	6	ounces dried cranberries
2	teaspoons vanilla extract	1	cup shelled pistachios

Preheat the oven to 350 degrees. Mix the butter, sugar, eggs, baking powder, vanilla, anise seed, and almonds until well blended. Stir in the flour gradually. When the mixture is smooth, stir in the cranberries and pistachios. This dough will be sticky but not difficult to handle. Divide the dough into four equal parts. Shape each section into a loaf about 15 inches long and 4 inches wide.

Bake the loaves for about 45 minutes on a baking sheet with sides. (If the dough begins to spread and become too flat during baking, reshape it with a spatula.) Remove the loaves from the oven and allow them to cool. When cool, cut each loaf into 1-inch slices. Place the slices back on the baking sheet, and bake for 10 to 15 minutes, or until golden.

PAT ALDIGHIERI | CORNISH, NEW HAMPSHIRE

Caramel Creams

Yield: 25 to 30 sandwich-style cookies

"Anytime I take these delicious cookies anywhere, I come home with an empty container and many recipe requests. My family and friends really like them. I think your readers will too."

Cookies:

1	cup (2 sticks) butter, softened (no substitutes)
2/3	cup firmly packed brown sugar
2	egg yolks
1/2	teaspoon vanilla extract
2 1/2	cups all-purpose flour
1/4	teaspoon salt
1/3	cup finely chopped pecans

Filling:

7 1/2	teaspoons butter (no substitutes)
1 1/2	cups confectioners' sugar
1/2	teaspoon vanilla extract
2	to 3 tablespoons whipping cream

For the cookies, cream the butter and brown sugar in a mixing bowl. Beat in the egg yolks and vanilla. In a separate bowl combine the flour, salt, and pecans. Gradually add to the creamed mixture. Shape into two 10-inch rolls. Wrap the rolls in plastic wrap and refrigerate for 2 hours.

Preheat the oven to 350 degrees. Unwrap and slice each roll into 25 to 30 cookies. Bake on an ungreased cookie sheet for 11 to 13 minutes, or until golden. Remove and cool on wire racks.

For the filling, melt the butter in a medium-size saucepan. Stir until golden brown. Remove from the heat. Add the confectioners' sugar, vanilla, and enough whipping cream to achieve spreading consistency. Spread on half of the cookies. Top with the remaining cookies.

JO ANN REID | SALISBURY, NORTH CAROLINA

Chocolate Mint Cookies

Yield: 66 cookies

"My grandma would always give us these cookies when we visited her—if she didn't eat all of them first. They were so mouth-watering—like all her food—and special because they were made with Grandma's loving hands and heart."

21/2	cups all-purpose flour	2	eggs
11/2	tablespoons baking powder	1	teaspoon vanilla extract
3/4	teaspoon salt	1	(10-ounce) package mint-flavored semi-sweet chocolate chips or 1 (12-ounce) package mint patties, finely chopped
1	plus 1/4 cups sugar		
3/4	cup vegetable oil		

In a small bowl combine the flour, baking powder, and salt. In a large bowl combine 1 cup of the sugar with the oil. Mix well. Beat in the eggs and vanilla. Gradually add the flour mixture. Stir in the chips. Chill the dough in the refrigerator for about 30 minutes.

Preheat the oven to 350 degrees. Grease a cookie sheet. Shape rounded teaspoons of the chilled dough into balls and roll them in the remaining 1/4 cup sugar. Place on the prepared cookie sheet and bake 8 to 10 minutes.

DEVONNE J. HOFFERT | MINOT, NORTH DAKOTA

Oatmeal Divine Cookies

Yield: 24 cookies

"I make these cookies around Christmas because they resemble snowflakes, but they are good any time of the year. The recipe was given to me more than thirty years ago."

1/2 cup (1 stick) butter (no substitutes)	1/4 teaspoon baking powder
1 cup uncooked quick oats	1/4 teaspoon salt
1 cup sugar	1/2 teaspoon vanilla extract
3 tablespoons all-purpose flour	1 egg

Preheat the oven to 350 degrees. Melt the butter in a mixing bowl in a microwave oven. Add the oats, sugar, flour, baking powder, salt, and vanilla to the butter and mix well. Beat the egg and add it to the dough. Mix until well blended.

Line a cookie sheet with aluminum foil. (This step is necessary to bake the cookies successfully.) Drop the dough 1/2 teaspoon at a time onto the foil. Leave several inches between each cookie, because they spread. Bake for 7 to 9 minutes, or until golden.

Remove the cookies from the oven and allow them to remain on the foil until cool. They will peel off the foil only after cooling. Cover the cookie sheet with new foil for each batch.

LUCY DAWSON-THOMPSON | URBANA, OHIO

Peanut Butter Cookies

Yield: 12 cookies

"All of my friends request the recipe when they taste these good and simple cookies."

1 cup peanut butter, creamy or chunky	1 egg, beaten
1 cup sugar	1 teaspoon vanilla extract

Preheat the oven to 325 degrees. Mix the peanut butter, sugar, egg, and vanilla until evenly blended. Drop 1-inch balls of the mixture onto an ungreased cookie sheet. Press with the tines of a fork to decorate. Bake for 12 to 15 minutes, or until golden.

JOANN VANDERBURG | ALEXANDER, ARKANSAS

Tips From Our Test Kitchen:

This super-easy recipe is tasty and so quick to prepare. If you like chocolate, try adding 6 ounces semi-sweet chips to the batter.

Czech Out West, Texas

In 1997, state lawmakers made it official: West, Texas—often called "West comma Texas" to differentiate it from the region of western Texas—is the home of the official Kolache of the state legislature.

West's 2,692 residents were pleased but not surprised. After all, folks regularly drive more than 100 miles to West so they can gorge on the Czech delicacy, an oh-so-light pastry puff filled with fruit (such as apricots, cherries, and prunes), cheese, or poppy seeds.

West has taken a Czech tradition and made it a Texas-size happening. On the Friday, Saturday, and Sunday before Labor Day, the town holds Westfest, a celebration of all things Czech, which draws 20,000 to 25,000 people. The community begins preparing in early summer. People fill their freezers with home-baked pastries, build floats, and refurbish booths where they'll sell all sorts of crafts and treats.

During the festival, attendees play in taroky tournaments (played with a special deck of cards); run in a 5K race; demonstrate chores performed by the early settlers, such as corn grinding and rope making; and pitch horseshoes and washers. Audiences delight at the sight of the Czechoslovakian Folk Dancers of West, and the Junior Historians of West High School, who perform folk dancing during the festival.

Dancing abounds, and polka bands perform on two stages. A Saturday morning parade winds through downtown. During the Polka Mass on Sunday, hymns are sung to the tunes of polkas and waltzes.

And then there's the food. Kolache Baking Contest rules specify that only made-from-scratch yeast dough may be entered. And sausage is served in a variety of ways—on a stick, in sandwiches, on a hotdog bun, and even in kolaches themselves.

In the Cultural Amphitheater, festivalgoers visit the genealogy booth to refer to Czech passenger lists and other family history resources. Today, at least 75 percent of West's population can trace its family back to the former Czechoslovakia. (In 1992, Czechoslovakia split into two countries: Slovakia and the Czech Republic.)

Czechs flooded into central Texas during the late nineteenth century because the state had plenty of land, and that appealed to the immigrants, who were mostly poor farmers. Gradually, some of the Czech newcomers began opening shops in town—meat markets, restaurants, and bakeries. West became a town where Tex-Czech culture thrived.

With newer eateries and bakeries taking their place beside venerable institutions, many drivers along the route between Dallas and Austin make a West Kolache Pit Stop.

And that's just fine with Westonians.

For more information, log on to www.westfest.com or call (254) 826-5058.

Andrea Gross is a writer based in Denver, Colorado.

Buffalo Chips

Yield: about 48 cookiess

*"I received this recipe from my seventy-eight-year-old mother. These cookies
are her favorite ones to bake."*

1	cup (2 sticks) butter or margarine		4	cups all-purpose flour
1	cup solid vegetable shortening		2	teaspoons baking soda
2	cups firmly packed brown sugar		2	teaspoons baking powder
2	cups granulated sugar		1	cup flaked coconut
4	eggs		1	cup chopped pecans
2	teaspoons vanilla extract		2	cups Rice Krispies cereal
2	cups uncooked quick oats		6	ounces chocolate or butterscotch chips

Preheat the oven to 350 degrees. In a very large mixing bowl cream the margarine and shortening with the brown sugar and granulated sugar. Add the eggs and vanilla and mix well. Stir
in the oats, flour, baking soda, and baking powder. When well blended, stir in the coconut,
pecans, Rice Krispies, and chocolate chips. (This batter is very heavy and will require using your
hands to mix it.) When the batter is thoroughly mixed, drop the batter by the 1/4 cup for each
cookie on a large, ungreased cookie sheet. Bake for 10 to 12 minutes, or until the edges are
golden if you prefer chewy cookies. For a crispy cookie, bake longer, for about 12 to 15 minutes. Allow the cookies to cool slightly while still on the baking sheet. They are large and break
easily while warm.

DORIS MORRISON | BISHOP, CALIFORNIA

Double Chocolate Oatmeal Cookies

Yield: 48 medium-size cookies

*"I've been baking and sharing these cookies for more than twenty years. My
family and friends call them 'Mama Hookie Cookies.'"*

11/2	cups sugar		1/3	cup cocoa powder
1	cup margarine, softened		1/2	teaspoon baking soda
1	egg		1/2	teaspoon salt
1	teaspoon vanilla extract		3	cups uncooked quick-cooking oats
11/4	cups all-purpose flour		6	ounces semi-sweet chocolate chips

Preheat the oven to 350 degrees. Lightly grease a cookie sheet. Cream together the sugar and margarine. Stir in the egg and vanilla. Sift together the flour, cocoa, baking soda, and salt. Stir into the creamed mixture. Add the oats and chocolate chips. If the dough is too stiff, add up to 1/4 cup water. Drop with a cookie dough scoop onto the prepared cookie sheet and bake for 10 to 12 minutes.

JOLENE HOOKIE | DAVID CITY, NEBRASKA

Date Cookies

Yield: 75 to 100 cookies

"I received this recipe from the late Dorothy Schwar, a member of my church in Emmaus, Pennsylvania. I'm thankful she shared her recipe with me. Every time I make these delicious cookies, I think of her."

1	cup (2 sticks) margarine	2 1/2	cups all-purpose flour
2	cups firmly packed light brown sugar	1	(10-ounce) container diced sugared dates
3	eggs	1	(10-ounce) package chopped English walnuts
1	teaspoon baking soda		
1/4	teaspoon salt		

Preheat the oven to 350 degrees. Grease a cookie sheet. Using an electric mixer, cream the margarine with the brown sugar. Add the eggs, soda, salt, and flour and mix well. Stir in the dates and walnuts. Drop the dough 1 teaspoonful at a time onto the prepared cookie sheet. Bake for 10 to 12 minutes.

MARILYN DECKER | EMMAUS, PENNSYLVANIA

Tips From Our Test Kitchen:

Reserve some chopped dates and walnuts to place on top of each cookie before baking. This gives them a chunky and appetizing look.

Charles Hires, a Philadelphia, Pennsylvania, pharmacist, introduced a new drink at the Philadelphia Centennial Exhibition in 1876. First selling it as a dry mixture, then as a liquid concentrate, he was soon bottling the popular drink—root beer.

Macadamia Nut Cookies

Yield: about 36 cookies

"I made this recipe up for my son, and he loved them. Each year at Christmas, it is a tradition for me to bake these cookies for him."

1 1/4	cups all-purpose flour	2	eggs
1	teaspoon baking soda	1	teaspoon vanilla extract
1/2	teaspoon salt	1	(12-ounce) bag white chocolate chips
1	cup (2 sticks) butter, softened	3	cups uncooked quick-cooking oats
3/4	cup brown sugar	1	cup chopped macadamia nuts
3/4	cup granulated sugar		

Preheat the oven to 350 degrees. Combine the flour, baking soda, and salt. In a separate bowl cream the butter with the brown sugar and granulated sugar. Add the eggs and vanilla to the creamed mixture. Stir in the dry ingredients until well mixed. Add the white chocolate chips, oats, and nuts. Allow the dough to rest 20 minutes.

Drop the dough 1 teaspoon at a time onto an ungreased cookie sheet. Bake for about 10 minutes, watching carefully to avoid overbaking. The cookies should be light brown.

MARLENE FINNSON | HAMILTON, NORTH DAKOTA

Tips From Our Test Kitchen:

Macadamia nut pieces can usually be found in the baking supply aisle at your grocery store. They are far less expensive than the whole nuts.

Magnificent Macaroons

Yield: about 30 cookies

"I found this recipe years ago. These macaroons are always delicious and have the added benefit of being very easy to prepare. My family and friends love them."

1	teaspoon vanilla extract	2/3	cup sweetened condensed milk
2	to 3 drops red food coloring	3	cups flaked coconut

Preheat the oven to 350 degrees. Grease a cookie sheet. Stir the vanilla and food coloring into the sweetened condensed milk until evenly blended. Fold in the coconut until well mixed. Drop the dough 1 teaspoon at a time on the prepared cookie sheet. Bake 8 to 10 minutes, or until a delicate brown. Cool on a flat surface.

MARY HERRON | MESHOPPEN, PENNSYLVANIA

Tips From Our Test Kitchen:

These cookies can be decorated with candied cherries or almonds. Try adding almond extract instead of the vanilla.

Raisin-Filled Cookies

Yield: 30 to 36 cookies

"My twin and I make these family favorites every year for our father. Allow about two hours to prepare them from start to finish."

Pastry:

1   cup sugar
1/2   cup (1 stick) butter or solid vegetable shortening
1   egg
1/2   cup milk
1   teaspoon vanilla extract
31/2   cups all-purpose flour
1   teaspoon baking soda
1   teaspoon cream of tartar

Filling:

2   tablespoons all-purpose flour
2   tablespoons lemon juice
1   cup plus 1 tablespoon water
2   cups golden raisins
1/4   cup chopped walnuts
1   cup sugar

Tips From Our Test Kitchen:

Be careful not to over-bake these cookies. They are meant to be a soft, old-fashioned treat.

For the pastry, beat together the sugar and butter in a large bowl. Stir in the egg, milk, and vanilla. Add the flour, baking soda, and cream of tartar. Roll into a large ball.

For the filling, blend together the flour, lemon juice, and 1 tablespoon water. Combine the raisins, walnuts, sugar, and remaining 1 cup water in a small saucepan. Add the flour mixture and stir until thick. Set aside to cool.

Preheat the oven to 350 degrees. Roll out the cookie dough on a well-floured surface until very thin. Using a cookie cutter or upside down glass, cut the dough into about 60 small circles. Spoon about 1 heaping teaspoon of the raisin filling on top of half of the dough circles. Cover each with another circle and seal the edges with your fingertips. Bake for 12 to 15 minutes, or until light golden.

JUDI BROWN | RISING SUN, MARYLAND

At the age of twenty-two, Samuel Kirk opened a store in Baltimore, Maryland, in April 1815 and began making silverware. His sterling silver cutlery sets were among the first to be manufactured in America.

Spring Garden Ranch Cookies

Yield: about 36 cookies

"My granddaughter Sydney and I came up with this recipe. We based it on a similar recipe that didn't have enough chocolate to suit us. The cookies are very popular at the ranch."

1/2	cup (1 stick) soft margarine	1/2	cup all-purpose flour
1 1/2	cups chocolate graham cracker crumbs	2	teaspoons baking powder
1/2	cup uncooked quick-cooking oats	1	tablespoon milk
1 1/3	cups flaked coconut	1	cup chopped walnuts
1	(14-ounce) can sweetened condensed milk (preferably chocolate)	2	cups semi-sweet chocolate chips

Preheat the oven to 350 degrees. Using a heavy-duty mixer, combine the margarine and graham cracker crumbs. Mix in the oats, coconut, and sweetened condensed milk. Add the flour, baking powder, and milk. Stir in the walnuts and chocolate chips by hand. This is a very dense batter. If you don't have a heavy-duty mixer, use your hands.

Drop by the rounded tablespoonful onto an ungreased cookie sheet. Bake nine cookies at a time for 7 to 9 minutes. Be careful not to overbake these cookies. They should be chewy.

ROGER DROTAR | LONGMONT, COLORADO

Thadalies (Italian Sugar Cookies)

Yield: 48 cookies

"These cookies are perfect for any festive occasion. Frost them with icing of different colors. They taste great and look beautiful."

6	eggs	1/2	cup milk
1	cup vegetable oil	5	cups all-purpose flour
1	cup sugar	5	teaspoons baking powder
1	teaspoon vanilla or almond extract		

Preheat the oven to 350 degrees. Beat the eggs, oil, sugar, and vanilla in a large mixing bowl. Add the milk, flour, and baking powder. The dough will be sticky. With floured hands, roll the dough into 1-inch balls. Bake on an ungreased cookie sheet for 7 to 8 minutes.

GLORIA PARSONS | SIDNEY, NEW YORK

Caramel Corn

Yield: 12 servings

"This caramel corn is so easy to make. It's the perfect snack for Halloween parties. Kids of all ages love it."

1	cup (2 sticks) butter (no substitutes)		1	teaspoon salt
2	cups firmly packed brown sugar		1	teaspoon baking soda
1/2	cup light corn syrup		71/2	quarts popped popcorn

Preheat the oven to 200 degrees. In a saucepan heat the butter, sugar, corn syrup, and salt. Stir occasionally. When the mixture comes to a full boil, cook for 5 minutes. Remove from the heat and stir in the baking soda. Pour the caramel mixture over the popcorn and mix until evenly coated. In a large, greased roasting pan bake the popcorn for 1 hour, stirring every 15 minutes.

PENNY HOUDEK | LITCHFIELD, MINNESOTA

Tips From Our Test Kitchen:

Maple-flavored syrup is a nice substitute for the corn syrup. For extra crunch, stir in 1 cup pecans or peanuts.

Ohio Buckeyes

Yield: 24 to 36 buckeyes

"The people I give these to always want more. My recipe is a bit different from others because it has graham crackers in it."

11/2	cups chunky peanut butter		11/2	teaspoons vanilla extract
24	ounces confectioners' sugar (11/2 boxes)		1/2	cup graham cracker crumbs
1	cup (2 sticks) margarine		12	ounces chocolate chunks or chocolate chips

Knead together the peanut butter, sugar, margarine, vanilla, and graham cracker crumbs. The mixture will be crumbly at first. Keep working with it until it's smooth. Then roll it into small balls about the size of a walnut.

Melt the chocolate over very low heat, stirring often. Remove from the heat as soon as the chocolate loses its shape and becomes glossy. Skewer each buckeye with a toothpick, and dip it into the chocolate, leaving a small uncoated circle at the top. Place on wax paper and chill.

RICHARD ANTAL | MEDINA, OHIO

Tips From Our Test Kitchen:

Buckeyes freeze well and make a great gift.

Pecan Bark

Yield: 48 or more pieces

"I've had this recipe for years. I like to make it with Keebler brand Cinnamon Crisp Crackers."

24	graham cracker squares	1	cup unsalted butter (no substitutes)
1	cup chopped pecans	1	cup firmly packed brown sugar

Preheat the oven to 350 degrees. Line a 15 x 10-inch cookie sheet with foil and lightly grease. Place the graham crackers on the cookie sheet in one layer. Evenly sprinkle the pecans over the top.

Melt the butter in a small saucepan. Add the brown sugar and stir until the mixture boils. Boil for 1 minute. Pour evenly over the graham crackers and pecans. Bake for 10 minutes. Remove from the oven and immediately place the hot cookie sheet in the freezer. Remove the pan after 1 hour and break the bark into pieces. This candy does not need to be refrigerated.

DOROTHY HUBERMAN | KILGORE, TEXAS

Alaska Almond Roca

Yield: 96 to 120 pieces

"This is my favorite candy recipe. It was given to me in 1950 by a neighbor. She picked up the recipe in Alaska."

1	cup sugar	1	tablespoon white corn syrup
1	cup (2 sticks) butter (no substitutes)	8	ounces slivered almonds
1/4	cup water	8	ounces milk chocolate chips

Lightly grease a jelly-roll pan. Put the sugar, butter, water, corn syrup, and almonds in a heavy skillet. Stir occasionally over medium heat until a candy thermometer registers 290 degrees. Watch carefully to be sure the candy does not burn. It will become a rich amber color and will form a hard ball when dropped by the spoonful into cold water. (Depending on the altitude, you may need to heat the candy to 310 degrees to achieve the same result.) The almonds will be toasted at this point. Pour the candy, while warm, onto the pan. Sprinkle the chocolate chips on top. Spread with a butter knife until the chocolate makes an even coating. Allow to cool. Break into bite-size pieces and store in an airtight container.

BARBARA ALLISON | WOODBURN, OREGON

One of America's foremost chefs, James Beard, was born May 5, 1903, in Portland, Oregon, and spent summers at the beach in Gearhart (pop. 1,027). He published *Hors D'oeuvres & Canapés* in 1940, the first major cookbook devoted to cocktail food, and had a segment on television's first cooking show in 1946.

Whoopie Pies

Yield: about 40 cookies

"About fifty years ago I received this recipe from my sister. Ever since, it's been a favorite. I have had so many requests for the recipe."

Cookies:

1/2	cup vegetable oil
1	cup granulated sugar
1/2	cup cocoa powder
1	cup milk
1	egg
2	cups all-purpose flour
11/2	teaspoons baking soda
1/2	teaspoon salt
1	teaspoon vanilla extract

Filling:

1	cup solid vegetable shortening
2	cups confectioners' sugar
2	cups marshmallow crème
1	teaspoon vanilla extract
3	to 6 tablespoons milk

For the cookies, beat together the oil, sugar, cocoa, milk, egg, flour, baking soda, salt, and vanilla until well mixed. Refrigerate for about 1 hour. Preheat the oven to 425 degrees. Drop the dough one teaspoon at a time onto an ungreased cookie sheet. Bake 5 to 10 minutes. Watch them carefully to prevent burning.

While the cookies cool, make the filling. Beat the shortening, sugar, marshmallow crème, vanilla, and 3 tablespoons milk together until fluffy. Add more milk (up to 6 tablespoons) if needed. Spoon a generous dollop of filling on the flat side of half the cooled cookies. Place another cookie on top of each to make a sandwich.

RUTH JOHNSON | DELAWARE, OHIO

Index

Mary Carter

Susan Fisher

Candace Floyd

Mary Carter is a longtime cook, food stylist, writer, and contributing food editor for *American Profile*.

Susan Fisher, recipe coordinator for *American Profile* magazine, has compiled four cookbooks for Publishing Group of America.

Candace Floyd, is the food editor of *Relish*, sister magazine of *American Profile*.